THE CONSPIRACY OF ALLUSION

STUDIES IN THE HISTORY
OF
CHRISTIAN THOUGHT

EDITED BY

HEIKO A. OBERMAN, Tucson, Arizona

IN COOPERATION WITH

ROBERT J. BAST, Knoxville, Tennessee

HENRY CHADWICK, Cambridge

BRIAN TIERNEY, Ithaca, New York

ARJO VANDERJAGT, Groningen

VOLUME XCVII

DOUGLAS KELLY

THE CONSPIRACY OF ALLUSION

THE CONSPIRACY OF ALLUSION

DESCRIPTION, REWRITING, AND AUTHORSHIP FROM MACROBIUS TO MEDIEVAL ROMANCE

BY

DOUGLAS KELLY

BRILL
LEIDEN · BOSTON · KÖLN
1999

This book is printed on acid-free paper.

Library of Congress Cataloging-in-Publication Data

Kelly, Douglas.
    The conspiracy of allusion : description, rewriting, and
authorship from Macrobius to medieval romance / by Douglas Kelly.
        p.   cm. — (Studies in the history of Christian thought, ISSN
0081–8607 ; v. 97)
    Includes bibliographical references and indexes.
    ISBN 9004115609 (alk. paper)
    1. Literature, Medieval—History and criticism.   2. Classical
literature—Adaptations—History and criticism.   3. Macrobius,
Ambrosius Aurelius Theodosius—Influence.   4. Macrobius, Ambrosius
Aurelius Theodosius—Allusions.   5. Literature, Medieval—Classical
influences.   6. Romances—History and criticism.   7. Description
(Rhetoric)   8. Rhetoric, Medieval.   9. Authorship.   10. Poetics.
I. Title.   II. Series.
PN681.5.K45 1999
809'.02—dc21
                                                                99–41484
                                                                    CIP

Die Deutsche Bibliothek - CIP-Einheitsaufnahme

Kelly, Douglas:
The conspiracy of allusion : description, rewriting and authorship
from Macrobius to medieval romance / by Douglas Kelly. – Leiden ;
Boston ; Köln : Brill, 1999
    (Studies in the history of Christian thought ; Vol. 97)
    ISBN 90–04–11560–9

                    ISSN   0081-8607
                    ISBN   90 04 11560 9

PRINTED IN THE NETHERLANDS

Ausus idem.

(Horace)

TABLE OF CONTENTS

PREFACE

Rhetoric is an art of conspiracy. It is an art of making a particular version of a story convincing over against different, even conflicting or contradictory versions of the same story. Conflicting versions of narratives are the basis of dispute in courts, one of the places the art of rhetoric still receives its most consistent application. Such rhetorical conspiracy animates Chrétien de Troyes's attack on the inaccurate, incomplete versions of Erec and Enide's story told by contemporary storytellers as well as his assertion at the end of *Yvain* that any change in his version of the romance will falsify it. Authors like Chrétien when retelling and rewriting received *matières*, along with those who imitated his stories, themes, motifs, and lines of verse, did so in a cultural context that favored rhetorical training. Daring to rewrite — Horace's *Ausus idem* — characterizes virtually all ancient and medieval writing that is based on scholastic paradigms and models, paradigms and models that are informed by the art of rhetoric.

Macrobius refers to the art of *conspiratio* in the Preface to his *Saturnalia*. Among the metaphors he employs to describe the composition of this work is that of a symphony of voices blending their breath in unison, underscoring in this way the *con-* (with) *spirare* (breathing) that enables (em)plotting: "tale hoc praesens opus volo: multae in illo artes, multa praecepta sint, multarum aetatum exempla, sed in unum conspirata" (*Sat* praef. 10)[1] [This is the kind of work I intend to write: it should contain many arts and many precepts as well as illustrations from many times, but all brought together into one harmonious whole.] Different voices sing the same song. Not only do different authors proffer different versions of a single story, but each individual author must negotiate among the many voices heard in order to arrive at a new version. Homer and Vergil, as Macrobius shows in Books Five and Six of the *Saturnalia*, provide examples. "Quid enim suavius," exclaims Macrobius, "quam duos praecipuos vates audire idem loquentes?" (*Sat* 5.3.16) [what is more sweet than hearing two exceptional poets saying the same thing?] Macrobius is here attributing to "conspiracy" something of its literal signification in Latin: the unison of different voices. His sense of *conspiratio* in this passage is,

---

[1] Cf. Hooley 1997 p. 253.

actually, an art of allusion — that is, "how one text quotes, comments, corrects, integrates, and rereads another text."[2] The Middle Ages raised the art of allusion to an art of poetry.

Now, "nothing guarantees that a medieval *ars poetica* will provide the best available guide to the processes of the fictional text."[3] At issue is interpretation — that is, can knowledge of a formal art of writing help us interpret texts that exemplify that art, appreciate their originality, and identify features of their composition that might otherwise have escaped notice or have been misunderstood? Doubts often spring from a Romantic view of the creative, imaginative, because inspired artist rather than from the view most prevalent in the Middle Ages, a view fostered by arts of poetry and prose, and relying on the medieval meaning of invention. Invention is taught by precept and treatise, at least when the young student begins to study rhetoric. But the constraints of precept, especially with the talented or gifted writer, inform habits of conception, and can turn constraint into awareness of a language's potential for original expression. When the student of the treatise becomes the observer of actual poetic models that he or she sets out to rewrite, either by imitation or emulation, the rhetorical intent to retell the same story comes into play; the author plots another version of a given matter or theme,[4] and, in so doing, he or she engages in the art of conspiracy rather than submitting to a burst of inspiration — that is, he or she engages in intertextual allusions that rewrite and even correct earlier voices rather than relying on inspiration whose only source is the creative imagination.[5]

My purpose here is to delineate this poetics of conspiracy and to illustrate its usefulness for interpretation of a number of specimen romances in French from the twelfth and early thirteenth centuries. The book begins with Chrétien de Troyes's reference in *Erec et Enide* to Macrobius, an early fifth-century author best known to medievalists for his *Commentary on the Dream of Scipio*. The commentary has

---

[2] Wills 1996 p. 15. On the variety of such citations in Macrobius's *Saturnalia*, see Fiocchi 1981.

[3] Pensom 1993 pp. 533-34. SunHee Gertz has suggested to me that *inspirare* seems to have precluded *conspirare* in our conception of invention. See also Moos 1976 pp. 111-14 and Abramowska 1985 pp. 45-46.

[4] See, for example, Fredborg 1987 pp. 87 and 89-92, and Blänsdorf 1995.

[5] For a contemporary analysis of some of these issues, but in a framework compatible, I think, with that developed in this book, see Attridge 1999.

generally been taken to be the source of Chrétien's reference, although, as I shall argue, this is doubtful; if the later writer (in this
case, Chrétien) makes only a more or less accurate paraphrase, this is
antithetical to the medieval art of poetry as we know it, which does
not teach how to recover or reconstruct a text, as in source scholarship. Rather, it teaches how to rewrite by drawing on an earlier
work's potential for new expression. Indeed, this "immanent poetics"[6] is what Macrobius meant by description, and it is the art of
description that Chrétien de Troyes says Macrobius taught him, description being the art of rewriting. This immanent or implicit poetics
lies in the arts of poetry themselves, projecting them into a larger
milieu of reading, instruction, and imitation.[7] Rewriting, therefore, is
the sphere within which medieval writers in the scholastic tradition
sought and achieved originality.

Thanks to Chrétien's allusions to Macrobius we can bring together
the source, medieval arts of poetry, and rewriting or reconfiguring of
topoi that both Macrobius and Chrétien suggest by description.
Macrobius's surviving works illustrate the art of description that important medieval writers actually practiced; it can be found anew in
their own works and used to interpret them. My book focuses on
practice in the especially crucial period from about 1150 to 1225
when the Latin and French languages were producing some of their
greatest and most representative works. Those works are rewrites.
They rewrite by description, that is, by topical invention. In this way,
they raise issues of interest to some aristocratic audiences during their
own time: war and combat, consent in love and marriage, and constancy in love and marriage.

If we seek to appreciate how romancers rewrote their predecessors,
we must be selective since rewriting presumes a new version of ante-
rior material. Therefore, we must choose to examine specific romances that reveal the practice of the art and illustrate how they used
it to achieve originality. Inevitably, this requires comparison based on
allusions in the rewritten work to its antecedent sources and models:
to be original is to be, if not unique, at least different. Such comparison allows us to recover the medieval art of writing in original compositions.

I referred to antecedent works as models. "Model" will be a key

---

[6] Roberts 1985; see Chapter Three.
[7] Gerritsen 1973 part 3 p. 11.

term in this study. It is preferable to that of "genre" since, as Thomas Haye as pointed out, medieval authors often construed rewriting in terms of models rather than of genres. A critical model for the Middle Ages was, for example, the *Aeneid*. It is in terms of models that medieval poets thought of their own rewriting, whether they relied on the same plot as the model or whether they adapted the art implicit in its composition to new matters — as we shall observe in the case of Huon de Mery, who rewrote Chrétien's motifs and themes in a new, allegorical matter.

***

Two institutions have greatly contributed to the realization of this project: the University of Wisconsin, which has supported my work for many decades with marvelous generosity and patience, and the Netherlands Institute for Advanced Study which made it possible for me to complete this book in an ideal setting for writing and research. I would also like to express especial thanks to Professor Heiko A. Oberman for accepting this work into his series *Studies in the History of Christian Thought*. In addition, I am especially indebted to several persons who have helped further this project. First and foremost, SunHee Gertz has faithfully read a first version of the manuscript and offered invaluable advice. Paul Rockwell provided essential information on the *Troie*'s lexicography. I am also indebted to Jeffrey Wills, my colleague in the Madison Classics Department, and to Jan Miernowski, my colleague in the French Department, for numerous helpful suggestions; while at the Netherlands Institute, Dennis Green, Johan Oosterman, and Frank Willaert were very forthcoming with their help and suggestions. I have, however, followed my own way in this book; therefore, it goes without saying that the responsibility for any surviving errors and misprisions is entirely my own.

D.K.
June 1998
Wassenaar, The Netherlands

INTRODUCTION

> So bietet Macrobius... einen aufschlußreichen
> Umriß der dichterischen Nachahmungsmög-
> lichkeiten.[1]

Near the end of Chrétien de Troyes's twelfth-century romance *Erec et Enide* the narrator intervenes to comment on a coronation robe he is about to describe.

> Lisant trovomes an l'estoire
> La description de la robe,
> Si an trai a garant Macrobe
> Qui au descrire mist s'antante,
> Que l'an ne die que je mante.
> Macrobes m'ansaingne a descrivre
> Si con je l'ai trové el livre,
> L'uevre del drap et le portret.
> Quatre fees l'avoient fet...
>
> *(Erec* v. 6736-44) [2]

[Reading we come to the place in the story that describes the robe. I rely on Macrobius's authority, he who applied himself to the art of description, so that no one can accuse me of lying. Macrobius teaches me how to describe the weaving and portraiture of the cloth as I have invented it in my book. Four fays had woven it....]

---

[1] Cizek 1994 p. 63 [Thus, Macrobius offers a revealing outline of the possibilities for poetic imitation].

[2] Roques's edition, based on ms. B. N. fr 794, is garbled; see Dembowski 1994 pp. 123-24. Could one punctuate as follows: "Qui au descrire mist s'antante. Que l'an ne die que je mante!"? [who applied himself to the art of description. Don't accuse me of lying!] On Chrétien's influence on description in French romance, see Kelly 1987. Hartmann von Aue does not include the coronation robe in his adaptation of *Erec*, and, therefore, does not mention Macrobius. On Hartmann's adaptation from a critical perspective similar to mine, see Worstbrock 1985.

By and large scholars have read Chrétien's words as a reference to Macrobius's *Commentary on Cicero's Dream of Scipio*. But they have been hard put to identify a specific passage in this late antique text which might have served as source for Chrétien's description.[3] I intend to question that identification here, since I am convinced that Chrétien has, instead, Macrobius's *Saturnalia* in mind, although not as a source from which he might have lifted a passage in order to translate it into French verse. We shall see that the commonplace modern notion of copying or paraphrasing a source is quite different from the way Chrétien and his contemporaries rewrote their sources.

Indeed, the syntax in the *Erec* passage referring to Macrobius does not support the usual interpretation of these lines according to which Chrétien lifted from Macrobius his description of the quadrivium in Erec's robe. My argument is based on the fact that the presumed masculine object of the verb *descrire* in v. 6739 — "Qui au descrire mist s'antante" — cannot refer to the feminine *robe* (v. 6737), and that there is no other suitable masculine antecedent to account for it. This obliges us, therefore, to seek a different interpretation of the phrase "au descrire." I believe an acceptable one is available if one takes *descrire* to be an infinitive noun introduced by the masculine definite article *le* in elision with *a* > *au*.[4] Jean-Marie Fritz interprets the passage in this way although he still implies that Chrétien has Macrobius's *Commentary on the Dream of Scipio* in mind rather than the *Saturnalia*: "... auteur du *Commentaire sur le Songe de Scipion*, œuvre très lue et étudiée durant le Moyen Age. Macrobe semble ici transmettre à Chrétien l'art de décrire plutôt que le contenu même de cette

---

[3] Hofer 1928, Hart 1981 pp. 259-65. Hunt 1981-82 p. 221 mentions Chrétien's reference to the art of description, not to the substance of the description, and suggests that he may have known the *Saturnalia*; but his article focuses primarily on the *Commentary*, which was probably more widely known in Chrétien's century. Some scholars have argued that Chrétien is referring to Martianus Capella's *Marriage of Mercury and Philology*, books VI to IX of which are devoted to the quadrivium. See especially Uitti 1981; Luttrell 1974 pp. 20-22 (who thinks that Alain's *Anticlaudianus* is Chrétien's source for the quadrivium; on this attribution, see Hunt 1978b p. 231). On Martianus Capella's treatment of the quadrivium, see LeMoine 1972 Chapters Six and Eight; Stahl 1971-77 vol. 1 pp. 125-227.

[4] See Kelly 1983 pp. 14-16. By contrast see *Erec* v. 6707-08: "Donc vuel je grant folie anprandre / Qui au descrire vuel antandre" [wherefore I attempt something really foolish by trying to describe it], in which the personal pronoun *le* in *au* (< *a le*) obviously refers to "son coronemant," or coronation, in v. 6706. Dembowski ed. *Erec* v. 6731 keeps the reading of B.N. fr. 794: "Qui an l'estoire mist s'antante." But he interprets *l'estoire* to mean "l'art de la représentation, de la description" (p. 1112 n. 4), which fits my interpretation of the other reading of this line based on *le descrire*.

description qui, elle, se trouve dans la mystérieuse *estoire*."[5] In other words, *le descrire*, or description, is the art that Chrétien says he learned from Macrobius.

The only discussion of an art of description in any of Macrobius's extant writings appears in Books IV through VI of the *Saturnalia*. It follows that Macrobius's *Saturnalia* gives us insight not only into Chrétien's art of description but also into medieval notions of the art of poetry as set forth in eleventh- and twelfth-century commentaries on Horace's *Art of Poetry* and in twelfth- and thirteenth-century treatises on literary composition like those by Matthew of Vendôme and Geoffrey of Vinsauf. More specifically, the *Saturnalia* gives us insight into the emergence and rewriting of twelfth- and thirteenth-century French romance and the art of rewriting, of conspiracy, that informs it.

To be sure, Chrétien may be referring to both the *Saturnalia* and the *Commentary*. This view is strengthened by Chrétien's depiction of the four arts of the quadrivium in Erec's robe. For, although Macrobius contains no source text (in the usual sense of a passage lifted and translated) which Chrétien used to describe Erec's coronation robe, it is certainly true that the quadrivium — arithmetic, geometry, music, and astronomy — are the principal arts or sciences treated in both the *Commentary* and the coronation robe.[6] Let us look at that description.

According to Chrétien, the quadrivial arts provide truth and delight. They permit one to marvel at the whole universe, measuring the length and breadth of the earth and the heavens. Nothing escapes their scrutiny, not even the smallest particles: the number of drops in the sea, of grains of sand on the shore, of stars in the sky, of leaves in the forest. Harmony in sound and voice offers delight, while the heavens reveal the past and future.[7]

---

[5] *Erec* ed. Fritz p. 509 n. 1; see as well as *Erec* ed. Carroll v. 6692, 6694 and 6696 notes (p. 337).

[6] See Englisch 1994 pp. 54-55; she discusses Macrobius's contribution to the arts of the quadrivium in Chapter Three of her book. For a thorough review of the place of the liberal arts in the twelfth century, including extensive bibliography, see Stahl 1971-77, Beaujouan 1982, and Luscombe 1989. Chrétien does not reflect what Beaujouan p. 484 calls the "advanced" twelfth-century "research" on the quadrivium, but only "the more popular representations of the world." Macrobius enjoyed authority during this period for astrological studies (Beaujouan 1982 p. 481); as we shall see, Chrétien treats astronomy as astrology.

[7] See *Erec* v. 6746-90.

Perhaps the most intriguing art is astronomy.

> La quarte [fée], qui aprés ovra,
> A mout buene oevre recovra;
> Car la mellor des arz i mist.
> D'astronomie s'antremist,
> Celi qui fet tante mervoille,
> Qui as estoiles se consoille
> Et a la lune et au soloil.
> An autre leu ne prant consoil
> De rien qui a feire li soit;
> Cil la consoillent bien a droit.
> De quan que ele les requiert,
> Et quan que fu et quan que iert,
> Li font certainnement savoir
> Sanz mantir et sanz decevoir.

(Erec v. 6777-90)

[The fourth fay added her work next, producing a very fine piece of work, for she placed the best of the arts in it. She undertook the representation of astronomy, she who accomplishes such wonders, consulting the stars, moon, and sun. She consults nowhere else in any of her assigned tasks. They rightly advise her on whatever she inquires of them — on all past and future events — they give her certain knowledge, without falsehood or deception.]

The stars are unfailing sources of truth regarding the past and future, offering counsel and, it would seem, direction to life. The measure and harmony of the universe is reflected in the order and direction of human life.[8]

The complementary disciplines of geometry, arithmetic, music, and astronomy are commonplace topics in the rhetorical sense of places from which arguments may be drawn. Chrétien did not need Macrobius in order to describe them in the matter-of-fact way he

---

[8] On the relationship between ethics and the seven arts, see Delhaye 1958 pp. 59-78. Unlike Chrétien, Macrobius does not emphasize astrology; see Englisch 1994 pp. 182-95. This may be because part of the *Saturnalia* is missing; see *Sat* 1.24.18 on Eustathius's enthusiasm for Vergil's treatment of astrology; cf. *Sat* 5.2.2.

does. Any clerically trained author who had received schooling would know as much as Chrétien tells us in his description of the four arts.[9] As we shall see, descriptions of any or all of the seven liberal arts are not uncommon in medieval Latin. Indeed, knowledge of the commonplace activities of the quadrivial arts is so widespread that even fairies in the Matter of Britain were familiar with them! But, like weaving pictures, describing in words requires training and skill. It is the *art* of such representation — the art of description — that Chrétien says he learned and put into practice by studying Macrobius.

That Chrétien learned to describe in a medieval classroom is even anticipated by Macrobius when he declines to analyze in detail Vergil's extensive rewriting of the fall of Troy because the subject was too commonplace to require his illustration[10]; as Macrobius writes: "Sed et haec et talia pueris decantata praetereo" (*Sat* 5.2.6) [But I shall pass over these subjects commonly declaimed by and for school boys]. Declaimed — and thus committed to memory for future imitation.[11] In ancient and medieval schools rewriting was learned by *praeexercitamina*. Description is one kind of *praeexercitamen* in Priscian's influential system.[12]

Clearly, the *Commentary* does not teach how to describe, although it does offer numerous examples of descriptions as well as instances of the noun and verb for describing. In this study, Chapter Two examines the semantic range of *descriptio/describere* in medieval Latin and in Macrobius's own use of the word in both his works. This will provide a context which will enable readers to gauge Chrétien's French examples as well as his use of the term *descrire* in *Erec*.

Thus, starting with Chrétien de Troyes's assertion that he learned the art of description from Macrobius, I shall, in the first part of this

---

[9] The quadrivium was not taught everywhere; see Lesne 1938-40 vol. 5 pp. 608-13. Venice ms. Marciana Z lat. 497 is a compilation of works on the liberal arts, including extracts from both of Macrobius's two major works and from Martianus Capella; see Newton 1962 pp. 264-65 and 275-76 as well as Munk Olsen 1991a p. 64 and note 177.

[10] Cf. *Doc* II.3.132-37. Glauche says that anthologies of pieces on Troy were common in the eleventh century (Glauche 1970 p. 95). I discuss some twelfth-century examples in Chapter Four.

[11] On *decantare* as *praelectio* and *imitatio*, see Ziolkowski 1985 pp. 94-95 and Mora-Lebrun 1994a pp. 53-54, who also refers to *Sat* 1.24.5. Macrobius's words do not preclude both reading to and by schoolboys, nor do they distinguish between reading Vergil himself and classroom imitations of Vergil.

[12] *Gram. lat* vol. 2 pp. 438-39.

book, develop the implications of this statement by delineating Macrobius's and Chrétien's uses of the term 'description' and its cognates in order to show how consonant their notion was with medieval statements on *descriptio* in composition. Just as reading Macrobius from this perspective reveals a chain of descriptive rewritings from Vergil to Homer, so too, we can find similar lines of descent from Vergil's *Aeneid* through Macrobius into the twelfth century and beyond. The second part of this book treats the practice of that art in French romance, including the adaptation of Vergil's epic, the *Roman d'Eneas*, and Chrétien's own first romance, *Erec et Enide*, in which the reference to Macrobius occurs. In other words, I shall examine how various twelfth- and thirteenth-century romances use the art of description which Chrétien and Macrobius refer to. From this demonstration emerge illustrations of rewriting as *descriptio*, the technique Chrétien says he learned from Macrobius — a technique we can use to interpret medieval romances in the very tradition which Macrobius and Chrétien de Troyes articulate and illustrate.

The Macrobius reference in Chrétien's *Erec* raises two sets of questions, the one narrow, the other broad. The narrow questions are: what works by Macrobius is Chrétien specifically referring to, and what 'art of description' could he learn from it or them? These questions rest on the hypothesis that Chrétien is in fact referring to one or more of Macrobius's writings, that he is not lying when he asserts that Macrobius taught him how to describe things like a coronation robe, and that he has specific features of description ("le descrire") in mind, features which in fact Macrobius treats and which Chrétien in turn uses in the amplification on Erec's coronation robe as well as elsewhere in his first Arthurian romance and in his subsequent romances.

Arguing for this hypothesis raises the broader set of questions: what is the art of description, and what relation exists between Macrobius's art of description and that art as it was taught and imitated in twelfth-century schools in which Chrétien and others might have studied Macrobius? To answer these questions, we must review not only available evidence on twelfth-century instruction in composition and its relation to Macrobius on description, but also evidence of description in Latin and the vernacular.

Chrétien's claim regarding Macrobius's influence leads to one particular question concerning the *Saturnalia*: how well known was this work in Chrétien's time? Scholarly opinion is not unanimous. A rather wide divergence of opinion, together with the relative paucity of studies of the *Saturnalia* vis-à-vis those on the *Commentary*, means that hypotheses on the *Saturnalia*'s uses and influence rest on shaky ground. No doubt, the most balanced assessment comes from the pen of R. W. Hunt: "Works like... Macrobius's *Saturnalia* were certainly available in France and England in the [twelfth century], and were no less certainly read and consulted; but to judge from the evidence of extant MSS and from references in library catalogues [on which see Chapter One, below], they were not to be found everywhere...."[13] Thus, nestled in the broader set of questions is the critical problem of whether Chrétien's practice of description fits Macrobius's discussion of the art and use of the word and its cognates, whether that art was known or widely practiced in the twelfth century, and how representative Macrobius's treatment of description was for Latin and vernacular literary composition in Chrétien's time.

One final feature of Erec's coronation robe requires further comment: the presence of the four arts of the quadrivium and the ceremonies surrounding the coronation. Is there implied here that union of liberal and moral training which Jaeger has shown in *The Envy of Angels* to be typical of eleventh- and early twelfth-century cathedral

---

[13] Hunt 1971 p. 55. Cf., for example, Lesne 1938-40: "Maintes collections renferment le Songe de Scipion avec le Commentaire de Macrobe et parfois les Saturnales" (vol. 4, p. 778); Silvestre 1963: "Les *Saturnales* furent plus répandues ou, en tout cas, plus utilisées que le commentaire sur le *Songe de Scipion*" (p. 171 n. 7; Dronke 1974 pp. 5-6 n. 2 finds Silvestre's opinion "seriously misleading"); Bernabei 1970: "The *Saturnalia* was read by many medieval authors who used parts of it in their works, but it cannot be said to have had a great impact on medieval literature; although the *Saturnalia* was used amply, it was not used extensively, and it does not seem to have affected the fundamental outlook of any medieval thinker" (p. 199); De Paolis 1986-88: "... la fortuna di Macrobio nel Medioevo... fu maggiore per I *Comm[entarii]* che per I *Sat[urnalia]*" (p. 112); Barker-Benfield and Marshall 1983: "Medieval enthusiasm for the *Commentary* reached its peak in the twelfth century, while the *Saturnalia* did not come fully into favour until the Renaissance"; however, "although the *Saturnalia* never attained the popularity given to the *Commentary*, nevertheless in the twelfth century the *Saturnalia* comes into its own with such writers as William of Conches, Giraldus Cambrensis, and John of Salisbury" (p. 234). May we add Chrétien de Troyes's name to this venerable list? (See as well the table showing the number of manuscripts they have identified for each between the ninth and the fifteenth centuries inclusive (p. 224). See also Ghellinck 1946 vol. 2 p. 83; Jeauneau 1960 pp. 22-23; Vernet 1975 pp. 104-105; Hunt 1981-82 pp. 215-16, 219-20; Lord 1996. For additional bibliography, see De Paolis 1986-88 pp. 105-254 and, subsequently, the annual *Medioevo latino*.

schools as well as integral to the education of princes?[14] Perhaps. However, this fact does not explain why Chrétien chose to represent neither the trivium nor all seven liberal arts in the robe, but only the arts of the quadrivium: geometry, arithmetic, music, and astronomy.[15] What is the significance of the quadrivium in the representation of a prince being crowned king?

To illustrate this point and anticipate my argument, let us look briefly at Macrobius's *Commentary*. The *Commentary* comments on an extract from Cicero's *De republica*, the *Somnium Scipionis*, which treats of the immortality of great leaders. Thus, Erec's fusion of prince and quadrivium mirrors Scipio Africanus's dream. More precisely, the dream includes a description of the universe which the quadrivial arts help explain. In particular it treats the past and future of heroes — the subject of Chrétien's Astronomy as well — suggesting that leaders like Scipio who upheld world order also find a place in the greater scheme of things.

Ideas like these were not new when Chrétien wrote the *Erec*. For example, John of Salisbury uses both of Macrobius's major works to develop his conception of an ideal courtier,[16] although he also castigates the very courtiers Chrétien and vernacular authors like him probably wrote for. And while vernacular audiences are not necessarily identifiable as readers of Latin, as we shall see in Chapters Three and Four, such audiences did have interest in just such commentary on social and moral conduct, as is exemplified by *Cligés*, the romance Chrétien wrote after *Erec*.

The *Cligés* Prologue begins in a sense where *Erec* leaves off.[17] That is, it abstracts from Erec as ruler crowned and wrapped in the learning of the quadrivium; Chrétien moves on to evoke a national order upheld by the twin ideals of *chevalerie* and *clergie*, a variant, which Chrétien probably invented, of the traditional theme of the *translatio studii et imperii*. Cicero's *Somnium* and Macrobius's *Commentary* could

---

[14] Jaeger 1994 and Haug 1989.

[15] This is the sequence in *Erec*; the commonplace arrangement seems to have been arithmetic, music, geometry, and astronomy (Beaujouan 1982 p. 463).

[16] Hunt 1981-82 pp. 215-16, and 218-19, Moos 1988b pp. 570-75, Jaeger 1994 Chapter Twelve.

[17] Frappier 1968 pp. 17 and 102-03, Hunt 1981-82 pp. 222-23, and Halász 1992 pp. 21-22 and 35. Dembowski 1994 argues convincingly that Chrétien's "il m'estuet a el antandre" (*Erec* v. 6942) [I have other matters to attend to] does not refer to the composition of *Cligés* since it is not the conclusion to *Erec* in most manuscripts.

well have provided Chrétien with a key model of sovereignty based on prowess and learning. In *Erec* and *Cligés*, Chrétien informed feudal France and Arthur's Britain with that model — they are conspired descriptions of it.

But I do not wish to press this emphasis on learning presented by the coronation robe description too far. The elementary level of the *Erec* descriptions of the quadrivial arts, and even the implicit link in Chrétien's collected works between the quadrivium adorning a knight in *Erec* and the motif of the translation of *chevalerie* and *clergie* in *Cligés* may simply function as aspects of the marvelous. *Chevalerie* in the twelfth century does not embrace a scholarly, well-educated group of young men.[18] It can bedeck itself with the marvels of *clergie* (for example, in the tent descriptions in the antique romances) just as it can with those of fairy without revealing any fundamental urge to explore either the seven liberal arts or necromancy. These subjects bore the trappings of the marvelous, not of the learned twelfth-century *renovatio*. The seven arts and necromancy are usually left to women in the romances.[19] When we find them combined in the education of young men, as in *Athis et Prophilias*, it is only knighthood that is of any use to them afterwards; one variant version of this romance even mocks scholars' fear and ineptitude on the battle field.[20] Chrétien may indeed have proffered another, perhaps more desirable, image of the warrior class, but an explicit connection to an education in the quadrivium is lacking.

Is one justified in making Macrobius an exemplary authority on the art of description for Chrétien and others in his time? I believe so. But the art of composition, and especially the art of description are taken up only in the *Saturnalia*, which offers a compendium of late antique poetics, a poetics which, as Curtius points out[21] and as we shall see, survived into the Middle Ages. Latinists themselves point to Macrobius's *Saturnalia* as an authority on imitation and emulation in

---

[18] See Barbero 1987 esp. Part II: "L'aristocrazia e la chiesa." Cf. Batany 1992. Burgess 1994 has shown that the word *chevalerie* in the twelfth century connoted little more than military prowess.

[19] See Medea in the *Troie* v. 1221-28, Melior in *Partonopeu* v. 4611-12, and the Pucelle aux blanches mains in the *Bel inconnu* v. 4937-41. All three know the liberal arts, but only magic is of any use to them.

[20] See Castellani 1996 and, in general, Barbero 1987 pp. 168-70.

[21] Curtius 1954 pp. 441-42.

classical and later antiquity.[22] Description, as Macrobius uses the
term in the *Saturnalia*, refers to imitation as an art of either open or
disguised allusion to and rewriting of antecedent material. The
wealth of examples in Macrobius helps us to know this art as it was
used elsewhere in Latin and in the vernacular, especially in the period after 1100. In this way, Macrobius takes us a long way towards
understanding that art and appreciating its application in Chrétien's
romances and elsewhere. Chrétien de Troyes was not doing anything
unusual in using Macrobius's instruction on description to invent
Erec's coronation robe. But, as we shall see, his use of the art permitted him to describe with the originality and skill that raise his works
above those of many of his contemporaries.

The first part of this book contains three chapters. The first chapter takes up external evidence for the availability and use of
Macrobius's *Saturnalia* in Chrétien's epoch (about 1100 to 1225), and
the contexts in which it was used. Such contexts provide important
clues as to what readers or students sought among the diverse topics
taken up in the *Saturnalia*. The second chapter focuses on the art of
description as Macrobius uses the word in Books IV to VI. It shows
the term's relation to sources, imitation, and originality in rewriting.
The third chapter has three goals. First, it surveys the practice of
description in compositions that span the pupil's progression from
elementary paraphrase through writing worthy in its own right to
serve as model of the art of description, while charting stages in
acquisition of the art of description that Chrétien may well have
followed himself before going on to write the masterpieces of French
romance that themselves became models for other vernacular writers.
Second, it bridges the time span between late antique description and
medieval description. Third, it treats the emergence of commentaries
on Horace's *Art of Poetry* in the eleventh and twelfth centuries, which
establish principles of composition that the better-known twelfth- and
thirteenth-century arts of poetry and prose set out more systematically. Macrobius on description fits easily into this framework. The
second half of my book encompasses three chapters, which move on
to description in Latin and the French vernacular. The first of these
treats the rewriting of Dares by Benoît de Sainte-Maure and Joseph

---

[22] See, for example, Pasquali 1951 pp. 14-15 and 17, Wlosok 1990 pp. 234 and n.
5, and 238 and n. 19, Cizek 1994 esp. p. 63, Vogt-Spira 1994, Wills 1996, and
Hooley 1997.

of Exeter; the second takes up description of the consent motif as it was rewritten in three related works: the *Roman d'Eneas*, *Erec*, and the *Bel inconnu*; and the third examines the art of insertion and description, with special attention to Huon de Mery's *Tournoiement Antechrist*, Jean Renart's *Roman de la rose* or *Guillaume de Dole*, Gerbert de Montreuil's *Roman de la violette*, and Jakemes's *Le Châtelain de Couci et la Dame de Fayel*.

Vernacular authors adapted explicitly and implicitly the medieval Latin art of writing to their own different languages and publics. Knowledge of that art assists us today in interpreting medieval rewriting. It also helps us appreciate the originality of authors we may admire, but whose full achievement has sometimes escaped our grasp.

CHAPTER ONE

MACROBIUS IN THE MIDDLE AGES

> Nel Medio Evo, insomma, proprio il modo di
> trasmissione delle opere... deve essere conside-
> rato il maggior responsabile della qualità della
> ricezione letteraria.
>
> (Maria Luisa Meneghetti)[1]

The late antique author Macrobius wrote the *Saturnalia* (*Sat*), the
Commentary on Cicero's Dream of Scipio (*ComSS*), a grammatical treatise
on Greek and Latin verbs, and perhaps a few other fragments.[2] He
was cited frequently as a moral, philosophical, and scientific authority, especially because of his neoplatonic world view, and quotes ascribed to him are found in florilegia and elsewhere.[3] Philippe de
Thaon refers to him in the *Comput* and Richard de Fournival owned
his two major works. Macrobius's theory of true and false dreams was
especially influential. It is referred to in French literature in the Prologue to the *Roman de la rose*, where Guillaume de Lorris bases his own
dream's veracity in part on Macrobius's authoritative treatment of
the subject at the beginning of the *Commentary*.[4] On the other hand,
Jean de Meun later denies the veracity of Guillaume's dream, again

---

[1] Meneghetti 1992 p. 25: In short, in the Middle Ages, the mode of transmission
of literary works should be considered primarily responsible for the quality of literary
reception.

[2] Flamant 1977 pp. 145-47; Marinone ed. *Sat* pp. 27-29; Marinone 1987 p. 299.
On Macrobius's dates, see Cameron 1966. The extant grammatical treatise is actu-
ally an Irish summary of an original which has been lost; see Bershin 1988 p. 34. The
summary shows that the original was a scientific study of verbs in the Greek and
Latin languages. For the text of the summary, see *Gram lat* vol. 5 pp. 595-655; cf.
Barker-Benfield 1983 p. 223.

[3] Paris BN lat 1860 (see Sanford 1924 p. 235), Paris BN lat 7647 = the *Florilegium
Gallicum* (see Burton 1983 pp. 44-49), Rome Bibl. Angelica 1985 = the *Florilegium
Angelicum* (see Rouse 1976 pp. 95 and 100) — all twelfth-century manuscripts. To be
sure, some attributions are spurious. Quotes also occur in glosses; see Hunt 1991,
where *Saturnalia* references occur in vol. 1, pp. 252, 265, 266, 272, and 275. French-
language references are discussed below.

[4] Kruger 1992. However, he was not the only source of dream theory, despite the
autority of the *ComSS*; see Bodenhem 1985 and Peden 1985.

referring to Macrobius's *Commentary*, but this time to establish its mendacity.[5] The *Commentary* is his best-known work today, as it apparently was in Chrétien's lifetime.

Although less well known in the twelfth century, the *Saturnalia* is more indicative of the art of rewriting in the Middle Ages than the *Commentary*. Macrobius himself says that he wrote the work for the education of his son (*Sat* praef. 1-2). It reports a fictitious three-day conversation among guests invited to celebrate the feast of the Saturnalia.[6] The topic of the three-day conversation is Vergil. Macrobius treats the *Aeneid* as an encyclopedic work.[7] As such, it could educate its readers in many different branches of learning. Indeed, the conversations that make up the three-day celebration turn on a variety of topics, from the calendar to the divinity and the origins of Roman customs. Books IV through VI, which will occupy us most here, treat Vergil's imitation of Homer, either by showing how the Roman poet adapts his Homeric source, or how intermediate Latin writers "translated" (in the word's three senses of 'translate,' 'transmit,' and 'transform') Homer's art to Vergil.[8] These books treat Vergil's imitation as 'description.' From them, Chrétien could have learned the art of description which he claims to imitate and apply in the composition of Erec's coronation robe.

But first two clarifications. Although I am convinced that Chrétien meant what he said — that Macrobius, and, more particularly, the *Saturnalia*, taught him how to describe — it is not necessary to suppose that Macrobius was the only source of instruction on description

---

[5] Kelly 1995a pp. 150-51.

[6] On the divisions of the *Saturnalia*, see Marinone ed. *Sat* pp. 36-41, Pieri 1977 pp. 43-75, and Irvine 1994 pp. 142-47. La Penna 1953 pp. 242-43 shows that only the three-day division can be traced back with certainty to Macrobius; the division into seven books was probably determined by the lacunae that separate each of the seven books (Marinone 1987 pp. 301-02).

[7] Cf. *Sat* 1.24.13. On the *Aeneid* as *sacrum poema*, see Herzog 1975 p. xv, esp. n. 2; Sinclair 1982 pp. 261-63; Klopsch 1980 p. 104; Berlioz 1985 pp. 81, 90, 105, 113, and 116; Wlosok 1990 pp. 486-87, esp. ns. 32-37; for reservations regarding this attribution in Macrobius's time, see Cameron 1977 pp. 23-24. On Vergil as source of universal knowledge for medieval readers before Chrétien's time, see Gibson 1975 pp. 9-10; on p. 12 she discusses Macrobius's *Commentary* as authority for this view.

[8] Macrobius did not invent this view of Vergilian imitation, but he did illustrate it in great detail; for an overview see (with additional bibliography) Wlosok 1990 pp. 476-88. On the controversy about Vergil's rewriting and even alleged plagiarism, see Pieri 1977 pp. 7-13 and Hathaway 1989 pp. 22-27 (including special reference to Macrobius).

available to Chrétien. In fact, he was not. Whatever Macrobius may have taught Chrétien, his treatment of description is typical, not original. Macrobius complements and, in many ways, clarifies and differentiates the modes of rewriting as description that we find in the medieval Latin tradition and in the emerging vernacular tradition of rewriting to which Chrétien himself contributed so much and served as model. Chrétien's reading and use of the art of description as set forth in the *Saturnalia* was not "reading against the grain" of his time.

Second, we must recognize that reference to Macrobius (or any other author) does not prove direct knowledge of the work referred to. For example, Alard de Cambrai names twenty of "Les plus maistres clers qui ains furent"[9] [the greatest master clerics of the past]; the last is Macrobius, right after Vergil (v. 75-80). Alard cites Macrobius on the virtues and vices, a subject on which the late Roman author was also an authority and a source.[10] But he knew Macrobius through Guillaume de Conche's *Moralium dogma philosophorum* or the Old French translation of it.[11] The moral maxims attributed to Macrobius may themselves have reached Guillaume through *florilegia*, although Macrobius's classification of the virtues in the *Commentary* was, as I said, widely known. In any case, we first need evidence that corroborates Chrétien's claim to have studied Macrobius's treatment of description. To do so, we need to delineate the environments in which Macrobius was studied during Chrétien's time. Such evidence will show that the *Saturnalia* was available to him.

Macrobius's Contextual Environment in the High Middle Ages

Let us begin by examining the reputation, availability, and influence of the *Saturnalia*, especially Books IV-VI, between 1100 and 1225. To do so we shall explore the "contextual environment" in which Macrobius survived and was read. I am using the term contextual environment in the sense proposed by Léopold Genicot. It is (1) the mode of insertion of a text in a given manuscript, whether as part of the original copy, as an added leaf or leaves, or in a manuscript that

---

[9] *Philosophie* v. 23.

[10] Holmberg ed. *Dogma* p. *9*; all the references identified in Alard's and Guillaume de Conches's treatises are to the *Commentary*. On Macrobius's contribution to ethical classifications, see Lottin 1942-49 vol. 1 p. 528 n. 1.

[11] Holmberg ed. *Dogma* pp. *9-10*, *33*, and *36*; Payen ed. *Philosophie* pp. 11-12.

binds together two or more originally separate manuscripts into one; and (2) the contents of a given manuscript, and the frequency of the same contents in other manuscripts.[12]

There are four main sources of information on the *Saturnalia*'s contextual environment: first, the manuscript tradition, including evidence of glossing and commentary, and the contents of manuscripts containing the *Saturnalia* that offer clues regarding the purpose for which the manuscript was written and used; second, medieval library catalogues, especially when these provide evidence as to context and uses of the catalogued manuscript; third, poetic anthologies, florilegia, and *libri manuales*, or excerpt collections,[13] to suggest what the anthologizer or the compiler was looking for in the *Saturnalia*; and fourth and last, medieval references to the *Saturnalia* like Chrétien's own that tell us whether it was known and how it was used. I shall take these topics up in order.

Manuscripts

By and large, the *Saturnalia* and the *Commentary* were transmitted separately until the late Middle Ages and Renaissance.[14] Only a few pre-thirteenth-century manuscripts contain both works.[15] Almost all manuscripts containing both are late medieval or early modern bindings of manuscripts that were originally separate.[16] No manuscript

---

[12] Genicot 1975 pp. 224-25. Cf. Kelly 1991 p. 122. Hexter 1988 pp. 26-35, Godman 1990a pp. 596-99, Moores 1990, and Atkinson 1994 offer excellent illustrations of the analysis of contextual environment in Genicot's sense.

[13] Including the *Saturnalia* itself: Books IV-VI provide a collection of excerpts from Vergil and numerous other writers. Some parts read like a string of quotations and have little or no commentation (e.g., *Sat* 5.4-10, 6.1.8-65); others interlace excerpts and commentary (e.g., *Sat* 5.11 and 13-14); still others are commentary with cross-references that contain no, or fewer, actual quotations (e.g., *Sat* 5.1.18-2.16, 5.15-17, 6.1.1-7). The medieval arts of poetry and prose treat quotations in a similar fashion; see Kelly 1991 p. 41.

[14] Barker-Benfield and Marshall 1983 p. 222; De Paolis 1986-88 p. 134, Jan ed. *Sat* vol. 1, p. lxii. This is borne out by comparing the list of *Sat* manuscripts in the Appendix to this chapter with the *ComSS* manuscripts listed in Eastwood 1994.

[15] Barker-Benfield and Marshall 1983 pp. 222-23. Naples VB 12, another twelfth-century manuscript, contains extracts from *Sat* and *ComSS* (Munk Olsen 1982-89 vol. 1, p. 243).

[16] See Barker-Benfield and Marshall 1983 p. 222 n. 1. The same may be true for Paris B.N. latin 6370 if Paris B.N. latin 6371 and Troyes 514 are analogous to it (Barker-Benfield and Marshall 1983 pp. 222-23). On later bindings, especially by Renaissance editors, see Barker-Benfield and Marshall 1983 p. 223.

contains a complete text of Macrobius's original *Saturnalia* (see the Appendix at the end of this chapter). Scholars agree that all the manuscripts of the incomplete *Saturnalia* derive from a single eighth- or ninth-century original.[17] Many — the so-called *mutili* — do not even contain all of the text still extant today. Among these, Books IV-VI are often missing, which suggests that they were viewed as different from the other more scientific or encyclopedic books.[18] In other words, the emphasis on composition in Books IV-VI distinguishes them from the philosophical, ethical, and scientific topics treated in the other books.[19]

Modern studies of Macrobius manuscripts emphasize their codicological rather than literary historical features, focusing on early specimens in order to recover the original text and neglecting most manuscripts dated after 1200.[20] But the literary historical aspects of manuscript transmission are important in determining the contextual environment of the different copies of the *Saturnalia*. Moreover, in the *Saturnalia* itself, the different topics taken up on different days meet diverse interests.

Importantly, some manuscripts collect related works that suggest the purpose for which they were read or used. Those with a decidedly poetic context — some of which contain canonical works bound together with arts of poetry and prose — may illustrate the *kind* of manuscript in which Chrétien read Macrobius.[21] Such manuscripts

---

[17] La Penna 1953 p. 234, Willis 1957 p. 158, Marinone ed., *Sat* p. 61, Barker-Benfield and Marshall 1983 pp. 234-35, De Paolis 1986-88 p. 135.

[18] La Penna 1953 p. 243, Willis 1957 p. 158, De Paolis 1986-88 p. 134, Barker-Benfield and Marshall 1983 p. 234.

[19] For overviews of the different subjects discussed in the *Saturnalia* and their order, see Marinone ed. *Sat* pp. 36-41; Marinone 1987 pp. 301-02. No known manuscript before 1225 contains only Books IV-VI. Paris BN lat. nouv. acq. 1907 contains only Book VI (Olmont 1907 p. 30 and Munk Olsen 1979-80 vol. 10 pp. 129-30); Bern Burgerbibl. 404 contains Books 5.13 through 7 (Munk Olsen 1982-89 vol. 1, p. 397). Contamination is common (Willis 1957 p. 154).

[20] But there are exceptions; see Willis 1957 pp. 153-54.

[21] For example: Cambridge Corpus Christi 71 contains both of Macrobius's works as well as works by Apuleius (*De dogmate Platonis, De mundo, De deo Socratis*) and two letters exchanged between Gerbert d'Aurillac and Adelbodus on mathematical subjects; see James 1912 vol. 1 pp. 149-51; Sanford 1924 p. 224 (§208); La Penna 1953 p. 242; Munk Olsen 1982-89, s.n. Apuleius C.15 and Cicero C.79. Similarly, Cambridge Bibl. Univ. 1213 contains the *Saturnalia*, Apuleius's *De deo Socratis*, sections of the *Florida* Book IV, some verses by Maximianus, and poems attributed to Lucan and Cicero; see Jan ed. *Sat* vol. 1, pp. lxxxi-lxxxii; La Penna 1953 p. 242; *Cambridge* 1980 vol. 2 p. 412; Munk Olsen 1982-89 s.n. Apuleius C.16, Florilegia C.10, Cicero C.681, Lucan C.23, Ovid C.16, Petronius C.4, and vol. 3^1 p. 60 and 3^2 p. 162.

suggest that the *Saturnalia* could be read either as an authority on the art of composition or for its more encyclopedic content.[22] The *Aeneid* itself was read as a poetic model in this way: "Si quis vero hec omnia studeat imitari, maximam scribendi peritiam consequitur; maxima etiam exempla et excogitationes aggrediendi honesta et fugiendi illicita per ea que narrantur habentur" (*ComBS* p. 2, ll. 17-19) [If one strives to imitate all these things, one acquires the greatest skill in writing. One also finds in its plot superb examples and thoughts for following what is right and avoiding what is wrong]. The dual intent is common in the Middle Ages, as we shall see below in the discussion of commentaries (see Chapter Three). Works of a philosophical or moral character like Bernardus Silvestris's *Cosmographia* or Jean de Hauville's *Architrenius* were also models of the medieval art of poetry.[23]

On the other hand, some manuscripts evince a rhetorical context. For example, in Escorial S.I.18 (thirteenth century) the *Saturnalia* follows Cicero's *De inventione* and the pseudo-Ciceronian *Rhetorica ad Herennium* as well as his *De natura deorum, De divinatione, De fato*, and *De officiis*[24]; this manuscript includes Books IV-VI of the *Saturnalia*.[25] Rhetorical manuscripts like these might also resemble, by their contextual environment, the kind Chrétien read and drew his ideas on the art of description from. These manuscripts are merely selected examples. Further study is necessary. Such study would examine not only *Saturnalia* glosses but also Vergil manuscripts to determine whether Macrobius was used to gloss his works, and in what ways.[26]

Of particular interest here as an example is Paris BN nouv. acq. lat. 1907, which contains excerpts from Vergil's *Aeneid* (fol. 4r°-9v°) in groups of verse separated by blanks that might be used for glossing,

---

Apuleius was a model for scientific and philosophical poetry in Chrétien's time, just as Bernardus Silvestris's *Cosmographia* was a model for the medieval poetic art; see Kelly 1991 pp. 57-64.

[22] Hathaway 1989 p. 24 treats Macrobius's borrowing of well-put phrasing and of material he deemed worth knowing.

[23] Kelly 1991 pp. 57-64.

[24] *Escorial* 1910-23 vol. 4 pp. 24-25. On the relation between rhetoric and poetics, see Curtius 1938, Moos 1976, Leotta 1988, Kelly 1991 pp. 52-53 and 60.

[25] Naples V.B.12 contains Cicero's *De inventione*, but only the first three books of the *Saturnalia*; see La Penna 1953 p. 239.

[26] Manuscripts containing glosses or scholia: Becker 1885 §§ 93 "ut glosas super Macrobium... transmittere" (p. 207, in a letter), 103:4 "glosse super Macrobium" (p. 223). A commentary on the *ComSS* was written by Guillaume de Conches (Jeauneau 1971).

and that also resemble sections of the *Saturnalia*'s Books V and VI, which list illustrations of Vergil's rewriting without comment. Thus, this manuscript contains excerpts from Book VI of the *Saturnalia* and Servius's commentary on the *Aeneid*, both of which treat Vergil's rewriting earlier Latin authors.[27] Likewise, Venice Marc. Z lat. 497 contains extracts from the *Saturnalia* together with others from Vergil in a vast collection on the liberal arts, thereby again exemplifying the frequency with which these arts were studied in their relation to Macrobius.[28]

Eleventh- and twelfth-century commentaries on Horace's *Art of Poetry* are also significant here, not only because Macrobius's name appears in them on occasion, but also — and more importantly — because their systematic interpretation of Horace's poem prepares the way for the twelfth- and thirteenth-century arts of poetry and prose, in which the kind of description Macrobius treats is so important.[29] Matthew of Vendôme in particular treats extensively the circumstantial topoi under description (*Ars vers* 1.77-113). This is a framework that users of the *Saturnalia* in manuscripts containing, for example, the *De inventione*[30] might quickly recognize. For example, Macrobius on Vergil's rewriting might influence later rewriting of, notably, the Trojan War, a topic recommended by Horace,[31] treated in part in Book II of the *Aeneid* (cf. *Sat* 5.5.1-14), and practiced in the medieval classroom (see Chapter Three). Strasbourg BN and Univ. 14, an eleventh century manuscript, binds Dares and Dictys with the *Saturnalia*, which suggests the relation of these works to major twelfth-century poems by Joseph of Exeter and Benoît de Sainte-Maure (see Chapter Four).

---

[27] See Olmont 1907 p. 30; Munk Olsen 1982-89 vol. 2 pp. 769 (= B.203), 819 (= Bc.71), and 866 (B.51). Before the end of the twelfth century, Vergil's works were almost always bound together (Munk Olsen 1985 pp. 38-40); Macrobius treats the *Eclogues* and the *Georgics* too.

[28] Newton 1962 pp. 264-66, Munk Olsen 1991a p. 64 and note 177.

[29] Friis-Jensen 1995b. On these commentaries, see Chapter Three.

[30] Brussels BR 10.057-10.062 (see Ward 1972 vol. 2 pp. 250-51). The *Saturnalia* is bound with Cicero's *De inventione* in the following manuscripts: Escorial S.1.18 and Vatican Borg. Lat. 326. Cf. Ward 1995 pp. 143 and 240-41. The *De inventione* is the principal source for Matthew's descriptive topoi (Faral 1924 pp. 75-85).

[31] *ArsPoet* v. 128-30; see Kelly 1998.

Library Catalogues

Richard de Fournival knew Macrobius. His case is intriguing since he was a vernacular author quite familiar with the Latin tradition; he wrote in French in a variety of registers, and one major medieval Latin poem has been attributed to him.[32] His library, which he catalogued in the *Biblionomia*, attests to his broad knowledge and interests, interests which reappear in his own writings. The *Biblionomia* is therefore especially important in determining contextual environment; it catalogues the library of a vernacular author, includes the *Saturnalia*, and arranges titles loosely according to subjects.[33] Sanford has called attention to four works in his library that contain Macrobius; one she calls a handbook on the art of writing, and another contains the *Saturnalia*.[34] This is not the manuscript that contains Fournival's complete copy of the *Saturnalia*, which is §88 in the *Biblionomia*. The latter has been identified as B.N. latin 6367 where it is bound with the *Commentary*; however, they were originally separate and were still so in Fournival's library.[35]

The *Biblionomia* divides Fournival's manuscripts into two broad categories: philosophy and poetry. Among the works Fournival catalogues under philosophy appear Martianus Capella's *Marriage of Mercury and Philology* and a treatise on astrology attributed to him, as well as another title attributed to him called "de sex reliquis artibus" (*Biblionomia* §§97-98)[36] [on the six remaining arts], presumably based on the trivium and quadrivium. Also included under philosophy are Alain de Lille's *Anticlaudianus* and *De planctu Naturae* (*Biblionomia* §§ 105-106), Bernardus Silvestris's *Cosmographia* (*Biblionomia* § 107), and Jean de Hauville's *Architrenius* (*Biblionomia* § 108).[37] On the other hand, under poetry in Fournival's library appear Vergil (*Biblionomia* § 109), Gautier de Châtillon's *Alexandreis* (*Biblionomia* § 113), and Ovid (*Biblio-*

---

[32] On the contested attribution of the *De vetula* to Richard, see Klopsch ed. *Vetula*, pp. 78-99.

[33] For an edition, see *Biblionomia*; on Fournival's library catalogue, see Rouse 1973.

[34] Sanford 1924 p. 197 (§ 325); the *Saturnalia* is in § 327 (p. 233)..

[35] See Rouse 1973 p. 266; *Biblionomia* §84, which also contained the *Saturnalia*, has not been identified in a modern library (cf. Sanford 1924 § 327; Rouse 1973).

[36] Leonardi 1959-60 does not list this title.

[37] Gervase of Melkley calls these works exemplary illustrations of the art of poetry and prose, and, therefore, worthy of imitation by his pupils (*ArsGM* pp. 1 and 3-4).

nomia §§ 117-20). Claudian's *In Rufinum* (*Biblionomia* § 122) also appears among the poets (unlike the *Anticlaudianus*, which is classified among the philosophers § 105), as well as Horace's *Art of Poetry* (*Biblionomia* § 125),[38] Prudentius's *Psychomachia* (*Biblionomia* § 128), Matthew of Vendôme's *Tobias* (*Biblionomia* § 131), and Petrus Riga's *Aurora* (*Biblionomia* § 132: "Petri Trecensis bybliotheca versificata").[39]

The classification of manuscripts in Richard de Fournival's library catalogue is not, and indeed could not be, entirely consistent. A given manuscript often contained more than one work, making its various contents difficult to classify, especially if first gathered to meet demands different from his own system of classification. Several sections may overlap in any given manuscript, in which case the catalogue heading may conform to only one general topic. For example, Cicero's *Topica* is classed under logic (*Biblionomia* §21[40]) whereas Boethius's commentary on the *Topica* falls under rhetoric (*Biblionomia* §35). In fact, the *Topica* and Boethius's commentary on it treat both logical and rhetorical topoi.[41] The *Saturnalia* itself appears twice, once in a florilegium comprising philosophical and moral precepts excerpted from the *Saturnalia* as well as writings by Jerome, Apuleius, Pliny the Younger, Cicero, Sidonius Apollinaris, Seneca, Aulus Gellius, and Plautus.[42] Metaphysical and ethical books comprise a subsection of philosophy. The complete *Saturnalia* is found in the section containing philosophers' works ("libros vagos phylosophorum," *Biblionomia* §88[43]). In Fournival's library it is catalogued between the

---

[38] The *ArsPoet* also appears among the grammar books (§ 11), bound together with what is probably Geoffrey of Vinsauf's *Poetria nova*: "Item Willermi de Witam poetica nova ad Innocentium papam tercium"; see *Poetria nova* ed. Faral 1924 v. 2099-2116, and Nims trans. p. 110. On this identification, see Kelly 1991 p. 117 n. 277. This manuscript precedes Matthew of Vendôme's *Summa de arte versificandi* (*Biblionomia* § 12); on this title for the *Ars versificatoria*, see Kelly 1966 p. 262 and Lennartz 1993 pp. 47-48.

[39] On the author's name and the poem's title, see Manitius 1911-31 vol. 3, p. 825.

[40] In a manuscript containing treatises on logic; see Rouse 1973 p. 259.

[41] Stump ed. *Top* and Vance 1987. Matthew's *Ars vers* 1.76 alludes to this distinction; see Bornscheuer 1976 pp. 170-71.

[42] *Biblionomia* §84; cf. Sanford 1924 § 327. It would be useful to determine whether excerpts from the *Saturnalia* include material from the lost, longer version like that which John of Salibury may have had at his disposal (Webb 1897; Courcelle 1948 p. 61 n. 4).

[43] This is the complete version of the *Saturnalia* Rouse 1973 p. 266 identifies as Paris BN lat 6367.

Commentary on the Somnium Scipionis (*Biblionomia* §87) and Aulus Gellius's *Noctes Atticae* (*Biblionomia* §89). That the *Saturnalia* precedes the *Noctes* makes sense, for Aulus Gellius's work is an eclectic collection of essays on diverse subjects, including commentary on Vergil which Macrobius too inserted into his own work.[44] Clearly, the titles included in this section fit philosophy in the broader sense of "knowledge" or "learning."

We may draw two conclusions from Fournival's system of classification and the works located under various topics in his catalogue — conclusions that point to the uses made of the *Saturnalia* itself. First, the division among the arts and sciences under the general heading of philosophy is typical and traditional. We proceed through the "tree of knowledge" from the trivium through the quadrivium and the higher physical, metaphysical, and ethical sciences to "philosophy." "Poetry" comprises a separate, subsidiary servant of the arts and sciences.[45] Second, since the disposition of works is not always consistent, a work like the *Saturnalia* can be viewed as a source of moral instruction and wisdom, a work of philosophy, as well as a commentary on Vergil's art of poetry and on the art of poetry in general; indeed, how it is read may depend on the context in which it is found and its context may depend on how complete it is in the given manuscript or whether it is excerpted or in a florilegium. Vergil for Macrobius is also a philosopher, a master of all arts and sciences. As poet, he appears in the *Biblionomia* not only with Horace and Ovid, but also with the *Cosmographia, Alexandreis, Tobias,* and the versified Bible *Aurora* — that is, with scientific, historical, and religious writings.[46] Interpreters of the *Aeneid* also refer to these contexts for reading Vergil,[47] contexts which correspond to those treated by Macrobius himself in the *Saturnalia*.

---

[44] Macrobius may have drawn on the *Noctes* for the *Saturnalia* using principles of adaptation like those he himself describes in analyzing Vergil's imitation of his models; see Lögdberg 1936 chapter One. However, Marinone ed. *Sat* pp. 47-49 (with additional bibliography) argues that the correspondences between the two works may derive from their common source.

[45] On trees of knowledge like that implicit in Fournival's arrangement of books, see Dahan 1980 pp. 175-85, with additional bibliography. On rhetoric in the classification, see Fredborg 1987 pp. 86-87.

[46] Vergil's complete works are in *Biblionomia* § 109.

[47] Baswell 1985 and 1995. Similarly, Radulphe de Longchamp reads the *Anticlaudianus* as a scientific work, breaking off his commentary when Alain de Lille's poem passes to other matters; see Sulowski ed. *In Anti* pp. xxxiii-xxxv.

The *Biblionomia* is a medieval library catalogue. Many such catalogues refer to "Macrobius" without designating a title.[48] Other catalogues simply name the *Saturnalia*, without always specifying whether it is complete, lacks certain books, or contains only excerpts.[49] Nonetheless, taking them together with the foregoing example of Fournival's library and the discussion below of poetic anthologies, we find that medieval library catalogues contain witnesses for the contextual environments in which the *Saturnalia* was read and studied in the Middle Ages, and, more to the point of this book, for the grammatical, rhetorical, and poetic contexts in which Chrétien might have used the work to learn how to describe. The *Saturnalia* was a major commentary on a canonical masterpiece and exemplar of the art of poetry, Vergil's *Aeneid*. It would certainly be consulted in studying Vergil. And it was available.

Anthologies, Florilegia, and libri manuales

The *Saturnalia*'s Books IV-VI read like a florilegium — so much so that actual *libri manuales* and florilegia seem to mirror how Macrobius presented Vergil and other poets.[50] The scribe of one of his manuscripts appended a poem as if to confirm the work as a kind of florilegium containing "Dulcia Virgilii dicta vel egregii / Ex studio

---

[48] See, for example, Becker 1885 §§ 25:3 (p. 57), 60:25 (p. 146), 74:179 (p. 177), 77:180 (p. 183), 80:75-77 (p. 192), 86:106 (p. 202), 112:87 (p. 229) immediately after two "Homeri" (112:81-82) and four "Vergilii II in IIII divisi" (112:83-86), 117:82 (p. 240), 121:1 (p. 247), 136:282 and 311 (pp. 284, 285); Manitius 1935 § 151 (pp. 227-32); Ogilvy 1967 pp. 196-97; Glauche 1970 pp. 94 and 96.

[49] Becker 1885 §§ 15:319 *Sat* (p. 35), 62:13 *Sat* (p. 147), 68:255 *ComSS* and *Sat* (p. 154), 79:222 *Sat* (p. 189), 80:93-94 *Sat* (p. 192), 86:105 *Sat* (p. 202), 127:145 *Sat* (p. 265), 136:338 *Sat* (p. 285). Becker p. 127:158 (p. 266) names "Macrobius super somnium scipionis," then, after several other titles and authors, "Macrobii II." Cf. Vernet 1975 pp. 104-105. Other catalogues identify the *ComSS*, while still others suggest excerpts from the *Saturnalia* — for example, Becker 1885 §§ 62:9 "proemium Macrobii" (p. 147). Jarrow contained the *Saturnalia* but not the *Commentary* (Jeauneau 1975 p. 33). Bede used the *Saturnalia* in his *De temporum ratione* (Ogilvy 1936 p. 62) and Bernard of Chartres in his commentary on *Timaeus* (*Glosae* ed. Dutton pp. 64-65). However, Bede knew both works; see Manitius 1911-31 vol. 1, pp. 77 and 80, and the "Index auctorum" in *Opera Bedae* vol. 3, pp. 779-80; but see Wright 1995 Study XI p. 362 n. 4, who contests this knowledge. Ogilvy 1967 states that "the Irish seem to have had the whole text," but that it reached England in some version only in the tenth or eleventh century; he admits that "the history of most of the [*Saturnalia*] MSS is obscure" (p. 196). For reservations on the "Irish connection" and Macrobius, see Jeauneau 1975 p. 34 and Holtz 1991 esp. pp. 89-94.

[50] Burton 1983 p. 47; Munk Olsen 1979-80.

cerpta ueterum congesta et in unum."[51] [illustrious Vergil's sweet
words diligently excerpted and collected] The author, a certain
Azelinus, is referring to poetic florilegia like that in *Saturnalia* Books
IV-VI. It is noteworthy that his bouquet metaphor is used much as
Macrobius does perfume and chorus metaphors in the Preface to the
Saturnalia (praef. 8-9).

Florilegia and *libri manuales* usually evince a moral context.[52] The
florilegia may not have been widely used to teach the art of writing.[53]
But it is different with the *libri manuales*. A notable exception is the
medieval arts of poetry and prose, especially those written in prose.
Like *Saturnalia*'s Books IV-VI, the prose treatises by Matthew of
Vendôme, Geoffrey of Vinsauf, Gervase of Melkley, and John of
Garland are laid out like commentaries on an anthology of excerpts.[54] Some manuscripts reinforce this impression by inserting
these arts in poetic anthologies.[55] Here too Macrobius's commentary
on representative passages from Vergil and other authors anticipates
and fits into the format of manuscripts containing treatises that teach
the art of poetry and prose. Among florilegia, those known as the
"Florilegium Macrobianum" are clearly relevant to this study. This
brief florilegium received its name because it is found inserted in the
Saturnalia in four different manuscripts.[56] Inserted either between
Saturnalia Books VI and VII or, in one instance, after Book VII, this
florilegium constitutes a small set of eight texts or extracts, including
poems attributed to Cicero and Lucan as well as others.

A number of the more general *libri manuales* dating from Chrétien's
period also contain excerpts from the *Saturnalia*. Eva Matthews Sanford identified numerous such compendia, grouping many of them
according to their context or predominant subject-matter, the contextual environment, of each manuscript.[57] Macrobius's place among

---

[51] Quoted from La Penna 1953 pp. 240-41.

[52] Sanford 1924 and Munk Olsen 1979-80 vol. 9 p. 56; cf. Hamasse 1990.

[53] See Munk Olsen 1982 pp. 160-64, who likens them to *aides-mémoire* and *vade mecum* rather than school books; but he also says that more work needs to be done on the question of their uses. Ward 1990 p. 21 suggests that they could have served as *materia* for *usus* (*chria*) in *exercitatio*.

[54] See Kelly 1991 p. 125.

[55] Kelly 1991 pp. 99-100. The best known example is the Glasgow anthology; see Faral 1936, Cizek 1994 pp. 154-56; Rigg et alii 1977-90 report other examples. I return to this subject in Chapter Three.

[56] Munk Olsen 1979-80 vol. 9 p. 51 and vol. 10 pp. 120-22.

[57] Sanford 1924 pp. 203-40.

them illustrates the diverse ways both the *Saturnalia* and the *Commentary* were read: they served as source books on rhetoric and dialectic, astronomy, natural history and medicine, and for proverbs and moral pedagogy. Closer to the subject of this study are those compendia that specialize in the language arts, including exercise books used by pupils, handbooks on the art of writing, and collections devoted to rhetoric or poetics.

In order to define the scope of pedagogical compendia Sanford takes Cassiodorus's definition of grammar: "Grammatica est peritia pulchre loquendi ex poetis illustratibusque oratoribus collecta"[58] [Grammar is the skill in speaking well, acquired from famous poets and orators]. She argues that "By Cassiodorus' definition all the libri [manuales] containing the works of poets and orators would belong"[59] under the head grammar. Grammar included study and imitation of canon authors. A glance at the index to Sanford's article will quickly convince the reader of how extensively Latin poets and prose-writers were copied whole or excerpted in such manuscripts. During Chrétien's time, Vergil is the most prominent author in these manuscripts.[60] Some *libri manuales* include Macrobius. Sanford states that he is especially prominent in rhetorical and dialectical *libri*.[61] These might include the private collections of poems authors owned and copied into.[62]

References to the Saturnalia

Up to the early thirteenth century, references to the *Saturnalia* rarely single out Books IV-VI. However, the *work as a whole* was known,[63] and it was available in medieval libraries (see notes 48-49). As we

---

[58] Sanford 1924 p. 195; cf. Thurot 1964.

[59] Sanford 1924 p. 196.

[60] Sanford 1924 pp. 200-01, 247-48; see as well Glauche 1970 passim on pp. 62-127; Munk Olsen 1985 pp. 37-38.

[61] "The writings of Cicero, Boethius, Apuleius, and Macrobius dominate, and with them are frequently found other works by the same authors, or connected with them, not dealing at all with rhetoric or dialectic" (Sanford 1924 p. 194, with references).

[62] Martin 1979 p. 70, Munk Olsen 1979-80 vol. 10 pp. 119-20, and Tilliette 1995. The practice continued among vernacular writers; see Willaert 1992 p. 118 and Champion 1907.

[63] On the question of knowledge and use of the *Saturnalia*, see Barker-Benfield 1983 pp. 233-34, with additional bibliography.

have seen, it was mined for Vergilian and other quotes for florilegia and quotations. Among twelfth-century Latin writers William of Malmesbury refers to both of Macrobius's major works;[64] John of Salisbury knew and used him. On the continent, in the Franco-German milieu of the school at Laon, Manegold of Lautenbach felt obliged to rise up against Macrobius's influential teachings because he judged them to be incompatible with the Bible.[65] Abelard used him too.[66]

How well known was Macrobius to Chrétien's French-speaking audiences? The first French language reference to Macrobius in Philippe de Thaon's *Comput* is even earlier than Chrétien's.[67] Philippe names Macrobius three times in this work, including what Philippe purports to be actual citations. The first reference to Macrobius appears in the discussion of the signs of the Zodiac. Philippe says that their invention is recounted "El *Sunge Scipiun*" (*Comput* v. 1189-94)[68]; he may be referring to the *ComSS* 1.21.[69] The third reference contains a Latin word allegorically drawn from Macrobius — "*coïtum*" — that is used in the sense of a solar eclipse (*Comput* v. 2719-24).[70]

It is the second reference, however, that is the most problematic. While proposing an allegorical reading of sheep horns, Philippe refers to archetypal ideas.

> De icest Macrobe dit
> Par veir en sun escrit,
> E si li posat num
> *Mundum archetipum.*
> E les furmes que il vit,

---

[64] Thomson 1975 esp. pp. 381-82; note on p. 382 this quote from the *Polyhistor*: "nam de taciturnitate Papirii pueri [= *Sat* 1.6.18-26], Macrobium Saturnaliorum narrasse quis nesciat?" [for who doesn't know that Macrobius related in the *Saturnalia* the boy Papirius's taciturnity?] For the fourteenth century and after, see Galand-Hallyn 1994 and Lord 1996.

[65] Hartmann 1970 pp. 57-60.

[66] Szövérffy 1983 pp. 239-40.

[67] "The *Comput* is datable, on internal evidence, to 1113 (or perhaps 1119)" (Short ed. *Comput* p. 1).

[68] Guillaume de Lorris refers to Macrobius as the author of Cicero's *Somnium Scipionis* (*Rose* v. 6-10), as does Jean de Meun (v. 18335-37 and 18389-94 — Nature is speaking).

[69] Calcidius also discusses the zodiac; for example, see *Timaeus* pp. 125-30.

[70] *ThLL* s.v. *coetus* col. 1444, ll. 15-18; and *MitW*, s.v. *coitus*, II col. 821 ll. 36-42. As early as 811, Dungal used Macrobius to explain eclipses to Charlemagne (Jeauneau 1975 p. 40).

Senz nul cuntredit,
'Ide[e]s' apelat.

(Comput v. 1517-23)[71]

[About this Macrobius speaks truthfully in his book, and he gave it the name *Archetypal World*. And the forms he saw he called 'ideas', without doubt.]

Although the *Commentary* contains a number of synonyms for *mundus archetypus* that refer to God's idea of the world before its material creation, the term *archetypus mundus* appears nowhere, although *idees* does.[72] Philippe seems to be confusing Macrobius with Calcidius, whose Commentary on Plato's *Timaeus* the *Thesaurus linguae latinae* refers to for its only example of the term *mundus archetypus.*[73]

The treatment of Macrobius would be incomplete without some discussion of problematic references to him in vernacular texts. We may begin with Philippe's inaccurate attribution. Philippe's confusion of Calcidius and Macrobius may not be unusual. Relying perhaps on memory or erroneous sources, he associated concepts found in Calcidius with Macrobius's discussion of those same concepts, albeit using different terminology. But such confusion has considerable implications for the interpretation of Chrétien's own Macrobius reference. It has been argued that Chrétien made the same kind of error by referring to his authority on the quadrivium.[74] To be sure, Macrobius refers here and there to the quadrivial arts.[75] But for a

---

[71] Curtius 1954 p. 118 n. 3 mentions two references to Macrobius in the *Comput*; on the *Timaeus* and Macrobius, see Hartmann 1970 pp. 72-74 and Viarre 1975 pp. 547-50. Marinone ed. *Sat* lists one borrowing from the *Timaeus* (p. 893) and corrects another, earlier attribution.

[72] *ComSS* 1.2.14, 1.12.11-12 (using ἰδέαι/*idea*), as does *Timaeus* pp. 32 l. 19 and 413 s.v. *idea*.

[73] *ThLL* s.v. *archetypos* col. 460 ll. 32-35. Calcidius's translation reads as follows: "similis esset uterque mundus; archetypus... sensibilis" (*Timaeus* p. 30 ll. 16-18) [similar would be each world; both archetypal and perceptible]. See also *MitW* s.v. *archetypus* col. 878 l. 59-879 l. 2. I am assuming that the words Philippe assigns to Macrobius did not occur in the fuller, now lost version that may still have been extant in the twelfth century (see note 42). Alard de Cambrai also ascribes to Macrobius statements by other authors (Hunt 1981-82 p. 226 n. 35); see Payen ed. *Philosophie* p. 316 s.v. "Macrobes." For additional references to Macrobius, see De Paolis 1986-88 pp. 232-39, Flutre 1962 p. 126, West 1969 p. 109, and Hüttig 1990.

[74] See above, Introduction n. 3.

[75] Englisch 1994.

systematic analysis and a more likely source, would not Chrétien have turned to Martianus Capella's *Marriage of Mercury and Philology*? A well-known authority in the Middle Ages,[76] this work treats the seven liberal arts in great detail, including, of course, the quadrivium Chrétien describes.

Certainly, Martianus Capella appears to have been widely read in medieval schools.[77] Moreover, some have suggested that Chrétien actually used the *Marriage of Mercury and Philology* as model for Erec's marriage and coronation, including the coronation robe and quadrivial figures on it.[78] If Chrétien read the *Saturnalia*, he certainly could have read Martianus Capella too. In fact, the two works complement one another nicely, as some library catalogues and manuscripts suggest.[79] Moreover, Martianus's treatment of grammar and rhetoric do complement other treatises and frame the *Saturnalia*'s discussion of Vergil's art of description.

That Chrétien consulted Martianus is indeed possible. But is it necessary?[80] Does the *Marriage* actually help us understand better the

---

[76] Wagner 1986 p. 19; see also the chapter on astronomy by Claudia Kern in Wagner 1986 pp. 229-32; Leonardi 1959-60 provides manuscript evidence; see also Wetherbee 1972 p. 144 and n. 38 (examples).

[77] Leonardi 1959-60 lists all known manuscripts. See also Glauche 1970 esp. pp. 76 and 88-89 and Lesne 1938-40 vol. 4, pp. 20-25; *De nuptiis*'s influence may have declined in the twelfth century (Glauche 1970 p. 123).

[78] Luttrell 1974 pp. 21-22 and Uitti 1981. Note, however, that manuscripts of the *De nuptiis*, like those of the *Saturnalia*, sometimes included only parts — notably, only Books I and II — and, therefore, not those on the quadrivium (Books VI-IX); see Leonardi 1959-60 and Jeauneau 1975 p. 36 n. 53.

[79] See also Jeauneau 1975, esp. p. 23: "Il n'est pas sans intérêt de noter que la fortune de Macrobe et celle de Martianus Capella, du IXᵉ au XIIᵉ siècle et même au delà, sont assez étroitement liées." Cf. Stahl 1965 p. 105: "conclusions that are drawn about Martianus become re-inforced when it is pointed out that in most cases they apply with equal force to Macrobius." LeMoine 1972 uses both Macrobius's works to interpret Martianus's *Marriage*; for the *Saturnalia* see pp. 94 n. 52, 113 n. 14, 134 n. 20, and 196 n. 25. Both are used to teach the liberal arts (Jeauneau 1975 p. 44). See Leonardi 1959 pp. 467 n. 128 and 475, and 1960 p. 519 s.v. "Macrobio." This close connection suggests how the one author might be mistaken for the other. Excerpts from both are found together in several *libri manuales*; see Sanford 1924 §§ 85, 117, 136, and 390.

[80] As I noted in the Introduction, Macrobius's description of Astronomy emphasizes her astrological role, whereas this side of her "character" is, if not totally eliminated, at least clearly subordinated in Macrobius and Martianus; see Stock 1972 pp. 166-67 and Englisch 1994 pp. 185-86; Stock also notes that astrology is an important subject for Chartrain poets like Bernardus Silvestris, but that it was also controversial. See also Donati 1990.

art of description Chrétien claims to have learned from Macrobius? There are two issues here. One is the identification of Chrétien's putative source for the description of the quadrivial arts in Erec's coronation robe. The other is the articulation of the art of description he used to represent them. That is to say, the *Erec* passage under discussion here points us towards both Chrétien's source *matière* and to his own artistic *sens*.[81] We must first deal with the question of Chrétien's sources for the matter and art of his description, then discuss the practice of the art in representative works. Let us therefore take up the argument that the *Marriage* is a source for Chrétien's description of the quadrivium.

Although Martianus Capella treats extensively the quadrivial arts and uses personifications to represent them, Chrétien's own version by comparison is an abbreviation so radical as to be perfunctory. Indeed, why would a clerically educated writer need to rely on any source to write what little Chrétien does about the four arts. Surely we do not need to imagine him diligently consulting Martianus Capella, Macrobius, or anyone else in order to write, for example, that Geometry

> esgarde et mesure,
> Con li ciaus et la terre dure,
> Si que de rien nule n'i faut,
> Et puis le bas et puis le haut,
> Et puis le le et puis le lonc;
> Et puis esgarde par selonc,
> Con la mers est lee et parfonde,
> Et si mesure tot le monde.

(*Erec* v. 6747-54)

[surveys and measures the extent of heaven and earth, leaving nothing out, first its height and depth, and then its length and breadth. Then she surveys as well the width and depth of the sea and in this way she measures the whole universe.]

But it would not be surprising if Chrétien remembered from his studies what Geometry does when he came to summarize her activi-

---

[81] On these important terms in Chrétien, see Kelly 1992 chapter Four.

ties.[82] He merely incorporated that acquired and recalled knowledge into his description of Erec's coronation robe. That is his art, and it is the art he says Macrobius taught him. Indeed, Chrétien does name Macrobius and there is no real disagreement among Chrétien manuscripts on the name Macrobius, which appears twice in this *Erec* passage[83]; more importantly, Macrobius alone illustrates extensively what Chrétien says he learned from him: literary description — that is, how to imitate models on all levels of composition, from the work to the word. Descriptions of the seven arts, or, alternately, of the trivium or the quadrivium, are not found only in Martianus Capella; they are common themes for *praeexercitamina* like those Chrétien may have written while reading Macrobius.[84] In these cases the trivium and quadrivium are descriptive models. In fact, the twelfth century witnessed a decline in Martianus's authority on the liberal arts in favor of more specialized handbooks and the kind of brief poems discussed here.[85]

More importantly here, Philippe de Thaon's reference to the 'archetypal world' recalls the *Saturnalia*'s analogy between divine creation and artistic invention. Although it was actually commonplace from the *Timaeus* on, Curtius traces this analogy back to Macrobius.[86] As is well known, Geoffrey of Vinsauf uses the adjective *archetypus* to describe artistic invention in the *Poetria nova*. Like God's *archetypus mundus*, the artist's *status archetypus* is a mental blueprint or model of

---

[82] Cf. the analogous case of Herbort von Fritzlar, who, according to Worstbrock 1963 p. 258, relies on "Reminiszensen aus der Schule" to describe the seven liberal arts in his Troy poem. Macrobius treats geometry rather briefly and with different emphases from those in Martianus; see Englisch 1994 p. 150-51. On the "relative maladresse" of the "description très peu théorique" of music in *Erec*, see Baumgartner 1998 esp. pp. 75-79.

[83] See Foerster ed. *Erec* v. 6738 var. and 6741 var.

[84] For examples, see MGH vol. 1 pp. 408-11, 544-47, and 629-30 and vol. 4 pp. 249-60 and 339-43; Wattenbach 1893 pp. 500-01; Walther 1926 p. 314; Lehmann 1935 pp. 32-33; Leonardi 1959 p. 467 n. 125; Leonardi 1961 pp. 152-68; Ward 1972 vol. 1 pp. 159-60; Wetherbee 1972 p. 144; and Camargo 1992 pp. 201-202. Bernardus Silvestris describes them briefly in his *Mathematicus* (Godman 1990a p. 617), as does Eberhard the German in his *Laborintus* v. 159-70 (Faral 1924 p. 343). Must we assume that all these authors went to Martianus Capella for matter or model? The Bible itself is read as a source book on the liberal arts by Cassiodorus; see Astell 1999 pp. 38-42.

[85] Leonardi 1959 pp. 470-78 and Glauche 1970 p. 123.

[86] Curtius 1954 pp. 441-42. Curtius also notes Macrobius's inclusion of Nature in the analogy in *Sat* 5.1.18. Cf. Mayer 1976 pp. 104-105; Homeyer 1970 p. 142 n. 2; and *Timaeus* p. 73 ll. 10-12.

the work to be written.[87] According to Macrobius, Vergil drew his 'archetypes' from Homer: "per omnem poesin suam hoc uno est praecipue usus archetypo" (*Sat* 5.13.40) [in all his poetic works he took this one author as his archetype or model]. Interestingly here, *Archetypus* occurs only in the *Saturnalia*, not in the *Commentary*.[88] But in the *Saturnalia*, 'archetype' is not the same as the "archetypal world" referred to in Philippe de Thaon's quote. Archetype meaning model was common in Latin from Classical times on.[89] Therefore, the *Saturnalia* is, if not the sole reference in the *Erec* passage, at least a major authority on the art of description. As we shall see in Chapter Five, it contains models for the *descrire* Chrétien says he practices in *Erec*, although those models are not the arts of the quadrivium.

This discussion of the archetype brings us around to a point made by Roger Pensom regarding the "incompatibilities" of neoplatonic notions of the archetype and the rational, prescriptive character of the arts and other documents like Macrobius's that liken the neoplatonic archetype to the artist's blueprint.[90] There is indeed a problem here, but it is more fundamental than Pensom suggests; it lies in the validity of the analogies medieval theoreticians and authors themselves make between their art and divine creation. However, although prescriptive rhetoric is often still seen as merely "reducible to grammar, that is that there exists a possible algorithmic method for the decoding of the meanings of fictional narrative,"[91] medieval writers actually saw both grammar and rhetoric as steps towards mastery in practicing these arts, if not their final stage.[92] Mastery

---

[87] In *Poetria nova* v. 45-49; see Kelly 1991 pp. 37 and 64-68. Geoffrey's model for poetic invention is architecture. *Archetypus* can also mean 'blueprint'; see *MitW* s.v. *archetypus* col. 879 ll. 6-8. On a possible link between Macrobius and the *Poetria nova*, see Cizek 1994 pp. 137-38 and 169.

[88] See Willis ed. *ComSS* p. 193 s.v. *archetypum*. Despite considerable effort in different places, I have been unable to locate M. C. Granados Fernández *Léxico de Macrobio*, listed in De Paolis 1986-88 p. 146.

[89] See also *Sat* 5.13.23. For examples of *archetypus* in classical Latin in the sense of a source which the writer imitated or used as a model, see *ThLL* s.v. *archetypos* col. 460 ll. 35-47 (B. with references to the *Sat* 5.13.23 and 40, 7.14.2). In the sense of ideas in God's mind, references in *ThLL* col. 460 ll. 32-35 are to Calcidius's translation of the *Timaeus* 38 and his commentary 272, 278, and 349; cf. *Timaeus* s.v. *archetypus* p. 409. See also Dziatzko 1895.

[90] Pensom 1993 p. 532.

[91] Pensom 1993 p. 533. Contrast his views with Bornscheuer 1976 pp. 54-56.

[92] Ziolkowski 1985 pp. 130-39 discusses the diverse ways in which grammar and rhetoric influenced education and were also stepping stones to salvation.

supposes the acquisition of a "habitual" way of writing that interpretation and appreciation (in the French sense of this word) can elicit from our texts and help us to understand how they were written and how they were meant to be read.[93]

Philippe de Thaon and Chrétien are evidence that Macrobius's *Saturnalia* was widely available in Chrétien's time, and that it was known not only to Latin but also to vernacular authors and, through them, to their audiences as an authority. More specifically, his works are present in manuscripts that link the *Saturnalia* with grammar, rhetoric, and poetics. Writers young and old are said to have read authors and tried to imitate them by rewriting and description. Poetic anthologies suggest the very contextual environment evident in Fournival's library and writings. As we have seen, some *Saturnalia* manuscripts also contain works that are bound elsewhere in poetic anthologies or with the well-known twelfth- and thirteenth-century arts of poetry and prose. Manuscripts containing these works also appear in close proximity in medieval library catalogues, suggesting thereby arrangement according to principles like those used by Fournival for his own library. Such groupings, whether in a single manuscript or in groups of manuscripts catalogued together, illustrate the range of medieval education on composition — from elementary treatises through imitations and borderline or "bridge works" to the masterpieces all sought to emulate. Macrobius's *Saturnalia* would fit into such a curriculum. It certainly seems to do so for Chrétien.

For these reasons, we may readily take Chrétien's reference to his use of Macrobius as a steppingstone to investigate ways he learned to write and, furthermore, to ways his works and the works of those who wrote in the same tradition may be read. Since Macrobius was available in Chrétien's time, and he did treat description, we may move on to look more closely at Macrobius on description to learn what heuristic value his writings have for the interpretation of Chrétien and other romances written in the tradition he helped found.

---

[93] See Vinaver 1964 pp. 493-94; Kelly 1991 pp. 87-88; and more generally Bornscheuer 1976 pp. 54-56. These stages are evoked in poem XVI from London BL Cotton Vitellius A.xii, edited by Boutemy 1937 p. 313.

APPENDIX:
SATURNALIA MANUSCRIPTS TO THE EARLY THIRTEENTH CENTURY

The following list of *Saturnalia* manuscripts is included to illustrate the fore-going discussion. I rely on evidence collected from a number of authoritative sources. Although it is still incomplete, the available evidence shows how extensively the *Saturnalia* was known. I have arranged the list by approximate century chronology and included whatever information I could find on how complete the *Saturnalia* is in each manuscript. "Complete" means a complete text as represented by the seven books in the standard editions. The source of my information is provided at the end of each item; in all cases I have consulted the treatment of *Saturnalia* manuscripts in the editions prepared by Marinone pp. 61-62 and Willis pp. vii-x. I also relied on the invaluable resources of the Institut de Recherche et d'Histoire des Textes in Paris. However, I have included only sources of information that present a consensus and that treat specifically the *Saturnalia*. Where no other precise source was available to me, I have indicated a reference to the files of the Institut de Recherche et d'Histoire des Textes as IRHT.

Late Eighth Century

Vienna BN series nova 37: fragments from 1.12-15. Lowe 1963 p. 21; Mazal and Unterkircher 1965 pp. 13-14; Barker-Benfield 1983 p. 234.

Ninth Century

Bamberg M.V.5 n. 9: to *Sat* 3.19.5. *Bamberg* 1895, vol. 1.2, p. 38-39; Marinone 1975 p. 507; Barker-Benfield 1983 p. 234.

Leiden Vos. Lat. Q2 (fragment). Barker-Benfield 1983 p. 233 n. 6; Eastwood 1994 p. 143 (dated 10th-11th century for *ComSS* folios).

Montpellier Ec. Méd. 225: *Sat* 1.12.21 to end of *Sat* 3. La Penna 1953 pp. 238-39; Willis 1954, Marinone 1975 p. 507, Barker-Benfield 1983 p. 234.

Naples BN V.B. 10 (9th-10th century): to *Sat* 7.5.2. Mueller 1895 cols. 27-29; La Penna 1953 p. 240; Marinone 1975 p. 506; Barker-Benfield 1983 p. 234.

Oxford Bodl. Auct. T II 27 (9th-10th century): to *Sat* 3.4.9. Lindsey 1900; Marinone 1975 p. 506; Munk Olsen 1982-89 vol. 1, p. 245; Eastwood 1994 p. 145. Barker-Benfield 1983 p. 234 dates this ms. 11th century.

Padua Bib. Antoniana 27: *Sat* 1.11.50-15.20. Marinone 1975 p. 507; Barker-Benfield 1983 p. 233 n. 4.

Vatican lat. 5207: *Sat* 1-3 incomplete (9th or 10th century): Sanford 1924 p.
   210; Marinone 1975 p. 507; Barker-Benfield 1983 p. 234.
Vatican reg. lat. 586. *Sat* 1.12.2,4-5.15.20. IRHT
Vatican reg. lat. 1650 (end of 9th or beginning of 10th century): *Sat* 1-3.
   Goetz 1890 p. iv; Mueller 1895 cols. 60-61; La Penna 1953 p. 239;
   Pellegrin 1973 pp. 279; Marinone 1975 p. 507; Pellegrin 1975-82 vol. 2.1
   pp. 337-38; Barker-Benfield 1983 p. 234.

Tenth Century

London BL Cotton Vitellinus C III: *Sat* 1-3. La Penna 1953 p. 239, Marinone 1975 p. 507; Barker-Benfield 1983 p. 235 dates this ms. 9th century.
Paris BN nouv. acq. lat. 1907: Olmont 1907 p. 30; Munk Olsen 1982-89
   vol. 2 p. 866 (extracts from *Sat* 6).
Vatican Pal. lat. 886: lengthy extracts from *Sat* 1-3. Perhaps 9th century.
   Goetz 1890 p. vi; Mueller 1895 col. 61; Tohill 1978 pp. 104-05; Pellegrin
   1975-82 vol. 2.2 pp. 62-64.
Vatican reg. lat. 2043: to *Sat* 7.14.11. La Penna 1953 p. 241; Marinone
   1975 p. 507; Pellegrin 1975-82 vol. 2.1 p. 490; Barker-Benfield 1983 p.
   235 dates this ms. 10th-11th century.

Eleventh Century

Bern Burgerbib. 514: *Sat* 7 only. Munk Olsen 1982-89 vol. 1, p. 153.
Paris BN lat. 6371: complete. Marinone 1975 p. 506; Munk Olsen 1982-89
   vol. 1 p. 257; Barker-Benfield 1983 pp. 222 and 234.
Strasbourg BN & Univ. 14: complete. *Strasbourg* 1923 pp. 5-6; La Penna
   1953 pp. 240-41; Marinone 1975 p. 506; Barker-Benfield 1983 p. 234.
Venice Marciana Z lat. 497: excerpts. End of century. Newton 1962; Munk
   Olsen 1991a p. 64.

Twelfth to Early Thirteenth Century

Bern Burgerbibl. 404 (late 11th or 12th century): *Sat* 5.13-*Sat* 7. Munk Olsen
   1982-89 vol. 1 p. 397.
Brussels BR 10.057-10.062: *Sat* 7 only. Perhaps 13th century. Munk Olsen
   1982-89 vol. 1, p. 158, and vol. 2, p. 319; Ward 1972 vol. 2 pp. 250-51.
Cambridge BU 1213 (= Ff.III.5): complete. 12th-13th century. *Cambridge*
   1980 vol. 2, p. 412; La Penna 1953 p. 242; Barker-Benfield 1983 p. 235.
Cambridge Corpus Christi 71: complete. James 1912 pp. 149-51; Sanford
   1924 p. 224; La Penna 1953 p. 242; Marinone 1975 p. 507; Munk Olsen
   1982-89 vol. 1, pp. 13-14; Barker-Benfield 1983 p. 222; Eastwood 1994
   p. 141.

Douai 749: abbreviated extract *Sat* 7.1.1-25. 12th-13th century. Boutemy 1939 p. 295; Jeudy 1989 p. 585.

Escorial E.III.18: complete, but only to *Sat* 1.17.6 from 12th-13th century. *Escorial* 1910-23 vol. 2 pp. 78-79; Willis 1957 p. 153; Marinone 1975 p. 507; Barker-Benfield 1983 p. 234-35.

Florence laur. plut. 51 n. 8: complete. 12th-13th century. Le Penna 1953 p. 241.

Florence laur. plut. 90 sup. 25: complete. 12th-13th century. Sanford 1924 p. 234; La Penna 1953 p. 242; Marinone 1975 p. 507; Munk Olsen 1982-89 vol. 2 pp. 851-52; Barker-Benfield 1983 p. 235.

London Harley 3859: complete. La Penna 1953 pp. 241-42; Marinone 1975 p. 507; Munk Olsen 1982-89 vol. 1 p. 215.

Madrid BN 7825: IRHT.

Munich Clm 22004: excerpts. Halm and Meyer 1969 vol. 4.4, p. 17; Munk Olsen 1982-89 vol. 2 p. 666.

Naples BN V.B. 12: *Sat* 1-3. Mueller 1895 col. 29; La Penna 1953 pp. 239-40; Munk Olsen 1982-89 vol. 1, p. 243.

Paris Arsenal 711: excerpts. 12th-13th century. Martin 1886 vol. 2 p. 51-52.

Paris BN lat 1860: extracts. Perhaps 13th century. Sanford 1924 p. 235; Lauer 1940 pp. 200-01.

Paris BN lat 7412: *Sat* 7 only. IRHT.

Paris BN lat 7647: excerpts in *Florilegium Gallicum*. Munk Olsen 1979-80 pp. 77-82; Burton 1983 pp. 46-49.

Paris BN lat 7710: *Sat* praef. 1-1.8.8. 12th or perhaps 13th century. La Penna 1953 p. 246.

Paris BN lat 16676: *Sat* 1-2, 7. 12th or perhaps 13th century. La Penna 1953 p. 244.

Rome Bibl. Angelica 1985: excerpts. Munk Olsen 1973 pp. 193-96; Rouse 1976 pp. 95 and 109-10; Munk Olsen 1979-80 vol. 9 pp. 104-06.

Troyes 514: complete. La Penna 1953 p. 241; Barker-Benfield 1983 p. 222; Eastwood 1994 p.147.

Vatican Borg. lat 326: extract from *Sat* 7. Munk Olsen 1982-89 vol. 1 pp. 455-56; Pellegrin 1975-82 vol. 1 pp. 231-33.

Vatican lat. 3417: *Sat* 1-4, 7. Carton 1965 p. 26; Munk Olsen 1973 p. 193; Marinone 1975 p. 507; Munk Olsen 1979-80 vol. 9 p. 107; Barker-Benfield 1983 p. 235.

Vatican Ottob. lat 1935: complete. 12th-13th century. Pellegrin 1975-82 vol. 1 pp. 702-03.

Vatican pal. lat. 957: excerpts from *Sat* praef. and 1-7. Pellegrin 1975-82 vol. 2 pp. 94-97.

CHAPTER TWO

MACROBIUS ON THE ART AND MODES OF DESCRIPTION

Non de nihilo fabulam fingit (*Saturnalia*)[1]

Although this chapter takes up Macrobius on description in some detail, I have endeavored to keep the context of twelfth-century romance on the reader's mind with illustrations not only from the *Saturnalia* but also from Chrétien's romances. A fuller interpretation of the use of description as rewriting is found in Chapters Four through Six.

The Description of Erec's Coronation Robe

Let us begin with the coronation robe in *Erec et Enide*, in which Chrétien attributes Macrobius's advice on description. Actually, to begin with a "small unit of discourse"[2] like this is entirely in keeping with Macrobius's own practice of illustrating Vergil's rewriting of Homer and his other sources. As we have seen, most scholars have treated the passage as a reference that points to Macrobius as a *source* for descriptive material on the quadrivium. According to Edmond Faral, Chrétien "prétend citer Macrobe, ce qui est faux."[3] Of course, Faral sought a source for Chrétien in the old sense of the term. In that sense, Chrétien's description would be a copy or paraphrase of a passage in Macrobius. In the twelfth century, however, copying or paraphrasing a source, as we shall see, is a sign of elementary or inferior work; it is hardly the *modus operandi* in an accomplished description. Faral goes on to say that Chrétien's Macrobius reference "n'exclut pas et même peut indiquer qu'il a suivi un modèle." Here, Faral has hit upon medieval poetic norms, for such models are pre-

---

[1] *Sat* 5.19.2 [He doesn't invent his story out of nothing].
[2] Quadlbauer 1962 p. 71; on the significance of such units or compositional blocks in medieval poetics, see Kelly 1991 pp. 85-88 and Vogt-Spira 1994 pp. 17-18.
[3] Faral 1913 p. 346.

cisely what interest Macrobius in Vergil's adaptations of Homer and other authors.

We cannot analyze Chrétien's rewriting as Macrobius did Vergil's because there is no clear indicator of who the French romancer's first authors are — the storytellers he refers to in the *Erec* Prologue — whereas Macrobius names and quotes authors and works we too can examine. Furthermore, according to Chrétien, no version of Erec's story prior to his own seems to be of the quality Macrobius attributes to most of Vergil's predecessors. The *conteurs*, he says, are wont to *depecier* and to *corronpre* (v. 21) their stories — to tear them apart and leave lacunae.[4] However, besides the well-known reference in the Prologue to "Cil qui de conter vivre vuelent" (*Erec* v. 22) [those who wish to gain their living by telling stories] and who told the story of Erec in high courts, in the passage referring to Macrobius Chrétien alludes to an *estoire* in which the description of the robe appears: "Lisant trovomes an l'estoire / La description de la robe" (v. 6736-37) [Reading in the *estoire*, we find the robe's description]. He goes on to say that four fairies skillfully wove the robe (v. 6744-45). Although we cannot compare Chrétien's version of the coronation robe with the oral *contes* mentioned in the Prologue or the *estoire* of this latter passage, which he says he knows, we can see what Macrobius has to say on the art of description so as to find out how Chrétien might have understood that art, and then look at *Erec* and other romances to see whether these actually reflect that art in their descriptions and whether such advice helps us appreciate them.

Since in *Erec* v. 6739 Chrétien refers specifically to *descrire* as a technique which he learned from Macrobius, we may start with the word for 'description' and cognates in the *Saturnalia*. Macrobius's use of *describere, descriptio*, and their cognates evinces a wider, more differentiated range of meanings than modern 'description' usually connotes; furthermore, his usage mirrors the semantic range of these words in classical and medieval Latin. We shall therefore begin by determining what meanings were available to Chrétien in Macrobius in order to identify the semantic range of Chrétien's own notion of description.

---

[4] See Kelly 1992 pp. 125-29. Macrobius uniformly appreciates the high quality of Vergil's Greek and Latin models, even when he thinks Vergil improves on them; see the examples in *Sat* 5.11-13.

Ethos and Pathos in Description

In classical and medieval rhetoric and poetics, description is anchored in topical invention.[5] That is, the author identifies (invention) those places (topoi) which he or she can elaborate upon (amplification) in order to represent persons, things, and actions as he or she intends for them to appear. Such description may focus on momentary features like emotions or it may dwell on constant features that are more habitual and not subject to rapid change. Of importance to description, as we shall see, is book IV of the *Saturnalia*, in which Macrobius uses the Greek term pathos (πάθος) to refer to strong movements of pity or indignant wrath (*Sat* 4.2.1). Its traditional partner, ethos (ἦθος) — which has to do with character, and refers to customary or habitual moods or states of mind — does not, however, appear in the extant *Saturnalia* manuscripts.

Since only part of the *Saturnalia* IV is extant, it has been conjectured that Macrobius treated ethos in the missing beginning.[6] The contrast between ethos and pathos is indeed commonplace in both rhetoric and poetics.[7] For example, Quintilian translates both words into Latin under *affectus* or emotion, which he then divides into pathos, or strong but transitory emotions, and ethos, or a constant state of mind.[8] Emphasis on pathos or ethos in description, then, will

---

[5] On this sense of description, see Linke 1880 pp. 37-42, Cizek 1989, and Kelly 1991 pp. 71-73. Cf. *ThLL* s.v. *descriptio*, esp. § II.

[6] See especially Vietti 1979; for examples of *affectus* as pathos in the *Saturnalia*, see Bestul 1975 p. 12.

[7] See Lausberg 1960 §§257.2a and 257.3, Cizek 1994 pp. 276-85, and Urbanek 1995 esp. pp. 23-27; cf. Flamant 1977 pp. 260-71 and Auerbach 1958 pp. 144-47. Bestul 1975 p. 15 n. 30 suggests that the treatment of *affectus* in Book IV may have contributed to the notion of Vergil's Wheel as an image of Material Style — that is, style based on social order or type; see Quadlbauer 1962 §46b-m. In Book 5, Macrobius identifies four *genera dicendi* which he finds in Vergil: *copiosum*, *breve*, *siccum*, and *pingue et floridum* (*Sat* 5.1.7-20). This leads him to assess poetic genius, including not only in art but also in learning, both of which contribute to the composition of Vergil's works. On the unusual number of four *genera*, see Quadlbauer 1962 §7 n. 15 and Quadlbauer 1984 p. 112. Actually, the four Macrobius refers to represent two sets of doubles: *copiosum-breve* and *siccum-pingue et floridum*; see Galant-Hallyn 1994 pp. 380-84. Perhaps there is an echo here of the differentiation by pairs common in ancient and medieval treatment of the *genera dicendi*; cf. Urbanek 1995. Macrobius also mentions but does not discuss a third pair: *maturus et gravis* and *ardens et erectus* (*Sat* 5.1.16-17). He favors a tempered blend of all three. For a list of adjectives used to characterize varieties of style in classical rhetoric, see Lausberg 1960 §1244 s.v. *stilus* (p. 818).

[8] Zundel 1989 pp. 4-5 s.v. *affectus*.

depend on whether the author seeks to represent momentary or constant features of a person, thing, or action.[9] For example, Erec's coronation robe is a feature of his coronation; it exemplifies his royalty. By contrast, we find pathos in the representation of Enide's grief when she thinks Erec is dead and count Limors forces her to marry him, or, again, in *Yvain*'s description of Laudine in mourning. In these cases Chrétien's description identifies emotions in each woman that momentarily alter their constant or "ethical" features.[10]

For instance, the "ethical" Laudine appears as the stereotype of human beauty.[11] Chrétien details her parts in a conventional catalogue that procedes from head to hands and breasts. An unparalleled beauty, which God alone could form, and then only once — she is virtually archetypal — and which Nature herself could not imitate, sparks Yvain's love with the habitual *coup de foudre*. Enide is no different; her rent robe evokes pity for her supreme beauty, a beauty which inspires Erec's love and leads to her acquiring royal garments befitting her unique excellence (*Erec* v. 402-41, 1554-1672). Yet Laudine is lacerating her beauty. The grief-stricken lady Yvain is falling in love with is emotionally distraught and physically *disjointe*. Paradoxically, then, her beauty inspires love at the very moment that beauty is being *depeciee* and *corronpue*. Macrobius too gives examples of descriptions that betoken physical violence and mental anguish.[12] Indeed, many of the devices Chrétien uses are singled out by Macrobius as well; *habitus*, for example, describes "outward appearances" that are the effect of inner violence and grief (*Sat* 4.1).[13] For

---

[9] Cf. the circumstantial topoi *habitus*, or a constant or habitual state of mind, and *affectio*, or a temporary or transitory feeling (*Ars vers* 1.85 and 87, *De inv* I.xxv.36).

[10] In *Perceval*, Chrétien contrasts Blancheflor's stereotyped beauty with the impoverishment in her besieged castle; the *amie* of the Orgueilleux de la Lande illustrates an analogous contrast between natural beauty and the deleterious effect of the weather on her complexion, the wretched clothes she must wear, and her sorry horse.

[11] *Yvain* v. 1146-65, 1462-1506. See Colby 1965 esp. pp. 159-64.

[12] *Sat* 4.1; cf. 4.4.19-21. These are illustrations of comparable techniques that suggest possible influence on Chrétien's art of description; they do not prove actual borrowing on Chrétien's part. On *Erec* descriptions, see Le Goff 1982 and Castellani 1993. In fact, the *Eneas* preceded him in incorporating Macrobian notions of pathos with ethos in adapting Vergil; see Blons-Pierre 1993 pp. 62-63; Mora 1996, esp. pp. 22-24 and 37-40.

[13] Macrobius's sense of *habitus* as an effect of pathos (*Sat* 4.1.3) is therefore different from Cicero's and Matthew of Vendôme's, for whom *habitus* is an "ethical" characteristic of human beings (*De inv* I.xxv.36 and *Ars vers* 1.85).

instance, Chrétien uses hyperbole and exclamation to amplify on Laudine's features. The *Saturnalia* exemplifies these devices in scenes from the *Aeneid* that are, actually, parallel to the ones we have been discussing in Chrétien. For example, Dido's grief when Aeneas leaves her is, like Laudine's, caused by the loss of a loved one (*Sat* 4.2.2 and 4.3.7). Of course, the French author diverges from the Roman poet in his application: Dido commits suicide, Laudine remarries, and Lunete is no Anna.[14] Importantly, the *Saturnalia* is consistent with and, indeed, reinforces traditional instruction on physical description with Vergilian examples that move conventional images like feminine beauty into new narrative settings, and Chrétien follows suit.[15]

Even more importantly here, Chrétien's description of Laudine in her mourning recalls several features of Erec's coronation robe. Chrétien first describes the funeral procession and Laudine's part in it. But before he describes her, he supplies a narrative intervention in which he emphasizes his representation of Laudine as a formal description.

> Mes sire Yvains oï les criz
> Et le duel, qui ja n'iert descriz;
> Que nus ne le porroit descrivre,
> Ne tes ne fu escriz an livre. (*Yvain* v. 1173-76)

[My lord Yvain heard the cries and the grief, which will never be described. For none could describe it, nor was anything like it recorded in a book.]

In Macrobius's language, the poet intervenes — "ex poetae quidem persona est" (*Sat* 4.6.18) [in the persona of the poet] — to comment on his own art of description in terms of the "inexpressibility commonplace" (*Unsagbarkeitstopos*): Laudine's words and grief are indescribable.[16] The subsequent description, which Chrétien does none-

---

[14] On the other hand, the cousin of the Dame de Fayel does have some of Anna's traits, as we shall see in Chapter Six.

[15] Another example is the plight of the three hundred *tisseuses* at the Castle of Pesme Aventure in *Yvain*, who were, perhaps, moving for medieval audiences because of their nobility.

[16] Here as elsewhere, I use the word commonplace to refer to conventional subject matter, whereas common place refers to topoi as places or features common to the kind of person, thing, or action being represented; this distinction corresponds to that betwen *locus* and *locus communis* as varieties of topoi (Bornscheuer 1976 pp. 67-68; cf. Moos 1988b esp. pp. ix and 422-26 and Vincensini 1996 pp. 311-34).

theless put into writing, is a moving account of conventional actions centering on a supernatural occurrence: blood spurts from Esclados's wounds as his corpse passes by Yvain who is protected from discovery by the invisibility made possible by a magic ring Lunete gave him. After Chrétien displays Laudine's anguish, he also shows her quieter but no less moving grief while reading a psalter and reflecting on her deceased husband's virtues. Both the violent as well as the calmer images evoke pathos in Macrobius's sense, as an *argumentum a causa* (*Sat* 4.4.1); Laudine's tears and lamentations like her religious reflection are proof of her grief. Indeed, earlier Chrétien's narrator draws just such an inference with respect to Yvain's presence. Thus, the blood from the wounds in Esclados's corpse

> . . . fu provance veraie,
> Qu'ancore estoit leanz sanz faille
> Cil, qui feite avoit la bataille,
> Et qui l'avoit mort et conquis. (*Yvain* v. 1182-85)

[was proof positive that, indubitably, the one who had fought, killed, and defeated him was still inside.]

In the *Yvain* example we have something approaching Macrobius's conception of pathos achieved by description (*descrivre*). It contrasts with the stereotyped beauty of Soredamors, which is eroticized in Alexandre's imagination by the analogy between her appearance and the invisible "arrowhead" of her nude body, eliciting pathos as Alexandre's desire to see the body he imagines through the arrow metaphor.[17]

Descriptio is a technique used to achieve ethos and pathos in medieval rhetoric and rhetorical poetics. Masters of the art like Chrétien could translate the *Saturnalia*'s analysis and illustrations of Vergil into their verse, since their habits were formed by numerous composition exercises, or *praeexercitamina*.[18] By the time Chrétien wrote *Erec* and *Yvain* those habits of describing would easily have become ingrained in his approach to the art. Indeed, the three conventional descriptions from *Erec*, *Cligès*, and *Yvain* exemplify how originality may none-

---

[17] Kelly 1987 p. 217.

[18] One finds violent illustrations of pathos inserted into a conventional ethos in *Philomena*; see Anne Berthelot ed. *Philomena* pp. 1392-94.

theless inform convention; a masterpiece is, in a sense, an inventive and skillfuly honed transformation of conventions.[19]

Description in Latin, with Special Reference to Macrobius

Descriptio has a broad range of meanings in Latin. These include pictorial illustrations; geometrical, astronomical, and architectural diagrams; written descriptions as such; copies; identification by epithets; topical invention; and descriptive narrative. *Descriptio* overlaps in meaning with rewriting as copying, paraphrasing, imitating, and emulating; that is, with any original description by which an antecedent matter, motif, or theme is rewritten in order to enhance, improve upon, or correct the prior version or versions.[20] According to one grammarian, narrative elaboration (*enarratio*) is itself "secundum poetae voluntatem unius cuiusque descriptionis explanatio"[21] [elaboration of each description in accordance with the poet's wish]. Likewise, narrative "nominatur quae rerum consequentium continet perspicuam et dilucidam cum gravitate expositionem" (*Ad Her* IV.xxxix.51) [is the name for the figure which contains a clear, lucid, and impressive exposition of the consequences of an act]. For example, a *gradus amoris* can set forth the narrative consequences of falling in love, a *gradus aetatum*, the stages in life that begin at birth. The stages in each *gradus* are topoi the writer will describe *secundum voluntatem*.

Macrobius uses the word *descriptio* in all these senses. The first, oldest meaning appears in the *Commentary* to refer to illustrations of the microcosm and macrocosm[22]; some manuscript illustrations are extant, notably those in Richard de Fournival's own copy.[23] Elsewhere in Macrobius, description refers to transcription, but not just in the narrow sense of "to transcribe": "si quid apparuerit unde

---

[19] I am using the term "masterpiece" in the sense of a consummate example of the medieval poetic art; see Kelly 1991 pp. 57-60.

[20] S.v. *describo* in *ThLL* col. 656-64; *descriptio* col. 664-67; and cognates (*descriptionalis, descriptiuncula, descriptivus, descriptor*) col. 667. Cf. Wattenbach 1896 pp. 266-67 and Glauche 1970 p. 91 (based on a letter from Gerbert, abbot of Tegernsee).

[21] S.v. *descriptio* in *ThLL* col. 666 ll. 20-21 from Victorinus's *Ars grammatica* (*Gram lat* vol. VI, p. 188).

[22] *ComSS* 1.22.12 (cf. p. 167); see also 1.17.1-5, 1.21.1-8 (cf. p. 164). *ThLL* s.v. *descriptio* § IA3 and s.v. *describo* § IB.

[23] See Barker-Benfield and Marshall 1983 p. 232.

sumptum sit, aliud tamen esse quam unde sumptum noscetur appa-
reat" (*Sat* praef. 6) [if something should reveal the source of a borrowing, let it nonetheless appear to be different from its source]. This
prescription is actually an argument for emulation, not for copying,
paraphrasing, or the "timid" imitation we find in school *praeexercitamina*. Although *descriptiones* can constitute classroom exercises, actual
mastery of the technique evinces a different standard, one that requires the writer to surpass the source author's achievement and
demonstrate how much better the source matter can be treated, or,
at least, how it may be treated in a different way. Such description is
truly original in Macrobius's context. Presumably the depiction of the
quadrivium in Erec's coronation robe is an effort to transform the
description of the same robe in Chrétien's original *estoire*, perhaps by
adding the personifications of the quadrivium to the fairies' artistry.

Original description implies both a source and a common model.
Such is the case, for example, when Macrobius uses the word 'description' to refer to Vergil's representation of the plague "de
descriptione pestilentiae" (*Sat* 6.2.7) in the *Georgics*[24]; Macrobius
names Lucretius as Vergil's source. The passages from both these
authors reveal the common model — "Nonne vobis videntur mem-
bra huius descriptionis ex uno fonte manasse?" (*Sat* 6.2.14) [does it
not seem to you as if the parts of this description flow from a common source?] — along with the originality of each author which the
juxtaposition of the common parts reveals. The reader is expected to
discern the common and original features, as Macrobius suggests by
the following mirror image: "nunc locos locis componere sedet
animo, ut unde formati sint quasi de speculo cognoscas" (*Sat* 6.2.1)
[now I propose to compare different passages in such a way that you
may perceive as in a mirror what he based his rewriting on].
Chrétien's treatment of stereotypical feminine beauty which we examined in the previous section illustrates this kind of originality when
rewriting the commonplace into new matter.

Macrobius's examples thus show Vergil rewriting his sources, his
verse not only using the source as model for a new description, but
also serving itself as a model for subsequent writing. According to
Macrobius, the new description is also an effort to realize the source's
model in a new way. Vergil may draw the new version out of a brief

---

[24] Note also "navigationem... describit" (*Sat* 5.2.10) [he described the sea voyage]
and "iter... descripsit" (*Sat* 5.2.12) [he described the voyage].

statement or a definition, or kind of definition, whose brevity gives space for the prolixity characteristic in the invention of a description,[25] especially in the sense of full and complete illustration, whether in pictorial or written modes, of a person, thing, or action.[26] Macrobius's examples of Vergil's borrowing show how the Roman poet improves on his models (*Sat* 5.11) as well as how models and a new version seem to him to be on a par (*Sat* 5.12); in other instances, Vergil falls short of his models (*Sat* 5.13).[27] The standard seems to be a full description, that is, a description "omnia quae in hac re eveniunt comprehendens" (*Sat* 5.11.25) [including all that happened in these circumstances]. A *plena descriptio* strives therefore to articulate all the relevant features of the person, thing, or action being described, as in this reference to chariot description: "nec ullam quadrigarum partem intactam reliquit, ut esset illi certaminis plena descriptio" (*Sat* 5.11.22) [nor did he fail to touch on every part of the chariots so as to provide a full description of the contest].

Such description of parts of a whole is a kind of enumeration. Catherine Croizy-Naquet has referred to this device as "énumération par enchaînement," which recalls the orthographic confusion of Old French *conte-conter* as "account-to account for" (*conte-compte* and their verbs in modern French).[28] It is such "enumeration" that Macrobius emphasizes in Vergilian descriptions, as in "descriptio et enumeratio" in catalogues (*Sat* 5.2.15), but also as recapitulation, or a full account in summary form of the main features of the object of description (*Sat* 5.11.25). Description may literally recount everything of importance, like a virtual index of the subject matter, as in Vergil's catalogue of the Trojan and Italian wars (*Sat* 5.2.15-17). Or it may specialize in order to distinguish an object from others of the same kind, as when Vergil uses arcane or unusual language in order to characterize different peoples and their actions (*Sat* 5.18.16, 5.19.1-14).

---

[25] Cizek 1994 pp. 134-36 and 144, Knapp 1975 pp. 58-60, and Kelly 1991 pp. 76-78.

[26] As in "complurium rerum vel nominum plena et in certam ordinem digesta perscriptio," s.v. *descriptio* (*ThLL* col. 665 ll. 16-17) [a complete account of numerous things or names, set out in a specific sequence], or s.v. *describere* (*ThLL* col. 658 l. 17): "diligenter ab initio usque ad finem perscribere," *ThLL* verb IE [thoroughly, diligently written out from beginning to end]. Matthew of Vendôme enunciates the same standard of whole and complete description in *Ars vers* 1.63, 74, 110, and 114.

[27] See in general Wlosok 1990 p. 487.

[28] Croizy-Naquet 1994 p. 82; see also pp. 60-61. She bases her observations on Andrieux-Reix 1987 pp. 157-59.

Thus, Macrobius draws fully on the meanings of *descriptio*, as outlined above. As his use of the word moves from the sense of copying to that of rewriting, it takes on more complex configurations. Such is the case when it connotes 'adaptation' by chains of authors and rewriters. Thus, *Saturnalia* VI shows not only how Vergil adapted Homer, but also how intermediate Latin authors transmitted Homeric models to Vergil after their own adaptations. Here Homer reaches Vergil by way of Ennius, Lucretius, and others. The student of Macrobius might easily compare Greek models in Book V and Latin models in Book VI with the same lines in Vergil.[29] Similarly, Chrétien is a link in the chain of texts that transmitted descriptions of the liberal arts or, in his case, the quadrivium — a chain that itself formed part of the *translatio* of *clergie* he evokes at the beginning of *Cligés*, the romance he wrote immediately after *Erec et Enide*.[30]

But before examining some lines of transmission of descriptive material in Chapter Three, let us first look at a specific instance of *descriptio* as Macrobius uses the word, its cognates, and related techniques. What we are after is Macrobius's contribution to our understanding of the art of description as medieval writers practiced it and as Chrétien himself says he learned it. The passage I shall examine explains how Vergil 'described' the sea storm in Book I of the *Aeneid*.[31] If we take the storm as extending from v. 50 when Juno propositions Aeolus to Neptune's intervention that ends at v. 157, we find parts of the description treated nine times in Books IV-VI. The tempest itself is described in *Aeneid* v. 81-123. "Nam et tempestas mira imitatione descripta est — versus utriusque [that is, of Vergil and Homer[32]] qui volet conferat" (*Sat* 5.2.13) [for the tempest is set

---

[29] For example (following Marinone ed. *Sat*), *Sat* 5.5.5 and 6.1.8 (= *Aen* 2.250), 5.13.14 and 6.2.28 (= *Aen* 1.416-18; cf. Marinone ed. *Sat* p. 687 n. 45), 5.6.15 and 6.1.31 (= *Aen* 4.585), 5.13.27 and 6.3.5 (= *Aen* 10.361), 5.1.12 and 6.7.18 (= *Aen* 11.770-71), 5.3.14 and 6.6.13 (= *Aen* 12.206-07), and 5.16.5 (reference not quoted) and 6.2.7 (= *Geor* 3.478-80).

[30] On such chains in romance, see Kelly 1992 pp. 92-93.

[31] This example has been chosen because of its prominence in Book 5; it recurs in medieval rewriting. See Chapter Three.

[32] Cf. "De quinto *Odysseae*" = *Odyssey* V, v. 282-389; see Marinone ed. *Sat* p. 524*n*7 and Willis ed. *Sat* p. 252 n. 23. Macrobius abbreviates his quote: "versus, quoniam utrobique multi sunt, non inserui: qui volet legere ex hoc versu habebit exordium: 'haec ubi dicta, cavum conversa cuspide montem,' et apud Homerum de quinto *Odysseae*..." (*Sat* 5.4.4) [since the lines are numerous in both works I have not quoted them; whoever wishes may read beginning with this line: "So he spoke, and, turning his spear... the hollow mountain...", and in Homer's *Odyssey* Book V...] Cf. Herescu 1932.

out in marvelous imitation — whoever wishes may compare the lines
in both authors]. This is precisely what Macrobius himself does with
the remaining quotations from this episode.[33]

"Tempestas Aeneae Aeolo concitante cum allocutione ducis res
suas conclamantis de Ulixis tempestate et allocutione descripta est, in
qua Aeoli locum Neptunus obtinuit." (*Sat* 5.4.4) [The tempest Aeolus
unleashed on Aeneas together with that leader's lament on his fate is
drawn from Ulysses's storm and lament, in which Neptune stands in
Aeolus's place.] "Descripta est" is clearly not merely 'described.' It is
"de-scripta est," that is, 'is drawn from' (as in Marinone's translation:
"è derivata da") 'written out from,' and thus 'modeled on.'[34] To
'describe' here means 'to derive from a source a model to reproduce
in the new version,' but with suitable modifications that improve
upon the antecedent and fit it to a new matter, understanding, intention, or context. Such appropriation makes the new version a new
work. "Hic opportune in opus suum quae prior vates dixerat transferendo fecit ut sua esse credantur" (*Sat* 5.3.16) [he transferred into
his own work the earlier poet's words so as to make them appear to
be his own words]. Clearly, Vergil is understood to have 'described'
the tempest in the *Odyssey* by drawing it from Homer's version and
adapting it to his own story. Importantly, the instigator of the storm
has changed: Vergil's Juno has replaced Homer's Neptune as first
cause of the storm. Moreover, Aeolus has been introduced to unleash
the storm's winds, and Neptune acquires a more positive role in the
Aeneid, since he stops the storm and calms the sea.[35]

Macrobius sees Homer's text as a tripartite model for Vergil that
links a sea storm produced by the winds, the hero's despair and
lament on his misfortune, and divine intervention. Providing an obvious topical order, a kind of *gradus tempestatis*, the tripartite model
functions not unlike a *gradus amoris* using the topoi *ante rem, cum re*, and
post rem (cf. as well "circa rem" *Sat* 4.5.1).[36] The tripartite model also

---

[33] *Aen* v. 65-66 : *Sat* 5.4.2, *Aen* v. 71-73 : *Sat* 5.4.3, *Aen* v. 81 : *Sat* 5.4.4, *Aen* v. 92
: *Sat* 5.3.9, *Aen* v. 94 : *Sat* 4.6.3, *Aen* v. 105 : *Sat* 6.6.7, *Aen* v. 135 : *Sat* 4.6.21 and
6.6.15, and *Aen* v. 137 : *Sat* 6.8.7.

[34] Davies translates *descripta est* here as "are taken from Homer's description,"
whereas Marinone renders it more precisely.

[35] See *Sat* 6.8.10; cf. *Sat* 4.3.15 and 4.6.21. In Homer's *Odyssey* Bk. V v. 291-393,
it is Athena who intervenes to calm the storm after Ino, Neptune's consort, tells
Odysseus where to swim to safety while Neptune is returning to his palace.

[36] This seems to point to the figural feature of topical markers; see Wills 1996 pp.
2-4. On tropes and figures as devices for amplification in topical invention, see Kelly
1991 pp. 71-78.

relies on the topoi of cause and effect (*a causa*; cf. *Sat* 4.4.1, 4.4.22, 4.5.3). Macrobius is showing in order (cf. "ab initio per ordinem," *Sat* 5.4.1) how Vergil wove Homeric threads into a new weave — "quod totum Homericis filis texuit," *Sat* 5.2.9 [which he wove entirely from Homeric threads]. Macrobius's analysis shows how Vergil's tempest is drawn out in wondrous imitation — *mira imitatione* (*Sat* 5.2.13) — of its model and source. Vergil's description here is emulation, or original imitation, by use of a tripartite model which he found in Homer.

Likewise, Chrétien implies that he intertwines Celtic and Latin matters in Erec's coronation robe. That is, in his *estoire*, Chrétien found a description of the coronation robe made by the fairies (*Erec* v. 6736-45); then, with the art he learned from Macrobius, he represented each fairy as portraying one of the quadrivial arts in the robe (v. 6744-46, 6756, 6770, 6777). Perhaps coincidentally, his description contains the three topoi Macrobius identified in Vergil: the coronation (*causa*), the fairies (*ante rem*), the weave (*cum re*), and the personifications of the quadrivium (*post rem*). Whatever Chrétien's sources may have been, his *conjointure* of fairies and quadrivium fits the Macrobian model of description, as he says that it should: "Macrobes m'ansaingne a descrivre...."[37]

Macrobius's analysis of Vergil's models also "foreshadows" Faral's interpretation of Chrétien's rewriting of an *Eneas* model in the anonymously composed romance written around 1165. Faral actually identifies elements in the description of Erec's coronation robe — the four fays, an exotic cloth,[38] including material from marvelous beasts,[39] and commonplace personifications of the four arts of the quadrivium — as occurring in the *Roman d'Eneas* too. Of course, there is no coronation robe in the coronation and marriage with which the *Eneas* concludes. But three of these features do appear in Camille's robe. And in some manuscripts the "missing" quadrivium is translated and transformed onto the wall of Dido's palace (see *Eneas* ed. Petit v. 433-35). If Chrétien described, that is, adapted, the *Eneas* in the sense of the art of description illustrated in the *Saturnalia*, he could have combined elements from Camille's robe with the four arts of the quadrivium, either because his manuscript of the *Eneas* suggested the

---

[37] And, we recall, as Faral 1913 p. 346 surmized.

[38] So exotic that the meaning of the word, *moire* (*Erec* v. 6735), is uncertain. On what follows see Faral 1913 pp. 345-46.

[39] See Burgess and Curry 1989 and 1991.

addition to him (two configurations drawn from the same source, but in a new *conjointure*) or because he drew on his own knowledge of the quadrivium to invent a fuller description. As such, both the *Eneas* and Chrétien illustrate original configurations of borrowed matter using a descriptive model which the new version partially rewrites and rearranges, adding to or deleting from the source. It also appears that such rewriting, or 'describing,' fits a larger narrative purpose indicated by the new subject-matter. That is, Vergil rewrites a Homeric model — the sea storm, an episode in Odysseus's wandering — to fit Aeneas's new, different quest for a homeland. Similarly, in *Erec*, Faral sees Chrétien taking a coronation scene found in the *Eneas*, but adding to it a robe modeled on other parts of the *Eneas* manuscript he may have read: what is *corrompu* and *depecié* in his model comes together in a new, complete *conjointure*.

To return to the *Saturnalia*, Macrobius goes on to discuss the art of description in Vergil's account of Aeneas's arrival in Carthage and Dido's banquet, which follows the seastorm. Here too he finds a model in Homer. "Venus in Nausicaae locum Alcinoi filiae successit; ipsa autem Dido refert speciem regis Alcinoi convivium celebrantis" (*Sat* 5.2.13)[40] [Venus takes the place of Nausicaa, Alcinous's daughter; Dido herself mirrors king Alcinous giving his banquet]. That is, Macrobius likens two banquet descriptions as mirror images ("operis speculo formatum est"), pointing out where appropriate rearrangement and adaptation of topical elements in Vergil reconfigure his Homeric model ("refert speciem") (*Sat* 5.2.13). Well might Macrobius ask: "Quid quod et omne opus Vergilianum velut de quodam Homerici operis speculo formatum est?" (*Sat* 5.2.13) [indeed, is not Vergil's entire work shaped as if to mirror the Homeric poem?].

Chrétien's art of description conforms to Macrobius's own examples of such artistry. Both illustrate rewriting by the four operations common in late antique and medieval transformation: addition, deletion, replacement, and transmutation. These operations refer to an art that transforms and recombines compositional blocks,[41] an art, that is, of *bele conjointure*. A new synthesis results from the combined operations of all four of these transformations.[42] As seen above, each

---

[40] On Christian poets who rewrote this scene in their biblical poems, see Mora-Lebrun 1994a p. 70 and Deproost 1992. John of Salisbury links the two descriptions in order to inveigh against intemperance in the *Policraticus*; see Poirion 1978 p. 217.

[41] See Cizek 1994 p. 124, esp. n. 19, with additional bibliography.

[42] Cizek 1994 pp. 122-25.

new version is an imitation. Vergil imitates a Homeric model — for example, the sea storm. Chrétien too imitates models, notably, the coronation scene at the end of the *Roman d'Eneas*. But each new version is also unique.

The Descriptive Model as Archetype: Imitation and Emulation

Macrobius presents Vergil studying Homer's descriptions as if they were poetic archetypes. The noun *archetypus* can also mean a 'blueprint,' and these meanings come together in the *Saturnalia*'s use of *archetypus* in the sense of 'model.' Indeed, Macrobius understands the entire *Aeneid* as a 'Homeric description,' that is, as an imitation in new matter of his Homeric model, the *Iliad* and the *Odyssey*:

> per omnem poesin suam hoc uno est praecipue usus archetypo. Acriter enim in Homerum oculos intendit ut aemularetur eius non modo magnitudinem sed et simplicitatem et praesentiam orationis et tacitam maiestatem. (*Sat* 5.13.40)[43]

> [who used him especially as his archetype or model in all his poetry. For he fixed his gaze intently on Homer in order to emulate not only his grandeur, but also his straightforward description, effective speech, and quiet dignity].

Generally speaking then, description for Macrobius is the imitation of archetypes, that is, models found like blueprints in antecedent writing.

Thus, the full and complete description of Aeneas's *iter* or *navigatio*, modeled on Odysseus's, can become a major instance of topical invention, requiring, for a *plena descriptio* as Macrobius understands the expression (cf. *Sat* 5.11.22), a full and complete elaboration of the topic *iter* qua *navigatio*. As Vergil wrote and everyone who has read the *Aeneid* knows,

---

[43] On *archetypus* as used here, see *ThLL* vol. 2, col. 460 s.v. *archetypos*. Geoffrey of Vinsauf uses the attribute *archetypus* to describe invention in the *Poetria nova* v. 48. On his use of the term as a metaphorical attribute rather than as a literal substantive, see Kelly 1991 p. 37 n. 2.

> Arma virumque cano, Troiae qui primus ab oris
> Italiam fato profugus Laviniaque venit
> litora — multum ille et terris iactatus et alto
> vi superum.... (*Aen* I.1-4)

[Arms I sing and the man who first from the castle of Troy, exiled by fate, came to Italy and Lavinian shores; much buffeted on sea and land by violence from above....]

Vergil's prologue emphasizes *iter* as *navigatio* leading from *bellum troianum* to *bellum italicum* by way of Carthage and Dido. Indeed, Macrobius quotes sequences in the *Saturnalia* that illustrate like a kind of *cento* or florilegium, Aeneas's *casus* and *labores* from Book I through Book XII.[44] In this way, he shows Vergil putting his whole poem together, from work to word, with an eye on Homeric models.[45] This is description as recomposition of a model.

Macrobius's survey of Vergil's borrowing, imitations, rewriting, and transformations — that is, of his descriptions — leads him to conclude that the entire *Aeneid*, as a whole and in its parts, is made from Homeric cloth; cut, adapted, rearranged, rewoven with new and old threads, it is transformed into a new and original work. An imitation of Homer and others, yet one which offers original, if not always successful, adaptations of its Homeric models. All of these operations illustrate 'description' as either imitation or emulation.

It is important, however, to distinguish between *imitatio* and *aemulatio*: they are not synonyms. *Imitatio* refers to the writer's attempt to reproduce a source as model in a new work. *Aemulatio* refers to the writer's attempt to outstrip the source's version of the model, in effect vying with it formally or substantively or both.[46] In the latter case we have the basic rhetorical conflict: the issue posed by two versions of a given subject matter; similarly, two orators may use an existing case as a model for interpreting a new one (*imitatio*) or seek to win approval for different versions of the same matter (*aemulatio*).[47]

Macrobius treats three major kinds of imitation common in gram-

---

[44] See Marinone's and Willis's notes to *Sat* 5.3.18-5.10.13, and 5.11.1-5.12.1. On Macrobius as compiler in the positive sense of the word in the Middle Ages, see Hathaway 1989 pp. 23-27.

[45] See Kelly 1991 pp. 64-68 on the scope of invention from word to work.

[46] Angelucci 1984 p. 108 and Cizek 1994 pp. 52-55.

[47] For the relevance of issues to romance composition, see Kelly 1992 pp. 209-10.

matical and rhetorical traditions from Greek antiquity to the end of the Middle Ages and beyond: paraphrase, or literal or slightly modified adoption of various lines; imitation, or a greater modification of borrowed material which still is recognizable as such; and, finally, emulation, or the adoption of material which the new author rewrites with originality.[48] For Macrobius, to describe is to draw out of an extant matter a model which can serve to reshape the same matter or a new matter. Reading Macrobius on description, Chrétien would have discovered the usefulness of recognizable paradigms for imitation and emulation. Indeed, it is such description as 'extraction' that Chrétien refers to in the *bele conjointure* passage of the *Erec* Prologue: "Et *tret* d'un conte d'avanture / Une mout bele conjointure" (*Erec* v. 13-14; my emphasis) [and he *draws* from a tale of adventure a very beautiful configuration].

The Saturnalia*'s Writing Program*

Macrobius's movement from the large fresco to the small unit of discourse or "compositional blocks" entails the gradual immersion of his readers into the particulars of Vergil's art of description. First he evokes the background by reference both to Vergil's vast knowledge (*Sat* 5.2.2) and to an epic cycle, written as it were *ab ovo*, and attributed to an ambiguous Pisandrus (*Sat* 5.2.4-5).[49] He then reviews the contents of the *Aeneid* before passing on to progressively smaller units of discourse. First come the large frescoes like the sea storm. These include, as we have seen, Homer's epics recounting the Trojan War (*Iliad*) and Odysseus's return voyage (*Odyssey*) which Vergil used for his own description of war and of *iter* as *navigatio*. In Book V of the *Saturnalia*, Macrobius summarizes Vergil's plot by comparing it with Homer's two epics (*Sat* 5.2.6-13) before moving on to the description of the sea storm and Dido's feast, as analyzed above. The immediate, relatively passive apprehension and appreciation of that art by a late-antique, but educated elite assumed to be thoroughly familiar with the masterpieces of Greek and Latin literature[50] will give way in the

---

[48] Cizek 1994 p. 63, with references to *Sat* 2.1-8, 4.1ff., and 6.1-60.

[49] On "Pisandrus," see Marinone ed. *Sat* pp. 510-11 n. 6.

[50] Whether such readers actually existed in the fifth century is doubtful; see Marinone 1987 p. 304.

medieval classroom to learning the art of description by study, interpretation, and imitation of Vergil and other authors.

Macrobius does not quote every text he analyzes. The *Saturnalia* often requires that one refer back to Vergil's text, as in allusions like: "locum loco similem lector inveniet" (*Sat* 5.7.4) [the reader will find the places that are similar]. For example, lengthy extracts could not be quoted in full, as with the sea storm referred to above (*Sat* 5.4.1-4), all of Book IV (*Sat* 5.17.4-6), along with epic catalogues in Books VII and X (*Sat* 5.15), the Cacus episode related by Evander during a feast in Book IX (*Sat* 5.14.16), and the Nisus and Euryalus episode (*Sat* 4.6.12). In these cases, Macrobius provides only the essential parts of long descriptions: "capita locorum, ubi longa narratio est, dixisse sufficiet ut quid unde natum sit lector inveniat" (*Sat* 5.7.7) [it will suffice to provide the high points of the passages where the development is lengthy, so that the reader may find the source of each]. *Inveniat* here is 'finding' by consulting Vergil's text,[51] suggesting that consultation of the text being commented on is common procedure in reading commentaries[52] and that Macrobius too relies on the audience's knowledge of Vergil or on their being able readily to obtain a copy of his epic and other poems when Macrobius refers to them.

I shall illustrate the complexity of Macrobius's analysis as well as its systematic movement from large segments towards the small unit of discourse by perhaps the best-known example today, the Dido episode in Book IV. For Macrobius, Vergil chose not to imitate an episode in Homer, but took the Medea episode in Apollonius of Rhodes's *Argonautica* (*Sat* 5.17.4-6) as his model. That is, Vergil invented Dido's story by inserting originally extraneous matter into his Homeric material.[53] To make his case, Macrobius quotes extensively from Book IV of the *Aeneid*, in effect jarring his reader's memory with reminders of its contents.[54] The running comparison of Vergil's Book

---

[51] See Marinone ed. *Sat* p. 53 and n. 4.

[52] Holtz 1985 p. 14, Munk Olsen 1985 pp. 35 and 40-42. Cf. Ward 1995 pp. 58-59.

[53] On this *bele conjointure*, see Kelly 1983 p. 26 and Foehr-Jansens 1997. On fictive insertions, see Moos 1976 pp. 118-25. On insertions in romance narratives, see Chapter Six, below.

[54] Marinone's "Indice analitico" (*Sat* p. 898) lists forty quotes or references to Book IV of the *Aeneid* in *Sat* Books 4-6, a considerable number even though Macrobius actually refers to Book 4 less often than to any other book in Vergil's epic. Willis ed. *ComSS* pp. 180-81 lists thirty-four passages from the *Aeneid*'s Book IV in the *Sat*, but one is erroneous because it actually refers to Book IV of the *Georgics* (see "454 sqq." for *Sat* 5.16.5).

IV with Homer includes four direct quotes plus a fifth in a recapitulation (*Sat* 5.6.9-15, 5.11.14), all of which the listener is expected to
relocate mentally in the *Aeneid*'s plot or find again in a manuscript
copy of the epic.

Some of these passages illustrate without explanation, thus requiring mental commentary on the reader's part. Others include explication of Vergil's rewriting from different points of view and in the light
of different techniques. For example, in one place Macrobius recalls
how, in *Aen* 4:177, Fama "ingreditur... solo et caput inter nubila
condit" (*Sat* 5.3.11) [walks the ground with head hidden in the clouds]
in order to illustrate Vergil's use of a Homeric image; later, with the
addition of v. 176: "Parva metu primo, mox sese attollit in auras, /
ingrediturque solo et caput inter nubila condit" (*Sat* 5.13.31) [at first
small out of fear, she soon lifts herself up to the skies, walking on the
ground while hiding her head in the clouds], Macrobius argues that
Vergil's imitation is inferior to his model because of incongruities in
this description of Fama: she is no longer a rumor when all can see her
for what she is. Elsewhere, Vergil adds a topical feature in order to be
more accurate and provide a learned justification lacking in Homer
(*Sat* 5.11.14-15). Still another passage (*Aen* 4, v. 513-14), which in Book
V is made to illustrate a Vergilian adaptation of Sophocles (*Sat* 5.19.9-
10), becomes in Book VI an illustration of Sophocles's passage filtered
through a Latin-language intermediary (*Sat* 6.6.9); the early Latin
source adds what the Greek version did not express. In this case
Vergil's rewrite approaches paraphrase. Regarding still another
Vergilian passage, the famous dawn image: "et iam prima novo
spargebat lumine terras / Tithoni croceum linquens Aurora cubile"
(*Aen* 4:584-85 = 9:459-60) [and already Aurora leaving the saffron
couch of Tithon spreads her first light over the lands], Macrobius first
shows that Vergil adapts the image from Homer (*Sat* 5.6.15, 5.9.11),
then, in Book VI, he argues again for a Latin filter: two lines, one from
Lucretius, the other from a text known today only as a fragment,
which Vergil, as Macrobius puts it elsewhere,[55] combine into one:

---

[55] For *Aen* 4:584-85, Marinone ed. *Sat* p. 663 n. 42 refers to both Lucretius *De
rerum natura* 2:144, and p. 665 n. 54 to a fragment. Cf. "de duobus unum fabricatus
est" (*Sat* 5.3.9) [he has made a single whole from two things]. Of course, the diverse
explanations of Vergil are more realistic in the context of the Saturnalian feast
because various speakers propose different interpretations of how Vergil rewrote and
what sources he used. But taken together in this way, they also illustrate diverse
features of the art of description as rewriting.

"Tithoni croceum linquens Aurora cubile" and "interea Oceani linquens Aurora cubile" (*Sat* 6.1.31). Not all multiple readings are in disagreement. For example, "quos ego... set motos praestat componere fluctus" (*Aen* 1.135) [whom — ! But better is it to calm the troubled waves] illustrates both indignant anger as pathos (*Sat* 4.6.20) and *intermissio*, or interruption as figure of speech (*Sat* 6.6.15).

These examples suggest the wide-ranging operations for description as rewriting. They require of the reader some amount of what we call textual analysis, or, in medieval terms, commenting and glossing, to identify and delineate the art by which an author models his or her rewriting of an antecedent work or fragment.[56] What Macrobius's illustrations suggest is a broad array of model descriptive operations by which Vergil rewrote Homer and other authors in his new matter. They also suggest how descriptive rewriting can make old matter new.

On Vergil's invention *de suo* Macrobius refers to topoi that fill out the representation of the person, thing, or action he is writing about. For example, in Dido's tirade against Aeneas when he leaves her, Macrobius identifies not only the topoi of delivery (*partitio*) and upbringing (*educatio*) which Vergil took from his Homeric model, he also notes the Roman poet's own addition of the nurture topos *nutritio* of the suckling tigers (*Sat* 5.11.14-19): "nec tibi diva parens, generis nec Dardanus auctor, / perfide, sed duris genuit te cautibus horrens / Caucasus, Hyrcanaeque admorunt ubera tigres" (*Aen* IV, v. 365-67)[57] [False one! No goddess was thy mother, nor was Dardanus founder of thy line, but rugged Caucasus on his flinty rocks begat thee, and Hyrcanian tigresses gave thee suck]. Diverse topical attributes thus bring out the very "soul" of a motif: "His praetermissis, quae animam parabolae dabant, velut exanimum in Latinis versibus corpus remansit" (*Sat* 5.13.30) [if those things are omitted, which constituted the soul of the comparison, the Latin verse survived much like a dead body]. If the adaptor fails to apprehend that "soul" the rewrite fails; it is a corpse that lacks the vitality of its source.

---

[56] Cf. Zumthor 1978. One is reminded of Marie de France on authors who take an obscure matter and, by "glossing," draw out its potential or hidden meaning (*Lais* "Prologue," v. 9-22). In antiquity, Vergil was said to write in this way (Pieri 1977 p. 9). On the concept of the "first author" in medieval imitation and rewriting, see Kelly 1992 p. 77; cf. Kelly 1988.

[57] Cf. *Iliad* XVI, v. 33-35. Wills 1996 pp. 26-28 identifies another Latin intermediary as Catullus.

While description is a wide-ranging technique, it often deals with very brief texts. In *Saturnalia* VI we come to the smallest units of descriptive discourse treated by Macrobius. These passages extend from the single word to no more than two lines of verse (cf. *Sat* 6.1.7). Paolo Angelucci has identified the two ways in Book VI by which *descriptio* as extraction and rewriting transfers material of such brief compass from one author to another: reprise, including echo as variation or restatement of no more than two lines of verse (*imitatio*); and imitation whereby passages containing only one or two lines of verse are rewritten in order to draw from them a potential not realized by the first author (*aemulatio*).[58] Most important for our subject is the model's potential for incremental restatement and reinterpretation.[59] *Saturnalia*'s Book VI locates reprises and imitations under the following heads: 'ornaments,' or *ornamenta*, which include both borrowing of neologisms and archaisms, and echoes in variant restatements; and 'flowers,' or *flores*, which include imitations that amplify or abbreviate passages longer than a line of verse.[60] In other words, *Saturnalia*'s Book VI treats only single words, a line of verse or less, and passages no more than two lines long (*verba, versus, loci*) that pass from Homer through earlier Latin adaptations to Vergil.

A Model for Original Description

Four features characterize Macrobius's art of description: the *auctor-imitator* dichotomy, *mutuatio*, *mutatio*, and reception. Let me explain these features briefly before analyzing them in greater detail.

Macrobius distinguishes consistently between *auctor* as source au-

---

[58] Angelucci 1984; cf. Pieri 1977 pp. 16-18, and Wills 1996.

[59] Angelucci 1984 p. 101: "*imitatio* indicava sempre un'operazione consistente nella riproposizione... di un preciso aspetto della sua immagine letteraria tramite elementi che per consistenza e significatività erano capaci di riproporla"; see also p. 102. On "immagine letteraria" in this sense, cf. Bernard of Chartres on the "auctorum imaginem" (*Metalogicon* I.24.83). For a full discussion of the different species of imitation, see Cizek 1994.

[60] Angelucci 1984 pp. 104-05 and Pieri 1977, esp. the latter's discussion of Macrobius's division of adaptations from Lucretius into *versus, loci*, and *verba*. On the possible relation between the term *flores* and medieval florilegia, see Angelucci 1984 pp. 107-108. Were florilegia used as set passages for rewriting? They did constitute lists of memorial topics (*copia*); see Cizek 1994 p. 257. But see also Munk Olsen's reservations, discussed above in Chapter One n. 53.

thor and *imitator* as rewriter. Although the distinction allows for the latter's originality, it includes the source model in invention and construes writing as original rewriting. The *imitator* first identifies source material. He or she then lifts the source material that will go into the new work; this is *mutuatio*. The source may be actual subject matter, or it may be a theme or a motif that will serve as a model for rewriting. *Mutuatio* is followed by *mutatio*. *Mutatio* refers to the principal operations in rewriting: invention, disposition, and *elocutio* as amplification or addition (*adiectio*), concentration or deletion *(detractio)*, substitution (*immutatio*), and transposition (*transmutatio*).[61] Finally, appreciation of the rewritten work rests in part on audience reception, an important factor when we come to the replacement of Latin-educated audiences with vernacular publics and patrons. Audiences include the following categories, which may overlap: other writers, learned critics, informed audiences, patrons, and ignorant audiences. Twelfth-century audiences may include those who know Latin and those who know one or more vernacular languages, a critical consideration since allusion is a not inconsequential factor in audience reception.

I shall discuss these four features of Macrobius on description while suggesting — in anticipation of the rest of this study — their cogency in the case of Chrétien de Troyes and some of his contemporaries. But first it is necessary to point out that there are clear and hazy areas in the scheme. The art of description itself is clearly marked out in ancient and medieval treatises and commentaries. However, as we move away from the sources and the author (in all Macrobius's senses) and towards *mutatio* and audience appreciation, matters become hazier and variables emerge. Ultimately, reception is an individual experience, regardless of the quality of the reception.

Author and Rewriter (auctor-imitator): *The Agents of Description*

In Macrobius's *Saturnalia* our word "author" refers to two or more agents: the first author and the rewriter or rewriters. As we have observed, books IV and V show how Vergil rewrote his Greek predecessors; book VI places Latin intermediaries between Homer and Vergil. These writers are paradigmatic of rewriting in Latin and, by

---

[61] Cf. Schmolke-Hasselmann 1980, esp. Part I, for analogous examples in Arthurian romance.

extension, vernacular traditions during the time Chrétien de Troyes wrote his romances.[62] Indeed, Chrétien himself appears to have used models from Latin, French, and Celtic traditions; his romances offered, in turn, models for writers who followed him.

I am distinguishing between "author" and "rewriter" in conformity with Macrobius's own use of *auctor* and *imitator*.[63] In the *Saturnalia* *auctor* as 'author' refers to first authors, that is, those who first wrote the works which provided models for later writers. An *imitator* imitates or emulates an author, as in "auctoris sui imitator" (*Sat* 5.14.16) [imitator of his source-author]. Nowhere does Macrobius identify Vergil as an *auctor*, that is, as the first to write something and become thereby an authority on a certain matter, practice, or usage. Not everyone agreed: "sunt qui aestiment hoc verbum 'umbracula' Vergilio auctore compositum..." (*Sat* 6.4.8) [some believe that the word *umbracula* was first made by Vergil...]. But Macrobius denies Vergil's "authorship"; the speaker, Servius, identifies a hitherto unnoticed antecedent instance of *umbracula* that he thinks Vergil knew and used (*Sat* 6.4.8). Thus, he is a rewriter whose authority derives from others whom he rewrites as *imitator*. Such arcane examples actually serve to enhance Vergil's poetry, since they emphasize his learning and, consequently, the educational value of everything he wrote. By *auctor*, Macrobius usually means Homer, as in: "omnia quae ab auctore transcripsit" (*Sat* 5.13.33) [all that he wrote out from his author],[64] but he also uses the term for other Greek writers that Vergil used as models[65] as well as his Latin models, as in: "ea... a nostris auctoribus sumpta" (*Sat* 6.3.1) [those subjects drawn from our authors].[66] I shall therefore use *auctor* and *imitator* to distinguish be-

---

[62] Knapp 1975; Kelly 1992 pp. 92-93; Mora-Lebrun 1994a and 1994b. I discuss some chains of authors in the following chapters.

[63] The meaning of *auctor* as source or first author is consistent throughout the *Saturnalia*'s Books 4-6; see *auctor* at 5.1.4, 5.2.2, 5.15.1, 5.19.31, 5.22.9, 6.1.5, 6.4.17, 6.7.16, and 6.8.17. By contrast, other designations are used indiscriminately to refer to both *auctores* and *imitatores*, albeit with special connotations dictated by the term used. From Books 4-6, see, for example, *fabricator* 5.11.16; *fictor* 5.21.16; *interpres* 5.11.5; *orator* 5.1.1 and 2, 5.1.5; *poeta* 4.4.7, 4.4.26, 4.5.7, 4.6.1, 4.6.18, 5.2.1, 5.2.10, 11, and 12, 5.3.16, 5.11.21, 5.13.5, 5.15.16, 5.16.12, 5.18.1, 4, and 14, 5.19.5, 5.20.2, 5, and 8, 5.21.6, 5.22.1, 4, and 10, 6.3.6 and 9, 6.4.2, 6.7.18, and 6.9.4; *rhetores* 4.4.12, 17, and 19, 4.6.3; and *vates* 5.3.16, 5.14.11, 5.16.10, 5.22.12, 6.4.1, and 6.6.1 and 2.

[64] See also *Sat* 5.13.1, 5.14.16, 5.16.4 and 12, 5.17.4-5.

[65] *Sat* 5.18.14 and 21, 5.19.11 and 14, 5.21.19, 5.22.10 and 12.

[66] See also *Sat* 5.19.16, 6.1.3, and 6.4.1.

tween a first author and later authors who imitate or emulate the first author.

Although Macrobius's usage is precise, it also has a wide range of specific applications. An intermediary can be both an *auctor* and an *imitator*, such that the choice of one or the other term nonetheless distinguishes clearly between model and imitation. *Imitator* can collectively designate all estimable poets who emulate their predecessors, or *auctores*. *Auctores* imitate one another too: "quod et nostri tam inter se quam a Graecis et Graecorum excellentes inter se saepe fecerunt.... possum pluribus edocere quantum se mutuo compilarint bibliothecae veteris auctores" (*Sat* 6.1.2-3) [which our Latin writers often did, borrowing both from one another and from the Greeks, just as did the best Greek writers.... I can demonstrate by several examples how extensively authors of old literature compiled material from one another's works]. *Auctor* here is first author, and that is how Macrobius uses the term. "Authors" in this sense means all those Vergil rewrites — they are authors as sources and as models for rewriting.[67] A source derives its authority, or *auctoritas*, from its antiquity.[68] Accordingly, Vergil became an author in this sense when he himself was rewritten; the *Roman d'Eneas* is an obvious example of an intermediary *auctor* for Chrétien, but he is also an *imitator* of Vergil (see Chapter Five).

For Macrobius, Vergil is a consummate *imitator* or rewriter. The *imitator* who rewrites an *auctor* is endowed with native talent and an artist trained to rewrite with originality and learning. Vergil himself possessed a mind capable of original invention because he was learned in all things.[69] For example, in a passage already quoted Macrobius shows how Vergil added a line of his own to his imitation of Homer in order to enhance Dido's condemnation of Aeneas's inhumanity in leaving her. Aeneas, she asserts, is not only of unnatural birth, he is also nurtured in an unnatural manner: "Hyrcanaeque admorunt ubera tigres" (*Aen* IV.367; see *Sat* 5.11.14-19) [Hircanian tigresses gave you suck]. Macrobius's comment was: "Addidit enim

---

[67] This corresponds to the medieval Latin sense of *auctor* as first author; see Chenu 1927 p. 83.

[68] Cf. *Sat* 5.18.4 ("antiquissimorum Graecorum more") and 11 ("ad probationem moris antiqui"), 5.19.6 and 23, 5.21.13, and 5.22.8 ("auctoritate Graecae vetustatis"); cf. 6.1.1-7 on reviving old Latin authors.

[69] Macrobius asserts as much in *Sat* 1.16.12, 1.24.8, 5.1.18-20, 5.2.2, and 5.18.21, and *ComSS* 1.6.44, 1.15.12, and 2.8.1. See, in general, Willis ed. *ComSS* pp. 184-85 for further examples.

de suo" (*Sat* 5.11.15) — "ad criminandos igitur mores defuit Homero quod Vergilius adiecit" (*Sat* 5.11.19) [For he added from his own invention.... Vergil therefore added what was lacking in Homer in order to condemn his actions]. Macrobius derives not only from the topos of family found in Homer ("nec tibi diva parens, generis nec Dardanus auctor, / perfide, sed duris genuit te cautibus horrens / Caucasus," *Aen* IV.365-67) [False one! no goddess was thy mother, nor was Dardanus founder of thy line, but rugged Caucasus on his flinty rocks begat thee], but also from *nutricatio/nutricatus*, or the milk of tigers, which has nefarious effect on Aeneas's humanity, as Macrobius explains at some length.[70] Moreover, Macrobius explains Vergil's original invention with a learned digression on *nutricatio/nutricatus* that also lauds the Roman poet's learning and genius. Thus, Vergil possesses the *sens* and *science* that is also characteristic of the good writer of romances.[71] That is, he applies his knowledge and abilities with what Chrétien calls *painne* and *antancion* and Macrobius terms *industria, diligentia, cautio, observatio*, and *iudicium*. He uses all these terms to characterize Vergil's artistry: diligence, care, caution, careful attention, and judgment.[72] These characteristics of the master poet focus on diligent, yet masterly — that is, sure and steady — rewriting of an authoritative masterpiece.

---

[70] "Plene Vergilius non partionem solam, sicut ille quem sequebatur [= *Iliad* XVI, v. 33-34], sed educationem quoque nutricationis tamquam belualem et asperam criminatus est" (*Sat* 5.11.15) [Vergil expands on the author he was following not only by condemning his birth but also the, as it were, savage, uncivilized nourishment he received]. To birth in the wild Caucasus (*locus a patria*), but not of divine and noble parentage (*locus a natura et maioribus*), as in Homer, Vergil adds the *locus a convictu*: "Hoc autem attributum dividitur in consuetudinem nutriture et in eos a quibus aliquis suam contrahit nutrituram" (*Ars vers* 1.83 [This attribute is divided into customary nourishment and the persons from whom one receives nourishment]; cf. *De inv* I.xxv.35, under *attributae personis in victu*: "apud quem et quo more et cuius arbitratu sit educatus" [with whom he was reared, in what tradition and under whose direction].

[71] Kelly 1992 pp. 106-25.

[72] For examples, see *Sat* 6.9.13 (*industria*), 6.7.6 (*diligentia*), 5.15.13 (*cautio*), 5.1.1 (*diligens observatio rhetoricae artis*), 6.1.6 (*iudicium transferendi*). Note the fine juxtaposition and contrast of haste and delay (*celeritas* and *tarditas*) in "monebat ut ad rem agendam simul adhiberetur et industriae celeritas et tarditas diligentiae, ex quibus duobus contrariis fit maturitas" (*Sat* 6.8.9) [he cautioned that in doing something one bring both deliberate speed and due process, from which two contraries emerges the opportune moment].

From Mutuatio *to* Mutatio: *the Stages in Description*

Macrobius uses similar terms that identify two distinct stages in descriptive imitation: *mutuatio* and *mutatio*. *Mutuatio* refers to the lifting of material from a source in order to locate and rewrite it in a new work.[73] The realigning and rewriting of such material is *mutatio*.[74] With these two terms, then, Macrobius articulates two stages in rewriting: the extraction and transfer of matter (*mutuatio*) and its relocation and transformation in a new work (*mutatio*). Not coincidentally, *describere* itself, as *de-scribere*, comprehends both *mutuari* and *mutare*.

The transfer of matter or models from one work to another may be obvious or hidden.[75] Importantly, transfer, or *translatio*, is one of the best-known topoi in medieval literature. Chrétien uses it in his celebrated account in *Cligés* of the 'translation' of *chevalerie* and *clergie* from Greece through Rome to France.[76] Book V of the *Saturnalia* is devoted in its entirety to one stage in the historic process Chrétien

---

[73] Including the verb *mutuari* and analogous terms like *addere* (*Sat* 5.11.15 = "addidit enim de suo" [he added by his own invention] and thus an instance of topical invention, 5.15.6, 5.20.15, 6.6.19, 6.9.10) and *adicere* (*Sat* 5.11.19, 21, and 25, 5.18.9, 5.22.10), *compilare* (*Sat* 6.1.3, 6.2.33; cf. Hathaway 1989), *haurire* (*Sat* 5.19.23), *inducere* (*Sat* 4.6.4, 5.15.6, 5.18.16, 5.19.4, 5, and 14, 5.21.17, 5.22.7 and 8, 6.2.32, 6.8.10 and 14), *inferre* (*Sat* 5.16.1, 5.20.10), *inserere* (*Sat* 5.13.33, 5.15.6, 6.1.1, 6.4.1 and 17), *sequi* (*Sat* 5.11.15, 5.16.4, 5.22.12, 6.3.6, 6.4.17), *subripere* (*Sat* 5.16.14), *sumere* (*Sat* 5.9.12, 5.13.23 and 39, 6.1.4 and 7, 6.3.1, 6.4.16), *trahere* (*Sat* 5.2.2, 5.19.6, 5.20.17, 5.22.7, 6.1.1 and 7, 6.2.4, 6.3.1 and 8; also *subtrahere* 5.13.16 and 5.17.7, and *trahere* in the sense of drawing from a topos, as in "ex hoc loco [i.e., *ex causa*] traxit affectum," *Sat* 4.4.3), *transcribere* (Sat 5.13.33, 5.17.7, 6.1.7, 6.2.30), *transferre* (*Sat* 5.2.17, 5.3.1 and 16, 5.13.2, 5.15.18, 5.22.15, 6.1.5 and 7, 6.2.1), and *usurpare* (*Sat* 5.17.15, 6.1.2, 6.4.5, 6.5.6, 6.6.1 and 8). This vocabulary suggests the potential range of meanings in Chrétien's own *traire d'un conte d'aventure* in the *Erec* prologue; on the significance of *trahere*, see Ward 1990 pp. 41-43.

[74] Including the verb *mutare* and analogous terms like *aemulare* (*Sat* 5.13.40, 5.14.15, 5.17.8, 5.19.8, 6.1.2), *artare* (*Sat* 5.1.8) and *augere* (*Sat* 4.2.6 and 10, 4.3.7, 4.4.2 and 19, 4.6.5 — all instances of amplification), *convertere* (*Sat* 6.1.2, 6.6.14), *deviare* (*Sat* 5.15.1), *dissimulare* (*Sat* 5.16.14), *excolere* (*Sat* 5.11.1, 6.1.5), *fabricare* (*Sat* 5.2.5, 5.3.9, 6.4.2), *farcire* (*Sat* 5.1.6), *fingere* (*Sat* 4.5.9 and 10, 5.2.14, 5.17.6, 5.19.2 = "non de nihilo fabulam fingit" [he didn't make up the fiction out of nothing], 6.5.1), *imitare* (*Sat* 5.14.7, 5.15.1, 5.16.12, 5.17.4 and 5, 6.1.6), *interpretare* (*Sat* 5.2.5, 5.17.12), *pingere* (*Sat* 5.11.11 and 22, 5.13.19 = *depinxit*), *ponere* (*Sat* 5.13.17 and 35, 5.16.14 = "Hoc Maro non narrationis sed parabolae loco posuit, ut aliud esse videretur" [Vergil didn't use it as narrative but metaphorically so as to make it appear different], 6.4.12, and *componere Sat* 5.22.4, 6.3.4, 6.9.5), *tractare* (*Sat* 4.6.10), and *vertere* (*Sat* 5.17.4). We can discern in these techniques the multiple features of *conjoindre* in *bele conjointure*.

[75] Courcelle 1948 p. 15, especially n. 3; cf. Cizek 1994 p. 107.

[76] See·Curtius 1954 pp. 38-39 and 388-89, Worstbrook 1965, Jongkees 1967.

evokes: Vergil's 'translation' of Homeric and other matter from Greek to Latin. Indeed, Macrobius evokes a kind of *translatio imperii et studii*, a transfer of *chevalerie* and *clergie* from Greece to Rome, in passages like:

> Quia cum tria haec ex aequo impossibilia putentur, vel Iovi fulmen vel Herculi clavam vel versum Homero subtrahere, quod etsi fieri possent, alium tamen nullum deceret vel fulmen praeter Iovem iacere, vel certare praeter Herculem robore, vel canere quod cecinit Homerus: his opportune in opus suum quae prior vates dixerat transferendo fecit ut sua esse credantur. (*Sat* 5.3.16).[77]

> [because since these three were felt to be equally impossible — to take away Jove's thunderbolt, Hercules's club, or a verse from Homer — which, although it might be done, it would in no way be decorous for anyone other than Jove to hurl a thunderbolt, or to fight with such arms other than Hercules, or to sing what Homer sang, all the same, Vergil transferred the words of that poet into his own work in such a way that it seemed as if he had written them himself.]

Just so, Chrétien brought Greco-Roman ideals (as he construed them) to France. The *translatio studii* inferred in *clergie* included the clerical art of description Chrétien learned from Macrobius. That art included invention as transfer of the invented material into a new opus.

Chrétien's is not the only voice in the twelfth and thirteenth centuries to evoke the art of *mutuatio* as transfer from one language into another. Others also reflect the ongoing art of description in a Macrobian context while suggesting how difficult it is to practice that art. Marie de France in the Prologue to her *Lais* evokes the recent successes of those who rewrote Latin literature in French — the ancient romances and Ovidian adaptations come to mind, including those Chrétien mentions in his *Cligés* prologue — only to turn aside from such *matière* in order to rewrite in French the material she knew in other languages like Celtic and English. Later, on a gloomier note,

---

[77] Cf. as in *Sat* 5.22.15: "ingentia poteram volumina de his quae a penitissima Graecorum doctrina transtulisset implere" [I could fill volumes with the material he transferred from the most profound learning of the Greeks].

Huon de Mery despairs of emulating Chrétien's and Raoul de Houdenc's fine French — no Vergil nor Chrétien he! Yet, his rewriting of these authors nonetheless constitutes a new blend of borrowed material in an allegorical psychomachia. From Macrobius's perspective, Huon imitated motifs, as illustrated in Book V but not short passages as in Book VI. I shall return to his *Tournoiement Antechrist* in Chapter Six.

Like Huon de Mery, Vergil's rewriting of Homer in Book V relies, according to Macrobius, for the most part on compositional blocks or small units of discourse. However, these units are located in and acquire their full significance from a model embracing a whole work: Homer's corpus of *Iliad* and *Odyssey* as models for Vergil's rewriting of them in the *Aeneid*. They also include appropriate, but additional and secondary material in Greek or Latin that he could use and transfer to the *Aeneid*. In practice, the concept suggests anew a basic feature of rhetorical invention: its working in all phases and levels of composition, from the totality of a work through its parts to details of sentence, phrasing, and vocabulary.[78] Thus, a pupil like the young Chrétien studying Macrobius on description could, with some assistance from the schoolmaster, place the *Saturnalia* in a familiar paradigm of invention — that is, the medieval rhetorical and poetic paradigm for original rewriting that the twelfth- and thirteenth-century arts of poetry teach.

Macrobius's analysis reminds us that imitation includes invention. It therefore presumes a new construe of sources in order to produce an original rewriting of them. Horace wrote, and medieval authors concurred and passed on his counsel, that "tuque / rectius Iliacum carmen deducis in actus, / quam si proferras ignota indictaque primus" (*ArsPoet* v. 128-30)[79] [and you are doing better in spinning into acts a song of Troy than if, for the first time, you were giving the world a theme unknown and unsung]. Macrobius shows Vergil practicing the same art — the art of description — with Homer's *materia*, notably in the *Aeneid*'s Book II that treats the Trojan War. Not only does the writer imitate and emulate models identified in

---

[78] See Kelly 1991 p. 38, and Kelly 1992 pp. 43-44.

[79] On this passage, see also the glosses and commentaries from the Middle Ages, which I have followed in my translation, and in the arts of poetry and prose. Horace anticipates Matthew of Vendôme's distinction between *materia executa* or *pertractata* and *materia illibata*; see Kelly 1969b pp. 127-28. I discuss these eleventh- and twelfth-century Horatian commentaries in Chapter Three.

another writer, he or she can do so with more than one source, or insert secondary material into a major source. These different insertions come together in the new opus which, then, is truly a whole greater than any of its parts and than the sum of its parts. The new and beautiful *conjointure* is a new and original version of familiar material; it may in fact be so original that the reader does not recognize the *materia* that went into it.

Mutuatio followed by *mutatio* informs several metaphors which Macrobius himself rewrites and combines in his Prologue in order to describe the composition of the *Saturnalia* itself. The best known of these metaphors is that of bees making honey with the nectar from various flowers. Macrobius also refers to the making of condiments, nourishment, the production of numbers out of other numbers, the confection of perfumes, and the blending of voices in a chorus (*Sat* praef. 5-9) to describe recomposition. All these metaphors suggest how Macrobius intended his own work to be read. We should not hold it against him if he has lifted so much from others (*Sat* praef. 4), since the new combination is new: "in unum conspirata" (*Sat* praef. 10) [fused into one whole]. I translate "in unum conspirata" as fusion following Marinone — "fusi in un tutto unico"; Davies translates: "informed by a single spirit." There is no English, French, or Italian word that catches in a positive sense the connotations of conspiracy, plotting, and blending of voices. But it is perhaps the bee metaphor beginning the sequence of images that conveys best the process of imitation and emulation that goes into plotting a work of this kind. "Apes enim quodam modo debemus imitari, quae vagantur et flores carpunt, deinde quicquid attulere disponunt ac per favos dividunt, et sucum varium in unum saporem mixtura quadam et proprietate spiritus sui mutant." (*Sat* praef. 5) [We ought somehow to imitate the bees, who fly about gathering from flowers, then arrange what they have gathered, dividing it up among the wax cells. In this way they transform various kinds of nectar into a single flavor in a certain blend which is unique to them.] In the *mixtura quaedam* lies the potential for originality and genius.

Of course, Macrobius himself found this comparison to bees in Seneca.[80] Other authorities may have inspired the other metaphors,

---

[80] Stackelberg 1956 pp. 257-77; Pigman 1980 pp. 4-6; Hooley 1997 pp. 251-56. Both John of Salisbury and Peter of Blois use the image (Stackelberg 1956 pp. 278-81). This "maîtrise du multiple" by "une ordonnance du foisonnement" is discussed by Gally 1996 (quote p. 168).

although none has been identified; if not, Macrobius did use the
model for transformation borrowed from Seneca to invent new metaphors *de suo*. But taken as a whole all these metaphors for recomposition come together to make us understand the place of sources and
their transformation in the composition of the *Saturnalia* — they are
"in unum conspirata." They are also descriptions in the broad context understood in the *Saturnalia*: rewriting as an *imitator* or original
invention *de suo* as *auctor*. Similarly, *mutatio* may, in medieval practice,
extend from elementary paraphrase to original transformation or
even virtual metamorphosis of the source into something totally new
in subject or mode.

Macrobius's interpretation of Vergil's rewriting of Homer coincides in language with Chrétien's own references to his *modus agendi* as
writer. The description of Erec's coronation, including his coronation
robe, is determined by Chrétien's construe of his matter. "Or
avaingne qu'avenir puet, / Ne leisserai que je ne die / Selonc mon
san une partie" (*Erec* v. 6710-12) [happen what may, I'll not fail to
tell part of it using my wit and skill.] Then follows the reference to
Macrobius on description. In other words, Chrétien's *san* makes his
art of description narrate the coronation. For the mind is informed
by what it contains, as Chrétien suggests in the case of the personification of Arithmetic.

> Onques nonbres ne l'an boisa,
> Ne ja n'an mantira de rien,
> Quant ele i viaut antandre bien;
> Teus est li sans d'arimetique.
> (*Erec* v. 6766-69)

[Numbers never befuddled her, nor will she ever err in using
them whenever she wants to apply herself assiduously to her
calculations. That is the wit and skill of Arithmetic.]

As is well known, Chrétien says he combines matter and meaning
(*matiere et san*), drawing forth a new configuration of the matter so as
to express that meaning in a new, fuller, and more complete plot.
Such 'drawing forth' involves imitation of a mental model for the
new work, followed by the careful involution of that model into the
new matter, including appropriate additions, deletions, and adapta-

tions.[81] The model is already present in the source. For example, in the reference to Erec's coronation robe, Chrétien notes that Macrobius taught him how to describe the robe as we find it in the romance. But the robe was already in what Chrétien calls his *estoire*: "Lisant trovomes an l'estoire / La description de la robe" (*Erec* v. 6736-37) [reading the story we find the robe's description]. We may therefore conjecture that this *estoire* told how the fairies wove the robe, or, at least, what the product of their weaving looked like. Chrétien, emulating their work in a fuller description, adds *de suo*, or "selonc" his *san/sans* "une partie" (v. 6711-12) — presumably, the description of the personifications of the quadrivium.

We have already noted that, taking the Trojan War as Vergil's matter, Macrobius reminds his readers that his subject is so well known that he need not elaborate — every school boy knows it (*Sat* 5.2.6). Chrétien too implies in his Prologue his audience's awareness of numerous, presumably oral, and (by his standards) defective *contes* about Erec and Enide. But neither Chrétien nor Vergil was writing a school exercise or declamation. They were inventing a masterpiece as they understood the term. Vergil emulated Homer and other models. In so doing he rewrote so as to surpass his model. So did Chrétien. Both are describing a model in new matter.

Homer's two epics relate both the Fall of Troy and the wanderings of Odysseus. According to Macrobius, Vergil adapts this scheme or model to his new hero, transferring the war to Italy and relating the wanderings of Aeneas before that war. Macrobius follows this narrative model from the broad lines of the plot into the minutiae of description in compositional blocks. Various operations integrate the Homeric model into the *Aeneid* configuration. These operations are part of the art of *mutatio* or rewriting that turns the borrowed material into a new work. At this stage of composition description occurs. In Macrobius, the fundamental descriptive techniques are invention, ordering, and topical amplification — in Macrobius's terminology, invention, reordering, and various species of *mutatio*: addition, deletion, replacement, and rearrangement. I shall discuss each of these techniques in turn.

---

[81] The term involution is borrowed from Wesley Trimpi 1983. I take it in the sense of topical invention in romance (Kelly 1992 p. 49).

Invention (inventio)

Invention is a three-fold operation according to Macrobius, drawing on source matter (*ab auctore*), from the writer's mind (*de suo*), and on skill in using the art (*ex arte*).[82] Such threefold invention is also suggested by Thomas d'Angleterre's account of how he collected, sifted, and combined the matter on the Tristan legend available to him.[83] As he states, the purpose of his new version is to offer a full and credible account of the Tristan story as his sources report it. They are *in unum conspirata*. Thomas also excludes an episode which, he thinks, lacks verisimilitude. How, he asks towards the end of the romance, could Governal have gone to Marc's court to fetch Iseut, even disguised as a pilgrim, and not be recognized? Everyone knew him. He opposes his own version to most other versions containing this episode.

> Il sunt del cunte forsveié
> E de la verur esluingné,
> E se ço ne volent granter,
> Ne voil vers eus estriver;
> Tengent le lur e jo le men:
> La raisun s'i pruvera ben!
>   (*Tristan* Douce v. 879-84)

[They have strayed from the plot and left its true version far behind. If they refuse to admit this, I don't wish to quarrel with them. Let them keep to their version and I'll follow mine. The plot's rationale will be demonstrated clearly in that way.]

Thomas gathers into his plot only those features which he deems worthy of imitation. He clearly intends to outstrip the other versions of the Tristan story, just as Chrétien did the storytellers in *Erec*. Both are following Macrobius's principles of imitation and emulation: "non de unius racemis vindemiam sibi fecit, sed bene in rem suam

---

[82] For *ab auctore*: "sic auctorem suum dissimulanter imitatur, ut loci inde descripti solam dispositionem mutet et faciat velut aliud videri" (*Sat* 5.16.12) [he imitated his author covertly, in such a way that, by changing only the disposition of the places from which he drew his version, he made it appear different]; *de suo*: "addidit enim de suo" (5.11.15) [he added by his own invention]; *de arte*: "ipse poetica disciplina a rerum medio coepit et ad initium post reversus est" (*Sat* 5.2.9) [using the poetic art, he began in the middle of his subject and then returned to its beginning].

[83] See Kelly 1969a and Kelly 1992 pp. 101-03.

vertit quidquid ubicumque invenit imitandum" (*Sat* 5.17.4)[84] [he didn't harvest his grapes from one vine, but turned to his purposes whatever he found worthy of imitation, wherever he found it]. In other words, invention for Marie, Chrétien, and Thomas d'Angleterre meant both literally finding the sources and plotting a new version of them.[85] In Chapter Four, we shall find the same technique being used by analyzing their contemporary, Benoît de Sainte-Maure.

A key word in Macrobius's language, and one that helps define how description proceeds from invention, is *formare*. *Formare* in Macrobius can translate 'to form' or 'to mould' as 'to model,' as in this rhetorical question: "quid quod et omne opus Vergilianum velut de quodam Homerici operis speculo formatum est?" (*Sat* 5.2.13) [nay, is not all Vergil's opus modeled on Homer as in a mirror?] The examples of the technique use verbs of description to delineate the modeling: notably, the sea storm, the Latin auxiliaries, which we have already noted (*Sat* 5.2.13-15), and Vergil's modeling ("formaverit") Dido on Medea in the *Argonautica* (*Sat* 5.17.4). Similarly, Palinurus's tomb is modeled on ("formata est") Patroclus's (*Sat* 5.7.9). In numerous other places Macrobius shows Vergil modeling his transmutation of Latin sources: "ut unde formati sint quasi de speculo cognoscas" (*Sat* 6.2.1)[86] [so that you might recognize whence they drew this model as if in a mirror image].

Reordering (ordo)

Homer related, first, the war between nations at Troy in the *Iliad* and, second, the return of the Greek warrior Odysseus to his home-

---

[84] Cf. the condiment metaphor Macrobius uses to describe the composition of the *Sat* praef 6: "in unius saporis usum varia libamenta confundit" [he blends various condiments into a single flavor], as well as that for the composition of one number from other numbers (*Sat* praef 8): "ex omnibus colligamus unde unum fiat" [we gather together from all of them the wherewithal for a single unit], or, finally, that of singing in harmony (*Sat* praef 9): "concentus ex dissonis" [harmony from discordant sounds]. All are apt images for Thomas's *en uni dire* and *unir* as assemblage of all Tristan material that produces a credible plot — once again, *in unum conspirata* (*Sat* praef 10).

[85] Do some of the "rough edges" in Chrétien's *Perceval* — for example, the abrupt change in chronology at the insertion of Perceval's Good Friday adventure — derive from the incomplete state of the romance? See Kelly 1971 p. 329 n. 2.

[86] In the illustrations that follow, Macrobius shows how one description is reformed in rewriting so as to produce an original imitation (*Sat* 6.2.7, 8, and 31, and 6.3.7-8).

land in the *Odyssey*. Vergil, for his part, adopts this scheme as model
while rearranging it to fit the demands of his new subject matter.
First, he relates Aeneas's voyage to Italy; then he recounts the Italian
wars for that homeland.

> Iam vero *Aeneis* ipsa nonne ab Homero sibi mutuata[87] est erro-
> rem primum ex *Odyssea*, deinde ex *Iliade* pugnas? Quia operis
> ordinem necessario rerum ordo mutavit, cum apud Homerum
> prius Iliacum bellum gestum sit, deinde revertenti de Troia error
> contigerit Ulixi, apud Maronem vero Aeneae navigatio bella
> quae postea in Italia sunt gesta praecesserit. (*Sat* 5.2.6)[88]

> [And indeed, did not the *Aeneid* itself draw, first, the wanderings
> from the *Odyssey*, then the combats from the *Iliad*? Because the
> order of events required a different order: in Homer the Trojan
> War was fought before Ulysses's return voyage from Troy took
> place, whereas in Vergil Aeneas's voyage preceded the wars
> fought subsequently in Italy.]

Vergil not only transferred his Homeric model, he also rearranged it
to fit his new subject matter.[89] In this way he achieved the combination of events and the order which Chrétien would associate with *bele
conjointure* and which medieval poetics understood as order. First the
poet carefully orders — "plots" — the work to be written. Geoffrey
of Vinsauf describes this operation in a manner that is consonant
with what Macrobius says about Vergil's practice.

---

[87] On *mutuari* as plundering in order to compile, see Moos 1988a and Hathaway
1989 p. 24.

[88] This is not the principle of natural and artificial order as it is usually applied to
Vergil. The traditional medieval sense occurs in *Sat* 5.2.9-12; see Quadlbauer 1977
pp. 75-86. On order in *materia* as distinguished from order in the work, see Kelly
1992 pp. 264-72.

[89] Thus, Macrobius does not fit Vergil's account of the Trojan War into the
traditional notion of artificial order based on narrative chronology. Nonetheless, his
summary does reproduce the artificial beginning in medias res of *Aeneid* Book I —
that is, before the earlier events related in Books II and III — which became the
exemplar of artificial order for the Middle Ages; on these developments, see Quadlbauer 1977. Macrobius represents an early phase in the gradual authorization of the
principle in the art of poetry; Quadlbauer 1989 esp. pp. 126 and 134 n. 43 on
Macrobius, and Cizek 1994 p. 169 on Horace and Macrobius. See also Wills 1996 p.
23.

Non manus ad calamum praeceps, non lingua sit ardens
Ad verbum: neutram manibus committe regendam
Fortunae; sed mens discreta praeambula facti,
Ut melius fortunet opus, suspendat earum
Officium, tractetque diu de themate secum.
Circinus interior mentis praecircinet omne
Materiae spatium.[90]   (*Poetria nova* v. 50-56)

[Let the poet's hand not be swift to take up the pen, nor his tongue be impatient to speak; trust neither hand nor tongue to the guidance of fortune. To ensure greater success for the work, let the discriminating mind, as a prelude to action, defer the operation of hand and tongue, and ponder long on the subject matter. Let the mind's interior compass first circle the whole extent of the material. (Nims)]

Such reflection reproduces an order, as suggested in the compass metaphor, which Geoffrey of Vinsauf develops from the foregoing architectural metaphor as follows: "Certus praelimitet ordo / Unde praearripiat cursum stylus, aut ubi Gades / Figat" (*Poetria nova* v. 56-58) [Let a definite order chart in advance at what point the pen will take up its course, or where it will fix its Cadiz (Nims)]. Indeed, architecture became a common metaphor for literary invention in the Middle Ages. Like Geoffrey of Vinsauf, Macrobius uses architectural images to refer to order in invention. The *Saturnalia* expresses construction by words such as *construere* (*Sat* 5.13.15), *moliri* (*Sat* 5.17.8), and *fabricare* (*Sat* 5.2.5, 5.3.9, 6.4.2). *Fabricare* is broad in meaning, extending the notion to any art and even to procreation.[91] But more pertinent to Macrobius's treatment of transfer and imitation are terms for extraction, weaving, and forming, techniques that are also prominent in Chrétien's description of Erec's coronation robe.[92]

---

[90] Note that this image of the compass drawing out the space of the whole work corresponds exactly to one of the first, proper meanings of *descriptio* as an illustrative diagram.

[91] Elsewhere, Macrobius introduces the Neoplatonic analogy of creation, procreation, and artistic recreation; see *Sat* 5.1.18-20; cf. *ComSS* 1.7-21 and Curtius 1954 p. 442.

[92] For example, "L'uevre del drap" (*Erec* v. 6735) and "A fil d'or ovree et tissue" (v. 6785).

In addition to these and similar to the architectural metaphor, the cartographic metaphor — "ubi Gades / Figat" — fits precisely into Macrobius's geographical landmarks for the beginning of the *Aeneid*, including the first line of verse locating the narrative at a mid-point between the Trojan shores and the Lavinian coast in Italy,[93] after which the *narratio* begins *a medio* with the departure of the Trojan fleet from Sicily (*Sat* 5.2.8). Likewise, the composition of the *Poetria nova* is likened to a cartographic project setting out a voyage positioned on the location of New Carthage or Cadiz.[94] Similarly, Gautier of Châtillon fits a cartographic image into two orders based on Alexander's vision of the world and the divine order centered on Jerusalem, of which Alexander understands and, indeed, knows nothing.[95]

Sequence and disposition are not the same thing, although both fall under and are varieties of order. Sequence is chronological, spatial, or topical order; disposition is the arrangement of that sequence in the written work. The latter kind of order as reordering or disposition is apparent to Macrobius in Vergil too; Vergil rewrote Homer in the light of his new material. This is a conception of order different from narrative sequence, but common in medieval poetics. In this scheme, the *ordo* of the work is either retained as the chronological sequence of events, or it is artfully altered so that the disposition of narrative parts does not follow narrative sequence. This latter order is termed the artificial order. Medieval texts often illustrated the scheme with the *Aeneid*. But, according to Macrobius, Vergil's own model for the two orders was Homer. In the following passage, it will be noted that the narrative is "described" as artificial, a technique Macrobius says is a feature of the art of poetry ("poetica disciplina," *Sat* 5.2.19).

> Ergo Ulixis errorem non incipit a Troiano litore describere, sed facit eum primo navigantem de insula Calypsonis, et ex persona sua perducit ad Phaeacas. Illic in convivio Alcinoi regis narrat ipse quem ad modum de Troia ad Calypsonem usque pervenerit. Post Phaeacas rursus Ulixis navigationem usque ad Ithacam ex persona propria poeta describit. Quem secutus Maro Aenean de Sicilia producit, cuius navigationem describendo

---

[93] On mid-point in the arts of poetry see Kelly 1991 p. 95 and 1992 pp. 66-67.
[94] Kelly 1991 p. 95.
[95] Kelly 1992 pp. 45-46.

perducit ad Libyam. Illic in convivio Didonis ipse narrat Aeneas usque ad Siciliam de Troia navigationem.... Post Africam quoque rursus poeta ex persona sua iter classis usque ad ipsam descripsit Italiam. (*Sat* 5.2.10-12)

[Therefore he does not begin by relating Ulysses's voyage from the Trojan shore, but shows him first sailing from Calypso's island, and brings him to the Phaeacians. There, at king Alcinous's banquet, Ulysses himself relates how he got from Troy to Calypso. After the Phaeacians the poet narrates in his own voice Ulysses's voyage to Ithaca. Following this plan Vergil brings Aeneas from Sicily by relating his voyage as far as Libya. There, during Dido's banquet, Aeneas himself relates the voyage from Troy as far as Sicily.... After the African sojourn the poet again narrates in his own voice the fleet's passage to Italy itself.]

Homer is again the model. Vergil has made old matter new and original by reordering that model. It has become his own property!

The Four Species of Mutatio

Macrobius treats Vergil's transformation of Homer and others as a full and complete *mutatio*: "sic dissimulanter imitatur, ut loci inde descripti solam dispositionem *mutet* et faciat velut aliud videri" (*Sat* 5.16.12; my emphasis) [thus does he disguise his imitation by merely rearranging the object of description and thereby making it appear different]. Such "mutation" or "metamorphosis" also has its species. The four kinds of rearrangement include *adiectio*, *detractio*, *immutatio*, and *transmutatio*. Cizek defines these four operations, all of which Macrobius treats, as follows: *adiectio* adds new elements to a prior whole; *detractio* deletes elements from it; *immutatio* combines *adiectio* and *detractio* when an original element is removed from the whole and a new one, which was formerly not a part of it, is inserted in its place; *transmutatio* rearranges elements of the whole.[96]

We may briefly illustrate the four kinds of adaptation as follows: *Adiectio*, or the insertion of a new matter into another, occurs when the *Eneas* author adds the Lavine romance to Vergil, when the *Troie* amalgamates Dares and Dictys, or when the Prose *Lancelot* brings together Lancelot and the Grail. *Detractio*, or the deletion of matter,

---

[96] Cizek 1994 p. 123.

occurs in Joseph of Exeter's *Ylias* when he eliminates most of the
battles referred to in Dares or when Thomas d'Angleterre eliminates
Governal as messenger to Iseut. *Immutatio*, or the replacement of one
matter by another, occurs in the *Queste del saint graal* when Lancelot is
removed as the best knight in the world and Galaad is put in his
place.[97] *Transmutatio*, or rearrangement, occurs when *ordo naturalis* replaces *ordo artificialis* at the beginning of the *Eneas*.

Mutatio also includes figural or tropical embellishment which may
heighten pathos or sustain ethos by the articulation of common
places, or topoi.[98] Macrobius gives examples of this in Book IV of the
Saturnalia; as we have observed, the incomplete Book IV may originally have contrasted its treatment of pathos with means for repre-
senting ethos. Thus, the rearrangement of a sequence of events in an
antecedent work may also adapt by means of rearrangement or in
the formal use of the medieval principle of natural and artificial order
(*Sat* 5.2.8), rearrangement (*Sat* 5.2.6, 5.16.12), subtraction, addition,
or substitution of specific components of a transferred passage,[99] use
of a Homeric model in a new matter (*Sat* 5.13.23), and the changing
of words by altering or rearranging their letters (*Sat* 5.21.18, 5.22.1-6,
6.2.1). In Book VI, Macrobius sums up the process of transmutation
of Vergil's Latin-language sources as follows:

> Denique et iudicio transferendi et modo imitandi consecutus est
> ut, quod apud illum legerimus alienum, aut illius esse malimus
> aut melius hic quam ubi natum est sonare miremur. Dicam ita-
> que primum quos ab aliis traxit vel ex dimidio sui versus vel
> paene solidos; post hoc locos integros cum parva quadam immu-
> tatione translatos sensusve ita transcriptos ut unde essent elu-
> ceret, immutatos alios ut tamen origo eorum non ignoraretur;
> post haec quaedam de his quae ab Homero sumpta sunt osten-
> dam non ipsum ab Homero tulisse, sed prius alios inde sump-
> sisse, et hunc ab illis, quos sine dubio legerat, transtulisse. (*Sat*
> 6.1.6-7)

> [Thus, by judicious transfers and imitation he brought it about
> that, in what we read from another source in his work, we prefer

---

[97] See Rockwell 1995 pp. 162-70.
[98] On what follows, see Cizek 1994 pp. 276-79. The tropes and figures actually
contain suggestions for rearrangement; see Kelly 1992 pp. 282-90.
[99] Cizek 1994 p. 63.

his version or we marvel that it sounds better than its source. Let me say that he took from others from a half to about a full line of verse, then full passages slightly changed and rewritten, but with their meaning left intact, so that their source might be obvious, but he transformed others without hiding their source; after these I shall show that he took them not from Homer, but rather that others borrowed from Homer and he in turn borrowed from these intermediary authors whom he surely read.]

This passage rehearses the broad sense of invention as transfer and imitation, extending from the single word through a line or two of verse (and, by implication, a line or two of a phrase or sentence) to lengthier places or passages in the source[100] and, ultimately, to the entire work. Invention here, as is customary in medieval composition, is a multi-leveled, ongoing process analogous to the architectural construction Geoffrey of Vinsauf uses to illustrate literary invention — including the removal, as it were, of a single stone from one edifice for inclusion in a new edifice where it will have a specific, but new place and function. All these techniques are features of the multifarious art of description Macrobius sets out in the *Saturnalia*.

Small Units of Discourse
Macrobius's sixth book treats small units of discourse, as in the tropical and figural embellishment we associate with the medieval arts of poetry. He distinguishes between two kinds of small discourse: *flores* and *ornamenta*.[101] *Flores* admit no, or very little, change of the transferred material. But exact copying is also strictly limited, not only by length — to no more than two lines of verse — but also by restriction to neologisms, archaisms, or formulaic expressions, that is, to words and expressions for which there is no way to state what is to be stated except in the language of the borrowed material (as in legal, religious, and other such formulae). *Ornamenta*, on the other hand, require transmutation. They should either be hidden or so skillfully contrived that they seem new; or they should openly emulate the original material so as to surpass it if the transfer is justifiable.[102]

---

[100] Angelucci 1984 pp. 103-13.
[101] Angelucci 1984.
[102] As in *ArsPoet*: "Aut famam sequere aut sibi convenientia finge" (v. 119) and "publica materies privati iuris erit, si / non circa vilem patulumque moraberis orbem" (v. 131-32) [Either follow tradition or invent what is self-consistent... In

Although Latin transfer can be verbatim, Greek transfers like those in Book V must involve some change simply because of translation from one language to another. This is also, obviously, the case for twelfth-century transfers from Latin into French, a process which Angelucci terms "echo."[103] An "echo" in this sense allows one to recognize the repetition, making it distinct, then, from the hidden transfer. Each technique offers the pleasure of intertextuality for the knowledgeable reader.[104] Perhaps the most striking example of this achievement for today's reader comes not from Homer but from the *Argonautica*, whose Medea metamorphoses into Vergil's Dido (*Sat* 5.17.4).

> Quod ita elegantius auctore digessit, ut fabula lascivientis Dido-
> nis, quam falsam novit universitas, per tot tamen saecula speciem
> veritatis obtineat et ita pro vero per ora omnium volitet.... Tan-
> tum valuit pulchritudo narrandi ut omnes... coniveant... fabulae,
> et intra conscientiam veri fidem prementes malint pro vero ce-
> lebrari quod pectoribus humanis dulcedo fingentis infudit. (*Sat*
> 5.17.5-6)

> [Thus he surpassed his source to such an extent that the tale of
> a Dido enflamed with love, which everyone knew to be false,
> assumed the appearance of truth and passed as true. Such was
> the beauty of the narrative that everyone accepts the story and,
> suppressing an awareness of the truth of the original version,
> prefers the fiction that causes so much pleasure.]

Transmutation — or metamorphosis — of this kind is therefore essential to the artistry of the new version. Indeed, a new context may suffice to make a common subject matter resonate differently from its first version. However, transmutation seems to imply more than just

---

ground open to all you will win private rights, if you do not linger along the easy and open pathway]. See Friis-Jensen 1990 pp. 353-54.

[103] Angelucci 1984 p. 107. On the varieties of what Angelucci terms "echo" — gemination, polyptoton, parallelism, and modification — see Wills 1996, esp. his Introduction.

[104] Cf. "Quid enim suavius quam duos praecipuos vates audire idem loquentes?" because "hic opportune in opus suum quae prior vates dixerat transferendo fecit ut sua esse credantur" (*Sat* 5.3.16). [What is more pleasing than to hear two outstanding poets saying the same thing?... the latter transferred the earlier poet's words into his own work with such skill that the borrowing seemed to be his own invention.]

a change in context; although Marie de France will seek the *surplus de sen* in the Ancients' works which she rewrites, she alludes to the effort and toil that went into her rewriting their old stories. Anything less is a failure, revealing "translationis sterilitas" (*Sat* 5.13.23) [sterility of the transfer]. Macrobius enumerates a number of these features "in quibus mihi visus sit gracilior auctore" (*Sat* 5.13.1) [in which he seems thinner than his source author]. This contrasts with those cases where Vergil made Homer's archetype express more fully its potential through rewriting: "Vergilium in transferendo densius excoluisse" (*Sat* 5.11.1) [Vergil in transferring the passage elaborated it more fully] and thus emerged as the "locupletior interpres" (*Sat.* 5.11.5) [the richer rewriter].

Importantly, the last example takes us to the more common images for the operation of transfer in Macrobius: transfer as extraction, relocation, and weaving, as conveyed by terms like *trahere, sumere, ponere, texere*, and others, with their compounds, derivatives, and synonyms.[105] Here composition includes compilation. One lengthy passage summarizes all these operations very clearly.

Dicturumne me putatis ea quae vulgo nota sunt, quod Theocritum sibi fecerit pastoralis operis auctorem, ruralis Hesiodum, et quod in ipsis *Georgicis* tempestatis serenitatisque signa de Arati *phaenomenis* traxerit, vel quod eversionem Troiae cum Sinone suo et equo ligneo ceterisque omnibus quae librum secundum faciunt a Pisandro ad verbum paene transcripserit, qui inter Graecos poetas eminet opere quod a nuptiis Iovis et Iunonis incipiens universas historias, quae mediis omnibus saeculis usque ad aetatem ipsius Pisandri contigerunt, in unam seriem coactas redegerit et unum ex diversis hiatibus temporum corpus effecerit, in quo opere inter historias ceteras interitus quoque Troiae in hunc modum relatus est, quae Maro fideliter interpretando[106] fabricatus sibi est Iliacae urbis ruinam? (*Sat* 5.2.4-5)

[Do you expect me to say what everyone knows? that he made Theocritus his source for the work on shepherds and Hesiod for

---

[105] See notes 73, 74, and 92, above.

[106] On *interpretatio* as fundamental to the art of description, see Cizek 1994 pp. 46-50 and Kelly 1992 pp. 56-58; and Macrobius's reference to Vergil as "locupletior interpres" (*Sat* 5.11.5), or more opulent rewriter of Homeric material. *Interpretatio* in the medieval arts of poetry has, besides its special sense of synonymous repetition, a more general sense of amplification as restatement, lengthening, and emphasis.

that on farming? that in the *Georgics* themselves he drew the
features of storm and calm from Aratus's *phaenomena*? that he
copied almost verbatim Pisander's destruction of Troy, including
Sinon, the wooden horse, and all the other things he put into
Book II — Pisander, who is known for beginning his universal
history with the marriage of Jupiter and Juno and continuing in
sequence through all ages up to his own epoch? In this work,
among other events, the fall of Troy is related in the way that
Vergil, faithfully rewriting, builds his own version of the destruction of the Trojan city.]

Can one not perceive Chrétien following such an example, reducing
the cyclical features of Wace or the *romans d'antiquité* as well as storytellers' tales to the marriage and quest of the *Erec et Enide conjointure*?
The *Eneas* will be an especially important "archetype" or model for
him, as we shall see in Chapter Five.

Reception

The foregoing quote shows that Macrobius's banquet is attended by
elite connoisseurs, not medieval schoolboys. Such people know their
Vergil and Homer as well as other major authors.[107] On the other
hand, the *Saturnalia*'s immediate intended audience is Macrobius's
own son, who was to use it as part of his education. This actually
brings the text closer to the audience of schoolboys in which Chrétien
seems to locate himself. We must therefore take up the issue of audience appreciation from the fifth through the twelfth centuries, including both Latin and vernacular audiences, especially the audience of
learners Macrobius intends and which Chrétien's words illustrate.

   Both Book V and Book VI contain a lengthy and sometimes detailed survey of Vergilian rewritings. In Book V the examples are
arranged by and large to fit the narrative sequences in the *Aeneid*;
they constitute a coherent series of descriptions and a kind of *aide-
mémoire* facilitating reference back to the complete *Aeneid*. In Book VI,
on the other hand, the comparative descriptions are grouped in sets
according to the Latin authors and, more loosely, into topical subjects like storms, battles, and so forth. In these passages the pupil can

---

[107] Marinone ed. *Sat* p. 53.

find illustrations where direct comparison is possible and the art can be appreciated, commented upon, and imitated. Many of the juxtapositions use passages which in Book V are traced back to Homer; in Book VI, however, Homer is filtered through Latin authors who used Homer directly before Vergil rewrote them as well as, or instead of, Homer. In addition, analogous topics found elsewhere would illustrate and enhance those in the *Saturnalia*. Ultimately pupils in good schools would be working in the preceptorial context John of Salisbury describes for Bernard of Chartres: appreciation of imitable topics in prescribed works and their imitation in classroom *preaeexercitamina*.

I shall treat these matters in Chapter Three. But I want to close this chapter with one special problem in reading Macrobius in the Middle Ages: the Greek quotations. Would not such passages, or their absence,[108] have made Macrobius's critical commentary on Homer and Vergil incomprehensible to twelfth-century readers like Chrétien? I don't think so. Macrobius almost always explains what Vergil does with his Homeric and other archetypes, and his words in the context of the well-known *materia troyana* would have been readily comprehensible or explicable by a teacher using glosses[109]; thus, it is possible to follow Macrobius's analysis of Vergil's *translatio* solely from the Latin text, since Macrobius tells us what Vergil did with his Greek authors. Careful reading, with magisterial commentary, and the availability of Vergil's *Aeneid* in the twelfth century, make the kind of study and imitation I am describing feasible for Chrétien de Troyes despite the Greek. In addition, the comparisons of Vergil's adaptations with Homer in Book V are supplemented by his adaptations of Latin writers in Book VI, where readers could compare the *auctor*'s and the *imitator*'s versions.

For instance, the examples from Latin in Book VI would have complemented and filled out Book V with clearer illustrations,[110] even though Ennius, Lucretius, and other early Latin writers Macrobius cites were not common in the medieval school curricula as we know them today.[111] What does finally give substance to the *Saturnalia*

---

[108] See Willis ed. *Sat* p. ix on manuscripts that have suppressed the Greek quotes.

[109] On Macrobius glosses, see Hunt 1981-82 pp. 214-15.

[110] We recall that Angelucci 1984 bases his analysis of Macrobius's instruction almost exclusively on *Sat* 6. This narrows the scope of his inquiry and taxonomy; cf. Cizek 1994.

[111] Curtius 1954 pp. 58-64, Glauche 1970, and Cizek 1994 pp. 28-30.

and explain its importance for the Middle Ages and Chrétien's own reading of it is the relatively stable instruction on writing and rewriting from Hellenistic to early modern times.[112] In this context it is once again important to emphasize the place of *oral* instruction that accompanied texts like the *Saturnalia* as they were transmitted to and through the Middle Ages.[113] This is the pedagogical context in which Chrétien de Troyes[114] would have read and studied Macrobius on the art of description.

---

[112] Cizek 1994.

[113] Jaeger 1994; on some of the arts of poetry as student transcriptions of the master's instruction, see Kelly 1991 pp. 111-12.

[114] Macrobius relies on memory or cross-reference for some illustrations; see Büchner 1961 p. 358. Cf. Friis-Jensen 1997 p. 57. Ward 1995 p. 68 notes that "glossators seem to have assumed that their audience had texts in front of them, or else had a good memory of these texts. They seldom incorporate into their glosses enough of the original text for the commentary to make much sense without a separate text at hand." The widespread study of Vergil and the availability of manuscripts of the *Aeneid* would have facilitated comparative consultation like that which Ward describes for commentaries and glosses of Cicero's *De inventione* and the *Rhetorica ad Herennium*; these treatises were also widely available, as Ward's investigations demonstrate; see Ward 1972 and 1995.

CHAPTER THREE

BRIDGES IN AND BETWEEN THE MEDIEVAL LATIN AND VERNACULAR TRADITIONS

> Faciebatque ut qui maiores imitabatur fieret posteris imitandus.
>
> (John of Salisbury)[1]

How influential was Macrobius's critical analysis of Vergil's use of *descriptio* and its derivatives on writers before Chrétien? Or, to raise a more pertinent question, how representative in the Middle Ages and for Chrétien de Troyes in particular was the art of description set forth by Macrobius? Various avenues of investigation are open. First, it is necessary to recover the actual instruction on description as Macrobius uses it in its full range of meanings, but especially in the sense of topical invention. I attempted to do so in the preceding chapter. Second, this art of description must be seen working in medieval writing. This will be the goal of this and the following chapters. This chapter in particular treats Macrobius's art of description as a model for interpreting medieval writing as rewriting, including the introduction of that art into early French writing. Therefore, the rest of this book attempts to show how Macrobius's notion of description can help us understand and appreciate the art not only of Chrétien de Troyes, but also of other medieval writers. By "writer," then, I mean Macrobius's *imitator*, or rewriter.

A bridge between Horace and Macrobius on the one hand and the late twelfth- and thirteenth-century arts of poetry and prose on the other is nonetheless available; it is found in commentaries on Horace.[2] The late eleventh and the twelfth centuries witnessed a resurgence in such commentaries, glosses, and scholia on the *Art of*

---

[1] *Metalogicon* 1.24.84-85: He succeeded in making those who imitated earlier writers themselves imitable. Cf. Tilliette 1985 pp. 140-41.

[2] Villa 1992b and Friis-Jensen 1997. On Horace in the Middle Ages, see as well Manitius 1893.

Poetry.[3] Although work on them has only recently begun in earnest,[4] many have been catalogued and some have been edited and studied. For example, the *Scholia Vindobonensia* on the *Art of Poetry*, in its authoritative statements about natural and artificial order, might provide a context for Macrobius's own discussion of this subject in the *Saturnalia*.[5] Recent editions of two other related twelfth-century commentaries identify chains of commentaries from the *Scholia Vindobonensia* to the medieval arts of poetry themselves,[6] which appeared before or during Chrétien's early years. Written in France and at least one of which was widely copied,[7] these commentaries were supposed to assist the reader or teacher in understanding and applying Horace's presumed instruction in practical, applicable (if occasionally erroneous) terms. They impose on Horace's *Art of Poetry* a recognizable outline with major concepts to which the twelfth- and thirteenth-century arts provide a more or less systematic framework — concepts like invention and imitation, natural and artificial order, amplification and abbreviation, and Material Style.[8]

---

[3] Munk Olsen 1991b pp. 110-14, Villa 1993, Friis-Jensen 1995b, and Friis-Jensen 1997.

[4] Horatian commentaries are available in the following editions: *Vindobonensia*, Friis-Jensen 1990 and 1997 pp. 53-55, Hajdú 1993. For a bibliography of glosses and commentaries through the twelfth century, see Munk Olsen 1982-89 vol. 1 pp. 422-23 and 428-35 and vol. 3.2 pp. 62, 63-64, and 190-91. The late-twelfth-century Saint-Omer art of poetry illustrates elementary description with Horace's *Art of Poetry*; see *ArtOmer*, esp. v. 7-12. It also stresses both art and imitation, v. 93-96; see the Introduction to this edition. For the period after the twelfth century, see Friis-Jensen 1988 pp. 82-83,Villa 1994 pp. 127-46, Friis-Jensen 1997 pp. 72-73, and Villa 1997 passim.

[5] See *Sat* 5.2.8-12. The editor of the *Scholia Vindobonensia* dates it in the ninth century (ed. Zechmeister pp. i-vi); this dating has recently been corrected to an eleventh-century date (Munk Olsen 1982-89 vol. 1 p. 52, Friis-Jensen 1990 p. 322, and Munk Olsen 1992 p. 203). The single manuscript of this commentary is of Austrian origin; its relation to the French commentaries remains to be determined (Friis-Jensen 1997 pp. 53-54; but see Prill 1987). The scholia in *Scholia* vol. 4 are also eleventh century (Friis-Jensen 1997 p. 53).

[6] On the arts of poetry and prose as virtual commentaries, see Kelly 1991 p. 125. Geoffrey of Vinsauf's *Poetria nova* produced its own commentary tradition (Woods 1991).

[7] Friis-Jensen 1990 pp. 329-30 identifies fourteen complete or partial manuscripts and four accessus that stand alone.

[8] Friis-Jensen 1990 pp. 324-29 and 1995b.

Description as Rewriting from Macrobius to the High Medieval Commentaries on Horace

As noted, Tony Hunt first suggested that Chrétien may have derived some ideas on rewriting from the *Saturnalia*[9]; other scholars have commented on the *Saturnalia*'s influence on or usefulness for readings and rewritings of Vergil from late antiquity to the Middle Ages.[10] The gradual evolution of the notion of compilation from its pejorative connotations in antiquity to that of original rewriting has been set forth by Neil Hathaway, and his discussion includes Macrobius's place in the evolution.[11] Chrétien's first *bele conjointure* is itself a beautiful compilation of stories about Erec and Enide. The scope of rewriting this implies — the work of scribes, compilers stricto sensu, commentators, imitators, and first authors — was commonplace by the thirteenth century.[12] Recent work on late antique and early medieval Latin authors has important implications for the French works, and I shall begin by summarizing it here in the context of Macrobius's ideas on description in rewriting.

It is useful to insist on the notion of model here, especially of the given text as model. Thomas Haye has recently shown that rather than the concept of genre, the model or the cluster or group of models is more relevant to actual practice and original reception in the Middle Ages. Textual models ("Textmuster"),[13] such as the *Aeneid*, make for a tradition of reception which, mutatis mutandis, overlaps with Jauss's analysis of genre building through reception, which is an essentially diachronic approach to the problem. Haye, on the other hand, is synchronically focused; that is, he is interested more in the way rewriters regard their textual models. This approach permits him to concentrate on specific prototypes and models in a time when most writers did not have access to a large library. Authors could rewrite given models; they could also conspire to bring

---

[9] See the Introduction n. 3.

[10] See esp. Courcelle 1984 p. 757 s.v. "Macrobe" (correct *Sat* p. 221 to 231), Pecere 1991 p. 64, Dronke 1985, Moos 1988b, Cizek 1994, and Mora-Lebrun 1994a and 1994b. These works treat Macrobius in passing; see the indexes in Moos 1988b and Cizek 1994.

[11] Hathaway 1989 esp. pp. 23-24 and 26-27; see also Baumgartner 1994.

[12] Hathaway 1989 p. 20, who also refers to work by Parkes and Minnis.

[13] Haye 1997 pp. 1-3; cf. Moos 1988a p. 767 n. 83, Ward 1990 pp. 44-47, and Blänsdorf 1995.

together several models in the same new work. Here too, Chrétien de Troyes provides a brilliant illustration in his notion of new and beautiful *conjointure*.

The combination allows for the full range of models we have observed in Vergil's rewriting, a range extending from work to word. This intertextuality avant la lettre on the level of rewriting sources is what Philippe Walter has in mind while discussing rewriting French romance.

> Les notions d'*intertexte* et d'*intertextualité* ne sont pas, comme on le pense parfois, des reformulations plus ou moins modernes, des vieux concepts de *source* et d'*influence*; elles mettent au contraire en évidence la matérialité et l'efficience de modèles textuels déjà constitués dans tout processus littéraire. De même qu'une phrase résulte toujours de modèles de phrases qui les préexistent, de même un texte résulte toujours de l'assimilation d'autres textes qui lui servent de matrice. Il va de soi cependant qu'il ne faut pas traduire cette efficacité des modèles préexistants en termes de déterminisme absolu. La liberté du créateur est grande....[14]

Early Christian writers adapted Vergilian models to the composition of Christian epic — an adaptation analogous to the rewriting of Homer and others that Macrobius discerned in Vergil. Michael Roberts has discussed the Christian and pagan branches of the tradition in late antiquity.[15] Importantly, Roberts notes the late antique tendency to reduce the composition of a work to episodic, descriptive fragments, more or less loosely strung together into a series of contiguous rather than continuous parts.[16] The *praeexercitamina* critical to schooling evince the same emphases on discrete parts. Priscian notes in his brief but influential treatise on this exercise topics like fable, narrative, common place, praise, and, most notably for our purposes here, description.[17] Such emphases led to an appreciation of modes of elaboration common in late antiquity and that still survive in medieval instruction on description. From the perspective of criticism, eleventh- and twelfth-century commentaries on Horace's *Art of Poetry* paved the way for the adaptation of preceptorial poetics in the better-known twelfth- and thirteenth-century treatises. Thus the Middle

---

[14] Walter 1990 pp. 188-89. Cf. Wills 1996 chap. 1.

[15] Roberts 1985 and 1989 respectively. Roberts uses Macrobius to interpret these developments; see esp. 1985 pp. 190 n. 83, 199, 201, and 1989 pp. 46, 54, 57, 62.

[16] On such "episodic construction," see Haidu 1983.

[17] *Praeexercitamina* (in *Gram lat* vol. 3). By description, he means both separate descriptive pieces and descriptions within fables and narratives (pp. 438-39).

Ages sustained features of late antique poetics we have observed in Macrobius too, specifically in terms of "immanent poetics"[18] discernible in the *modus agendi* of model texts and "small units of composition" that were preferred over longer works or that were emphasized as rather discrete parts of larger works.[19] By "immanent poetics" Roberts means a critic's own scrutiny of the texts themselves to determine what features of the art of poetry they illustrate, thereby following in the steps of authors and pupils from antiquity into early modern times. For example, Bernard of Chartres had his own pupils scrutinize their authors in order to imitate their "immanent poetics." Gervase of Melkley's students did this by studying Bernardus Silvestris's *Cosmographia* and Jean of Hauville's *Architrenius*. Immanent poetics, in other words, is discerning the art of poetry and prose in a given work that can be imitated in subsequent writing. Pupils and authors who have advanced beyond the treatises and the classroom rewrite with originality by heeding the implications of the poetics immanent in the writers they rewrite. In this respect, Macrobius exemplifies the line of late antique and early Christian authors who cultivated the classical literary habit of reading, imitating and, then, passing on their writing for imitation and emulation by succeeding generations of school-trained writers.[20]

Late antiquity also saw the emergence of Christian poetry that conformed to the immanent poetics of ancient and contemporary pagan texts, but that took an entirely new source as model, the Bible. School boys read, interpreted, and imitated these Christian epics, notably those by Sedulius, Iuvencus, Prudentius, and Proba, throughout the Middle Ages.[21] But Biblical matter required harmo-

---

[18] Roberts 1989 p. 5. Cf. Moos 1991 p. 304 on a poetics as "ein begrenzt gültiges Verhaltensmodell in einem bestimmten raum-zeitlichen Rahmen," a model that "aus den Texten selbst erst descriptiv erschlossen werden [soll]."

[19] Roberts 1989 p. 55. This is what Quadlbauer terms the "Tendenz zur kleinen Einheit."

[20] On the learned quality of Christian emulation of Vergil and other pagan authors, see Manitius 1911-31 vol. 1 pp. 4-5, Curtius 1954 pp. 453-57, Thraede 1962, Fuhrmann 1967, Quadlbauer 1974, Roberts 1985 pp. 67-74. Emulation here means competition not with the biblical source, but with pagan matter, meaning, and art; see Herzog 1975 pp. xlv-xlvi and Angelucci 1990 pp. 47-78.

[21] Iuvencus, Sedulius, Arator, Prudentius, and others may be standard works in medieval schools (see Curtius 1954 pp. 58-61 and Glauche 1970 esp. pp. 80 and 110-12), but not in the arts of poetry and prose. For example, Matthew cites Prudentius only once (*Ars vers* 1.71). Gervase refers to none of them. Eberhard the German names Sedulius, Arator, and Prudentius (*Laborintus* v. 655-60).

nizing as well as adornment in order to conform to classical standards. The rhetorical operations made God's Word more accessible to
the refined ears of Romans hovering before conversion or eager to
understand in their own traditionally rhetoricized language the new
faith they adopted.[22] These adaptations determined as well how medieval authors would be trained to write in the schools where Christian poets supplemented or replaced pagan authors. Their art conforms to instruction that we find in contemporary rhetorics and
grammars; it is also evident in Macrobius's reading of Vergil. What
Roberts summarizes as "abbreviation, transposition and amplification" reflects the modes of rewriting which Cizek identified in the
antique tradition and which we have seen in Macrobius as well:
addition, deletion, replacement, and rearrangement.[23] With the Bible
as source matter, rewriting has constraints for the writer that did not
impinge on Vergil; however, the difficulties of harmonization which
Roberts analyzes do resemble the kind Chrétien confronted in deriving *sens* and a *bele conjointure* from the different versions of a *conte
d'aventure*. The Gospels had to be harmonized, contradictions real or
apparent had to be smoothed out, and lacunae in the Old Testament
like those in the creation of Adam and Eve or of the Flood had to be
completed by various kinds of transposition, amplification, or abbreviation.[24] Nevertheless, to teach such harmonizing, the *praeexercitamina*
were still the foundation for the art which the Christian rewriters of
the Bible mastered and practiced.[25] In other words, Vergil still provided the "implicit art," the immanent poetics, for which Macrobius
again offers evidence.

As Roberts has shown, Christian epic bifurcated in mode of treating its sources, according to whether it rewrote Old Testament or
New Testament matter.[26] The former led to an emphasis on narrative continuity pointing towards the new dispensation that the appearance of the Messiah would signify. New Testament narrative, on

---

[22] Herzog 1975 pp. xl-xlv.
[23] Roberts 1985 p. 3 and Quadlbauer 1974. Roberts 1985 pp. 38-39 uses the term
"paraphrase" to refer to all these operations; his sense of the word is therefore
broader than the narrower, more elementary kind of paraphrase I have been referring to. Numerous illustrations in his book make excellent reading alongside
Macrobius as an introduction to medieval adaptations of late-Roman rewriting.
[24] See Roberts 1985 pp. 127-35.
[25] Roberts 1985 pp. 23 and 69-74.
[26] Roberts 1985 Chapter Six.

the other hand, tended to pull narrative sequence apart into discrete episodes susceptible of independent allegorical deepening. This bifurcation prepared the way for and played against the two major poetic modes in medieval literary writing which went beyond the smaller compositional unit. For example, biblical narrative progression pointing to the Christian dispensation informs Gautier de Châtillon's *Alexandreis* and, to a lesser extent, Joseph of Exeter's *Ylias*; respectively, each recounts in straightforward chronology the life of Alexander the Great and the causes and events of the Trojan War. Allegorical deepening and fragmentation, on the other hand, is more evident in Alain de Lille's and Jean de Hauville's allegorical epics focusing on the New Man, either in his potential and perfection or in his struggle to find a way amid the conflicting and disjunctive poles of vices and virtues. Vernacular authors use these modes too while adapting them to secular contexts like those in Chrétien's romances and in Guillaume de Lorris's part of the *Roman de la rose*.

Returning to the late antique Christian writers, we can see how their adaptation of the Latin literary tradition to Christian writing was crucial to the survival of the late antique art of poetry. They carried over principles of imitation Macrobius discusses in Vergil to their own works, just as contemporary pagan poets were doing. They were doing so, furthermore, for an educated public that was still capable of appreciating the ancient echoes in the new, Christian setting. This public disappears in the later Roman world as pagan authors disappear from schools,[27] even though Christian epic continues to be read and imitated.[28] The Christian writers are in effect links in the chain between Vergil and the twelfth-century writers, links analogous to the Latin writers Macrobius identifies between Vergil and Homer in Book VI of the *Saturnalia*. Pupils could read, study, and imitate the adaptations these authors made of one another much as Macrobius does with intermediary Latin authors. Even where antique writers disappeared for a time from the schoolroom canon, their reintroduction after the Carolingian revival or even later generates an intertextual dynamics much as Christian writers did when they echoed classical writing in their new contexts.

Let me pause briefly to comment on this feature because it is important in the transmission of antique matter to the Middle Ages.

---

[27] Cf. Glauche 1970 pp. 5-9, Mora-Lebrun 1994a.
[28] Glauche 1970 pp. 7-8, 23-24; Mora-Lebrun 1994a.

Where schools became Christian and pagan authors were temporarily set aside, late antique audiences capable of appreciating the rewriting of Vergil or others in Prudentius or Iuvencus gradually disappeared too. However, after the Carolingian revival of interest in pagan authors, those familiar with early Christian literature returned to Vergil, and they could hear in his works echoes from Christian authors. Thus, reception was not simply linear, and the play of allusions remained intact. Christian authors let their Latin-educated publics hear Vergil resonate with a *surplus de sen chrétien*. Indeed, such echoes might reinforce the conviction that Vergil anticipated the Christian revelation, thereby privileging the readings of the Fourth Eclogue or the reference to Marcellus's death in the *Aeneid* as Christian allegories. Allusion was still an important element in rewriting and its reception.[29]

Indeed, in the twelfth century the model of Christian epic still influenced the teaching of composition in the schools. Christian writers like Sedulius, Iuvencus, and Prudentius belong to the twelfth-century canon, especially because they adapt pagan works to Christian matter.[30] Just as these Christian writers adapted a pagan art to new subjects, so too Bernard of Chartres taught composition as rewriting by imitation, and the pagan writers return to prominence as sources and models for rewriting. Not surprisingly, Chrétien and his contemporaries adapted both pagan and Christian works to social and moral issues of importance to their aristocratic patrons and audiences. Chrétien's *Philomena* is probably one of these works, suggesting perhaps that Chrétien belongs not with a cleric's *translatio studii*, but to the transmission of the *curiales*, that is, those authors whom John of Salisbury and Peter of Blois castigated for their worldly writings.[31]

With Macrobius in hand, as Chrétien suggests, what features might pupils be drawn to in reading Vergil and Ovid on the one hand (to name the obvious writers) and Iuvencus or Arator on the other? In particular, what features of 'description' might be focused on in their imitations? Studies of late antique and early medieval Latin literature both Christian and secular can help us here, since scholars have not infrequently relied on Macrobius to define the

---

[29] Mora-Lebrun 1985 pp. 91-95.

[30] Glauche 1970 pp. 101-27. Matthew of Vendôme carries this tradition into the late twelfth century with his *Tobias* (Herzog 1975 p. xx n. 33). Matthew's *Tobias* was also a model for writing (*Laborintus* v. 663-64).

[31] Peter of Blois remains ambiguous on this score; see Godman 1990.

modus agendi of these writers.[32] Mora-Lebrun in particular has noted the recurrence of Aeneas's sea storm and Dido's banquet as descriptive model during this period; she finds these scenes rewritten in Iuvencus, Proba, and the *Bella Parisiacis urbis* by Abbon of Saint-Germain.[33] This holds true into the twelfth century when Chrétien was learning to write, and later, when the *Saturnalia* not only shows how other authors rewrote models but even serves itself as a model for rewriting.[34]

Medieval Models of Description

The crucial period for the evaluation of a high medieval art of poetry and prose comes after 1000. The study of authors for their "immanent poetics" was pursued in elementary classrooms like Bernard of Chartres's. Instruction in composition still relied on preceptorial treatises in grammar and rhetoric inherited from antiquity. For grammars, the range spanned from introductions like Donatus's to treatises on versification.[35] Instruction on rhetoric relied largely on Cicero's *De inventione* and the pseudo-Ciceronian *Rhetorica ad Herennium*.[36] But the only available work on the art of poetry was Horace's *Art of Poetry* — hardly a beginner's reader! It became necessary, therefore, to make it accessible as a functional art of poetry, stimulating the writing of commentaries. Such commentaries set forth systematic readings of the *Art of Poetry* by adapting traditional glossing to the

---

[32] See, for example, Pasquali 1951 pp. 14-15 and 17; Wlosok 1990 p. 234 esp. n. 5, 238 and n. 19; Cizek 1994 esp. pp. 63 and 137-38.

[33] Mora-Lebrun 1994a pp. 70, 74-75, 151; she finds it in the *Waltharius* on p. 165 n. 130.

[34] Bourgain 1985 p. 176, Klopsch 1985 pp. 152-53, Anderson 1988 pp. 55-56, 81-82; cf. Hexter 1988, Ward 1995 pp. 52-53, De Rentiis 1996 p. 49 n. 11. It is also noteworthy that the *Saturnalia* provided Abelard with a model for one of his poems and that the treatment of the four cardinal virtues in the *Commentary* was interpolated into an eleventh-century saint's life in prose (Szövérffy 1983 pp. 239-40 and Renaud 1976 pp. 255 and 273-74); Saxo Grammaticus used Macrobius in his *Gesta Danorum*, most notably for a catalogue of warriors (Friis-Jensen 1987 pp. 23-24 and passim), as did Milo of Saint Amand in *De sobrietate* (Godman 1987 p. 178; cf. Pack 1981). On John of Salisbury, see Moos 1988a esp. pp. 751-55. Manitius 1911-31 passim reports numerous examples of authors who cite or otherwise use Macrobius, but his indications are often uncertain by modern standards of identification.

[35] Thurot 1964 pp. 3-58; cf. Holtz 1981.

[36] Curtius 1954 pp. 74-75, Ward 1995.

demands of verse writing and art prose as well as to the compositional categories available in standard treatises on rhetoric. Recent scholarship has been paying more attention to these commentaries, as they appear to form the basis for the composition of treatises in the later twelfth and early thirteenth centuries that renew the treatment in Horace's old art, or *poetria vetus*, through *poetria nova*.[37]

These treatises are "graded" in the sense that they are adapted to the level of achievement the pupils have reached; thus, they imply progress from one level of proficiency to another in reading and imitating canon authors. The goal is to advance the pupil to that "immanent poetics," the understanding at which a poet reading canonical texts can rewrite them, in consonance with the poetics the texts themselves illustrate.

How was this poetics taught in medieval classrooms? By and large, the evidence suggests that imitation was the goal. In his early thirteenth-century art of versifying Gervase of Melkley states that Bernardus Silvestris's *Cosmographia* and Jean de Hauville's *Architrenius* could teach the aspiring literary artist all he or she needed to know in order to write well.[38] The same holds true for other works Gervase locates among the masterpieces on which he bases his treatise. Practice in imitation of such authors, he asserts, perfects the talented mind. Analogous statements elsewhere suggest how authors were read and imitated in medieval classes in grammar and rhetoric.[39] The masterpieces (among them Vergil's *Aeneid* held pride of place[40]) illustrated the kind of good writing that the pupils were to imitate. Vergil is an illustration not only for Gervase, but probably for Bernardus Silvestris himself,[41] since the commentary on the *Aeneid* ascribed to Bernardus states that Vergil's epic can teach how to write well.[42]

---

[37] Curtius 1954 p. 163.

[38] *ArsGM* p. 3, ll. 24-25: "Cuius... libelli [= *Architrenius*] sola sufficit inspectio studiosa rudem animum informare" [Intense study of his book suffices to educate the unformed mind]. On Gervase's opinion of the *Cosmographia* as fullest treatment of the art of poetry and prose, see Kelly 1991 pp. 57-64 and Fraker 1993. The verse arts could also be read as immanent poetics; see Woods 1991 and Purcell 1993.

[39] See also Ward 1972 vol. 1 chap. 3 and 4. Eberhard the German's *Laborintus* v. 597-686 contains a list of imitable school authors.

[40] Glauche 1970, Munk Olsen 1985, Worstbrock 1985 pp. 29-30, and Cizek 1994 pp. 25-26 n. 46 (with additional bibliography).

[41] For the *Cosmographia*, see Wetherbee trans. pp. 31-32, 35-36, and 48-49; Wetherbee 1972 p. 167, and Dronke 1985 p. 327. For others, see Tilliette 1985.

[42] *ComBS* pp. 1, ll. 1-14, and 2, ll. 15-20. Cf. Jeauneau 1971 esp. pp. 100-01 and Brinkmann 1980 pp. 293-94 on Macrobius's influence on the conception of poetry as

And, of course, the *Saturnalia* itself is about Vergil's art of imitation as description.

Bernardus Silvestris, or the pseudo-Bernardus, treats such imitation in a commentary on Martianus Capella's *Marriage of Mercury and Philology*. The *accessus* to this commentary states that Martianus's third *modus agendi* was imitation. Now, the *vitae Boethii* had passed on to the eleventh and twelfth centuries the view that Boethius imitated Martianus by writing a prosimetrum.[43] But the commentator extends Boethius's models to include Vergil: Martianus imitated Vergil, and was imitated in turn by Boethius. Furthermore, he modifies the model from formal alternation of verse and prose to the thematic motif of guidance to an ideal.[44] In other words, the commentator is proposing an explanation of Boethius's imitation. In fact, each author in this chain rewrites and thus passes on for imitation the very model Macrobius claims Vergil himself took from Homer. That is, each work shows the progress of a certain figure — the "hero" — struggling towards a goal under the direction of a wise guide (cf. *Sat* 5.2.6-12).

Auctoris vero imitatio est, quia Maronem emulatur. Sicut enim apud illum ducitur Eneas per inferos comite Sibilla usque ad Anchisem, ita et hic Mercurius per mundi regiones Virtute comite ad Iovem. Ita quoque et in libro *De Consolatione* scandit Boetius per falsa bona ad summum bonum duce Philosophia. Que quidem tres figure fere idem exprimunt.[45]

---

allegory and learning; cf. Lerer 1982 and Zintzen 1988 esp. pp. 416-21. For other medieval references to Vergil imitating Homer, see Wlosok 1990 pp. 494-95 ns. 52-53. Medieval commentaries on Horace's works also influence the double goal of both moral and poetic illustration; see Friis-Jensen 1988 and Quint 1988 p. 25.

[43] *ComCP* p. 4; see also *Vita Boetii* pp. xxxi and xxxiii, Silk ed. *ComCP* p. xix n. 2 and Esposito 1913 pp. 111-12. The *accessus* also refer to Boethius's imitation of the prosimetrum genre in Martianus; see *Accessus* pp. 47, 65, 78, and 108; references in some of these passages to other imitations, including Vergil's of Homer, may have inspired the Martianus Commentator's gloss. On the genre prosimetrum, see LeMoine 1972, Gruber 1981, Dronke 1994, Pabst 1994, and Ziolkowski 1997.

[44] Cf. Wetherbee 1972 p. 8 and Gruber 1981 p. 209. After 1000, there is greater emphasis on the first two books of the *De nuptiis* (Leonardi 1959 pp. 466 and 473-75).

[45] *ComMC*, 2.114-19 (p. 47); see also Wetherbee 1972 pp. 124-25, Dronke 1974, Dronke 1985 pp. 326-27, Ziolkowski 1985 pp. 9-10, and Moos 1993 pp. 448-50. On the relevance of this passage to the composition of Alain de Lille's *Anticlaudianus*, see Simpson 1992 pp. 158-60.

[It is truly an imitation of the author because he emulates Vergil. For just as in the latter the Sibyl accompanies Aeneas through Hades to Anchises, so in this work Mercury passes through the regions of the universe to Jove in the company of Virtue. Similarly, in the *Consolation of Philosophy* Boethius rises through the false goods to the supreme good led by Philosophy. These three figures express practically the same thing.]

The technique is hardly different from Macrobius's reading of Vergil's adaptation of Homer: conflict followed by quest under the guidance of pedagogical figures like Hector, Venus, Anchises, and the Cumaean Sybil. The commentator's examples show as well that the same model can be used for an episode (Aeneas's descent into Hades), a larger segment (Mercury's voyage to the Empyrean), and a whole work (Boethius's *Consolation*).

Let us examine more closely the Martianus commentary's use of *figura* in the passage just cited. The Commentary's modern editor points out that *figura* is used here in the sense of *involucrum*.[46] The commentator indeed defines "figura" elsewhere as "oratio quam involucrum dicere solent" (*ComMC* § 2.70-71 [p. 43]) [A "figure" is discourse which is customarily termed an "involucrum"]. He goes on to say that there are two kinds of involucrum: allegory — discourse which uses historical narrative to veil a true meaning that is different from its surface meaning — and integumentum — or a fable covering a true meaning (*ComMC* 2.71-75 [p. 45]). According to this distinction, among the analogous *figurae* the commentator names, the *Aeneid* is an allegorical involucrum using the historical biography of Aeneas, whereas the *Consolation* and the *Marriage of Mercury and Philology* are integumenta because their letter is fictional. The distinctions are traditional; they are authorized by Macrobius, among others.[47] Allegory suits scriptural, integumentum philosophical discourse. Vergil is the Commentator's example, just as he had been Macrobius's (*ComSS* 1.3.17-20).[48] In the Vergil-Martianus-Boethius chain, imitation occurs when the subsequent work rewrites a model found

---

[46] Westra ed. *ComMC* pp. 23-33; Westra relies on Macrobius's use of the term in the *ComSS*. Cf. Simpson 1992 pp. 115-18 on *forma* and pp. 140-52 on the two orders, and Villa 1992a pp. 44-45.

[47] Wetherbee 1972 pp. 37-38 and Dronke 1974 chap. 1 and 1985. On *ComSS* 1.2.17, see Stock 1972 pp. 31-62.

[48] Curtius 1954 pp. 441-42.

in its predecesor. We saw an example of this in Macrobius's analysis of Vergil's description of Dido's banquet, for which the model is the banquet given to Odysseus by Alcinous in the *Odyssey*. This also illustrates one sense of *descriptio* we found in Macrobius — drawing a pattern, model, or other scheme from a "source." In each of the three works named by the commentator — the *Aeneid*, the *Marriage*, and the *Consolation*, and in Homer according to Macrobius — the model shows one agent passing through various regions as moving towards a goal with the guidance of another agent or agents. The Martianus Commentator's *figura* is Macrobius's *species*, a term which, in Macrobius, refers to the form or image of something — "Dido refert speciem regis" (*Sat* 5.2.13)[49] [Dido reproduces the king's image] — or a "speciem veritatis" (*Sat* 5.17.5) [the form of truth], a form that can be reproduced in different subject matter. This is the kind of imitation — imitation of, as it were, a species — that the Martianus commentator saw successfully practiced in Vergil, Martianus Capella, and Boethius. All relate a quest — for a homeland, wisdom, or the Supreme Good. The goal of each trajectory or quest is, in Boethius's expression, a summum bonum that defines the diverse surface narratives and the figural motifs or models beneath the literal surface.

Thus, Macrobius's analysis of Vergil's art places Homer and the early Latin writers in the tradition which the Martianus commentator extends from Vergil through Martianus Capella to Boethius. These works illustrate anew Macrobius's statement on Vergil's originality: "hic opportune in opus suum quae prior vates dixerat transferendo fecit ut sua esse credantur" (*Sat* 5.3.16)[50] [he skillfully transfers into his work things the earlier author had said and, in doing so, made them seem to be his own words]. The result is not patchwork compilation, but the harmonious combination of parts — Macrobius's *species* because it mirrors the source's *imago* or *figura* — in a new matter. The model is imitated in the shape of a new work. The vocabulary Macrobius uses to describe Vergil's art of imitation conforms to the poetic *modus agendi* throughout the Middle Ages: the

---

[49] In *ComSS* 1.6.20, *species* refers to the ideas in God's mind. *Species* is therefore analogous to Geoffrey of Vinsauf's use of *archetypus* to refer to the artist's mental conception of the work to be written, since Macrobius uses the same term in this sense in the *Saturnalia*; see Chapter Two.

[50] See also *Sat* 5.13.33, 5.16.5 and 12.

Aeneid mirrors Homer. David Anderson has recently put it very effectively.

> Within this broad mirroring of Homer's narrative, Vergil arranges scenes and motifs of Homeric inspiration. Although they are modified, their origin is easily recognized. Vergil's art is to be admired in part for its skillful transformations within these familiar structures *speciem refert mira imitatione* [Macrobius]. He composes his scenes by the 'admirable imitation' that arranges characters and actions by analogy to their well-known models.[51]

This is what Macrobius refers to as "conspiracy" — "in unum conspirata."[52]

Links in the chain of authors and imitators — *auctores* and *imitatores* in Macrobius's sense of, respectively, first or model author and rewriter — appear after the Martianus commentary who use the guided quest model.[53] Bernardus himself uses it in the *Cosmographia* to relate Nature's search for Urania, a human soul, and, finally, Physis in the Garden of Granusion.[54] Likewise, Alain de Lille's *Anticlaudianus* recounts a complex progression from Nature's complaint through the voyage through the Heavens and back to the New Man's victory over Allecto's assembled vices. So too, Jean de Hauville's *Architrenius* relates the Arch-Weeper's wayward quest for enlightenment. The Weeper has, to be sure, false goals; therefore, like Boethius's prisoner, he gets off to a bad start.[55] But such antiphrasis is, as we have seen, common in rewriting. We come across it again in Jean de Meun's *Roman de la rose*, which rewrites the model for the *gradus amoris* in Guillaume de Lorris according to the model for false goods in Boethius's *Consolation of Philosophy*.[56] In so doing, Jean adds the French *Rose* to the Greek and Latin chain Homer-Vergil-Martianus-Boethius-Alain. I shall return to French adaptations of the guided-journey model below.

---

[51] Anderson 1988 pp. 55-56. Cf. Wills 1996 pp. 23 and 296 on "mirroring" in both complete works and in the small unit of discourse.

[52] Cf. *Sat* 5.1.13, 5.2.5, 5.13.13 and 15.

[53] See Haye 1997 p. 2 on "Textketten."

[54] Stock 1972 pp. 163-87.

[55] Wetherbee 1972 pp. 244-47.

[56] See Kelly 1995a, esp. pp. 38-44; in the *Cité des dames* Christine de Pizan suggests reading the *Rose* this way (*Cité* p. 624).

Description and Classroom Compositions

A caveat is in order at this point. Rolf Köhn has pointed out that our knowledge of medieval education between the elementary and advanced or university level is based on ideal descriptions like that in the *Metalogicon* or lists of recommended readings, not on actual curricula in most schools, about which we know very little.[57] Very good schools did exist, as the accomplishments of some medieval writers seem to demonstrate — notably Bernardus Silvestris, Alain de Lille, and, indeed, Chrétien de Troyes himself! So what actually happened in good medieval classrooms like those in which Chrétien may have studied Vergil and Macrobius? To answer this question we must go back to the basics. Fortunately, recent scholarship can help us here.

On the most elementary classroom level, a pupil acquires mastery of Latin. Here the transition occurs from the pupil's native tongue to the language of grammar.[58] This stage is reflected in some manuscripts by means of interlinear and marginal glosses, many of them being in a vernacular.[59] So too, the transition to literary models begins here as well. For example, to learn the names of botanical words, the pupil may read an extract from Bernardus Silvestris's *Cosmographia* which contains a virtual catalogue of plant names.[60] If the pupil later imitates this *descriptio*, the model text would not present serious obstacles to understanding or to rewriting; it was also a small glossary of plant names. The pupil might even have memorized it. Macrobius's *Saturnalia* might itself provide vocabulary,[61] as some glosses show.

---

[57] Köhn 1986 esp. pp. 211-14; see also Murphy 1961, McGregor 1978, and Kelly 1998b; on lay literature, see Schmidt 1977 and Wendehorst 1986.

[58] We recall that *grammatica* refers to the Latin language (Curtius 1954 p. 36).

[59] See Hunt 1991 vol. 1 pp. 3-18 for a recent survey of the subject of vernacular glosses, with extensive bibliography.

[60] For use of Book I, par. 3 in this way, see Hunt 1991 vol. 1 pp. 51 and 157-58. I recall that the *Cosmographia* could be read as a full and complete art of poetry.

[61] Hunt 1991 vol. 1 pp. 252, 260, 262, 265, 266, 272, and 275 identifies a few citations from the *Saturnalia* among the glosses he edits. The quotes are not numerous, and may not derive directly from the original, but rather come by way of florilegia, commentaries, or quotes. They do show, however, that the *Saturnalia* was not unheard of even on the relatively elementary level of language acquisition (cf. Ward 1995 pp. 216-17). Philippe de Thaon may have consulted such lists in writing the *Comput*. The *Saturnalia* might have been a source for Greek words, especially when these were rewritten in Latin letters (see Hunt 1991 vol. 1 p. 293), but it would not have been a significant factor in literary composition since Greek words were important mainly for scriptural exegesis. See Bischoff 1967-81 vol. 2, p. 249 and Berschin 1988 esp. pp. 31, 43-44, and 98.

According to John of Salisbury, Bernard of Chartres's instruction furthered both interpretation and imitation through daily exercises in speaking and writing; its goal is progressive mastery of correct language, versification, and tropical and figural ornamentation.[62] This would have been standard procedure in the better medieval schools.[63] There are, importantly, striking similarities between Bernard of Chartres's art of imitation and Macrobius's commentary on Vergil's imitations. The only difference — but an important one for this study — lies in the fact that Bernard starts his pupils out on composition whereas Vergil's imitation of Homer is considered a consummate masterpiece.[64] Bernard's pupils are still at the stage of practicing daily exercises in the form of *praeexercitamina* and oral declamations (*Metalogicon* 1.24.76-80).

'Daily exercise' must be understood properly. Scholars have noted that careful glossing of grammatical, figural, and tropical minutiae may be intense only in short passages, especially at the beginning of a manuscript.[65] For instructional purposes, this suggests that the *praelectio* with commentary dealt only with sample passages, like Servius's intensive commentary on the first twelve lines of the *Aeneid*.[66] However, with such introductory commentary as a guide and as a model, the pupil could — mutatis mutandis — analyze any set passage in imitation of the prescribed way. The result would be a gloss, somewhat analogous to assigned textual analysis today like, for example, *explication de texte*. Such formal analysis or explication of a set piece, if successful by the standards of time and place, would demonstrate the student's ability to explicate any passage in the work. The early or elementary preparation for such imitation brings us back to the "Tendenz zur kleinen Einheit," or "tendency to focus on the small unit of discourse" or compositional block, that Franz Quadlbauer identified as critical, a tendency characteristic of both glossing and rewriting in *praeexercitamina*. The habits of imitation Bernard instilled

---

[62] *Metalogicon* 1.24.85-89; cf. "et eorum iubebat uestigia imitari" (1.24.78-79) [and he required them to follow in their predecessors' footsteps]. On the pre-treatise stage of oral instruction in the arts, see Moos 1991 pp. 304-07.

[63] Leotta 1988 p. 104 and Ward 1990 pp. 21-22.

[64] Cf. Leotta 1988 pp. 120-27.

[65] Schmidt 1977 p. 178, Baswell 1985 p. 186 n. 17, Bourgain 1985 p. 170, and Ward 1995 p. 66.

[66] See Parkes 1994.

in his pupils[67] would, by daily exercise, become ingrained as they went on to write more accomplished works and, in some cases, masterpieces. These became habits of invention that also instilled intertextual reading habits.[68]

More importantly, in Bernard of Chartres's kind of school, explication is not only commentary, it is also rewriting by imitation. The Chartrain master wanted his pupils not only to explicate but also to rewrite the assigned text or a topic in that text.[69] He wanted them to do what Macrobius thought Vergil did with Homer: practice original, imitable rewriting. Such rewriting is also a kind of explication: it elicits a *surplus de sen* embedded in the author imitated, a Macrobian *species* or Bernardian *figura* susceptible of being rewritten or even of involution into a new matter. These features of rewriting no doubt inspired the Martianus commentator's interpretation of the *Marriage*'s relation to the *Aeneid* and the *Consolation*.

Good rewriting must go beyond the paraphrase and compilation of passages characteristic of the elementary stage of composition. Bernard of Chartres was categorical on this point (*Metalogicon* 1.24.80-85).[70] He wanted his pupils to imitate the source author's *imago*, another term for Macrobius's *species* and the Martianus commentator's *figura*, also containing the model to be used in the new work. What that image might be is suggested in the reference above to Martianus Capella: "Que quidem tres figure fere idem exprimunt." [Which three figures express essentially the same thing.] That is, an *imago*, like a *figura* or *species*, is identifiable by its configuration, by the concrete elements that define it and which it shares with its antecedents. This informing shape is, for example, the model of guided progress towards a goal which Macrobius and the Martianus commentator

---

[67] See *Metalogicon* I.24.76-92. For illustrations of commentary on an advanced level, see Friis-Jensen 1997 pp. 57-71 on medieval commentaries on Horace's lyric poetry.

[68] Vinaver 1964 p. 493.

[69] On what follows, see Kelly 1991 pp. 50-52.

[70] Matthew of Vendôme was just as emphatic; see the *Ars vers* Prologue 7 on "pannorum assutores" (patchworkers) and 4.1. Even on this elementary level, paraphrase "reformats" the original (see *ArsGM* on *idemptitas*; cf. Glauche 1970 p. 4). On artistic paraphrase as *praeexercitamina* in antiquity and its relation to imitation and emulation, see Roberts 1985 chapters Two and Three. We recall that Macrobius allows paraphrase or repetition only within strict limits: neologisms, archaic words or expressions, and formulaic or purely descriptive or sententious passages (Angelucci 1984 pp. 106-107; see Chapter Two).

identify in Vergil, Martianus, and Boethius, or the model for the sea storm and banquet which Macrobius reads as Vergil's having modeled on Homer. Each model is the model of something that contains the essential components or topoi — the archetype as blueprint — which the accomplished artist identifies and amplifies or abbreviates according to his or her intention and comprehension. In a treatise even as elementary as Marbod of Rennes's *De ornamentis verborum*, the ability to identify topoi is a sign of the writer who has progressed from mastery of the rules inscribed in treatises to more nearly original imitation of models — that is, to the art of poetry and prose implicit in the works he or she rewrites.[71]

Matthew of Vendôme's instruction on imitation in the *Ars versificatoria* is analogous to Bernard's. His pupils should imitate extant texts, not merely paraphrase them. The Horatian 'unfaithful translator'[72] is Matthew's ideal,[73] especially if the successful new version is imitable in its own right. This is possible along the lines Gervase suggests: embellishing (*idemptitas*[74]), analogous reshaping or retelling (*similitudo*[75]), or antithesis and antiphrasis (*contrarietas*[76]). In Matthew's *Ars versificatoria*, however, *descriptio* is, as topical invention,[77] the means to provide a full, coherent, and suitable representation of persons, things, and actions — a *plena descriptio* in Macrobius's sense of the

---

[71] Leotta 1988 pp.122-24. Once again, we encounter "immanent poetics," for, as Leotta points out, Marbod invites the accomplished pupil to move beyond the formal use of figures of thought and diction and enter the true realm of poetry: topical invention. At this stage, the pupil will learn, for example, that "no instance of a figure is comprehensible by itself but must be seen amidst the company it keeps" (Wills 1996 p. 2).

[72] Horace's "unfaithful translator" has received some attention lately: Copeland 1991 pp. 168-78, Pratt 1991, Fleming 1993, Kelly 1997a; cf. Croizy-Naquet 1994 pp. 197-98. The basic analysis of the Horatian passage is Schwartz 1944.

[73] *Ars vers* 4.1; see as well *Doc* II.3.137.

[74] *Idemptitas*, as Gervase uses the term, is a kind of paraphrase, but on a very elementary level (Purcell 1991 pp. 76-83). On the elementary level of Gervase's treatise, see Kelly 1991 p. 63. Paraphrase seems suitable for beginners who are just learning to rewrite, but not yet to invent.

[75] As in the Vergil-Martianus-Boethius chain. See Purcell 1987 and 1991 pp. 83-85.

[76] As in the *Anticlaudianus* and Jean's *Rose*; each of these works writes an antiphrasis of its model source, Claudian's *In Rufinum* and Guillaume de Lorris's *Roman de la rose* respectively. See Purcell 1991 pp. 85-89.

[77] Despite the "school-masterly" mode of instruction which is not always consistent in its terminology (Wills 1996 pp. 9-10; cf. Quadlbauer 1986 p. 426 on, e.g., *proprietates* and *attributa*) or in elucidation (Quadlbauer 1986 pp. 444-45 n. 46).

expression. As such, the writer, or "describer," may well imitate both actual models or may choose to invent his or her own mental models of appropriate or customary actions. The latter is especially important if the antecedent model appears incomplete or confusing by the standards of description (*Ars vers* 1.38-40, 4.13). In these latter cases, as we have seen, imitation becomes emulation (*aemulatio*). The new author seeks to outstrip the less successful achievement of the predecessor, as, for example, Matthew of Vendôme himself counsels, citing Ovid as his authority: "Emendaturus, si licuisset, erat" (*Ars vers* 4.13)[78] [it would have been corrected if it had been allowed]. No doubt, Matthew's "school-masterly" rules for invention represent constraints. But they may also reveal a language's potential. The right poet can produce a masterpiece according to the same standards.[79]

Twelfth-Century Commentaries on Horace's Art of Poetry

The dates of the arts of poetry and prose raise an issue to which it is now time to turn. With the exception of Matthew of Vendôme's *Ars versificatoria*, these treatises are all thirteenth-century works; Matthew's is usually dated about 1175.[80] The question naturally arises: how did authors, including the young Chrétien, acquire the formal conception of and practice in composition that these treatises codify before they were available? Macrobius provides the answer proposed here. Yet, since Macrobius can hardly be read alone, or on an elementary level, Chrétien must have integrated his reading of Macrobius into what he would have studied and practiced beforehand. Certainly, since at least the classical era, the instruction in grammar and rhetoric which lies behind the arts of poetry themselves, had been a part of

---

[78] Cf. *Ars vers* 4.13: "Hucusque dictum est quomodo superflua debent resecari, sequitur quomodo minus dicta debeant suppleri" [Up to now I have discussed discussed how superfluous language may be eliminated. What follows concerns how *what is incomplete may be completed* (Galyon)].

[79] In general, see Vinaver 1964 pp. 487-95; Bornscheuer 1976 pp. 54-57; Quadlbauer 1986 pp. 434-36; on imitation of Horace in the eleventh-century *Ecbasis captivi*, see Quadlbauer 1980a pp. 139-43, Quint 1988 pp. 125-39, and, more generally, pp. 139-241. Godman 1990b p. 159 refers to emulation as "a context for writing that transcends its prescriptions." See also Godman 1990a on emulation as a kind of transcendence.

[80] Faral 1924 p. 3, Friis-Jensen 1990 p. 322.

the school training. Moreover, for poetic composition, Horace's *Art of Poetry*, which the later treatises use and adapt, was available. Indeed, several features of Horace's poem help explain Chrétien's own terminology and compositional techniques.[81] But the *Art of Poetry* is likewise hardly elementary fare. Even a pupil proficient enough to read Macrobius or Martianus Capella would surely require help in reading Horace's poem as a guide to rewriting.

The so-called "*Materia*-Commentary" on Horace's *Art of Poetry* probably influenced the arts of poetry most directly.[82] Karsten Friis-Jensen dates its composition between 1125 and 1175, with Matthew of Vendôme's *Ars versificatoria* as *terminus ante quem*,[83] since Matthew appears to have used the Commentary in writing his treatise. The "*Materia* Commentary" itself uses earlier, less widely disseminated commentaries like the "Zürich Commentary" and the *Scholia Vindobonensia*.[84] Taken together, they reveal on-going systematization and elaboration of Horace's *Art of Poetry*, the so-called *poetria vetus*, that finds its full realization in Geoffrey of Vinsauf's early thirteenth-century *Poetria nova*. Importantly, the diligent pupil would find in both Macrobius and the commentaries on Horace a common sense of description as the art of imitation. Macrobius may well have been Bernard of Chartres's model,[85] since he had his pupils imitate their authors in much the same way, just as Macrobius surely was Chrétien de Troyes's.

Bernard of Chartres wanted his pupils to develop habits of composition and, in doing so, to acquire sensitivity to qualities of language and artistry like those Macrobius analyzes in the *Saturnalia*. He there-

---

[81] Cf. Villa 1993 p. 201-202 and 1997 pp. 31-32 on Chrétien's *conjointure* and Leiden BPL 28, originally in the library of Saint-Pierre's of Beauvais where Chrétien says he found the *livre* he used to write *Cligés*; on this manuscript see as well Munk Olsen 1982-89 vol. 1 pp. 456-57. For additional analogies between Latin and vernacular statements, see Villa 1997 pp. 23 and 30-32.

[82] Friis-Jensen 1995b; it remains influential into the Renaissance (Friis-Jensen 1995a pp. 232-39). In fact, it and other Horace commentaries are found alongside the *Poetria nova* and its commentaries in some manuscripts; see Woods ed. *PNCom* pp. xl-xli and xliv-xlv.

[83] Friis-Jensen 1990 p. 322.

[84] Friis-Jensen 1990 pp. 322-23, Villa 1992a pp. 56-59, Hajdú 1993 pp. 241-43; cf. Friis-Jensen 1997. See as well Curcio 1907 and Massaro 1978.

[85] Bernard of Chartres uses the *Saturnalia* in one place (*Glosae* 3.222 p. 154). However, as Dutton ed. *Glosae* p. 64 points out, Bernard cites the *ComSS* more often, no doubt because he is commenting on the *Timaeus*, which is more closely related in subject-matter to the *ComSS*.

fore had them practice imitation in daily exercises. Similarly, Macrobius's critical survey inculcates, by its breadth and variety, an awareness of the possibilities of excellent imitation: "haec quidem iudicio legentium relinquenda sunt, ut ipsi aestiment quid debeant de utriusque collatione sentire" (*Sat* 5.11.1; see as well 5.13.27, 6.6.20) [these matters are left to the readers' judgment so that they might evaluate the quality of each comparison]. Such evaluation is required in Bernard of Chartres's ideal classroom.

The Horace commentaries also stress the use of extant material as source and model for rewriting. Following Horace, they recommend rewriting commonplace matter like the Trojan War rather than matter that is totally new; but even when the matter is new, the rewriting must make it conform to contemporary expectations. The two kinds of matter are codified by Matthew of Vendôme as *materia propinqua* or *executa* on the one hand and *materia illibata* on the other.[86] Finally, they illustrate rewriting as imitation or emulation with the example of the *Iliacum carmen* — the story of the Trojan War and its aftermath. Chrétien de Troyes would have been able to find examples of the *Iliacum carmen* or episodes from it on various levels of composition in his own time.

Horace's admonition to treat the Trojan War in new ways did not go unheeded (*ArsPoet* v. 128-30). The return to prominence of Horace's *Art of Poetry* in the eleventh and twelfth centuries gave this admonition the weight of authority. In fact, Latin poems on Troy proliferate during these centuries, and continue to do so into the thirteenth century. Indeed, they proliferate on all levels, from *prae-exercitamina* to masterpieces.[87] This resurgence coincides with a resurgence of interest in Macrobius, at least judging by the number of manuscripts that we know to have been copied during the same period.[88] The *Aeneid* is still the primary work in the high medieval canon[89]; and, as Macrobius strives to show in all the detail we have observed, Vergil did indeed rewrite the *Iliacum carmen*. In other words, the *Aeneid* is a specimen piece for Horace's admonition; it became thereafter a model for the art of rewriting as twelfth-century commentators interpreted it. Macrobius's *Saturnalia* is an authority on that art.

---

[86] Kelly 1969b pp. 127-28.
[87] Henkel 1993 pp. 40-41.
[88] See the Appendix to Chapter One.
[89] See Glauche 1970 and Munk Olsen 1985.

The burden of Horace's admonition is to make familiar subject matter new. To do so, the writer must make the earlier *materia* recognizable or verisimilar — "aut famam sequere aut sibi convenientia finge" (*ArsPoet* v. 119) [either follow tradition or invent what is self-consistent]. Characters should conform to their traditional features or acquire credible new ones. The student could appreciate this by comparing, for example, Horace's illustration of the topos of the ages of life with Macrobius's.[90] To be original, shift emphasis and the tonality of the work will be transformed. No *fidus interpres*, the new author will "unfaithfully" develop the old story and its public will be able to recognize and appreciate the originality of the new version. To be sure, "difficile est proprie communia dicere" (*ArsPoet* v. 128) [it is hard to treat in your own way what is common]; still it has been and can be done. Macrobius offers what he considered an excellent example in his discussion of Vergil's invention of the affair between Aeneas and Dido. Drawing the model of incontinence from the account of Jason's and Medea's affair in Apollonius of Rhodes's *Argonautica* and adding (*adiectio*) it to his *materia*, Vergil is able to mirror the *species veritatis*, or outline of truth in his source, a model that renders, in rhetorical context but as in a picture, a credible and thus convincing representation of a fictional past action (*Sat* 5.17.4-5).

Before evaluating twelfth-century masterpieces of which Dares was *auctor*, let us return to the classroom to see how the Trojan War was faring there. The poems in the Glasgow "rhetorical anthology" have been dated to about 1225, thereby falling within our time frame. This anthology illustrates the art of composition in several *praeexercitamina* associated with rhetorical invention as the High Middle Ages understood it, and their pedagogical emphasis is still closer to preceptorial imitation rather than to original emulation. The Glasgow manuscript's "contextual environment" includes arts of poetry and various specimens of that art, some of which appear to be student compositions while others are specimens by masters. There are three Troy pieces: "Quis partus Troie" (*Anth* § 6), "Bella minans Asye" (*Anth* § 22), along with a version of the widely known "Pergama flere uolo" (*Anth* § 30). Their features are typical of the Horatian and Macrobian tradition. They rewrite the Trojan War. Furthermore, they abbreviate, focusing on some major feature rather than unwind-

---

[90] *ArsPoet* v. 156-78 and *Sat* 4.3.1-5; cf. *Ars vers* 1.41-42 and 82 on "diversitas etatis."

ing the whole tale from its beginning. Macrobius too points out how Vergil related only Aeneas's biography rather than going back to the beginnings, as in one of his alleged models, a universal or cyclic history attributed to an obscure Pisander (see Chapter Two). Finally, the major actions are set forth, that is, described, in a manner consonant with description as Macrobius understands it in the *Saturnalia*.

For example, the first Troy poem, "Quis partus Troie" (*Anth* § 6), is a 50-line piece on the destruction of Troy; it is, therefore, an *Iliacum carmen*. But it focuses on Paris as the cause of the destruction, especially because he awarded Venus the apple designated for the "most beautiful."[91]

> Quis partus Troie, cuius ruit illa ruina,
>> quomodo, quoue dolo, me recreare iuuat.
> Troia parit Paridem, Paridis ruit illa ruina,
>> Scipridis ingenio, Palladiique dolo. (v. 1-4)

[Who is Troy's offspring? Who caused its fall? How? By what deceit? These things it pleases me to recreate. Troy bore Paris and Paris caused its ruin through Venus's stratagem and the betrayal of the Palladium.]

These opening lines allude to the three principal narrative moments in the poem: the birth and banishment of Paris, his return to Troy and the Judgment that prepared for the abduction of Helen, and the betrayal of the city to the Greeks. Artificial order is evident, since the conclusion — "illa ruina" — comes before the intercourse with Helen that is related in the poem's last line: "quam furatur? eam. cui sociatur? ei" (v. 50) [whom did he abduct? Her. To whom is he united? To her].

Furthermore, this poem is amplified in an interrogative mode recalling the staple dictum for topical invention in the Middle Ages: *quis quid ubi quibus auxiliis cur quomodo quando?* (*Ars vers* 1.116) [who? what? where? by what means? why? how? when?]. *Qui* and *quomodo* are in the first two lines cited above, *quid* in v. 5-6: "Quid regina? parit; quid rex? iubet adnichilari / partum; quid famulus? fronde recondit eum" [What does the queen do? She gives birth to him. What does the king do? He orders the child to be put to death. What

---

[91] Cf. "magis apta" (v. 38, 45, and 46) and "pulchrior" (v. 44).

does the servant do? He hides the child under leaves], *cur* in v. 37:
"Quis iecit pomum? Discordia. cur? qui derat" [Who throws the
apple? Discord. Why? Because she was not included in the celebra-
tion], and *unde* as a variant of *cur* in v. 39: "Que sunt que certant?
Pallas, Iuno, Venus. unde? / de se" [Who are the contestants? Pallas,
Juno, and Venus. Whence their strife? They themselves]. These are
only some examples of how the author moves forward from topical
question to narrative answer in order to relate Paris's biography and
the fall of Troy. The topical questions are obvious here; but they are
not inconspicuous elsewhere.

Bridge Works in Medieval Poetics

Is this description as Macrobius understands the art? Without men-
tioning Macrobius, Tony Hunt has dealt with this issue in his study
of the relationship between two of Chrétien de Troyes's romances
and several examples of medieval Latin *comediae*.[92] These are the narratives which Hunt calls "bridge works." The *comediae* illustrate a level
of accomplishment beyond study of the art of poetry and prose and,
consequently, beyond school exercises like "Quis partus Troie." As
such, the *comediae* are not of the same caliber as the masterpieces
extolled in those same arts of poetry. Rather they can be seen to
bridge the gap between masterpieces and *praeexercitamina* and function
as further evidence of the progress of scholastic writers beyond the
usual classroom performance.[93] Chrétien's Ovidiana would also fall
into this category.

The Macrobian sense of immanent poetics is perceptible in the
bridge works. Indeed, the medieval Latin *comediae*, which modeled
their art on Ovidian examples could, Hunt argues, have served in
turn as models for Chrétien de Troyes. Although not a necessary
conclusion, Hunt's analysis of parallel passages does frequently remind the reader of Macrobius's own interpretation of Vergil's adaptation of Homer. For example (the translations are in the note[94]):

---

[92] Hunt 1978a; cf. Gerritsen 1973 Lecture 2, Dronke 1986, and Camargo 1994.
[93] See Kelly 1991 pp. 61-64. Some are in *accessus* and catalogues — for example,
Pamphilus; see Glauche 1970 p. 121.
[94] I have not translated in the text because it would make less apparent the
similarity between Hunt's analysis and Macrobius's of model texts in two or more
works. The translations are (with line numbers to identify them): (85): "As is appar-

The psychological processes described in *De nuntio sagaci* 64-72 contain the seeds[95] of the entire set of interview scenes in *Le chevaliers au lion*. Even the messenger's description of the girl's beauty (*De nunt.* 85: 'Vt res ostendit, tibi nil natura negauit') is echoed by Chrestien's description of Laudine: 'Onques mes si desmesurer / An biauté ne se pot Nature' (1492-93). In both works the lady insists on knowing what the go-between is driving at (*De nunt.* 67 ff., *Yv.* 1678 ff.), but when enlightened, becomes angry and indignant:

> Absit quod dicis! O laxa licencia verbis!
> Es sane mentis quod me non affore sentis?
> Vere nil sentis; da talia frivola ventis;
> Vt tam magna petas nondum mea postulat etas;
> ...
> Tolle, precor, tolle; bene scis me talia nolle. (96-101)

> 'Ore oi', fet ele, 'desreison
> La plus grant, qui onques fust dite.
> Fui! plainne de mal esperite,
> Fui! garce fole et enuieuse!
> Ne dire ja mes tel oiseuse.
> Ne ja mes devant moi ne vaingnes,
> Por quoi de lui parole taingnes!' (1710-16)

The messenger now assures the lady 'nullum tibi dedecus opto' (102) and Laudine realizes that 'Ne sa honte ne son enui / Ne li loeroit ele mie' (1746-47). The lady now replies, 'At, nimis astute, michi reddis et

---

ent, Nature denied you nothing." (1492-93): "Never did Nature so immoderately produce beauty." (96-101): "No! Oh! idle verbal licence! Are you in your right mind? don't you see that I am standing in front of you? Indeed you perceive nothing. Stop asking for such frivolities. The great things you are asking for are not suitable for a person my age... Desist, I beseech you to desist. You know I don't want such things." (1710-16): "'Now,' she exclaims, 'I hear the greatest folly ever uttered. Away with you! you are possessed by the devil. Away! you foolish, distressing trollope. Don't ever say such frivolous things to me again; don't ever come to talk to me about him again!'" (102): "I'm not asking you for anything improper." (1746-47): "She would not recommend anything that would cause her shame or distress." (112): "Ah! You're a sharp one! You give me clever answers!" (130): "I know what you're after: you seem to want to deceive me." (1700 f.): "I think you are out to deceive me; you want to trick me with words."

[95] Cf. Macrobius's "accepto brevi semine..."(*Sat* 5.11.22) [receiving the small seed] from Homer, Geoffrey of Vinsauf's "Sic surgit permulta seges de semine pauco" (*Poetria nova* v. 687) [In this way, plentiful harvest springs from a little seed [Nims]], and Chrétien's well-known use of *semer/semence* in *Perceval*: "En tel liu sa semence espande / Que fruit a .c. doubles li rande" (v. 3-4) [let him sow in a place from which is harvested a hundred-fold], on which see Pickens 1985 pp. 235-40 and Kelly 1992 pp. 19-21.

omnia... caute' (112) and 'Sencio quid queris: me fallere uelle uideres!'
(130). Similarly, Laudine retorts, 'Il m'est avis, que tu m'agueites, / Si
me viaus a parole prandre' (1700 f.)."[96]

Chrétien emulates material like this while rewriting and adapting it
to vernacular romance.

> Here again we recognize the essential point that the romance and the
> *comedia* share many points of style, technique and invention, owing
> naturally enough to their common origin in the schoolroom, but that
> the common features are differentiated in function. The much more
> ambitious context of Chrestien's romances raises *fabliau* material to a
> more complex existence in which effects are less immediate and clear-
> cut. This greater ambitiousness of the romance is doubtless linked with
> the status and culture of its patrons.[97]

Hunt does not claim that Chrétien actually used the *comediae* passages
he cites. However, what he does demonstrate convincingly is that
Chrétien's romances and the *comediae* share techniques which were
part of the standard instruction and art deriving from twelfth-century
practice in composition exercises.[98] If we extend that influence to
include actual imitation as modeling, then Hunt's article in effect
illustrates the kind of rewriting common in the scholastic tradition, a
tradition that links description as a practice with Horace's *Art of
Poetry*, Macrobius's *Saturnalia*, and Chrétien de Troyes.

The techniques Macrobius saw in Vergil's rewriting of Homer and
others were actually practiced in twelfth-century Latin and vernacular composition. These features of what Chrétien terms description
can assist us in explaining these works as they were composed and as
they were received by contemporary audiences.

Hunt's distinction between source and convention in rewriting is
analogous to Bart Besamusca's distinction between what he calls specific intertextuality and generic intertextuality, a distinction we can
adapt to the art of rewriting in the Middle Ages. Indeed, Besamusca
develops Matilda Bruckner's distinction between "specific contacts

---

[96] Hunt 1978a pp. 140-41; for additional parallels, see Cohen ed. *Comédie* passim.
[97] Hunt 1978a p. 146.
[98] Cf. Hunt 1978a p. 135. "Of course, many of these details are Ovidian commonplaces, but the important thing is to note that they have come together in a
dramatic, literary work before Chrestien wrote his romances," and thus they contain
the "seeds" (p. 140), the motifs, or the elements (p. 154) of models Chrétien used in
his *matière de Bretagne*.

between romances" and contacts "mediated by the model of... tradition."[99] Specific contact supposes the actual rewriting of a preceding work; this is what Macrobius means when he discusses Vergil's rewriting of Homeric material. On the other hand, some material became commonplace so that one may speak of a tradition within which an author rewrites traditional material. In Hunt's example, the classroom becomes the source of commonplace models that Chrétien carries from Latin into French, as we see, for example, in Chrétien's description of the quadrivium.

Description as Topical Invention

To understand description as topical invention, we must return again briefly to classroom basics. In the earliest extant art of poetry and prose, Matthew of Vendôme begins with description. I have dealt with this instruction in detail elsewhere,[100] so I shall merely summarize here for the present context. Matthew's conception of description is topical invention based on the identification of circumstantial topoi in persons, things, and actions. Such topoi are the attributes that identify and distinguish the kind of person, thing, or action represented. Rewriters choose from among the topoi those that can articulate their own intentions with regards to the person, thing, or action.

On the level of treatises like Matthew's, representative topoi are given to the pupil for practice. The topoi for a human being are variously articulated in examples so as to reveal differences in, for example, social rank, age, gender, profession, nationality, and place of residence (*Ars vers* 1.41-43, 46). In addition, the person, thing, or action chosen should emphasize the predominant features in the proposed work. Such exercises are authorized in quotations from Horace that are in turn corroborated by commentaries on his *Art of Poetry* and illustrated through excerpts from Ovid and others.[101] The pupil examining Matthew's typical descriptions in light of the precepts will

---

[99] Bruckner 1987 p. 224 and Besamusca 1993 pp. 16-17.

[100] Kelly 1987, 1991 pp. 71-78, and 1992 pp. 49-61.

[101] Franco Munari has provided exhaustive information on Matthew's illustrations in his edition of the *Ars versificatoria*; less thoroughgoing, but still useful identification of quotes is found in the other editions of the arts of poetry, in many of the translations of them, and in Sedgwick 1928. Useful illustrations of selective rewriting of commonplace models are found in Godman 1990.

note the choice of appropriate topoi and their specialized articulation, which is to fit each of the types illustrated (*Ars vers* 1.60-75). Various recommendations guide the pupil in scrutinizing them, including actual common places (topoi, loci, lieux) that the author may select and amplify in composition. The illustrations of these topoi are drawn from canonical writings, including Vergil, as well as from Matthew's own works, including the model descriptions that precede formal instruction (see especially *Ars vers* 1.46-58 and 107-11).

These examples also show how the pupil acquired the habit of thinking and inventing in terms of topoi. It is not a difficult habit to acquire. It is not hard to imagine, moreover, that when he or she moves to the stage of "immanent poetics," the manner of invention will still obtain because it has become habitual. Matthew also illustrates this by means of his criticism of Ovid's omission of stages in a *gradus amoris* (*Ars vers* 4.13). More importantly here, this criticism enables us to judge at what level Macrobius's *Saturnalia* will be accessible, and how Hunt's comparison of passages from Latin comedies and Chrétien's romances operates. We have seen how Vergil is alleged to scrutinize Homer's description of a sea storm and then rewrite its common places in the *Aeneid*. To the extent that the author expects the audience to recognize the rewriting, the poetics of allusion comes into play as well.

Imitation and Allusion in the French Tradition

We have now identified Macrobius's place in high medieval poetics. But what of Chrétien's French tradition? Of course, we cannot expect vernacular audiences to have the fine sense of allusion Roman audiences possessed or that medieval schooling fostered. Still, the reliance on allusion in topical invention could be cultivated among connoisseurs of the new writing. There is evidence for this, starting with Chrétien himself. Apart from his own statement in *Erec et Enide*, we have noted Jean de Meun's thirteenth-century imitation of Boethius in the *Roman de la rose*, which places the French poet in the line of the *translatio figurae*, a translation in this case of the guided quest motif that is anchored in Homer. This model recurs not infrequently in major medieval works after Jean's *Rose*. One fifteenth-century commentator claims that Dante uses it in the *Divine Comedy* to

imitate both Vergil and Jean de Meun.[102] Christine de Pizan introduces similar guides towards her own goals in no less than three
nearly contemporary works: the Sibyl in the *Chemin de long estude*,
Ladies France, Opinion, and Philosophy in the *Avision Christine*, and
Ladies Reason, Rectitude, and Justice in the *Cité des dames*. All her
guides to enlightenment and self-knowledge inform three different
images that articulate that knowledge: the quest as *chemin*, the vision,
and the founding of a city. Perhaps coincidentally, these three images
occur as well in Vergil and the chain of authors whom readers in the
Middle Ages believed imitated Vergil.[103]

Interestingly, Jean de Meun's imitation adapts the quest motif by
antiphrasis; it is a regression or "wrong road taken."[104] To be sure,
Amant literally proceeds in the company of various guides towards
the rose which he set out to pluck. Yet the truth underlying the fable
suggests the opposite of the surface carnality, by means of an implicit
Boethian (and Vergilian) model of the quest for a *summum bonum*
founded on virtue, making the poem an example of allegorical
antiphrasis.[105] The fiction in which Amant rejects Reason runs contrary to the model journey towards a goal in Vergil, Martianus

---

[102] Badel 1980 pp. 486-87.

[103] Christine de Pizan also imitated Dante; see her *Chemin* v. 1125-52. On
Macrobius and Dante, see Rabuse 1958 and 1976, Raby 1966, and Hübner 1995
pp. 12-13. These images also occur in Chrétien de Troyes's romances. They belong
to the "great public images," that is, in Tuve's words (1966 pp. 21-22), "the ways we
have developed to refer to things too complex to state in full, though experienced by
all of us. There are not very many such great public images (quest, pilgrimage,
marriage, death, birth, purgation, for example)...."

[104] The *Anticlaudianus* rewrites by *contrarietas* Claudian's *In Rufinum*; see Bossuat ed.
Anticlaudianus pp. 34-35.

[105] Christine de Pizan also suggests reading the *Rose*'s misogyny on two levels. As
her Reason puts it: "Et des pouettes dont tu parles, ne sces tu pas bien que ilz ont
parlé en plusieurs choses en maniere de fable et se veullent aucunes foiz entendre au
contraire de ce que leurs diz demonstrent? Et les puet on prendre par la rigle de
grammaire qui se nomme antifrasis qui s'entant... si comme on diroit tel est mauvais,
c'est a dire que il est bon, et aussi a l'opposite. Si te conseille que tu faces ton prouffit
de leurs diz et que tu l'entendes ainsi, quel que fust leur entente, es lieux ou ilz
blasment les femmes." (*Cité* p. 624). [Furthermore, don't you know that the poets you
mention spoke on a number of topics through fables and that they did so on occasion
in such a way that one might understand them in a sense contrary to their literal
meaning. They can be interpreted using the grammatical principle antiphrasis, as if
one were to say that someone is bad, meaning that he or she is good, and in this way
produce an opposite meaning. I advise you to profit from what they say by reading
them in that way, whatever their intent may have been, in those passages in which
they attack women.]

Capella, and Boethius; yet it complements them too by suggesting what might have become of Aeneas had he remained with Dido, of Mercury had he rejected the company of Virtue, or of Boethius had he spurned the counsel of Philosophy. Although their mode changes as well as their content, all these works relate a guided voyage towards a golden, desirable goal. The differences turn on whether its glitter comes from false gold, gilding, or pure ore.

Rewriting by antiphrasis in the *Roman de la rose* recalls Gervase of Melkley's three varieties of imitation: *idemptitas, similitudo*, or *contrarietas*[106] — that is, paraphrase, analogy, or antiphrasis. Gervase applies these procedures to a complete or incomplete *sententia* which may have both a literal and a figurative meaning (*ArsGM* p. 6:3-5). As in the examples from the Martianus commentary, analogues tell a single truth — "fere idem exprimunt" as *idemptitas*. Further, the works in the chain of authors identified by the Bernardus Commentary are *similitudines*, or comparable, in that they teach the way to a supreme good variously identified as Rome, understanding, or sufficiency. And finally, in Jean de Meun's adaptation of the scheme, a comparable story tells a contrary truth, or *contrarietas*, which, as Christine de Pizan suggests, harmonizes by allegorical antiphrasis with the literal truth and goal. The technique is recognizable in terms of Macrobius's *auctor-imitator* correlation by *mutuatio, mutatio*, and reception.[107]

But rewriting in French introduces variables that are absent in the Latin tradition. For example, Jean de Meun could not rely on his audience's knowledge of Boethius because the intended lay audience would not necessarily know Latin, or the Latin tradition; moreover, Jean thought that Boethius was not yet available in French.[108] Poetic allusion to that tradition was therefore risky. At least, that is what we may surmise both from Jean's call for a translation of Boethius as well as from interventions like Benoît de Sainte Maure's in which he says that he is relating the well-known story of the Trojan War for those ignorant of Latin and who, therefore, were excluded from that knowledgeable group (*Troie* v. 37-39). Their implied audiences could

---

[106] *ArsGM* p. 6, ll. 6-9. Cf. *Sat* 4.5 (*locus a simili*), 5.3.1 ("versus ad verbum paene translatos"), 5.16.12 ("faciat velut aliud videri"), 6.1.7 ("locos integros cum parva immutatione translatos"), and 6.2.1 ("quaedam immutando verba tamquam fuco alio tinctos") and 4 ("eundem colorem ac paene similem sonum loci utriusque").

[107] Cf. Demats 1973 pp. 19-26 and Cizek 1994 pp. 122-25, 156-61.

[108] Kelly 1995a p. 163 n. 18. For a recent survey, including dating of the French translations of the *De consolatione*, see Atkinson 1994.

not appreciate allusions to Boethius or to Dares and Dictys the way a Latin audience might understand such allusions. However, the latter would know about vernacular traditions like those of King Arthur which, for example, Joseph of Exeter refers to in the *Ylias*: "Sic Britonum ridenda fides et credulus error / Arturum exspectat exspectabitque perenne" (*Ylias* Bk. III, v. 472-73)[109] [Just so is the laughable gullibility and mistaken belief of the Britons who await the return of King Arthur now and will always go on doing so (Bate)]. By the same token, Benoît's and Jean's vernacular audience could in all likelihood appreciate references to Aeneas's story or to the Theban war because the romances of *Thèbes* and *Eneas* were available.[110] Nonetheless, times were changing and a new, vernacular audience was emerging. This implied vernacular audience is presumed to be intelligent. The *Thèbes* author distinguishes it from ignoble, presumably vulgar publics incapable of understanding the romance (*Thèbes* v. 13-20). These publics would include those whom Benoît describes as being ignorant of Latin.

Let me briefly illustrate the contrast between Latin and vernacular audiences with another well-known example that is both contemporary with and analogous to the evidence from Benoît and Joseph: Thomas d'Angleterre's allusion to Breri's version of the Tristan story.

Thomas alludes — as Joseph and Wace did to Arthur[111] — to the multiple versions of the Tristan and Iseut story known in the French-speaking world at the time he was writing. He also singles out an

---

[109] Another allusion to Arthur appears in the surviving fragment of Joseph's *Antiocheis*, v. 16 (p. 212 in Gompf ed. *Ylias*). The BN lat. ms. 15015 glosses on the *Ylias* do not explain the Arthur allusion. We may therefore assume that the allusion was deemed readily comprehensible. The glosses distinguish elsewhere between familiar material, which the reader will know, and unfamiliar material, which is explained. For example, on Semele's fate, "Nota est fabula" (*Ylias* ed. Riddehough p. 349 to v. 537); but the birth of Erichthonius, although said to be known, and the contest between Paris's bull and Mars disguised as a bull, are explained (*Ylias* ed. Riddehough pp. 348 to v. 510 and 350 to v. 580). The commentary also singles out another apparently contemporary example in Joseph's castigation of the Balearic soothsayer (*Ylias* Bk. IV, v. 231-37; see the commentary *Ylias* ed. Riddehough p. 374 to v. 236). Similar examples occur in glosses to Gautier de Châtillon's *Alexandreis*: one late-thirteenth-century gloss explains Paris's declaration of eternal love to Oenone (*Alex* p. 369 to v. 459), but leaves out the account of the Judgment of Paris because it was well known: "sed notissima est hec fabula, unde non est necesse ipsam hic scribi" (*Alex* p. 370 to v. 461) [but this fable is very well known; hence, it isn't necessary to relate it here].

[110] Monfrin 1985.

[111] On these allusions, see Loomis 1959 chap. 6.

authoritative version, Breri's, which he chose to follow, while not neglecting the others.[112] Thomas assumed that his implied audience was familiar with many versions of his story. Similarly, Joseph could assume his Latinate audience's knowledge of different versions of the Trojan War like those to which Benoît also alludes (*Troie* v. 42-44). But unlike Thomas, Benoît does not assume his audience's knowledge of them because they are written in Latin (*Troie* v. 129-34). All three authors, moreover, reconciled differences among their versions much as the early Christian poets had to do when rewriting biblical matter. In Thomas's case, he excludes an episode recounting Governal's clandestine visit to Marc's court to fetch Iseut on the grounds that everyone would have recognized him. Like Thomas, Benoît and Joseph chose different versions of the horse by which Troy was betrayed. Benoît followed Dictys (and Vergil) by relating the ruse of the Trojan horse (*Troie* v. 25893-925). Joseph kept to Dares's version according to which the Scaean Gate — which had a horse's head sculpted on top and was also Antenor's dwelling — functioned as the nocturnal entry point to the Greeks, opened to them by Antenor and the other Trojan traitors (*Ylias* Bk. VI, v. 712-38). These examples illustrate the winnowing and sifting that went on in both Latin and twelfth-century vernacular rewriting.

Let us now turn back to what is extant of the beginnings to get some grasp of the earliest vernacular audiences and thereby sketch what may have been available as models. The *Sainte Eulalie* illustrates the passage from Latin to vernacular composition. This work seems to have been written along the lines of the Council of Tours of 813, which allowed using the vernacular in sermons for the sake of those who could not understand Latin and hence could not profit from hearing in their own idiom.[113] Interestingly, the late ninth-century *Sainte Eulalie* appears in a Valenciennes manuscript together with another short poem in Latin on the same saint.[114] Is the Latin version

[112] See Gallais 1967 and Kelly 1992 pp. 101-03; Gerritsen 1995 pp. 158-61 shows how stories passed by word of mouth from one individual to another.

[113] Pope 1952 p. 12, Herman 1996; but see as well Wright 1982 esp. pp. 127-35 and 1997 and McKitterick 1989. Whether *Sainte-Eulalie* is in "vernacular Latin," as Wright and McKitterick argue, or early Romance or French, the difference is not directly relevant here; even if the manuscript's two versions of the Eulalie legend are, the one in Carolingian and the other in "vernacular" Latin, the former is still unintelligible to those who do not understand reformed Carolingian pronunciation. The issue of *lay* literacy is hardly resolved by the two works.

[114] See Dion 1990 pp. 10 and 49-50.

the source of the French version? It certainly isn't a clear case whereby the vernacular version attempts a faithful translation or paraphrase of the Latin version.

The Latin sequence is a song of praise; Eulalie's trials and martyrdom are only briefly alluded to, suggesting that its readers or listeners, at mass or in the refectory, are presumed to know the life and martyrdom that justify epideictic description.[115] The French version is quite different.[116] After briefly describing the complementary physical and spiritual beauty of the saint, the poem goes on to relate a conventional *gradus sanctitatis*, suggesting that its public is unfamiliar with the story since, unlike the Latin version, the saint's life is recounted episode by episode. The conclusion confirms faith in God's grace through the saint's intercession. Here Eulalie is a *sancta adiutrix*. Clearly, the French version meets the recommendation of the 813 Council of Tours to deliver sermons in the vernacular so that the laity might better understand what was said or, in the case of the *Sainte Eulalie*, sung.

The dichotomy between *litterati* and *illiterati* distinguishes between those educated in the Latin language and thus knowledgeable and those who were not, a dichotomy defining issues in early vernacular writing.[117] Although many vernacular authors wrote in conformity with the Latin art, they adapted what they wrote for vernacular audiences, as is the case with *Sainte Eulalie*.[118] In other words, the French writer is rewriting, not merely copying or translating. The Latin version is in epideictic mode, the French version in narrative mode. It abbreviates what the Latin model amplifies, the panegyric description, but lengthens what the model treats briefly, the saint's martyrdom. As such, the French poem conforms to the Macrobian and rhetorical principles that will be put into practice later by Bernard of Chartres's pupils: they will imitate, but also recreate the

---

[115] Do we have here the distinction between the 'imitable saint' and the 'helping saint' (see Gier 1977 pp. 18-19)? Whereas the Latin version seeks the saint's intercession for *Famulos* ("dō famulantib:—"), or servants of the Lord like her, the vernacular version refers only to "nos," or sinners in the secular world in need of her intercession (*Eulalie* p. 51 stanza 14); see also Leupin 1988 p. 456.

[116] Cf. Leupin 1988 pp. 464-68.

[117] On this distinction, see Grundmann 1958; for the changes in style occasioned by the rise of a lay, but Latin reading public, see Schmidt 1977.

[118] See Poirion 1986 p. 12; cf. Hartmann 1970 pp. 119-23 and Schmidt 1977, and Zink 1996 on vernacular narrative elaboration of Saint Bernard's parables when they are rewritten in French.

received *materia* to fit new emphases, new intentions, and new audiences. The audience is perhaps the primary concern in rewriting when *materia* passes from a clerical to a lay audience.

The Latin and French lives of Eulalie highlight Macrobius's use of *auctor* and *imitator* as first author and rewriter. They also illustrate lifting and transformation — *mutuatio* and *mutatio* — for an intended audience. They have therefore a place in vernacular rewriting as imitation and invention that was already in place in the ninth century when the French and Latin versions of this work were written.[119] Scribal intervention while copying manuscripts, especially when such intervention actually leads to original rewriting (as in the *Eulalie* example), continues to play a major role in composition in the High Middle Ages when French literary writing emerged on a grand scale. For example, Aimé Petit has shown how the *Eneas* adapts Vergil to the Ovidian motif of the lady falling in love with a man — in this case, a besieger — from Ovid's *Metamorphoses*[120]; the French romance thus combines two matters much as Vergil himself did, according to Macrobius, when he used the *Argonautica*'s Medea model to tell the story of Dido's love. Later scribes did the same, even reverting to earlier versions to correct later rewriting. For example, the Ovidian motif for falling in love was borrowed subsequently by a thirteenth-century scribe of the *Roman de Thèbes* to amplify Parthonopeus's courtship of Antigone.[121] Similarly, a fourteenth-century scribe of *Eneas* makes his version conform more closely to Vergil — a correction of the vernacular tradition in favor of the first author, or *auctor* in Macrobius's sense of the word.[122]

These texts exemplify varieties of bridge works. As we mentioned earlier, Tony Hunt used this term to refer to the relation between Chrétien de Troyes's romances and twelfth-century Latin *comediae*.[123]

---

[119] My point holds even if we take the French *Eulalie* as first version and the Latin text as its imitation; on Hucbald of Rheims as possible author or inspiration for the vernacular version, see Wright 1982 pp. 133-34.

[120] Petit 1985b pp. 407-12.

[121] Petit 1985b pp. 381-85.

[122] Triaud 1985 esp. pp. 180-87; cf. also Petit 1985b pp. 414-15 and 1996. *Eneas* ed. Petit is an edition of this manuscript.

[123] Hunt's article emphasizes the performance of these works as well as their vernacular counterparts. I have not done so here, although orality is certainly an important, albeit elusive aspect of reading in Latin and French. There is some interesting material on oral performance and mime in some twelfth-century commentaries on Horace's *Art of Poetry*. See especially Friis-Jensen 1990 pp. 348 (§81), 353 (§125), 357 (§179:19), 359 (§193), and 364 (§260:5), where the reference to a

We recall that the *comediae* are bridge works, that is, "those few works... which seem to represent bridges between" Latin and French traditions in the twelfth and thirteenth centuries.[124] Moreover, Hunt rejects two traditional views of this relationship between the two traditions. The first, based on continuity, sees the vernacular tradition flowing out from and continuing the Latin tradition, the view most commonly associated with Curtius.[125] What a tradition is can be a problem in itself. As Ardis Butterfield has cogently observed, "the term 'tradition' is often and perhaps inevitably used loosely, as a post-facto gathering together of works in the mind of a critic rather than a collection of works perceived as such by any of the authors themselves."[126] The other view postulates an opposition between Latin and vernacular, clerical and popular, oral and written.[127] For his part, Hunt views the Latin and French traditions as contiguous.[128] This means that "mutual interference" among specific works took place at various times and places, under diverse circumstances, and in both directions between Latin and French. The "contiguity of the two literary traditions" obliges the scholar to examine specific, but often diverse instances of bridging. In this way we are able to assess originality and the quality of rewriting in contemporary medieval terms. Furthermore, we can see vernacular authors pursuing the "immanent poetics" of specific works which they imitate by paraphrase, analogy, or antiphrasis. The Macrobian features of rewriting (*mutatio*) — addition, deletion, replacement, and transformation — loom large in these poetics.

Besides its theoretical validity, the bridge work has a practical interpretative advantage over the two other models based on, respec-

---

reader and mimes on p. 353 may well describe how the *comediae* were staged. This gloss is not found in earlier Horace commentaries that have been edited. Cf. Gouttebroze 1995.

[124] Hunt 1978a p. 120.

[125] Cf. Curtius 1954 p. 9: "Ohne diesen lateinischen Hintergrund sind die volkssprachlichen Literaturen des Mittelalters unverständlich."

[126] Butterfield 1997 p. 69.

[127] See, for example, Stock 1983 chap. 1.

[128] On what follows, see Hunt 1978a p. 120-22. Hunt's conception of the bridge work is valid for relations between Latin and other vernacular traditions as well as for relations among the vernaculars themselves and among separate traditions that may exist within a single vernacular, as Bec 1977 pp. 30-33 suggests. For example, there are bridge works in French between romance traditions and those of the chansons de geste; see Kay 1995 p. 5 on the "mutual interference between the two genres," and Bec 1977 pp. 40-43, who recall implicitly Hunt's notion of the mutual interference of contiguous traditions.

tively, continuity and opposition that have dominated views on Latin-French relations in the high medieval period. It makes us focus on precisely those instances where "interference" does occur in specific works and on its modalities and scope, as Hunt did with the medieval Latin *comediae*, bridging classroom *praeexercitamina* and French romance.[129] Although he admits that the Latin works could have directly influenced Chrétien's romances, he notes that this is not necessary to justify the concept of the bridge work, since topical models were readily available in Chrétien's time. More importantly, the bridge work suggests ways by which traditional clerical *materia* and art were adapted in vernacular works for aristocratic patrons and audiences who probably did not know Latin well or at all and had different tastes and predilections. Of course, these audiences did not need to know the Latin models in order to appreciate romance. But it is obvious that knowledge of the *comediae* helps us interpret and appreciate the quality of Chrétien's art of writing, prior to the "performance" as public or private reading.[130]

French versus Latin Rewriting

Twelfth-century authors made a conscious choice either to write in Latin and thus produce works illustrated in the twelfth-century canon by authors like Bernardus Silvestris and Joseph of Exeter, or to write in the vernacular, like Chrétien de Troyes and Benoît de Sainte-Maure. As Marie de France puts it,[131]

> ... començai a penser
> D'aukune bone estoire faire
> E de latin en romaunz traire;
> Mais ne me fust guaires de pris:
> Itant s'en sunt altre entremis! (*Lais* Pro v. 28-32)

[I began to think about writing some good story, drawing it from Latin into French. But it would hardly have redounded to my credit since so many others have already done so!]

---

[129] Hunt 1978a p. 121-22.
[130] On this sense of performance, see Huot 1987 pp. 304, Butterfield 1997 p. 79, and note 123 above.
[131] See also Hurst 1995.

Another twelfth-century author evokes this moment more dramatically; the anonymous author of *Partonopeu de Blois* recalls his controversial decision to write in French rather than in Latin in the following manner.[132]

> Cil clerc dïent que n'est pas sens
> D'escrire estoire d'antif tens
> Quant jo nes escris en latin,
> Et que je pert mon tans enfin.
> *(Partonopeu* v. 77-80)

[Clerics say that it isn't smart to write a story of bygone days unless I do so in Latin, and that in the final analysis I'm wasting my time.]

He felt he had a choice; yet, obviously, emerging twelfth-century aristocratic audiences of French narratives were not taken seriously by those favoring Latin. Nonetheless, the *Partonopeu* poet's romance was a success and served itself to make bridges to other vernacular languages by adaptation.[133] In addition, the *Partonopeu* illustrates and corroborates Hunt's analysis of the informed, educated choices made by twelfth-century writers when turning from Latin to the vernacular.

Convincingly, Hunt identifies four groupings under which bridges between Latin and French may be categorized. First, there is reciprocity between Latin and vernacular works observable at those moments when the subject matter and art of one language pass from the one tradition to the other. To Hunt's specimen texts, the Latin *comediae* and Chrétien's romances, we might also add the central place held by Benoît's *Troie*. Like the other antique romances, it is a conduit for Latin *materia* and art into French vernacular as well as a bridge to other works in French, Latin, and other vernaculars.[134]

Second, Hunt's emphasis on *ovidiana* in the medieval Latin tradition underscores Ovid's well-known influence on early French writ-

---

[132] Bruckner 1993 p. 113. Dante's *Divine Comedy* received the same criticism; see Villa 1997 p. 25.

[133] Fourrier 1960 pp. 316-17; see as well Smith and Gildea ed. *Partonopeu* vol. 2:2 pp. 1-13.

[134] See Greif 1886, Stohlmann ed. *Hist Troy* pp. 166-72, Eisenhut 1983, Nolan 1992, Jappé 1996, Jung 1996 ch. 4, and Jung 1997. Cf. Brunner 1989. Klebs 1899 (esp. pp. 325-33) provides a useful survey — intertextuality *avant la lettre* — of Latin and vernacular adaptations of the Apollonius of Tyre subject matter.

ing, not only in Ovidian adaptations like *Philomena*, *Narcisse*, or *Pyrame et Tisbé*, but also in works modeled on Ovidian material in the antique romances, Chrétien, and elsewhere. Chrétien and Marie de France drew on this tradition; but, like the *Partonopeu* author, they also branched off from it in new directions. In Marie's case, this occurred initially because so many had already mined the Latin material. If she wished to treat a new subject matter, she needed to find new material; accordingly, she turned to vernacular traditions for the stories she rewrote in her *Lais*.[135]

Third, since his 1978 article, Hunt has identified stages in the training of the potential Latin and French writer as well as the moment at which they part ways — the moment illustrated so strikingly by the *Partonopeu* poet. In the beginning reading with glosses prevailed in elementary grammar courses. As the student gradually became more accomplished,[136] instruction such as that which Chrétien found in Macrobius was normal; in his case, this holds whether this learning occurred before he undertook to write the *ovidiana* and the Marc and Iseut poem referred to in the *Cligés* prologue or at the same time.

Fourth and last, we come to the moment when the vernacular art of writing met new, vernacular linguistic and social demands. Although this new vernacular line of transmission continued to harken back to and draw on the Latin art and artistic habits for specific rewriting while adapting to a new language and new audiences, a new vernacular tradition more independent of the Latin art of poetry is emerging. Philippe de Remi, for example, speaks of his lack of Latin compositional training (*Manekine* v. 30-33; cf. p. 388 note); his writing seems directly beholden only to vernacular models.[137]

These bridges allow us to add to the picture sketched by Hunt, who focused on the *comediae*.[138] The *comediae* do not give a full and complete picture for several reasons. First, the tone of these works is not the same as that of most romances. In Material Style they are to romance roughly what Molière's farces are to his high comedies.

---

[135] Nonetheless, Marie did return to the Latin-language tradition for sources in the *Fables* and *Espurgatoire Saint-Patrice*.

[136] Hunt 1978a p. 156 n. 104 identifies debate poems and *comediae* as progressively more advanced stages in composition. Cf. Edwards 1993. Epitomes also would seem to have a place in the scheme, either as sources for invention or as abbreviated compositions; see Otis 1936.

[137] Kelly 1987 pp. 208-09.

[138] On *novus*, cf. Méla 1989 pp. 8-15.

Although relatively sophisticated works, they only border on highly polished works, generally accepted as masterpieces. To complete the notion of the bridge we need to take account of other modes of treatment, including elementary and intermediate productions like those one finds, for example, in poetic anthologies. Finally, we must consider the often sharp contrasts between tastes of clerical and court audiences when analogous subjects are treated. These are the audiences Chrétien himself tries to link and bridge with his celebrated union of *chevalerie* and *clergie*, a combination he appears to anticipate in adorning the knight and king Erec with the splendors of the quadrivium and by referring to Macrobius's art of description. Here, the aristocratic microcosm finds its place beneath the quadrivial macrocosm, and it does so in the French language.

However, it is well not to press this "humanistic" feature of Chrétien's translation image too far. By and large, the nobility did not admire its clerics.[139] *Clergie* is often linked to magic in the romances, and the fruits of knowledge appear more often than not as belonging to the marvelous rather than learning. After all, "grammar" became "glamor" in popular usage. Hence, Melior's education in *Partonopeu*, which combines the liberal arts with necromancy, probably reflects the uneducated, but not necessarily unintelligent aristocratic audience's views of clerical hocus pocus. Chrétien too combined Macrobius and the quadrivium with fairy art. *Clergie* might well have connoted this conception of clerical learning as more marvelous than educational.

Medieval poets inherited from antiquity a poetics of allusion, a poetics which the *Saturnalia* illustrates particularly well.[140] This is doubtless another reason why Chrétien acknowledges Macrobius's influence on his art of description. Allusion is generally understood today as "a reference, without explicit identification, to a person, place, or event, or to another literary work or passage."[141] The last variety — "reference... to another literary work or passage" — is the sense that medieval writers in the Latin tradition knew and used for allusions. It is in this sense that it passed into the French tradition as well. Clearly, a body of works had to be written and become better known if French audiences were to amass a storehouse of memory

---

[139] Barbero 1987 pp. 131-242.
[140] Pasquali 1951 and Tilliette 1985 p. 139.
[141] Abrams 1993 p. 8.

that vernacular texts could activate by engaging the play of allusion in writing new works. To take an obvious example, they needed to know who Arthur was before allusions to him would be meaningful. In order to grasp what Chrétien and his peers did by bringing Latin compositional norms into French romance, we need reliable indicators. We need identifiable sources or models so that we may study what imitators did with their models while determining whether such imitation fits Macrobian schemes for rewriting. To that end, I propose to examine a number of specimen texts in the context of description illustrated by Macrobius's interpretation of Vergil's rewriting of his Greek and Latin antecedents. In this way, we move from generalizations about composition to specific texts that illustrate allusive description.

To show that vernacular adaptations conform to the traditional Latin scheme for imitation and rewriting, but with adaptations for contemporary vernacular audiences, I propose in the following chapters to examine how these adaptations occurred in the transition from Latin to a vernacular matter, audiences, and poetics. Chapter Four focuses on two aspects of descriptive rewriting: the bridge work as representative of the progressive acquisition of the art of description and the art of allusion which articulates the special intertextual relationships that obtain between the first work and its rewriting — relationships that Macrobius elaborated upon in his discussion of Vergil's rewriting of his Greek and Latin predecessors. A comparison of Benoît de Sainte-Maure's *Roman de Troie* and Joseph of Exeter's *Ylias*, which were apparently written independently of one another, will allow us to contrast Latin and vernacular rewriting by observing how both authors rewrote Dares. The contrast brings out more sharply the implications of the dichotomy we have already seen in the case of the Latin and French *Eulalie*, since the *Troie* rewrites Dares in the French vernacular and the *Ylias* rewrites him in Latin.

Chapter Five passes from Latin to vernacular sources to follow the rewriting of the consent motif from its absence in Vergil's *Aeneid* to its introduction in the *Roman d'Eneas* and the subsequent rewriting of the motif in Chrétien's *Erec et Enide* and Renaut de Beaujeu's *Bel Inconnu*. Both *Erec* and the *Bel Inconnu* allude to their predecessors and thereby alert audiences to reflect on different versions of the motif. The *Bel inconnu* brings us to the end of the twelfth century, by which time a vernacular tradition of rewriting with its own sets of real or potential allusions has emerged.

Among the major innovations in the thirteenth century is the insertion of troubadour and *trouvère* lyric as well as other genres into the romance mode. Chapter Six examines some features of the non-lyric insertion in Huon de Mery's *Tournoiement Antechrist* and the anonymous *Cristal et Clarie*; it then focuses on the *conjointure* of lyric and narrative modes in Gerbert de Montreuil's *Roman de la violette*, Jakemes's *Roman du Châtelain de Coucy et de la Dame de Fayel*, and Jean Renart's *Guillaume de Dole* or *Roman de la rose*. All these works permit revision of current terminology on the insertion. These romances illustrate not only inserted lyrics but also inserted quotes and narrative investment of pre-arranged lyric pieces. The chapter pays special attention to the motif of the distraught lover.

In other words, each following chapter examines an aspect of description treated in the *Saturnalia*. In Chapter Four on the *Troie* and the *Ylias* we explore rewriting of an extant source. This permits us to see how the rewriter, in Macrobius's sense of *imitator*, uses effectively the operations characteristic of description. Just as Macrobius compared Greek and Latin works as well as those in Latin, we can appreciate the effect of different languages, different contexts, and different implied audiences on the Latin and French rewriting of the same Latin source. Chapter Five's works do not have an extant source except for the *Eneas*; but all three use allusion to refer to motifs used in a prior work — notably consent in a *gradus amoris* — in order to underscore new and original descriptions of the motif which the allusions help us to appreciate. Finally, in Chapter Six, we examine insertions that are either hidden or identified as such. When identified, the source is literally inserted into the main matter, or arranged in such a way that narrative matter can be wrapped around it. Here allusion and quotation inform the alert vernacular audience. The modern reader can also see that the Latin art of description as rewriting has been fully assimilated and adapted to the French language.

The next three chapters do not attempt overarching interpretations of the romances they treat. Rather their works represent specimens of the art of rewriting as Macrobius and medieval poetics articulate it. Therefore, they should be read as illustrations of the art of description; they show how specific writers rewrite their antecedent models. Since, however, description as topical invention includes reinterpetation of themes and motifs in sources, each chapter also uses such a theme or motif as part of the interpretation. In Chapter Four, the theme is the description of destiny and fortune in the rewriting of Dares's *De excidio Troiae*. Chapter Five treats the theme of consent in love, whether such consent is to marriage, an affair, or only sexual intercourse. The final chapter explores the ways several thirteenth-century narratives insert the model of the betrayed male lover, whether he is a husband or an unmarried lover, and whether the infidelity is real or supposed. I have chosen these works and the topical emphases because they belong to a chain of rewriting, and because they have not hitherto received the attention they deserve in interpreting these works.

Most of the romances treated are not Arthurian. This is a deliberate attempt to enlarge the scope of romance criticism beyond the Matter of Britain on which there is abundant critical scholarship.[142] Furthermore, although the choice of specific themes or motifs has been in part influenced by current historical studies,[143] my study is not a historical interpretation of these works. Historians can evaluate the evidence of romance, bearing in mind the caveat implied by romancers themselves: it may be unsafe to speak the truth outright about contemporary mores.[144]

---

[142] Good examples of studies of allusion in French romance are Schmolke-Hasselmann 1980 and 1983, Kennedy 1986, Combarieu 1996, and Rockwell 1997. For allusion in the topoi of time and place, see Morris 1988.

[143] For example, Faber 1974, Contamine 1980, Duby 1981, Brooke 1989, Brundage 1987, and Martin 1996.

[144] Kelly 1992 pp. 121, 312-13, and 346 n. 146; cf. Brooke 1989 pp. 173-79.

CHAPTER FOUR

TROY IN LATIN AND FRENCH
JOSEPH OF EXETER'S *YLIAS* AND
BENOÎT DE SAINTE-MAURE'S *ROMAN DE TROIE*

Spiritum furoris habens in naribus.[1]

A chronicle of the city of Bruges relates that the Duke of Burgundy was standing one day in the square, sword in hand, when an old baker approached him and, bowing, wished him welcome. The prince raised his sword and struck the baker dead. Shortly thereafter a cooper dared approach the prince and was killed in the same way. When the townspeople saw this, they rushed back to their dwellings, and, seizing weapons, returned to the square ready to fight.[2] More clearly than many, I think, this episode illustrates the "petite acheison," the small cause or slight provocation that can unleash fury and violence.

Petites acheisons also give rise to the fury that motivates the Trojan War, as Benoît de Sainte-Maure and Joseph of Exeter relate it. Indeed, both authors add to the image of Troy transferred to the West, which was traditional before their time,[3] more "small causes" of the War: Peleus's desire to destroy a potential usurper, Jason, by sending him in search of the Golden Fleece, along with Laomedon's angry refusal of hospitality to Jason's Argonauts. Anger breeds yet more anger; a domino effect builds up, enhancing the fury provoked by these beginnings and leading to the destruction of both Trojans and Greeks. In this way, among others, these twelfth-century authors describe this war while rewriting the standard version they found in Dares's *De excidio*. In so doing, they follow Horace's advice and Vergil's example — they rewrite a poem of Troy instead of telling something completely new.

---

[1] Snorting fury. *Chronique* p. 1002.
[2] *Brugge* pp. 24-25.
[3] Cohen 1941 pp. 16-29; cf. Worstbrock 1963 pp. 252-53, Homeyer 1982, and Beaune 1985 esp. chap. 1.

The systematization of Horace's instruction in his eleventh- and twelfth-century commentaries, and the codification of that commentary in the twelfth- and thirteenth-century arts of poetry, are now well known. But what about actual practice? To answer that question, we may well turn to the versions of the Trojan War by Benoît and Joseph, masterpieces by twelfth-century standards, to illustrate diverse approaches to rewriting like those we have observed in the Latin and French versions of the *Sainte Eulalie*. Whereas Benoît amplifies on the plot he found in Dares in great detail and with considerable diversity for audiences who do not know the Latin tradition, Joseph seems far more interested in description, relying on his audience's being familiar with the events described.

Description in Joseph's Ylias

The topical questioning that we observed in the Glasgow Anthology's composition exercises appears in Joseph of Exeter's *Ylias* as well. An obvious example introduces the portrait gallery of Greeks and Trojans in Book IV. "Nunc utinam, quo quisque animo, quo fulserit ore, / Quis membris inscriptus honos, quis pectora motus / Extulerit, meminisse queam" (*Ylias* Bk. IV, v. 35-37)[4] [Oh, that I could now recall with what courage and with what beauty each one was resplendent, what dignity graced their limbs, what emotions stirred their hearts (Esler).] Joseph also describes by topical invention. "The conduct of the story was the last thing he troubled about; in fact he seems... mainly concerned to get away from the story and concentrate on speeches, descriptions, rhetorical outbursts and moral and theological disquisitions."[5] Let us therefore examine description in the Latin and French poems, taking description in terms of Macrobius's broad semantic range, and beginning with the later, but more topical descriptions in the *Ylias*.

The use of descriptions is certainly obvious even from an outline of the *Ylias*. On the most superficial level, Joseph seems to be following a dictum like Geoffrey of Vinsauf's to amplify what the source treats

---

[4] For other examples, see *Ylias* Bk. I, v. 152; II, v. 15-23 and 492; III, v. 201 and 415-16; IV, v. 489-90; VI, v. 33-34, 325, and 436. Cf. Bate ed. *Ylias* p.181 n. 492 and Bate 1971 p. 228.

[5] Sedgwick 1930 pp. 59-60.

briefly, but shorten what it treats at length.[6] The war itself is abbreviated to part of Book IV, Book V, and part of Book VI, as is Antenor's embassy to the Greeks to seek Hesione's return in Book II. Joseph himself emphasizes the small unit of discourse that we have observed in Macrobius's analysis of Vergil and in the school exercises. This was, of course, facilitated by the brevity of Dares's own account of the Trojan War.

But Joseph is not merely versifying Dares's brief annals of the war. Rather he presents a series of discrete panels linked by a thin narrative thread that at times abbreviates even Dares's own skeletal account. Indeed, Christine Ratkowitsch's analysis of the descriptive digression on Teutras's tomb should caution us not to jump to conclusions about the length of Joseph's epic. Relocating emphases and making use of amplification signal Joseph's originality in rewriting Dares; this is a kind of *immutatio* whereby the *imitator* amplifies an *auctor*'s brevity or vice-versa. We have seen instances of such transformations in Macrobius's analysis of Vergil's rewriting. However, one feature of Joseph's art deserves special attention here: the purpose of the descriptions he does amplify. For example, although Antenor's expedition is at first even more succinct than in Dares, and although Joseph follows a slightly different order of events (*transmutatio*), Antenor's pause at Telamon's is described more fully and pointedly. (*Ylias* Bk. II, v. 68-74).[7] Antenor arrives precisely at the moment the Greek is about to marry Hesione. The joys of the wedding celebration contrast sharply with Hesione's grief at being compelled to marry and endure the kisses which Telamon forces upon her in front of Antenor (*Ylias* Bk. II v. 138-54, 184-87). Telamon's emphatic refusal to return Hesione aborts any reconciliation between the Trojans and the Greeks. The conventionally described marriage celebration includes songs of victory over the Trojans followed by Hesione's grief as token of predatory warfare and Telamon's angry refusal to give her up.

Joseph's debt to school exercises shows as well in his description of the principal protagonists in the war.[8] He does not include all those whom Dares describes, but he does keep some who have no obvious

---

[6] See *Doc* II.3.133-34. The precept was Horatian; see *Doc* II.3.137 and the "*Materia* Commentary" on these lines in Friis-Jensen 1990 pp. 353-54.

[7] Cf. *De exc* pp. 6, l. 22-7, l.25.

[8] Sedgwick 1930 pp. 55-59.

place at this point in the epic, or even anywhere else in it. For example, Briseida has no role in the *Ylias*; Joseph even eliminates her inconstant heart, thereby illustrating the exercise of *detractio*. Castor and Pollux are already dead by the time Joseph describes them, and Pyrrhus would have been only about five years old at the outbreak of the war.[9] However, true to the interrogative mode of topical invention, Joseph promises a full description of the "outer" and "inner" features of each person he will describe: "quo quisque animo" and "quo... ore" (*Ylias* Bk. IV, v. 35-42). The combination of *honos* and *motus pectoris* allows for the traditional distinction between ethos and pathos, a distinction that will loom large in Joseph's moral evaluation of the war and its protagonists, and which is evident as well in the description of Hesione's wedding, where the display of triumph contrasts movingly with Hesione's subjugation to her undesired wedding.

Joseph's summary statement that he will describe, in traditionally complementary terms, the outer and inner person, is exact. Each portrait is a model of inner and outer nobility, whatever slight differences there may be in color of hair, complexion, age, or inherent virtue. Even the occasional physical defect in no way detracts from the nobility of the Greeks and Trojans portrayed by Joseph — that is, the "membris inscriptus honos." In fact, all these descriptions focus more on ethos than on pathos; the latter comes to the fore in the war itself, especially as a *furor* that is not typical of their ethical character, but is certainly a pathos-induced product of war. Accordingly, not even Hector's stuttering and crossed eyes prevent him from being eloquent or from wreaking havoc on the field of battle, and they certainly do not diminish his nobility.[10] The women are masculine or virtuous; these are virtual synonyms for Joseph, reflecting their common etymon in Latin. Even Briseida has lost the mutability which Dares gave her; her joined eyebrows make her distinct, but they do not make her less comely (as in Benoît). She stands as a perfect example of feminine nobility: "Diviciis forme certant insignia

---

[9] See Ratkowitsch 1991 p. 349 n. 75. Dares justifies including the twins by alluding to the reports of those who knew them (*De exc* p. 14, ll. 12-13); Joseph has none of this. He also relocates their description at the end of his catalogue, just before Helen's, which is the last; in Dares, they come first, followed immediately by Helen. Moreover, Joseph deletes Dares's catalogues of Greek and Trojan divisions (*De exc* pp. 17-19 and 22-23); see Cizek 1994 p. 145.

[10] I wonder if there is an implicit reflection of those abnormalities characteristic of Melusine's sons and which seem to have fascinated medieval nobility; see Milin 1995 and Taylor 1996.

morum" (*Ylias* Bk. IV, v. 160) [the nobility of her character vies with the treasures of her beauty (Esler)]. *Simplex munditia*, she poses to be admired but has no story.

Helen's description is the exception. It is also the longest, and Joseph moves it to the end of his portrait gallery, thereby exemplifying his hand at *transmutatio*. Helen is indeed the only one to have a true defect: in the *Ylias*, her lust is the cause of the entire war. "Sic Helenen totam pars unica mergit et ipsum / Excitat in cladem regnis certantibus orbem" (*Ylias* Bk. IV, v. 206-07) [Thus a single part engulfs all of Helen's virtues and drives the whole world to disaster in the struggles of two kingdoms (Esler)]. The defective "part" is her liver, the seat — as the Commentator reminds us — of lust.[11] Thus, all the noble features that Joseph so carefully delineates in this longest of the portraits are of no avail against the perverse influence of her liver when in Paris's presence.

But Helen is not the only cause of Troy's fall. Just as damning, perhaps more so, some Trojans are prepared to betray their city. Notably, Joseph maps out the betrayal with topical interrogatives. "Hiis hilaris Frix certus abit, quaque hostis in urbem / Captet iter, quando veniat, que signa movendi / Militis, et cauto dispensat singula nutu" (*Ylias* Bk. VI, v. 729-31) [Reassured by these gestures, the Trojan cheerfully departs, after carefully arranging all the details: at what point the enemy will make their way into the city, when they are to come, what will be the signal to move the army (Esler)]: *qua* — on what road will the Greeks approach Troy? *quando* — when will they stealthily arrive? *que signa* — by which signs will they be guided into the city? These lines prepare readers for the capture of Troy. For knowledgeable readers, they rehearse the path the Greeks will take after the traitor lights the way. By recasting Dares in this way, Joseph in effect interrogates his source in order to rewrite it. That is, he questions the material to see how it might be explained. The questions are chosen, of course, because their answers describe the course and context of the war as Joseph construes it. Sometimes the questions are set out, as here; on other occasions, they are implicit, and we must reconstruct them if we want to understand his invention. One might easily reduce those questions to the formulaic topical scheme *Quis quid ubi...*, but they do not have to be stereotyped, since all possible questions might not be useful for a given *transmutatio* and

---

[11] *Ylias* ed. Riddehough pp. 372-73.

since others might occur to the rewriter as he or she partakes in *transmutatio*. In rewriting, a new author might elicit answers not answered by the source, as Macrobius shows Vergil doing with Homeric material. This is similar to what Matthew of Vendôme had in mind when reading Ovid and finding an incomplete *gradus amoris*, critiquing according to the standards he adopted from the *Materia*-Commentary.[12] In both medieval texts, instruction focuses the description on the predominant characteristic of the person or thing described; it assigns a role to that person — or rather, to that *persona*. The role also orients the narrative.

> Taken together, these techniques act to create a world in which the essential oneness of man, beast, [i]nanimate object, and abstraction is more significant than the differences between them. Since any individual thing is only an illustrative example of some idea, specific human beings can be thought of and referred to in terms of the abstractions which they exemplify, as appropriately as by their own names. Conversely, nouns which normally refer to single persons, such as "king," "citizen," or "soldier," can designate the condition in general rather than the individual who occupies that condition, because any single king, citizen, or soldier is important primarily as a living embodiment of the *ideals* of kingship, citizenship, or soldier-ship.[13]

This is precisely what Matthew of Vendôme teaches. Esler goes on to show the *Ylias*'s use of indirection to designate such persons. Indirection is achieved by circumlocution, a variety of amplification. Those who are named by a circumlocution identify authorial interpretation, and amplification articulates that interpretation. For example, Joseph prefers patronymics to personal names.[14] Achilles is Aeacides just as Agamemnon and Menelaus are Atrides. They are sons of their fathers and live to continue their noble line, or *race*, which was the early connotation of family. Indirection thus refers to someone or something by naming its attributes, which are articulated by topical questions. Indirection also occurs in descriptions that identify a person's role in the plot. We have seen this in the departure of the Trojan

---

[12] *Ars vers* 1.38-49; cf. also Friis-Jensen 1990 on obscure brevity (pp. 337 § 3 and 341 § 25) and incompletion (pp. 338 § 6 and 343 §§ 32 and 35).

[13] Esler trans. *Ylias* p. 110; Esler's emphasis (my correction of "ananimate" to "[i]nanimate"). On the distinction between the exemplary and the abstract, see Moos 1988 p. ix.

[14] Amplification includes patronymics. Cf. *Ars vers* 1.82 *locus a cognatione*, Gompf ed. *Ylias* "Namenindex," Bloch 1983 pp. 78-79, and Cizek 1994 pp. 301-02. On circumlocution as amplification, see Faral 1924 p. 68.

traitor from the Greek camp, where he has plotted and sworn the betrayal. The Trojan Antenor then returns to Troy on a route drawn in conformity with the treasonous act to follow (*Ylias* Bk. 6 v. 729-31). All of this — it should be emphasized — for an audience quite familiar with Dares. It is allusion for an audience of connoisseurs.

A fine appreciation of the allusive power of description is also found in Christine Ratkowitsch's analysis of Teutras's tomb. This particular description contains topical features modeled on the fates of Trojans and Greeks throughout the epic.[15] The ekphrasis is not only a description, it is also a digression which, as narrative, does not, in and of itself, justify amplification. But, as Ratkowitsch points out, it provides a model for the fate of all the participants in the Trojan War — it is a virtual *mise en abyme* of future events. Both the four ages of life (for which Horace and Macrobius may have provided the model[16]) and the inscription on the tomb state, or rather restate, in indirect interrogative mode the image of life as subject to fate, fortune, and chance.

> Hec super exiguo breviter collecta sigillo
> Fata viri, quis regis honos, quis funeris auctor,
> Quod fatum, que causa, patentque hoc singula scripto:
> "Dux Teutras, Mesis decus arvis, passus Achillem
> Ense necem sensit sceptri defensor aviti." (*Ylias* Bk. IV, v. 488-92)

> [In addition to these scenes, a simple inscription briefly describes the man's fate, his glory as king, who caused his death, how he met it and why; the details are given in these words: "King Teuthras, the glory of Mysia, succumbed to Achilles, meeting his death by the sword in defense of the sceptre of his ancestors." (Esler)]

Not surprisingly, epitaphs were a common activity of the medieval poet and were, indeed, a topic for *praeexercitamina* in the schools.[17]

---

[15] Ratkowitsch 1991 p. 349; for her analysis of the ekphrasis, see pp. 323-30. Ekphrasis is prominent in the antique romances; see Mora-Lebrun 1997.

[16] Ratkowitsch 1991 p. 327-29; *Sat* 4.3.1-5.

[17] Faral 1913 pp. 100 and 114; see, for examples, *MGH* s. v. *epitaphia*, vol. 1 p. 651, vol. 2 p. 719, and vol. 3 p. 804, *Beiträge* §§ 22, 23, and 215, and Rigg 1977-90 passim. They continue to be used in vernacular romance; see Trachsler 1996. Tent and shield decoration served a similar purpose in the *romans d'antiquité* (Baumgartner 1988).

I would add an example which Esler alludes to but does not treat in detail.[18] When Priam returns to Troy after Laomedon's death, he reconstructs a city more splendid and impregnable than before. At the end of the description of the reconstructed city Joseph names a small mound on which an altar to Jupiter stands (*Ylias* Bk. I, v. 545-49). At this fatal altar, as readers of Dares would know, Pyrrhus slaughters Priam in Book VI (v. 787-88; see *De exc* p. 6, ll. 11-12 and p. 49, l. 18). The irony is obvious, irony that is brought to the attention of knowledgeable readers by means of the description.

We now have a sense for the descriptions that abound in the *Ylias*. They are there for knowledgeable readers with a nimble memory. The object of description betokens the fate of those associated with the object. I shall return to the issue of fate and fortune in the *Ylias* in a moment.

As we discovered in Chapter Two, Macrobius's analysis of *descriptio* in Vergil includes four major features: distinction between first author (*auctor*) and rewriter (*imitator*); selection of sources (*mutuatio*); adaptation of sources (*mutatio*), or invention, especially topical invention whereby the rewriter adapts source material to a new or original version using the procedures characteristic of such invention in medieval rhetoric and poetics; and, finally, the implied audience. I shall take up each of these features of the *Ylias* in this order.

First Author and Rewriter (auctor-imitator)

Medieval writers commonly refer to the *Ylias* as "Dares," that is, by the name of its first author (Macrobius's *auctor*),[19] although they know that the poem is by Joseph. For example, when recommending the *Ylias* as a model for rewriting, Gervase of Melkley refers to it as "Dares"; elsewhere he notes that "Ioseph in Darete suo... inquit"[20] [Joseph says in his "Dares"...]. Likewise, the pupil using Gervase's treatise knew the name of the first author, Dares, and that of the twelfth-century rewriter Joseph as well as the various titles by which they were known — *Dares*, *Ylias*, and *De bello troyano*.[21] Identification

---

[18] Esler trans. *Ylias* pp. 40-41.
[19] See Gompf ed. *Ylias* p. 6.
[20] Gompf ed. *Ylias* pp. 9 and 14. The reference to Dares in *ArsGM* p. 252 s.v. "Dares (Phrygius)," 84.8 is erroneous; the passage refers to the "Phrygian" Paris, and is from the *Architrenius*.
[21] Gompf ed. *Ylias* pp. 6-19.

of a narrative by the first author (*auctor*) is not unusual. One twelfth-century poet writing on the Trojan War distinguishes between himself and the first author, Dares, whom the medieval poet is rewriting in verse. He denies any originality by remaining anonymous, attributing his twelfth-century product to Dares (*Hist Troy* p. 266, ll. 12-17). Similarly, Guido de Columnis's *De destructione Troyae* identifies its *auctores* as Dares and Dictys but not its intermediate *scriptor* Benoît, although he is obviously relying on the French author to rewrite the Trojan War.[22] No extant manuscript of the *Ylias* contains Dares, but there is evidence that some lost manuscripts did include versions by both Dares and Joseph; in these cases, it was possible to compare while reading them.[23]

Selection (mutuatio)

Joseph is selective in his choice of *materia*. Wilhelm Greif has set out in detail, book by book, what Joseph used and what he set aside.[24] For example, Dares's description of the counsel to determine what to do about Antenor's failure to bring back Hesione is omitted in Joseph, evincing *detractio*, in order to link more emphatically Priam's call to war and Paris's account of the dream in which he awarded the golden apple to Venus;[25] Joseph thus suppresses details of the council related in Dares but amplifies the Judgment. The principal abbreviations in the *Ylias* occur in the battles, which Joseph compresses into a simpler narrative that obscures the ten-year chronology which explains and justifies the numerous, sometimes lengthy battles reported

---

[22] See *Historia* p. 4. Like Macrobius in *Sat* 5, Guido is identifying only the first author rather than intermediate authors, as in *Sat* 6. Cf. *Beiträge* § 388 for another example, and Moos 1976 p. 110 on the *De bello troyano*.

[23] Gompf ed. *Ylias* pp. 14-15 (nos. 13-14); Stohlmann ed. *Hist Troy* pp. 201-02. On the special relation between prose and verse versions of the same matter, see Curtius 1954 pp. 157-58.

[24] Joseph includes material suggesting that he used a manuscript close to Meister's *G* (= Sankt Gallen Stiftsbibliothek 197), which contains a summary of Dictys similar to Joseph's conclusion (Meister ed. *De exc* pp. vi-vii, Greif 1886 p. 131; on this manuscript, see Stohlmann ed. *Hist Troy* pp. 41-52, Munk Olsen 1982-89 vol. 1 pp. 376-77 and 382). Bate ed. *Ylias* identifies the chapters in Dares which Joseph rewrites in the notes to his edition and translation. See also Sarradin 1878, esp. chap. 5.

[25] Greif 1886 p. 132. On Venus's role in the *Ylias*, see Dunkle 1987 pp. 208-10. The operation is similar to that used in rewriting the Bible in Christian epic; see Roberts 1985.

by Dares and amplified by Benoît.[26] Joseph also draws on another
source to rewrite the battles he otherwise abbreviates or excises from
Dares, most notably, Statius.[27] Thus, like Vergil in Macrobius's interpretation, Joseph of Exeter looked beyond his first author for models
of combat, apparently seeking out models that invoke the horror of
war,[28] and clerically condemning combat not directed against non-
Christians (cf. *Ylias* Bk. VI, v. 962-69).

Since Greif's study, other scholars have identified near quotations
or echoes in the *Ylias*, in effect replicating the scale treated in Macrobius's Book VI — that is, the adaptation of passages of no more than
one or two lines.[29] Especially prominent are Joseph's use of Vergil,
Juvenal, and Boethius. Thus, Vergil provides the motif of destiny and
fortune, Juvenal illustrates the satirical mode, and Boethius sets the
moral standard and world view that reconciles the seemingly incon-
gruous blend of epic and satirical modes in the *Ylias*. For example,
Joseph's conception of destiny seems to echo that expressed by
Aeneas: "Venerat extremi revoluto stamine pensi / Fatorum
promissa dies, decimusque rotabat / Sferatum Titana labor" (*Ylias*
Bk. VI, v. 660-62) [The day promised by the Fates had come, the
thread of the last allotted skein having run out, and the tenth year of
war brought the hoped-for day (Esler)]. Likewise, Macrobius comments on two versions of the destiny motif in Vergil (*Sat* 5.1.8-11), the
one to illustrate brevity — "campos ubi Troia fuit" (*Aen* III, v. 11)
[the plains where once was Troy] — and the other prolixity.

> venit summa dies et ineluctabile tempus
> Dardaniae. Fuimus Troes, fuit Ilium et ingens
> gloria Teucrorum, ferus omnia Iuppiter Argos
> transtulit; incensa Danai dominantur in urbe.
>   (*Aen* II, v. 324-27)

[It is come — the last day and inevitable hour for Troy. We
Trojans are not, Ilium is not, and the great glory of the
Teucrians; in wrath Jupiter has taken all away to Argos; our city
is aflame, and in it the Greeks are lords.]

---

[26] Greif 1886 pp. 137-40.

[27] Greif 1886 pp. 136-37 and 139.

[28] Especially Statius; see Greif 1886 passim.

[29] Greif 1886, Sedgwick 1930, Riddehough ed. Notes pp. 197-224 (see also those
to the Paris commentary, pp. 430-45), Gompf ed. *Ylias* notes passim and Ratkowitsch
1991 pp. 350-52.

Clearly, Joseph's insertions or amplifications illustrate the variety of sources he draws on to complete and interpret his rewriting of Dares.

Adaptation (mutatio)

In Joseph's scheme of things this last day was not inevitable, as it was for Vergil's Aeneas.

> Florebant Asie fines, florebat opimis
> Troia suis et rege potens et milite tuta,
> Nec superos nec fata timens. Victoria Graium
> Mentito Calcante[30] brevi cessisset, at hostis
> Indigena et, qua nil gravius, privata nocendi
> Copia Testoriden vatem facit; invidet ipse,
> Ipse urbem civis aperit. (*Ylias* Bk. VI, v. 740-46)

[The lands of Asia were flourishing, Troy was flourishing in her own wealth, powerful in her king and secure in her army, fearing neither gods nor Fates. The victory of the Greeks would quickly have come to naught, giving the lie to Calchas; but the enemy within, and the power of private individuals to subvert — than which nothing is more dangerous — make a true prophet of the son of Thestor. It is the citizens, the citizens themselves, who hate their own city and open its gates to the enemy. (Esler)]

Treachery and usurpation bring down Troy, not ineluctable destiny. This is a major transformation of the traditional explanation for the fall of Troy. The key to such adaptation in the *Ylias* — *mutatio* — is the most important kind of adaptation in Joseph's poem. It reveals the originality of the new version as well as the social, moral, and political context in which it is to be read. Recognition of sources and the comparison of them with their adaptation enhances the quality and significance of such contextualized reception. What did Joseph abbreviate or delete? What did he add or amplify? Why did he make these adaptations?

To answer these questions, let us begin with the abbreviations and deletions. Joseph reduces Dares's annals of the ten year war to a few exemplary combats and deaths. Book IV relates only the combat in

---

[30] On my correction of text, see Gompf's Index p. 232 s.v. "Calcas."

Mysia; yet it amplifies Teutras's death and his tomb in a paradigmatic digression that anticipates Troy's fate in Teutras's. Obviously,
for Joseph, the admonition to lengthen what is brief and abbreviate
what is lengthy in the source is not a perfunctory operation. In Book
V, a series of major deaths culminates in Hector's own death, exemplifying *gradatio*; Book VI relates Achilles's death at mid-point and the
death of Priam and destruction of Troy itself at the end. These adaptations illustrate two senses of the term "description" in Macrobius.
First, description appears as a summary statement of what happens.[31]
But as a summary, it also emphasizes that device for abbreviation in
Geoffrey of Vinsauf's sense of that term: "Plurima perstringat paucis
expressa locutrix / Emphasis" (*Poetria nova* v. 693-94) [Let emphasis
be spokesman, saying much in few words (Nims)]. Thus, "manus
artificis multas ita conflet in unam, / Mentis ut intuitu multae vi-
deantur in una. / Hac brevitate potes longum succingere thema"
(*Poetria nova* v. 700-702) [Let the craftsman's skill effect a fusion of
many concepts in one, so that many may be seen in a single glance of
the mind (Nims)]. Macrobius too refers to brevity as a desirable feature of rewriting (*Sat* 5.1.7), using Sallust as his exemplar. Accordingly, we can see that Joseph greatly reduces the battles he found in
Dares to the point that, in Geoffrey's words, they all seem to blend
into one.

   Geoffrey's *Documentum* gives additional information on the art and
aims of abbreviation of particular relevance to the reading of the
Ylias. According to the *Documentum*, there are two kinds of emphasis.
The first kind occurs when one refers to a characteristic feature of a
person or thing rather than to a name, as in "Clementia vestra meae
subveniat necessitati" (*Doc* II.2.33) [may your clemency assist my
need]. The second kind occurs when the name of a person or thing
stands for a character trait, as in "Medea est ipsum scelus" (*Doc*
II.2.34) [Medea is crime itself]. Joseph's use of patronymics illustrates
such emphasis. More importantly, he not only compressed Dares into
a few indistinctly separated battles, he also focused on specific individuals who exemplify the *furor* that drives all the warriors into com-

---

[31] See the Admont commentary in *Ylias* ed. Riddehough p. 448: "Est...
descrip[sio] breuis summatim futuri tractatus comprehensio" [description is a brief
summation of what is to be treated]; if one deletes the adjective *futurus*, such description becomes a definition of an abbreviated plot — abbreviated in comparison to the
length of its source, and thus analogous to the plot summary Benoît inserts between
the *Troie*'s prologue and narrative.

bat, a madness exposing them to whatever destiny, fortune, or chance may do with them.

Joseph added to or amplified whatever revealed his sense of the conflict. For, as all the arts of poetry state, dilation should stress what is paramount in a person, thing, or action.[32] Macrobius shows that Vergil is remarkable mostly for his amplifications.[33] Similarly, when Joseph comes to certain parts of his matter neglected by the first author, he expands on those features, devoting his amplifications to the fury of war. He is specific from the outset.

> Iam libera Marti
> Laxat frena Furor, stimulat Bellona volentes,
> Mars cogit dubios. Ingens per castra furentis
> Interpres animi clamor tonat, arma capessunt,
> Arma fremunt, augent lituique tubeque tumultum
> Et responsuris invitant vocibus Eccho. (*Ylias* Bk. IV, v. 512-17)

[Now fury gives Mars free rein; Bellona spurs on the willing, Mars coerces those who hang back; through the camp thunders a mighty shout, expressing their furious mood; they snatch up their arms with a roar. Trumpets and clarions increase the tumult, and Echo urges them on with responsive cries. (Esler)]

This passage shows men possessed; it emphasizes the furious passions of war by activating the gods of war and by dilating the fury that drives all combatants, both brave and cowardly, into violence.

Framing the furor and dominating the entire poem are the powers of fate and fortune. They are diversely named or personified, and their context allows for a wide range of meanings within the semantic fields of words like *fatum* and *fata*, *fortuna*, *casus*, and the verb *destinare*.[34] Despite more or less obvious differences in semantic range that occur in specific instances,[35] the vocabulary for fortune and fate tends to be

---

[32] *ArsPoet* v. 114-18 and 156-78; *Ars vers* 1.39-40, 42, 44-46, and 65-71; *Poetria nova* v. 1842-51, as in the examples v. 554-667; *Doc* II.3.138-39.

[33] See the references in *Sat* Book IV to *augere* (4.2.6, 4.2.10, 4.3.7, 4.4.2, 4.4.19, 4.5.3, 4.5.4, 4.6.1, and 4.6.5) and *minuere* (4.5.4 and 4.5.5).

[34] For example, *fatum* (*fata*) Bk. I v. 1, 70, 96, 101-02, 136, etc.; *fortuna* Bk. I v. 42, 226, 238, 471, etc.; *casus* Bk. I v. 75, 225, 463, II v. 39, 222, etc.

[35] For example, Ratkowitsch 1991 p. 349 n. 76 identifies *fortuna* as the motif that best expresses the meaning of the *Ylias*. This is true if one allows the word to include the range of meanings suggested by the words in the immediately preceding note,

used interchangeably in most cases. For example, the following brief, but representative passage regarding Priam's military expedition during which the first destruction of Troy occurs includes a number of "fortune words" without significantly discriminating among them.

> Hiis aberat Priamus aliam servatus in iram
> Fatorum casusque alios. Cui Marte secundo
> Eoos populata Friges victoria leta
> Faveret et reduci comites plausere triumphi.[36]
>
> (*Ylias* Bk. I, v. 462-65)

[Priam had been absent from this war, preserved for other misfortunes and a different wrath of the fates. Joyous victory had blessed him with a successful campaign to ravage Eastern Phrygia and his comrades applauded him on his triumphal return (Bate).]

But, as so often in the *Ylias*, good fortune draws the heedless victim to his or her fate.[37] The same holds for Priam, as Joseph again evokes the wide range of meanings that jumble together as fate and fortune cooperate.

> Dura hominum Lachesis! Sors perfida! Luditur anceps
> Imperium: Priamus natales ampliat agros,
> Troia ruit; sceptroque novus dum queritur orbis,
> Sceptri nutat honos; faustos in regna meatus
> Fata dabant reduci[,][38] sed dira, sed aspera donis
> Invidit Fortuna suis, que, cum ardua donet,
> Gustatos graviore favor ulciscitur ira. (*Ylias* I, v. 466-72)

[O harsh fates of men! O perfidious chance! His double empire is mocked. Priam increases his native lands while Troy itself falls. While new territory is sought for his rule the glory of that rule is tottering. The fates were giving him a successful return journey to his kingdom but cruel, harsh chance begrudges him her gifts (Bate).]

---

where *fatum/fata* occur more frequently. Joseph's usage corresponds to practice in contemporary Latin historiography; see Mégier 1997 esp. pp. 61-62 and 65.

[36] Ironically, the Greeks' own shout of victory ("penetrantque ad sidera plausu," Bk. I v. 461) [Their shouts reach the sky (Bate)] is still ringing in the public's ears.

[37] This is true for Hector and Achilles; see Ratkowitsch 1991 pp. 341-43, 345-46.

[38] As in Bate's edition.

As this passage shows, Fate and Fortune are personified and exemplified, and thus even assume the shape and special concerns of specific gods and goddesses.

Indeed, goddesses are instrumental in carrying out the will of fate, as the Fates become Atropos, Clotho, and Lachesis, Erinis and Allecto, or the Parcae.[39] Fortune follows gods or goddesses as they intervene in their own various ways in the course of events, even to the point of determining how battles and combats turn out. Especially obvious is the case of Hector, on whom Juno and Minerva[40] avenge their defeat in the Judgment of Paris by facilitating the designs of Fortune intent on destroying Troy and the major obstacle to that destruction, Hector. Achilles was reluctant to engage Hector; however, on the fatal day, "Iuno negantem / Sollicitat, stimulat Pallas pariterque precantes / Prebent hec animos, hec iras, utraque vires." (*Ylias* Bk. V, v. 487-89)[41] [despite his reluctance he is encouraged by Juno and goaded on by Pallas; the entreaties of both inspire him, the one with courage, the other with wrath, and both with strength. (Esler)] Of course, Venus is the principal source of conflict in the poem; but she disappears when violence begins and is not present at any battle.

Personified or deified agents are ambiguous too as to whether they act in conformity with fate or whether they intervene for their own purposes and, thus, function haphazardly, as fortune itself can. But whatever their roles, they are essentially diabolic powers, at least by implication; Joseph explains oracles in this way.[42] But he does not insist on this identification as much as later writers will, preferring, like Boethius in the *De consolatione*, to stress the human features of passion in relation to destiny and fortune. Most combattants have to

---

[39] See these names in Gompf ed. *Ylias* "Namenindex."

[40] Minerva here is not the intellectual ideal of the philosophers but represents both war, art, and learning (cf. Bate ed. *Ylias* p. 180 to v. 343 note); in this she comes closer to the warlike Pallas of the *Eneas* (Poirion 1978 p. 215).

[41] Cf. Ratkowitsch 1991 p. 342. Joseph does not fault Homer for introducing them into combat as do Dares and Benoît de Sainte-Maure, but he does attack the pagans' false faith (for example, *Ylias* Bk. 6 v. 922-25). On the gods in the anonymous *Historia Troyana*, see Stohlmann ed. pp. 144-45.

[42] *Ylias* Bk. IV v. 238-40, where *hostis* = the devil; cf. Σ p. 374: "assignat causam quare huiusmodi pronostica quandoque prouentum habeant... Diabolo ministrante" to v. 239 (238 in Riddehough's edition) and "insidians... hostis... fallit" [he explains why such predictions sometimes are true... the Devil is the agent.... The watchful devil... deceives].

die, and their fate is absolutely certain. But in the *Ylias* men, blind to all else (*mens ceca, Ylias* Bk. I, v. 107), seek death and, in so doing, form ("creavit", *Ylias* Bk. I, v. 107) their own idols, allegorically speaking, only to become victims to fate before their time in pursuit of false goods like those Boethius identifies and condemns. The gods, which Joseph describes as projections of the self through human imagination and art, cooperate as men do with fate, fortune, and chance to undo even the best — those like, for example, Agamemnon (or, indeed, Boethius himself), who almost seems to escape destruction. Thus, when Agamemnon agrees to cooperate in achieving the goals of the Greek expedition by surrendering his command of the army to Palamede — showing in exemplary fashion that he is prepared to subordinate personal glory to the goals of the common expedition — his reasoning is unimpeachable; indeed, it contrasts sharply with the self-seeking glory of most heroes on both sides, including Palamede, who wants to replace him. "Nil refert," Agamemnon exclaims, "quis, ubi, quando, sed qualiter et quid / Factum. Durabunt actus et transiet actor." (*Ylias* Bk. VI, v. 33-34) [It matters not at all by whom, where, or when the deed is done, but what is done and how: the acts will endure, though their author will pass away (Esler)] Prudently, Agamemnon chooses to rest on his own possessions: "Hiis addit se iure frui potiore Micenis / Et stabilem regnare domi" (*Ylias* Bk. VI, v. 35-36) [To these considerations he adds that he can now exercise a firmer control over Mycenae, and enjoy a stable reign at home (Esler)]. The irony is profound. Teutras's tomb stands as a reminder of the uncertainty of justice, as does Palamede's own swift demise bringing Agamemnon back into command.[43] In the *Ylias*, this is not justice, but fate. At the end of the war, the Mycenaean king returns to his "stable" and "just" realm only to be assassinated. Joseph's irony is vicious.

> Quid, stulte, superbis?
> Ultima felices etas facit. En habet Argos
> Nil bellis questus, nil equore passus Atrides;
> Victorem coniunx iugulum secat, audet adulter
> Insidiis mactare ducem. (*Ylias* Bk.VI, v. 924-28)

---

[43] Ratkowitsch 1991 pp. 342 and 343.

[Why do you exult, foolish one? Only the last age makes happy men: lo, the son of Atreus has Argos, he has suffered no losses in the war nor at sea; but his wife slits the conqueror's throat, and her seducer boldly slaughters his king by treachery. (Esler)]

These lines are clearly Boethian allusions.[44]

The supreme irony of fate is, however, no doubt illustrated best in Helen. She alone comes through unscathed to glory in her achievements. "Quin ipsa superbit / Accendisse duces, lacerasse in prelia mundum, / Infamem forme titulum lucrata pudende." (*Ylias* Bk. VI, v. 956-58) [But she is proud to have inflamed the kings and torn the world apart in war, and she is rewarded with the infamous renown of a shameful beauty (Esler).] Like Venus, she takes her prize, then escapes from the violence she causes.[45]

Human fury aids and abets fate and fortune. Heedless of reason or moderation, *furor* drives its victims to action in the *Ylias*; with *mens ceca*, mortals remain oblivious to the right path. Indeed, they are predetermined to failure by ignorance of the true faith. Joseph underscores the absence of true faith, or *veri sacra fides*, that alone can liberate men from fate and fortune, yet recourse to faith exceeds the grasp of Greeks and Trojans born before Christ.[46] Still they had another source of stability and direction: sufficiency. Awareness of this virtue, which was not denied the pagans, could guide them in resisting the assembled powers of fate and fortune as well as opening their eyes to their own errors and misprisions. Yet, evoking the origin of the whole Trojan tragedy, Joseph comments wryly on Peleus's envy and Jason's avarice: "Egeste sic Ditis opes, quas ambitus audax, / Quas predo pallens Stigiis extorquet ab antris, / Sufficiunt?" (*Ylias* Bk. I, v. 65-67) [Did not the riches of Pluto, mined from the earth and hewn out of the Stygian caves by the bold ambition of the pallid plundering miner, suffice? (Bate)] The Boethian theme of sufficiency rings loud and clear in the admonitory lines that follow.

---

[44] Cf. King 1985 pp. 54-60 and Ratkowitsch 1991 pp. 347-48.

[45] See *Ylias* Bk. II, v. 435-42, and Dunkle 1987 pp. 212-13. The fact that Minerva faults Venus for this habit does not make it less true in the *Ylias*. Ratkowitsch 1991 p. 340 refers to Helen's "moral fall." However, there is no evidence that her fall causes her any physical or moral anguish, except by implication; cf. Boethius: "In quo perspicuum est numquam bonis praemia, numquam sua sceleribus deesse supplicia." (*De cons* IV Pr 3, 1) [wherefore it is obvious that the good never lack rewards, while the evil never escape punishment.]

[46] *Ylias* Bk. I v. 6-7, 27-29, 107; IV v. 215-45; VI v. 922-23.

> Cui iam satis est, quod regna, quod urbes
> Ipsaque quod pateant rapiendis Tartara gazis?
> Itur in ignotos fluctus ultroque procellis
> Insultare iuvat et soli vivere fato. (*Ylias* Bk. I, v. 67-70)

[For whom now then is it enough that kingdoms, cities and even Hell itself allow their riches to be stolen? Men ventured into unknown waters and moreover rejoiced in facing storms and living by fate alone (Bate).]

Soli vivere fato models everyone's conduct in the *Ylias*. Whether the fate comes from without or within, it is essentially the same when blind minds live for the false goods of insufficiency. Boethius names five such false goods: power, fame, wealth, honor, and bodily pleasure; we find them all sought after in the *Ylias*. Since these powers prevail where Christian faith is lacking, and since they depend on changeable Fortune, who destributes her favors and blows indiscriminately, all the participants in the war, including even those who exercise some rational moderation of their violence, are victims of what happens, whether as good or bad fortune. Hence, Helen's escape. Similarly, Aeneas, Antenor, and Telephus happen — "fortunately" — to survive unscathed.

Importantly here, Joseph's *modus agendi* recalls that of the *prae-exercitamina*. That is, he chooses in Dares the sections he wishes to amplify in the light of a Boethian Christian ethic while reducing or eliminating others that do not usefully exemplify that ethic. An extremely thin line of narrative links these "purple patches."[47] For example, the ten-year war which occupies most of Dares's *De excidio* is set forth only in exemplary portraits in the last two books of the *Ylias*, illustrating rather than detailing all the events in the war. This is quite different from Benoît's approach, and the difference is important.

Four moments dominate the last two books of the *Ylias*: Teutras's death at the end of Book IV, Hector's death at the end of Book V, Achilles's death at the mid-point of Book VI, and Priam's death at its end. The battles that surround these events illustrate mounting and subsiding *furor*. The action is violent, the actors grow ever more mad.

---

[47] On the positive sense of "purple patches" in medieval poetics, see Quadlbauer 1980b.

Joseph sums it up, illustrating *summa facti* as topos,[48] when we near the end of Book V and Hector's death:

> Gaudia Martis
> Horrida deliciasque truces effervere passim
> Aspiceres. Fluit huic in vultus pulchra genarum
> Rapta dies, mento hic linguaque et nare recisa
> Informes aperit rictus; hiis auris adempta,
> Hiis manus, hiis nutat humerus. Pars viscera lapsa
> Sustentat retinente manu, pars poplite ceso
> Labitur, at manibus nitens sese eripit hosti.
> Hinc capitum largus stagnat cruor, inde relicti
> In cumulum surgunt trunci currusque retardant.[49]
>
> (*Ylias* Bk. V, v. 368-77)

[Everywhere you would have seen Mars' terrible joys and grim delights seething. One man's handsome eyes are torn from their sockets and slide down over his face; another, his nose, tongue, and chin slashed off, opens a deformed maw; others are deprived of an ear, others of a hand, another's shoulder is ready to fall; some support their torn-out entrails with restraining hands; some, their legs cut off, escape the enemy's clutches by dragging themselves along on their hands. Here, blood running from heads forms a pool; over there severed limbs, left behind, rise in a heap and impede the chariots (Esler).]

Benoît scatters scenes like this throughout the *Troie*, as we shall see. But unlike his French predecessor, Joseph emphasizes the physical conflict in one nightmarish summation that accumulates and focuses the violence and madness of conflict. There is no sense of *dulce et decorum est pro patria mori* — we are closer to Statius, but also to Wilfred Owen in the *Ylias*'s depiction of martial violence.

This passage also illustrates how the treatises' admonition to stress what is neglected by the first author but eliminate what seems superfluous can be effective. The annals of conflict in Dares reveal little of the savage fury with which men slaughter and maim one another.

---

[48] See *Ars vers* 1.95.

[49] Gompf ed. *Ylias* p. 171 note finds a model for v. 373 in Ovid's *Metamorphoses*. Riddehough ed. *Ylias* p. 213 to v. 372ᵃ (= v. 373 in Gompf's edition) notes Sidonius and the *Alexandreis*. On this passage, see Riddehough 1949 p. 389.

Joseph portrays a single yet commonplace description of violence that is meted out equally on both sides: "ita cedes / Alternant hinc inde pares et funera librant" (Bk. V, v. 355-56) [thus equal slaughter occurs, now on one side, now on the other, and the casualties are balanced (Esler)]. All of this results from and heightens as well the sense of fury.

In the midst of this violence, Fortune works her ways, setting Hector up for a fall (Bk. V, v. 402-07) by blinding him to the fate she reveals to him in Andromache's dream.[50] Joseph's description of her sleep also functions as a model for the prophetic dream. Holding tight to her husband, questioning him on the day's events, "sopita," Andromache "marito / Incubat" (Bk. V, v. 429-30) — falling asleep she clings to her husband. But *incubare* is a word rich with semantic potential in the *Ylias*. It suggests Andromache lying prone on her husband. Her physical intimacy recalls Helen after she surrenders to her lust, flinging herself onto Paris — "pectore toto / Incumbens gremium solvit" (Bk. III, v. 330-31)[51] [lying on him with her whole body, she opens her legs (Bate)]. But Andromache is overcome by fear, not lust; her fears may be "effeminate" in Joseph's eyes (Bk. V, v. 446-47), but her dreams while clinging to Hector are prophetic. Indeed, *incubare* has not only sexual overtones, it also connotes sleeping in a temple in order to have a prophetic dream. Andromache, literally and figuratively brooding on her husband, learns his fate — a fate she is unable to prevent because of Hector's own incredulity, so that she herself goes mad with frustration (Bk. V, v. 449).

Insofar as Dares offers a reason for the fall of Troy, it lies in the domino effect deriving from Peleus's fear of Jason (*De exc* p. 3, ll. 4-8). This fear inspires him to send Jason on the expedition to the Golden Fleece, hoping and, indeed, confident that his nephew will die in the effort. The unfortunate stop at Troy is merely an adventure on that quest, but an adventure which, because of Laomedon's inhospitality, leads by cause and effect to war and the two destructions of Troy.

---

[50] The Commentary to v. 428 in Riddehough ed. *Ylias* p. 395 explains how Andromache passes from *insomnium* to *somnium* — that is, from the erroneous dreams of first stage sleeping to the true revelations of deep sleep.

[51] On the fury of lust evoked in this description, see Bate ed. *Ylias* p. 192 note to v. 330-33. Both he and Gompf note the allusion to Vergil *Aeneid* I, v. 717-22, where Dido begins to forget her deceased husband; on this "fabula lascivientis Didonis," see *Sat* 5.17.5 [the fable of a lusting Dido]. On Joseph's use of the stereotype of feminine beauty illustrated by Matthew's portrait of "Helen," see Tilliette 1993.

Hence, the human origin or first cause is the fear shared by both Peleus and Laomedon that they will lose their lands. The abductions of Hesione and of Helen are topical stages in war, part of the spiraling chain of events leading to the fall of Troy as well as to the diverse Greek catastrophes.

Joseph changes all this. For him, Helen is the cause of the war, and lust explains her actions. To be sure, Helen is also Venus's agent, and her own fate mirrors Venus's own skill in slipping away from any violence which she causes. Moreover, Venus personifies lust in the *Ylias* just as Helen exemplifies it; the goddess's role fits, by indirection, into Joseph's Christian world insofar as gods and goddesses exist only as projected vices or as devils. More importantly here, to make Helen out as cause of the war Joseph must rewrite Dares. He therefore expounds on her guilt but abbreviates Peleus's by obscuring his motivation. In Joseph, Jason and his comrades set out for the Golden Fleece because they are young men eager for adventure. "Casus pelagi coniurat in omnes / Pars mirata ratem, pars fame prona petende, / Pars mundum visura novum gentesque remotas." (*Ylias* Bk. I, v. 75-77) [A common oath, whatever the dangers of the sea, was sworn by some who admired the boat, others keen on earning fame and others who wanted to see a new world and distant peoples (Bate).] Only upon their successful return do we learn of Peleus's distress, as a narrator's afterthought (Bk. I, v. 218-47); indeed, his interior monologue is itself obscure enough for the Σ glossator to add an explanation based on Dares.[52] The fate of Hesione, the Judgment of Paris, and the war itself are all evoked, to be sure. And, although Helen is cast in as lurid a light as possible — and she certainly appears to be lusty — her happy fate is typical of Venus's own power and of how even difficult deities proclaim the ways of fate and fortune.

> Omnifico vultu mentita favorem
> Amplexum in planctus solvit, defederat urbes,
> Arces frangit et in subitum rapit omnia Martem.
> Cum ventum in cedes, cedit; cum prelia fervent,
> Frigescit. Tunc arma iuvant, tunc Pallas in usu
> Et Venus in probris. Commercia turpia: molles

---

[52] See Riddehough ed. *Ylias* p. 332 to v. 210 (v. 218 in Gompf's edition).

Exacuit, duros emasculat et rapit orbem
In predam, cui preda venit. (*Ylias* Bk. II, v. 435-42)

[With her changeable face she lies when she offers you her protection, she turns love into grief. She causes cities to break trea-
ties, destroys citadels and drives everything into sudden conflict.
When the actual fighting starts she leaves; in the heat of battle
she grows cold. That is when weapons are useful, that is when
Pallas is needed and Venus is reviled. Her changes are disgust-
ing: she makes the weak brave, emasculates the hard men and
makes the world her prey when she comes as prey for it (Bate).]

Venus is goddess of love, not of violence. Still, she knows how to use
violence to achieve her own ends. Helen is no different. After quickly
relating the disastrous return of the Greek heroes, Joseph catches her
moment of proud introspection after returning unscathed to Sparta.
She glories in the role fate cast her in — to set the world on fire! (*Ylias*
Bk. VI, v. 956-57)

In the world of the *Ylias*, it is humanity's blind, furious addiction to
Boethius's false goods that does Troy in and, ultimately, the Greeks
themselves. Helen personifies addiction to pleasure; Paris and, ultimately, Troy itself and most of the Greeks are her victims. Motivation for war is also responsibility for war, as in Helen's case. It is
useful to envisage the cause of Joseph's version of the Trojan War not
in terms of Helen or of Peleus's fear, *chiquenaudes* that set events in
motion, but rather in terms of the four Aristotelian causes already
familiar in Joseph's time from the *accessus* tradition.[53] The four causes
— efficient, formal, material, and final— translate into persons responsible for actions in Joseph's Christian world view. In this scheme
four agents are responsible for the war and, ultimately, the destruction of Troy and of the Greeks themselves. They are, in order,
Peleus, Laomedon, Helen, and Paris. The first cause and, therefore,
the one who begins the plot[54] — albeit rather obscurely, as we have

---

[53] See, for example, Minnis 1984 pp. 28-29.
[54] In the *Ovide moralisé*, a tradition surfaces that both Joseph and Benoît ignore.
According to this tradition, Laomedon causes the first destruction of Troy and the
ensuing events when he refuses to pay Neptune and Apollo the reward he promised
them when they built Troy. In this scheme, Laomedon is the first cause and is
sufficient himself to explain all that follows; see Demats 1973 pp. 83-84, Jung 1996
pp. 621-28, and Possamaï-Perez 1997 pp. 100-101.

observed — is Peleus. By sending Jason in quest of the Golden Fleece, he begins the concatenation of events that lead to the ensuing catastrophes. Interestingly, Peleus's betrayal of Jason aborts because Jason achieves his quest. Thus, although Peleus puts events into motion as efficient cause, his action is not sufficient to account for all that follows. Choices are made independently of Peleus, and these multiply the causes. Peleus's betrayal — his inhospitality to his nephew — is a model for Laomedon's own inhospitality to the Greeks. Hence, inhospitality, as formal cause, models so much inhospitality to come — for example, that shown to Antenor by the Greeks or to Ulysses and Diomede by the Trojans. Laomedon's betrayal breaks a universal custom and awakens in the Greeks, especially Hercules, a desire for vengeance that precipitates the first destruction and sack of Troy. As part of the spoils of war, Hesione is abducted,[55] and Hercules gives her to Telamon as reward for entering Troy first. When Priam attempts to retrieve his sister the Greeks refuse; indeed, they deny any hospitality to his messenger Antenor while Telamon forces Hesione to marry him against her will. The betrayal of Hesione is a betrayal of the Trojans, who decide thereupon to take vengeance. At this point Helen enters the plot. Her beauty, surely a material cause, attracts Paris, and her lust makes her willingly meet his passion. Paris thereby realizes his own destiny as final cause: he is Troy's firebrand. Hecuba dreamed of this before his birth, and Priam unsuccessfully tried to escape fate by having his son exposed after birth (cf. *Ylias* Bk.III, v. 155-59).[56]

In all four causes, even those involving destiny, Joseph retains the option of exercising free will that is necessary for individual responsibility. Refusal to heed warnings or assume responsibility is paradigmatic in all these cases. The domination of passion — *furor* — is almost universal. For this reason Joseph did not need to distinguish between the different manifestations of powers like fate or destiny, fortune, and chance; all of them depend on human irrationality. Even in cases where such rationality is apparent — for example, in the cases of Agamemnon or Cassandra — the harm done is the fault

---

[55] On abduction as a motif in the Troy legend, see Kelly 1995b pp. 232-33; cf. Bate ed. *Ylias* p. 188 note to v. 155.

[56] As with the traditional account of Laomedon's betrayal of the gods, neither Joseph nor Benoît make anything of Paris's betrayal of Oenone, who appears in neither work; she is mentioned in Dictys as his wife, which makes Helen Paris's concubine, as Dictys makes no reference to their marriage.

and responsibility of others; this conforms to the Boethian concept of true happiness denied even to the good. Helen's escape from harm is another indication that these irrational powers do not preclude happiness of a kind. Is Helen one of the "successfully" evil, that is, one who, as Boethius phrases it,[57] seems to escape punishment and live on happily? Joseph does not answer this implied question.

Implied Audiences

Joseph's rewriting of Dares is obviously thoroughgoing and systematic. To see how his implied audience, learned in Latin and its canonical authors, heard his *Ylias*, we may go back to the epic's beginning and its topical questions.

> Quid memorem Esonide duras incumbere leges
> Oëte imperio, quid semina iacta, quid hostes
> Terrigenas Martisque boves sevique draconis
> Excubias? (*Ylias* Bk. I, v. 182-85)

> [Why should I recount the harsh terms imposed on Jason, son of Aeson, by Aeetes' orders, or the seeds that were sown, or the earthborn adversaries, or the bulls of Mars, or the watchfulness of the cruel dragon? (Bate)]

Unlike the Glasgow *praeexercitamina*, Joseph does not literally answer his topical questions. His implied audience already knows the answers, educated as it was on the Trojan War, no doubt familiar with Dares, Vergil, and the *Ilias latina* as well as with shorter poems that treat different features of that war, some of which they might have written themselves. Joseph "assumes that his reader is already so intimately acquainted with classical mythology that even the most allusive and compressed reference will call to mind all the details of a story with sufficient clarity."[58] This stands in stark contrast to Benoît's *Roman de Troie*. This fundamental difference occurs because Benoît's

---

[57] *De cons* Book 4 Prose 4.

[58] Esler trans. *Ylias* p. 83. The audience would have to be elite by twelfth-century standards (cf. Riddehough 1947). The Commentaries on the *Ylias* suggest proficient readers who, nonetheless, fall short of the high standards Esler evokes. Ziolkowski 1985 treats audiences for which play on even recondite grammatical terminology was a source of both humor and moral admonition.

implied audience is a vernacular audience ignorant of Latin. He himself points out in the *Troie* Prologue that he is telling the Trojan War, which is extant in many versions, for audiences that do not know Latin and cannot therefore read those works (*Troie* v. 33-39).[59] Further evidence of this radical difference between the Latin and the vernacular audiences is the virtual resumé of Dares and Dictys which Benoît inserts between the Prologue and the actual plot (*Troie* v. 145-709). Joseph's Latin language audience apparently does not require a resumé. He seems to assume that it already knows or can quickly consult Dares and Dictys. For those who need additional help, there are some commentaries.[60]

Description in Benoît's Troie

However, if we recall Chrétien's reference to the art of description, a different question arises. Is Benoît's *art* the same as Joseph's and different only insofar as they imply different audiences? Both poets are retelling the story of the Trojan War. Both rely on Dares, although neither merely paraphrases him. Yet each *describes* the Trojan War differently — and I am using *describe* with the broad range of Latin meanings we identified in Chapter Two of this study. Joseph's descriptions are conventional by the standards of twelfth-century Latin poetics. A. K. Bate judges this to be a fatal flaw. For, he asserts, while the French vernacular writers at Henry II's court were discovering the value of narrative, the Latin writers doggedly continued to immerse themselves in descriptive flourish.[61] We must therefore search for Benoît's "immanent poetics" as we have done for Joseph's.

Both Benoît and Joseph evoke the immoderation exemplified by Jason's voyage to Colchis. His is the first boat to venture out to sea. Perhaps coincidentally, Benoît likens his own romance and his goals

---

[59] On this "hierarchy of interpretations," see Sullivan 1985 (quote p. 353), and Baumgartner 1987 pp. 42-44.

[60] On the Joseph commentaries, see Riddehough ed. *Ylias* pp. 300-17; the Commentator thinks Joseph left them out because the events were too "fabulous" (*fabulosa*) (p. 331). Strasbourg BN and Univ 14, an eleventh-century manuscript, contains Dares and Dictys together with all of the extant *Saturnalia* (La Penna 1953 p. 240, Munk Olsen 1982-89 vol. 1 pp. 377 and 382).

[61] Bate 1991 pp. 8-9 and Zink 1981; cf. Zink 1984 and 1996 p. 37 on this "tendance constante de la littérature française face à ses modèles latins" to emphasize their narrative potential.

as writer to the traditional motif of writing as a sea voyage.[62] His *Roman de Troie* too is a colossal, perhaps immoderate, undertaking. He inserts other tales in the vernacular into it, by allusions to their events. The *Troie* embraces in this way Oedipus's family and Thebes, the overthrow of the Latin Turnus by the Trojan Eneas, and the violent loves of the Ovidian adaptations of the same epoch: *Narcisse* and, by implication, *Pyrame et Tisbé* and Chrétien's *Philomena*. Benoît had even larger goals in mind: a universal history he never wrote.[63]

The *uevre de Troie*, of which Emmanuèle Baumgartner has shown the rich significance in Benoît's romance, is in part an effort to recount past deeds in all their moral and social significance.

> Il faut sans doute mettre la polyvalence du mot *uevre* chez Benoît au débit d'une langue au vocabulaire théorique encore indigent. Mais on peut aussi y lire l'expression consciente d'une recherche qui sous-tend à cette date, et pour longtemps, l'écriture de l'histoire: l'adéquation entre les "faits" et les "dits", entre "les œuvres" et l'"œuvre", qui en est la transposition langagière aussi exacte que possible. Et ne serait-ce pas en outre une trace manifeste du projet d'écriture de Benoît: tisser une trame narrative qui englobe tout ce que l'on peut dire sur *l'uevre* de Troie, tout en retravaillant les formes alors existantes de discours littéraires, en explorant les techniques et les ressources d'une langue, d'un mode d'écriture, ce "roman", alors en quête de sa littérarité?[64]

Benoît has constant recourse to his sources, derives from them a *surplus de sen* that others had neglected, and relies extensively on amplification to express that meaning. He rewrites, in other words, by topical invention. Using techniques available to Benoît from his Latin language training, we can discern in his "literarity" the work of description in a new language. At the same time, by comparing his art of description with Joseph of Exeter's, we can appreciate better the originality of this fourth among the twelfth century's great French authors: Chrétien, Marie de France, to be sure, the largely lost French Tristan poems, but also Benoît himself.

Since it is fairly certain that Joseph did not use Benoît's romance in writing his epic, the *Ylias* and the *Troie* form both new, independent, and original versions of Dares. Benoît's romance is obviously a narrative amplification of Dares. This is in fact one of the major differences between it and the *Ylias*, since Joseph tends to amplify his

---

[62] Baumgartner 1996a, esp. p. 19. Cf. Lieberg 1969.
[63] Baumgartner 1996a pp. 27-28.
[64] Baumgartner 1996a pp. 15-16; see as well in this context Rollo 1995.

own insertions more than he does material in his primary source. Benoît's narrative elaboration of Dares is so extensive that he felt compelled to preface the romance with a plot summary in which he relates "a bries moz / De queus faiz iert li livres toz" (*Troie* v. 145-46)[65] [the book's contents in a few words]. Surprisingly, the summary fits better than the actual narrative what Benoît seems to promise in the lines immediately preceding it.

> Ci vueil l'estoire comencier:
> Le latin sivrai a la letre,
> Nule autre rien n'i voudrai metre,
> S'ensi non com jol truis escrit. (*Troie* v. 138-41)

[Here I wish to begin the plot. I follow the Latin source; I do not intend to insert anything other than as I find it there.]

How can this be so if, for example, the battles are amplified well beyond anything in Dares or love episodes like Briseida's emerge as if *ex nihilo*? To be sure, Benoît does provide for some novelty: "Ne di mie qu'aucun bon dit / N'i mete, se faire le sai, / Mais la matire en ensivrai." (*Troie* v. 142-44) [I don't say that I won't include some good word, if I know how to set it out, but I will follow my source.[66]] Still, "aucun bon dit" hardly resolves the problematic relationship between the romance and the source or sources Benoît claims to transcribe faithfully.

I have pointed out elsewhere that these words are similar to those in the Prologue to the anonymous Latin poem on the Trojan War written after Benoît's romance, the so-called *Historia Troyana*.[67] Unlike the *Ylias*, this poem is based on Dares and, perhaps, on the French romance too. Its author refuses to divulge his own name because, he claims, everything he writes is in Dares; his poem is less original than either Benoît or Joseph and falls, therefore, in the domain of paraphrase despite its formal amplifications and the versification[68]: "Non ego sum, quoniam nil fingo, poeta vocandus" (*Hist Troy* v. 12) [Since I invent nothing I must not be called a poet]. He sets forth his art of

---

[65] This is further evidence of his audience's ignorance of Dares; otherwise, no one would have needed a summary.

[66] My translation is explained by the interpretation that follows it.

[67] See Kelly 1988 p. 34.

[68] On its sources, see Stohlmann ed. *Hist Troy* pp. 20-76 and 150-72.

rewriting in a prose prologue which the poem's editor believes to be authentic.

> Quia vero in ordinata Troyani belli historia Daretem Frigium auctorem habui, additis tamen quibusdam per preparacionem et per etopoiiam, quod personarum loquencium informacionem dicunt, hoc opusculum illius nomine inscribendum esse statui. (*Hist Troy* p. 266, ll. 12-17).[69]

> [Since Dares Phrygius was my source author in setting out the account of the Trojan War, with the addition only of a few things that anticipate the plot to follow and speeches that characterize the speakers, I decided to identify him as author of this little work.]

Dares is his *auctor* in Macrobius's sense of "first author" and source.

Since Benoît projects an audience to whom the Trojan War is entirely new, allusions like those common in Joseph would not be possible unless they refer to narrative works available in French. For example, even if Benoît actually used Vergil's *Aeneid*, his allusions to it would be comprehensible to his implied French audience doubtless only as allusions to the *Roman d'Eneas*. If an allusion were not found there, then it might still tell us something about Benoît's art, but not about the audience's response. For example, the following lines can recall the plot of the *Eneas*.

> E Eneas s'en fu alez,
> Ensi com vos oï avez,
> Par mainte mer o sa navie,
> Tant qu'il remest en Lombardie. (*Troie* v. 28253-56)[70]

> [And Eneas set out, as you have heard tell, over many a sea with his fleet until he came to rest in Lombardy.]

"Lombardy" itself signals the *Eneas*'s geography, not Vergil's. This does not, of course, reconcile the divergence between Benoît's account of Eneas's departure and that conforming more closely to

---

[69] See Stohlmann ed. *Hist Troy* pp. 15-20 and 333.

[70] Paris Arsenal 3342 (= A²) gives information on Eneas's descendants; see *Troie* vol. 4 pp. 436-37 and Jung 1996 p. 146.

Vergil's in the *Eneas*. Alert members of his audience might have noted and discussed the difference, especially if the two works were in the same manuscript.[71]

Likewise, Benoît alludes to the *Roman de Thèbes*. When Diomede, Tydeus's son, comes with Ulysses to persuade Achilles to return to combat, Achilles refers to Diomede's father and the war against Thebes. But again, the audience would probably not have known Statius and, therefore, probably relied on the version found in the *Thèbes* to appreciate the allusion. Tydeus, according to Achilles, fought well, but:

> Puis en ot itel guerredon
> Qu'uns mauvais guarz le geta mort.
> A grant pechié e a grant tort
> Fist maint riche regne eissillier,
> Dont les homes fist detrenchier
> Al siege ou il les assembla. (*Troie* v. 19770-75)

[Then as reward for his efforts a worthless scum killed him. He wrongly and unjustly destroyed many a noble kingdom, by having the men slaughtered at the siege he gathered them at.]

Achilles's condemnation of Tydeus's death, which is fully detailed in the *Thèbes* (v. 6365-6896), buttresses his argument regarding the harm caused by the siege of Troy. Achilles's reading of Tydeus's life is therefore colored by his own goals: to end the war so that he can marry Polyxena. Every other reference in the *Troie* to the *fiz Tydeüs* is laudatory.[72] But allusions even to the *romans d'antiquité* are as rare in the *Troie* as are Joseph's allusions to Arthur in the *Ylias*.

At this point, it is useful to examine Benoît's *Troie* under the four heads used for the *Ylias*: the *auctor-imitator* dichotomy, *mutuatio*, *mutatio*, and, finally, the implied audience.

---

[71] See Jung 1996 pp. 117, 147, and 205; cf. also pp. 195 and 251. The Dutch adapter of the *Troie* was such an alert reader; see, for example, Jongen 1994 pp. 111-14. Although Benoît says that he is writing for those who do not know Latin, this does not preclude the presence of persons familiar with the Latin tradition in his audiences and, thus, their more complex reception of his romance. But I am treating the *Troie* from the perspective of the audience Benoît *implies* by his statement about those who do not know the Trojan War because they do not know Latin.

[72] For these allusions, see *Troie* vol. V, p. 91 s.v. "Tydeüs". On manuscripts containing both *Thèbes* and *Troie*, see Jung 1996.

*First Author and Rewriter (*Auctor-imitator*)*

Benoît might have known Macrobius. He knew Latin and had studied the canon authors. Even his audience might have recognized the
name, since Philippe de Thaon refers to him in poems addressed to
Eleanor of Aquitaine, whom Benoît himself surely addresses as the
"riche dame de riche rei" (*Troie* v. 13468) [the noble lady and wife of
a noble king]. In any case, Benoît refers to his principal sources
mostly as *autor*[73]; he has no other designation for a "writer" other
than *clerc*. For example, both Homer and Dares are identified as
"clerks" because they authored their accounts of the Trojan War
(*Troie* v. 45 and 99).[74] Other writers are also distinguished as clerk, as
is Sallust (*Troie* v. 80), or by their education in the liberal arts, like
Sallust's alleged nephew Cornelius (*Troie* v. 84), who, Benoît says,
translated Dares from Greek into Latin. But Cornelius is not designated as an "autor," unlike, for example, Dictys (*Troie* v. 24422), who
was also a "clers sages e bien apris / E sciëntos de grant memoire"
(*Troie* v. 24398-99) [a wise, well educated, and learned cleric]. To be
sure, the term *escrivain* existed in French but, until the sixteenth century, it seems to have denoted only a scribe.[75] Benoît never uses
escrivain in the *Troie*, nor any analogous word such as *conteor*, which
does appear in elsewhere, albeit in a pejorative sense. Nor does
Benoît identify himself as a writer except indirectly through certain
verbs or nouns that refer to his art, as when he claims to follow the
Latin text without attempting to add anything to it. (*Troie* v. 138-41)

Apparently, Benoît keeps Macrobius's sense of author as an authority whose truth a rewriter like Benoît may not gainsay although
he or she may, he implies, add something here and there (*Troie* v.
142-44) It is difficult to interpret the words "aucun bon dit" in these
lines. They seem to mean that he will add to his *matière*, as when he
inserts other sources into Dares; but they can also mean that he will
elaborate on his *matière* by amplifications. Both operations are present
in the *Troie*. Indeed, both are implicit in the range of meanings we
have found for 'description' in both Latin and French in Benoît's
time, evident, for example, both in Chrétien's use of *descrivre* and his
art as well is in Joseph's own rewriting of Dares in the *Ylias*.

---

[73] *Troie* s.v. "Autor" vol. 5 pp. 36-37 and 113.
[74] See also *Troie* s.v. "clerc" vol. 5 p. 129.
[75] Cf. Tobler-Lommatzsch s.v. *escrivain*. Niemeyer s.v. *descriptor*: "écrivain, narra-
teur, historien." See now Stiennon 1995.

To begin, however, it seems prudent to note where Benoît does not amplify Dares. The portraits in Benoît's catalogue are modeled closely on what he found in Dares.

> Beneeiz dit, qui rien n'i lait
> De quant que Daires li retrait,
> Qu'ici endreit voust demostrer
> E les semblances reconter
> E la forme qu'aveit chascuns,
> Qu'a ses ieuz les vit uns a uns. (*Troie* v. 5093-98)

[Benoît announces (for he omits nothing found in Dares) that he would like to describe and relate the appearances and shape of each of them; for he saw them one by one with his own eyes.]

These descriptions are actually carefully imbedded in the historiographic fiction of Dares as eye-witness. It seems that the portraits are credible because, in the time and space of the war, the Trojan historian went out to observe the persons he describes (*Troie* v. 5099-5104). Unlike Dares, Benoît uses a historiographic mode,[76] in contrast to the descriptive mode used in Joseph (cf. *pictura, Ylias* Bk. IV, v. 41). Perhaps this accounts for the less idealized portraits Benoît models on Dares: Ajax's awkwardness, Ulysses's mendacity, Pyrrhus's obesity and stuttering, Polidarius's obesity and melancholy, Briseida's joined eyebrows and inconstancy, Hector's strabismus and stuttering, Eneas's deceptiveness, Antenor's mockery, and, perhaps, Hecuba's masculinity. These features found in Dares are deleted in the *Ylias*. They certainly have little place in the *Troie*'s plot: strabismus, obesity, and awkwardness do not diminish the prowess of Hector, Pyrrhus, or Ajax, although Briseida's and Eneas's changeability does motivate their actions. These features are true, according to Benoît, because Dares wanted a full narrative — "S'estoire voleit faire pleine" (*Troie* v. 5105) [he wanted to make his account full and complete] — whereas Joseph's goal was to display the power or "virtue" of his principal actors through poetic eloquence ("eloquii virtus," Bk. IV, v. 38).

In Benoît 'to describe' can by synonymous with or overlap in meaning with *conter* and its compounds,[77] as, for example, in "Por

---

[76] Kelly 1992 pp. 85-92; cf. Croizy-Naquet 1994 pp. 216-26.
[77] Cf. "recontee lor façon" (*Troie* v. 5580) [related their appearance].

descrire, por aconter / Quel paveillon ot Achillès" (*Troie* v. 7598-99) [to describe, to tell what kind of pavilion Achilles had], and with near synonyms like *dire*, as in:

> De la beauté Polixenain
> Vos porreit l'om parler en vain:
> Ne porreit pas estre descrite,
> Ne par mei ne par autre dite. (*Troie* v. 5541-44)

[To relate to you Polyxena's beauty would be a vain effort: neither I nor anyone else could describe or express it.]

In referring to seven mountains as part of his *mappa mundi*, Benoît suggests the topical character of such topography: "Qui direit les descripcions," he begins, then continues with an implied "that is to say" amplified from interrogative topoi:

> En queus lieus n'en queus regions
> Il sont, ne queus fleuves i cort,
> Li queus en naist, li queus en sort,
> Come il sont haut, com bien il tienent
> Ne com granz choses i avienent,
> A grant merveille vos vendreit
> Com faitement ço avendreit. (*Troie* v. 23251-58)

[You would wonder greatly at how this could happen if someone were to make descriptions of them: in what places or regions they are found, what rivers flow there, which ones have their source there and which flow out from them, how high they are and how much space they occupy, and what great things happen there.]

The last feature is important. It shows that for Benoît description includes customary actions, a fact which Catherine Croizy-Naquet has pointed to in the case of urban descriptions in the *romans d'antiquité*.[78] Since Troy exists in both legend and history as the site of the ten-year siege, the descriptions of the more than twenty battles during that siege are, properly speaking, part of the tale he relates, even though Dares hardly ever provides details about them.

---

[78] Croizy-Naquet 1994 pp. 65-71.

Benoît is, therefore, an *imitator* as *descriptor* in the sense of author, historian. His authorities — or *auctores*, especially Dares — provided the material which he then recast and interpreted. It is his description that he is proud of. Like Chrétien concluding *Yvain*,[79] critics should not touch the *Troie* less they do it harm — "Quar teus i voudreit afaitier, / Qui tost i porreit empeirier" (*Troie* v. 30313-14) [for someone might do something to it that could quickly make it worse]. Here we confront a major problem in the production of the *Troie*. Martin Gosman has defined it as the, as it were, give-and-take between fidelity to sources and a certain reluctance to enter into the problems posed by the source for contemporary audiences.[80]

Selection (mutuatio)

From the foregoing analysis, it is clear that Benoît asserts fidelity to sources, both in the general contents of the *Troie* and in the treatment of specific episodes. His references include name identification — Dares and Dictys[81] — and more ambiguous references to the *autor* or *autors* who author, authorize, or give authority to the version of the Trojan War that Benoît himself relates. Various attempts have been made, with some success, to identify some of Benoît's episodic sources.[82] For example, Ovid has been identified for some of the topoi of falling in love and comparisons like that of Achilles with Narcissus, which remind us of the analogy between Chrétien's amplifications and those in Latin bridge works. Furthermore, we cannot exclude the possibility that Benoît drew on commentaries or glosses of Dares, Dictys, or other works like those available for Joseph's *Ylias* or Gautier de Châtillon's *Alexandreis*.[83]

Benoît also professed his learning in a digression on a *mappa mundi* at the outset to the introduction of the Amazons in order to locate their realm, Femenie. Yet here as elsewhere in romances where the

---

[79] *Yvain* v. 6817-18: "... ja plus n'an orroiz conter, / S'an n'i viaut mançonge ajoster" [you will hear no more told about him unless someone decides to add lies to the story].

[80] Gosman 1996. An obvious example is Ajax Telamon, who dies, as in Dares, but is still alive later, as in Dictys (see *Troie* s.v. "Aiaus" vol. 5 p. 20).

[81] See Greif 1886 p. 15 and notes (based on Joly's, not Constans's edition).

[82] Greif 1886 p. 55 (at § 5, with cross-references).

[83] Mora 1985 and Cormier 1988 and 1989 have suggested the usefulness of such commentary and glossing in explaining certain features of the *Roman d'Eneas*.

issue of imparting knowledge comes up, the lesson is provided not for learning but for wonder or *émerveillement*.[84] In the *Troie*, of course, Benoît only outlines what he would like to set forth in greater detail; still, his words suggest the topoi of topographies or geographical description (*Troie* v. 23169, 23251).

> Qu'en tot le mont n'avra partie,
> Ou qu'ele seit, que jo ne die
> Quel est, com grant e com bien tient,
> Ne qu'il i a ne qu'i avient,
> Quel nature ont li element,
> Quel les contrees, quel la gent. (*Troie* v. 23207-12)

[For no place on earth, wherever it may be, would I leave out, relating what it is, how big it is and how much space it occupies, what is found and what takes place there, what its climate is, what countries it includes and what peoples.]

Benoît would relate these marvels much as Philippe de Thaon and others did, to bedazzle rather than educate: "Ne com granz choses i avienent, / A grant merveille vos vendreit / Com faitement ço avendreit." (*Troie* v. 23256-58)[85] [what great adventures occur there, you would wonder how they could happen.] Note that such description would include "adventures" characteristic of the region to be described. Such events in the *Troie* include the battles that make up the ten-year siege and serve as part of the topical features in descriptions of places.

As the geographical descriptions imply, Benoît's description of the siege of Troy is full and complete. Unlike the *Ylias*, it includes all the warring parties and all the battles identified by Dares; furthermore, Benoît details the return of the Greeks according to Dictys, unlike Joseph who either did not use Dictys or else reduced him to a schematic outline analogous in scope to, but shorter in length than, Benoît's summary outline of the parts of the world he would like to describe.

---

[84] See Kelly 1992 chapter Five.
[85] See as well *Troie* v. 23243 and 23266.

Adaptation (mutatio)

Description relies on invention, and invention for Benoît is not just a prescribed technique; it also requires wit or *engin*. As he says in concluding the topical questions for a geography which are quoted above: "Tot en dirai, se jol comenz, / Qu'a ço sofist bien nostre engenz" (*Troie* v. 23213-14) [I'll relate everything once I start, for our wit is up to the task]. That wit, as ingenuity, will, therefore, seek to answer the kinds of questions the subject matter calls for as the author understands or chooses to understand it. That is to say that Benoît's originality will consist in providing answers to the topical questions raised by his *matière* and his answers reveal the significance of his sources. Horace had, we recall, recommended the Trojan War as subject matter. But he also wanted it to be rewritten with originality. Thus, Joseph of Exeter had put the war into the context of the true faith and human fury, abbreviating Dares's plot so as to emphasize these two themes, as we have seen. This is what abbreviation should do. On the other hand, amplification also emphasizes to some extent by lengthening what is implied in the source.[86] The operation is possible by topical invention, that is, the interrogatory mode that questions the sources, then provides answers in conformity with the context chosen for the new version of the sources. Topical invention relies on *ingenium*; with it the author draws *de suo* what is merely implicit in the first author. The art is the same as that which Macrobius discerns in Vergil's rewriting of Homer's Trojan matter.

Like Joseph, Benoît sees in Dares and Dictys the power of fate or destiny aided by human blindness, a blindness aided and abetted by the play of fortune and chance. But unlike in the *Ylias*, these powers play better defined, complementary roles in the *Troie*. Benoît uses a number of readily recognizable words to refer to them, like *aventure*, *sort*, *fortune*, and *destinee*. Although the semantic range of each word may overlap with that of the others — Benoît does not arrange them into a precise terminology — he does use them in context to represent rather precisely one of three senses: destiny or fate, fortune regularly oscillating from good to bad, and haphazard chance.

Let us begin with destiny. Destiny as fate stands over all. However, it can be eschewed by rational or intelligent human intervention. The

---

[86] Bornscheuer 1976 pp. 73-75. For a good illustration of the operations of addition, deletion, substitution, and rearrangement in one episode of the *Troie*, see Croizy-Naquet 1997.

most obvious manifestation of destiny is the ten-year war itself. Apollo announces to both Calcas and Achilles that the Greeks will win if they persevere for the entire ten years; Calcas reminds the Greeks of this whenever they think of giving up.[87] Benoît's Calcas is right; Joseph, we recall, represents his prophecies as false. In the *Troie*, *destinee* takes precedence or dominates over all other powers evoked to account for what happens. It does not depend on the gods although they know it by foreknowledge and can use it to achieve their own ends. Humans can know it as well if the gods deign to communicate with them — hence the importance of oracles in this romance. We may observe this in the predictions of Calcas, Cassandra, Helenus, Panthus, and, perhaps, Calypso and Circe, as well as those in which the gods directly inform a human through dreams, as with Hecuba and Andromache.

Yet both Greeks and Trojans have a choice. They can at any moment settle their differences by deliberation and compromise. Priam knows this when he sends Antenor to propose the return of Hesione. The Greeks themselves know it when, with their landing on the Trojan shore, they send Diomede and Ulysses to Troy before the war begins in earnest. Likewise, as in the *Ylias*, Agamemnon is in Benoît the one sensible Greek. He wishes to avoid any overweening pride that might attract the anger of the gods. He also recognizes that, if Laomedon started the enmity between Greeks and Trojans, as the Greeks think, they themselves are not innocent because they refused to return Hesione and are even now invading Priam's realm, having just seized a Trojan castle as well as the island fortress of Tenedos. Mutual responsibility for the misfortune calls for the mutual settlement of differences. An exchange of Hesione for Helen would settle matters. Yet, although the idea floats in the air and we hear no objection even from Telamon, it is never negotiated by either side. The Greeks want the return of Helen or there will be war (*Troie* v. 6185-95). The Trojans have been unable to get Hesione back and so there will be war (*Troie* v. 6349-58). No one acts on the obvious compromise — which becomes thereby a *surplus de sen* in Marie de France's sense of the expression — and destiny fills the gap left open by human silence.[88]

---

[87] See *Troie* v. 12775-78, 19924-53, and 25572-75. On fortune and destiny in the *Troie*, see also Suard 1992 pp. 179-84.

[88] On such "gaps" or "ellipses" in the narrative, see Gosman 1992a pp. 57 and 63.

This fact is important because it shows that humans may escape their destiny in the *Troie*. Destiny is, therefore, not necessarily inevitable, but contingent on whether humans heed warnings given to them by the gods or others; choice is possible among several available scenarios. For example, Troy will fall if Paris abducts Helen and the war lasts ten years. The Trojans know the former condition, the Greeks know the latter. And, although the Greeks are, from day to day, less successful on the battlefield than the Trojans, suing for truce more often[89] and suffering the effects, for example, of bad weather, disease, and the stench of decaying corpses, still they win by persevering through the tenth year of the war. The Trojans know that Paris must not bring Helen to Troy, yet they allow him to do so. Although Priam's sons are more successful in combat, their deaths are foreboding. The Trojans persevere in following their destiny into the fatal tenth year.

Destiny's operations are evident in passing events too. At the end of the second battle, the Greeks have been routed, and Hector is intent on burning their ships. Had he done so, the war would have ended in less than a year with a Trojan victory (*Troie* v. 10164-86). But he meets resistance from Ajax Telamon, who is the bastard son of Hesione and, therefore, Hector's nephew. Ironically, family bonds preclude victory as Hector terminates the second battle in deference to his relative (*Troie* v. 10175-86; see also v. 10121-24). Here destiny is at work; Hector confuses family loyalty with loyalty to his larger family and to Troy.

Thus, the "ellipse" in Gosman's sense illustrated by the Greek and Trojan failure to achieve a compromise allows destiny to continue its course. The acquaintance with Ajax Telamon does not bring the young man's mother back to Troy, but it does save the Greeks from defeat. They seek truces more often than the Trojans do because of their misfortunes, while the latter lose the sole agents capable of defending Troy. Deiphobus, Hector, Troilus, and finally Paris die one after the other. Even Ajax Telamon no longer serves. His own fate illustrates as well the force of destiny, since he dies while killing Paris after having gone mad and fighting "in the nude": "Toz nuz

---

[89] See *Troie* v. 10309, 12843, 15216, 16610-11, 19379-80, 20164, and 20871; the Trojans ask for a truce v. 14570, 17346-47, and 21799-800. Beginning with the twentieth battle, the Trojans refuse twice to leave the city to do battle (v. 23117-19 and 24379-87).

vueut estre a la bataille. / S'il ne s'i guarde, il fait que fous" (*Troie* v. 22612-13)[90] [He goes to battle without any armor. If he doesn't take care he acts like a mad man].

This brings us to Gosman's discussion of the "problematization of romance narrative" in the *romans d'antiquité*. "Il faut faire remarquer que toute problématisation exige soit une forte poussée du méta-commentaire (auctoriel ou actoriel), soit une complication signifiante de l'intrigue et/ou de sa distribution, soit une introduction (une *inventio*) d'éléments étrangers à la trame originelle. Ou une combinaison de ces trois possibilités."[91] The *Troie* contains all of these possibilities. In fact, the problems Gosman identifies in the *Troie* are typical of the romance mode and are probably basic to romance reception.[92]

We may illustrate this fact with the Briseida interpolation. For convenience, I shall treat Gosman's three features in reverse order. First, the Briseida episode is clearly an *inventio* in the sense that it includes material largely foreign to both Dares and Dictys[93] ; yet Briseida is not totally foreign insofar as Dares includes a Briseida in his Greek catalogue (*De exc* p. 17, ll. 7-10)[94] and Dictys alludes to a Trojan woman whom Diomede is bringing back to Argos after the siege, which motivates his wife Aegiale's enmity (*Ephem* p. 120, ll. 11-18). Now, the report of Diomede's — and Agamemnon's — return with Trojan wives is false (*Ephem* p. 120, l. 13: "falsis nuntiis"). It is merely part of Nauplus's plot to avenge his son Palamede whom he believes the Greeks treacherously killed. This is not to say that each did not bring back a Trojan concubine, as Agamemnon does with Cassandra; whether a woman actually accompanies Diomede is not said in Dictys and it is irrelevant in Agamemnon's case. In Dictys the report is false because these women are not *wives* and, therefore, no real threat to either Aegiale and Clytemnestra, that is, to the wives the returning heroes already have.[95] By making Briseida a Trojan

---

[90] On such nudity in the sense of wearing little or no armor, see Petit 1985b pp. 880-81 n. 125.

[91] Gosman 1992a p. 56.

[92] Vinaver 1964 pp. 500-02; Bruckner 1986.

[93] On what follows, see Kelly 1995b; cf. Gosman 1992a p. 62.

[94] She moves from one catalogue to the other in later adaptations; see Williams 1984 p. 62.

[95] Clytemnestra has, of course, already taken a lover, but that complication, found in Dictys, is not directly relevant to the Briseida invention.

and inventing her affair with Troilus, and then by transferring her to the Greek camp and narrating her new relation with Diomede that, after some time, produces a new affair, Benoît is truly introducing material foreign to both Dares and Dictys and, as far as we can tell, to any other version of the Trojan War prior to Benoît. Benoît is truly the *auctor* of the Briseida story he tells — he invented it *de suo*.

Let us turn now to Gosman's second kind of problematization: that is, the Briseida story also entails a significant complication in the plot and its arrangement. First, it lends new significance to the conflict between Troilus and Diomede. In Dares there is only one combat between the two men; in it Troilus wounds Diomede (*De exc* p. 37, l. 8). Dares mentions no other specific encounter between them, referring only to Troilus's overall victories and to Diomede's subsequent attempt, partly as a result of those victories, to persuade Achilles to return to the fight — the latter had been *recreant* because the Greeks will not desist and, therefore, he cannot marry Polyxena.

The Briseida episode has repercussions elsewhere too. By making her Calcas's daughter — another of Benoît's inventions — she becomes involved in the larger issue of Troy's fate. Her delivery to the Greeks is part of an exchange of prisoners, whereby Briseida is exchanged for Antenor. This has two implications for the *Troie*'s destiny as Benoît plots it: Antenor will himself betray Priam just as Briseida will be unfaithful to Troilus; but she betrays Troy because her father imposes the decision on her. Calcas as turncoat actually follows the will of Apollo, who knows Troy's destiny. Antenor's betrayal is part of that destiny.

This brings us to Gosman's final point on metacommentary. The metacommentary on the Briseida episode sets up a conflict between Benoît as narrator and a *riche dame* with respect to Briseida's constancy. Indeed, the narrator expresses a misogynist's evaluation of Briseida's conduct *avant la lettre*, that is, before telling her story, based on the presumption that she, like any woman, will be unfaithful after only three or four days in the Greek camp. The presumption is belied by the ensuing narrative. By introducing the *riche dame*, a *fame fort*,[96] a more sympathetic evaluation of Briseida's conduct than the narrator's is conveyed. Briseida's change of heart also illustrates changes caused by the war itself. Benoît describes these not so much in terms

---

[96] See Latzke 1979, Kelly 1995b pp. 228-29.

of Macrobius's sudden changes, or pathos (the kind Briseida would have undergone had she been false in the three or four days projected by her unreliable narrator[97]), but the gradual changes that are part of the ethos of prolonged war.

How does Benoît *describe* the Trojan War? As we shall see, he amplifies while following the plot lines dictated by Dares and Dictys. What topoi are appropriate to the descriptive amplification of war? How does Benoît articulate them? We can use Matthew of Vendôme's *loci* for *negotia* to answer these questions since his scheme fits the twelfth-century approach in Ciceronian and Horatian commentaries. Several topoi are amplified in Benoît. The summary of events (*summa facti*) at the beginning not only gives the audience a quick view of the long and sometimes complex plot, it also lets the audience know the significance of the interspersed predictions of what will happen, notably those by Calcas, Cassandra, Helenus, and Panthus, as well as those uttered towards the end of the romance — the premonitions of the Trojans themselves as they grimly prepare to fight to the bitter end (Priam, Antimachus) or negotiate betrayal with the enemy when defeat seems inevitable (Antenor, Aeneas). The narrator himself not infrequently calls attention to the inevitability of Troy's destiny in spite of individual free will. Furthermore, Dares and Dictys provide the outline of events prior to, during, and after the war (*ante rem*, *cum re*, *post rem*). Time (*tempus*) and place (*locus*) are also clearly expressed in the sources as ten years[98] and the site of Troy itself. More significant in accounting for Benoît's originality are the causes of the war, the means used to bring about and prosecute the war, and the quality of the war itself (*causa facti, facultas faciendi, qualitas faciendi*).

Causes — for we must use the plural for the *Troie* — include not only the chain of causes and effects we observed in the *Ylias* and that begin with Peleus, but also an important distinction between human and inhuman causes. Both destiny and *petite acheison* are fundamental factors in what happens. Like Joseph, Benoît reads out of Dares a concatenation of causes — a virtual domino effect —that begins with small things which snowball until both Trojans and Greeks are scat-

---

[97] And thus unlike Laudine in Chrétien's account of her change of heart; I return to this in Chapter Five.

[98] Benoît's chronology is very careful, although much of it comes from Dares; see Eley 1994 and Kelly 1995b p. 235 n. 29.

tered and destroyed. The first causes are human. There is a foresee-
able pattern which human will can escape by terminating the conflicts peacefully. But this does not happen, sometimes for obscure but
human reasons (Gosman's ellipses); as a result, destiny is free to work
itself out, aided and abetted by the turns of fortune, the play of
chance, human blindness, irrationality, and even sense of honor.

The first cause (*causa faciendi*) is Peleus's betrayal of Jason, which is
more explicitly portrayed than in the *Ylias*. The plot aborts, but not
before Laomedon's refusal of hospitality. Hercules and the Greeks
avenge their honor by sacking and destroying Troy, killing Laomedon and most of his family, and abducting Hesione.[99] Priam alone
survives with his family because, as in Joseph, he happened to be
away on a military expedition. Priam's attempt to reach a peaceful
settlement with the Greeks by the return of Hesione meets with
Greek hostility and intransigence. Paris's abduction of Helen brings
on the second Greek invasion, and the war begins in earnest. This fits
the narrator's own interpretation of events inserted after the account
of the first Greek invasion.

> L'uevre e la chanson[100] vos ai dite,
> Si com jo l'ai trovee escrite,
> Saveir par com faite acheison
> Avint ceste destrucion.
> Par assez petit d'uevre mut,
> Mais mout par monta puis e crut:
> Onques chose, si com jo truis,
> A tant n'ala ne ainz ne puis. (*Troie* v. 2827-34)

[I've told you the enterprise and the work as I find it written
down — that is to say, the cause of the destruction. It started as
quite a small undertaking, but it rose and grew considerably
thereafter. Never did anything have such great consequences, as
far as I know, either before or after.]

From *petite acheison* (cf. *Troie* v. 2837) to *grant destrucion*, Benoît describes
the stages by which small causes gradually precipitate the great

---

[99] Peleus leads the expedition, a sign that he has relinquished his realm to Jason
and accepted his new life as a Greek seeking vengeance.

[100] A number of manuscripts replace "la chanson" by *l'acheison*; see *Troie* v. 2827
var.

events that realize destiny. Once again we discover human causes to the sequence of events. The origin of the Trojan War in Benoît as in Dares and Dictys is Peleus. Peleus fears Jason's prowess, just as Laomedon fears the Greeks. Both actually fear most the loss of their *honor* — and "honor" to them may include their lands, the source of their family's power (see *Troie* v. 3768-69).

When honor is offended, the offended seek revenge (*facultas faciendi*). Revenge is the means to restore or confirm honor. In the *Troie* revenge leads to war; in war, the winner carries off booty, including women, which quickens a desire for further revenge among the victims. Peleus's attempt to rid himself of Jason fails; but he does not pursue his efforts after Jason's success. Jason himself never learns his uncle's motives and, therefore, has no reason to feel offended, especially because he acquires Peleus's realm, or *honor*, as reward for his quest (*Troie* v. 2053-54). In contrast, the abduction of Medea during the expedition is carried out with her consent. The abduction ultimately has terrible consequences; Benoît chooses not to relate them, but rather transfers the motif to Troy and the death of Priam's children.[101] The quest for the Golden Fleece also introduces another motif that is common in romance: hospitality.[102] However, Laomedon refuses hospitality. The Greeks feel that their honor is offended by his refusal, so they plan and execute the first destruction of Troy to avenge themselves by destroying Trojan honor and restoring their own. These features — offense to honor, war, and revenge — provide the *figura* or topical outline for the stage *ante rem* and a model for the lengthier development of the same motifs in the *cum re* and *post rem* phases of the plot. Greek perseverance and Trojan losses culminate in the second destruction of Troy after Antenor's and Eneas's betrayal of the city, an action analogous to Peleus's attempt to save his patrimony by eliminating a perceived internal threat to it.

Antenor and Eneas attempt to save and even enlarge their honor (in both senses of the word) by betraying their feudal lord. Their actions become the model for the strife that breaks out among the Greeks after the war is won, in the *post rem* phase of the plot: the Greek return.[103] Benoît continues to elaborate on these topical schemes when he turns to Dictys as source. The feudal strife illus-

---

[101] Kelly 1984b pp. 172-75.
[102] Bruckner 1980.
[103] Kelly 1997b pp. 59-60 and 63-64.

trated by Antenor's betrayal of Priam surfaces in the Greek camp when the spoils of war are divided — who deserves the Palladion? — as well as in Nauplus's assumption that Ulysses and Diomede treacherously killed his son Palamede. Not only does Nauplus avenge himself by causing the destruction of the returning Greek fleet, he also inflames internecine strife in Diomede's marriage and Agamemnon's family. Hermione's jealousy due to Orestes's love for Andromache and Ulysses's vengeance on Penelope's suitors provide similar plots. Ulysses himself dies later when his bastard son, Telegonus, unwittingly kills his father in rage because he is denied access to — his father! As in the *Ylias*, Helen alone escapes unscathed, although Benoît does not permit himself the misogynist observations that we find in Joseph of Exeter. I shall return to Helen below.

Let us first turn to Ulysses. His death at Telegonus's hands is paradigmatic and, therefore, topically interesting. I shall examine it more closely, while putting the episode into the context of Briseida's story. Ulysses's character is clearly set out in both Dares's and Benoît's portraits.

> Mout par ert de grant sen guarniz.
> Merveilles esteit beaus parliers,
> Mais en dis mile chevaliers
> N'en aveit un plus tricheor:
> Ja veir ne deïst a nul jor.
> De sa boche isseit granz gabeis,
> Mais mout ert sages e corteis. (*Troie* v. 5204-10)[104]

[He possessed great wit and intelligence. He was a wonderfully gifted speaker, but none among a thousand knights was his equal in trickery. He never spoke the truth. His speech was full of humor and boasting, but he himself was very prudent and courteous.]

Perhaps Ulysses is the best example of Benoît's conception of one leading an ideal life. For at his death,

---

[104] Cf. Dares: "Ulixem firmum dolosum ore hilari statura media eloquentem sapientem" (*De exc* p. 16, ll. 18-19) [Ulysses is firm, deceitful, of pleasing features, medium height, eloquent, and prudent]. On the meaning of many of these epithets, see Vielliard 1994 pp. 290-94.

> Mout par esteit granz sis aez,
> Maint jor e maint an ot vescu:
> Por quant si ert de grant vertu
> Et de grant force ancore al jor. (*Troie* v. 30252-55)

[He was very old, he had lived a long time. But he was in his prime and was very strong at the time of his death.]

Indeed, one might surmise that no one in the *Troie* had a better life than Ulysses did, although Circe, Telegonus's mother, knew Ulysses's tragic "destinee" (*Troie* v. 30288).

Like Ulysses, the Greeks too have a destiny which they do not escape after the war.

> Ensi com jo vos ai conté
> E come es Livres ai trové
> Avint de cest destruiement.
> Dès ore orreiz com faitement
> Ravindrent lor grant encombrier
> E lor damage grant e fier.
> Dès ore orreiz lor destinees:
> Quant jos vos avrai recontees,
> Ne direiz pas qu'a nule gent
> Avenist onc plus malement.
> Tuit alerent puis, ço lison,
> A duel e a perdicion. (*Troie* v. 26591-602)

[Thus did their great destruction take place as I have told you, just as I find it in the books. Now you will hear how the Greeks came to harm and destruction great and awful. Now you will hear their fates. When you have heard my tale you must admit that no people ever had worse misfortune. As we read, all came to grief and perdition.]

Even Ulysses, who by his wits escapes many unfortunate obstacles that emerge on his homeward journey, cannot, in the end, escape his fate. To be sure, he returns home safe and sound despite "Fortune e Male Destinee" (*Troie* v. 28615). Penelope has been faithful, and Fortune has placed him high on her wheel: "Dès or li est prospre Fortune, / Dès or li est joiose e liee" (*Troie* v. 29050-51) [From now on Fortune, joyous and happy, shows him her bounty]. But ultimately, Ulysses cannot escape his destiny: death at his own son's hand.[105] Although the alternation of good and bad fortune informs the course of Ulysses's life, destiny stands above it and actually uses fortune to realize its own predetermined ends — "la destinee / Que li esteit determinee" (*Troie* v. 29973-74) [the destiny that had been fixed for him]; even Circe, Telegonus's mother, cannot prevent his death even though she knows it in advance (*Troie* v. 30288). Fury once again facilitates the inevitable as Ulysses turns against Tele-machus and forgets his bastard son (v. 30150-51).

Priam also illustrates the hold of destiny. Although he knew per-fectly well the destiny that awaited Troy due to Paris's actions, his understanding of the calamity singles out only the commonplace of Fortune's raising and lowering kings.

> Haï! Fortune dolorose,
> Come estes pesme e tenebrose!
> Tant me fustes ja liee e bele,
> Sor le plus haut de la roële
> M'aseïstes et me posastes;
> Mais, puis que vos reporpensastes,
> Trop laidement, senz demorer,
> Me ravez fait jus devaler,
> Qu'el plus bas sui desoz voz piez,
> Povre, vis e desconseilliez,
> Senz espeir e senz atendance
> D'aveir mais joie n'alejance,
> Senz resordre, senz redressier. (*Troie* v. 25215-27)

[Ah! grievous Fortune, how terrible and dark you are! You were once so blithe and fine towards me, you seated me at the top of your wheel. But, once you changed your mind, you brought me down low with unseemly haste so that I now lie at the bottom at your feet, poor, vile, and distraught, hopeless, deprived of any expectation of ever experiencing again joy or relief, and unable to rise up or stand.]

To be located at the bottom of Fortune's wheel does not preclude rising once again. Priam's despair, however, redefines his bad fortune

---

[105] *Troie* v. 29973-74, 30228-29, and 30288.

as immutable, suggesting the effect of destiny's crushing power rather than Fortune's wheel.

Yet Priam knew his fate and could have avoided it. For example, he could have given Helen back to the Greeks. Or he could have restrained Hector during the tenth battle. For destiny had various options depending on the ability to deal effectively with her warnings that usually characterizes Ulysses. Yet, Andromache's dream and Cassandra's pronouncements are not enough to keep Hector from going to battle. Matters would have been different for Troy had he remained inactive. If Hector

> vesquist dous anz o mais,
> Destruit fussent si enemi;
> Mais Aventure nel sofri
> Ne Envie ne Destinee. (*Troie* v. 16840-43)

[had lived two or more years longer his enemies would have been destroyed. But neither adventure, greed, nor destiny permitted it.]

Since in the *Troie*, "Granz maus vient par poi d'acheison" (*Troie* v. 17551) [A small cause causes great harm], *envie* in the foregoing passage makes sense only if one considers Hector's desire for booty, hence my translation of the word as "greed." The moment of distraction when Hector tries to seize booty exposes him to Achilles's spear and the Greek warrior seizes the opportunity.

This observation occurs when Benoît prepares to relate Achilles's own death. The "poi d'acheison" is Achilles's sudden passion for Polyxena. Here one sees how the fortuitous may also have its place in what is predetermined. Similarly, the powers of chance, fortune, or destiny conspire to bring about the inevitable fall. Hector could have prevented it. By showing courtesy to his enemy and relative Ajax Telamon — the *petite acheison* — he gave a *chiquenaude* to Troy's fate. Yet he did no wrong, and it is hard to see how he could have known the baneful consequences of his courtesy.

Similarly, Ajax Telamon is reluctant to cross the line between his Greek and Trojan kin. Both his and Hector's actions are rational and derive from sincere affection: "Mout se baisierent ambedui, / Mout s'acolerent e joïrent / E lor chiers aveirs s'entrofrirent" (*Troie* v. 10140-42) [both kissed, embraced, and welcomed one another, and they offered their valuable possessions to one another]. But a ten-year war cannot but eat away at such affection. Hector himself evinces madness even when he is forewarned by his wife, the gods, Cassandra, and even Priam, of the fatality that must ensue if he goes out to the tenth battle. As we have seen, Ajax Telamon is so far gone in the twentieth battle that he foolishly sallies forth "in the nude." Yet his madness carries him forward until, finally, Paris — his kinsman and brother of Hector — dislocates his spine with an arrow. Mortally wounded, Ajax Telamon loses all reason (*Troie* v. 22791), hacking down Trojans right and left. He finally reaches Paris, seizes him in his strong arms, and, driving his sword repeatedly into his lovely face, packs his uncle off to Hades and away from Helen — "Por li morreiz, e jo si faz" (*Troie* v. 22813) [you die for her and so do I]. Borne back to his tent, Ajax Telamon dies snapping furiously at his parting soul with his teeth as if trying to eat it (*Troie* v. 22836).

Three topics are evoked by the events just singled out: the moral drift of the war, the sense and place of *Envie* in relation to Destiny and Fortune, and Helen as cause of the war (*qualitas faciendi*). It is important to examine them as well.

Joseph's view of the war's violence and immorality is presented almost ekphrastically. That is, he discards Dares's rather careful annal-like chronology in order to show in the two sequences of Books V and VI the fury that hurls the major combatants down the road to destruction. Benoît, on the other hand, retains Dares's chronology. This allows him to use the twenty-three battles to enhance pathos as the prolonged carnage drives the Trojans to defeat and the Greeks to destruction resembling what we today call ethnic cleansing. The multiple wrongs, the numerous *petites acheisons*, accumulate, and by the narrative weave that alternately binds together various groups only to come apart through the ongoing events of war, they snowball in the minds and actions of the protagonists. A complex narrative *gradatio* carries the war from its relatively human, albeit irrational beginnings to the rage and horror that mark a denouement extending from the sack of Troy to the death of Ulysses. There is a nemesis in this that fits Benoît's notion of destiny.

Nemesis is retributive justice. It functions to abort Peleus's plans to get rid of Jason by sending him in search of the Golden Fleece just as it does Laomedon's inhospitality. The failure to settle matters by returning Hesione and Helen to their kin is another manifestation of it, and Destiny, Adventure, and Fortune all cooperate as features of

Nemesis to bring down Troy and destroy the Greeks. The concept of
nemesis was available to the Middle Ages in Macrobius's *Saturnalia*,
where Nemesis represents one feature of the divinity: "Nemesis quae
contra superbiam colitur" (*Sat* 1.22.1)[106] [Nemesis who is worshipped
as the enemy of pride]. In the *Troie* the excesses of pride lead to
vengeance, and the acts of vengeance provide the stages leading up
to defeat and destruction.

Nevertheless, in the *Troie*, the principal vice seems to derive not so
much from pride itself as from *envie*. The word has a broad range of
meanings in this romance. Let me begin by looking at Guido delle
Colonne's adaptation of the *Troie*. There it is clearly seen as a human
weakness or vice that serves the purpose of evil destiny. Commenting
on Laomedon's refusal to allow Jason's Argonauts to stop on the
Trojan shore, Guido continues by expanding on the *inuida fatorum
series*[107] that can destroy humans even when they live in peace. Here
Nemesis is no longer merely just retribution, it is an ineluctable pro-
pensity in humans to decline from a state of happiness. In such a
world there is no felicity in Boethius's sense of the word; there is only
the fatal envy of happiness shared by humans and the powers of fate.
As Guido says regarding Hesione's fate:

> Nam inuida fatorum series, felicium inimica, summa in summi-
> tate manere diutius semper negat, et vt status hominum deducat
> habilius in ruinam, per insensibiles et cecas insidias potentiores
> immittit et inducit ad casum, a friuola et inopinabili materia
> causam trahens ne prouisione perhabita per cautele subsidium
> ualeant se tueri. (*Historia* p. 43)

> [For the envious course of the fates which is hostile to the fortu-
> nate refuses them the right to remain on high any longer; in
> order therefore to draw men more effectively down into ruin, it
> drives and pulls the more powerful with imperceptible and hid-
> den guile, luring them to misfortune for some frivolous, unex-
> pected reason lest they protect themselves by making provision
> against it through some stratagem.]

---

[106] Cf. Herter 1935 col. 2366-68; the *Novum Glossarium* gives only one example
(from Papias) *NGlos* s.v. *nemesis*.
[107] See Fichte 1995 p. 194 n. 6 and Mégier 1997 p. 64.

Guido has summed up in this addition to Benoît the role of *petites acheisons* in undoing the best laid plans, as, for example, when Priam reconstructs Troy or when Ulysses defends himself against patricide: "Par assez petit d'uevre mut, / Mais mout par monta puis e crut" (*Troie* v. 2831-32) [it began as quite a small thing, but rose and grew considerably thereafter].

There is one exception to this grim scenario: Helen. Benoît's last words about her recount her marvelous life, but say nothing of any suffering after her return to Menelaus, just as Joseph too evokes Helen's happy fate with no suggestion of any suffering or grief. In both works everyone great and small throngs about her to marvel at the cause of so much woe and destruction. But Benoît is silent on her feelings at this point.

Implied Audiences

The *Ylias* was regarded as a masterpiece and was recommended for imitation in some arts of poetry and prose; its audience was presumed to be educated, both in the sense of being proficient in Latin[108] and knowledgeable enough about earlier literature to be able to appreciate the work's allusions and originality. Joseph could therefore rely on a summary plot into which he inserted or, in medieval terms, out of which he drew major amplifications that integrated new material — themes from Juvenal and Boethius, motifs, quotes, and echoes from a variety of antique and medieval authors — into a truly new version of the Trojan War. With these additions, his audience could appreciate how fully he realized Horace's admonition to write an original version of Homer's song.

Benoît practices the same art. He draws not only on Dares but also on other sources, most notably Dictys, to complete his work. But — and this is a major difference from Joseph — Benoît's implied audience does not know Latin and is presumed to be ignorant of authors familiar to those who had received a good schooling: "Ceste estoire n'est pas usee, / N'en guaires lieus nen est trovee: / Ja retraite ne fust ancore" (*Troie* v. 129-31) [This story isn't widely known, nor is it

---

[108] Despite the uncertain quality of much medieval schooling, there were obviously very proficient readers and speakers of Latin in the twelfth century; see Schmidt 1977 pp. 170-72. A suitable audience for Joseph might be composed of those who, together with Pope Eugene II, listened to a reading of Bernardus Silvestris's *Cosmographia*; on this public reading, see Dronke ed. *Cos* p. 2.

found in many places. It would not yet have been related]. For example, Benoît's implied audience does not even know Dares. It follows that the rewriting that modern scholarship can detect in the *Troie* can indeed tell us about Benoît's art of writing, but it cannot be presumed as part of the reception by his implied audience. Nonetheless, his originality was so great that the *Troie*'s version of the Trojan War had a lasting impact on future Latin and vernacular writing. The Trojan War is no longer just the source of great families in Europe. It is also the account of the destruction of a great and proud patrimony. The falsity of the invention is offset by the plausibility of the plot. Benoît succeeded much as Vergil did in making his audiences prefer the fable to the truth (cf. *Sat* 5.17.6).

CHAPTER FIVE

THE ISSUE AND TOPICS OF CONSENT IN *ENEAS*, *EREC*, AND THE *BEL INCONNU*

> Fille es de roïne et de roi,
> Segnor te donra endroit toi,
> Alques t'estuet por ce soffrir.
> — Et se il n'est a ton plaisir,
> Qu'en feras tu, s'il ne te plaist?[1]
> (*Cristal et Clarie*)

Medieval rewriting established chains of works whose authors rewrite one or more antecedents much as Macrobius maintains that Vergil did Homer and others.[2] The material rewritten may be a complete work, like the rewriting of Dares by Benoît and Joseph, of Chrétien's *Charrette* in the *Prose Lancelot*, or of his *Erec* and *Yvain* by Hartmann von Aue. Or it may entail rewriting a part of an earlier work, such as motifs, images, or smaller units of discourse,[3] as when Vergil rewrote, according to Macrobius, the Jason and Medea affair in Book IV of the *Aeneid*. Examples of this latter kind are not rare in twelfth- and thirteenth-century literature. It is this kind of rewriting that this chapter will treat.

In Chapter Four it was possible to study closely how Benoît and Joseph rewrote their sources because the sources are known and extant. In this chapter, this is possible only for the *Roman d'Eneas*, since the alleged sources of *Erec et Enide* and the *Bel Inconnu* are no longer extant. As a result, it is possible to treat only the motifs which these works borrow from one another. Accordingly, we shall examine here both *mutuatio* and *mutatio* in the treatment of some of these motifs. Each of our authors alludes clearly and distinctly to the source of the motifs, thus alerting the knowledgeable public to their new ver-

---

[1] *Cristal* v. 8095-99. You are the daughter of royal parents. Your father will give you a husband; you must be a bit patient. — And if you don't like the person chosen? What will you do about it if he doesn't suit you?

[2] Kelly 1992 pp. 92-93.

[3] Lacy 1996; Haug 1992, esp. chapters Five, Six, and Seven, discusses Chrétien's originality in relation to German romance; see also Haug 1989 pp. 15-21 on *Ruodlieb*.

sions of familar commonplaces. The motif all these authors rewrite is the *gradus amoris* — a feature of romance, to be sure — but applied specifically in these works to the issue of consent in that commonplace sequence.

Consent as a Moral and Social Issue in Gradus amoris

Mastery of the art of description comes as one acquires skill in re-inventing and deploying commonplace schemes with originality, cogency, and moral and social relevance. One such scheme, the *gradus amoris*, is also a commonplace motif in many medieval romances, where it often yields original, unexpected rewritings that are as remarkable as Benoît's and Joseph's version of Dares's plain prose.[4] Matthew of Vendôme prescribes this device for rewriting Ovid in order to include the stages the Roman poet omitted (*Ars vers* 4.13). The stages in the scheme are, however, not hard and fast. Matthew names six[5] : sight, lust, approach, conversation, flattery, and consummation. He is referring to a scheme like that in Jean de Meun's *Roman de la rose*. An author can insist on those stages which seem appropriate to the matter he or she is treating. But other stages are possible. For example, lust suggests an immediate physical desire; however, reflection on the qualities observed in the other may move the emotions away from mere lust towards love, or at least to a different kind of lust. If we interiorize in this way not only the sentiments of the observer but also the virtues of the loved one, a different quality of love emerges, one which medieval romances evoke as, for example, *fine amour, bone amour,* and *amour par amours.* If marriage ensues, the final stage may exemplify not only mutually desired sexual intercourse, Matthew's "votiva duorum congressio,"[6] as for Erec and Enide, but also more feudal concerns like dowry, parents' rights, consent, and so forth. All of these potential versions of the *gradus amoris* suggest the kind of originality that is possible with mastery of

---

[4] Kelly 1983.

[5] The most common number is five; see Friedman 1965.

[6] Matthew's "votiva *duorum* congressio" means shared consumption of physical desire. Matters would obviously be different, in different ways, if only the aggressor enjoyed the consummation — for example, in rape (in Chrétien's *Philomena*), premature ejaculation (Paris in the *Ylias*), or forced marriage (Hesione). On these issues, see Schnell 1985.

topical invention in rewriting; they also suggest the real moral and social concerns of contemporary medieval audiences.

Focusing on consent is consistent with Matthew's instruction on selectivity in description (*Ars vers* 1.64-75). For example, various stages in the *gradus amoris* imply consent. Indeed, the moment of and grounds for consent may well identify the kind or quality of desire depicted. In the twelfth century consent was not an idle topic. Recent studies have made us aware of the struggle between ecclesiastical and parental authority in this matter.[7] The clashes between the two authorities seem to have been major, and their reflection in the literature of the court could therefore be compelling and even fraught with tension. How, for example, did contemporary court audiences respond to the conflict between Lavine's parents regarding Eneas or Turnus as potential son-in-law, or to Lavine's own initiatives after consenting to love and marry only Eneas? Similarly, how did they respond to Erec, a prince who decides on his own whom he will marry and promises feudal rights to Enide's parents without once consulting his own father or Enide herself? When he returns home after marriage to Enide, neither his father nor mother raises the issue of parental authority in selection of a spouse, unlike the parallel situation in the *Eneas*, where it matters very much.[8] What did the same audiences make of Enide's *parole* and the interference with their nightly and daily *votiva duorum congressio*, or of Erec's unilateral response of changing his wife's status from *fame* and *amie*, implying their essential equality (as in *Erec* v. 1507-13), to that of wife alone, implying male domination? Here we can perceive the master artist treating a traditional motif, the *gradus amoris*, in a new way, and against a compelling backdrop of current marital issues.[9]

In this chapter, I propose to examine the issue of consent in several related romances. But rather than impose a contemporary reading of marriage into my interpretation of them, I shall let the texts

---

[7] See especially Duby 1981, and, in his wake or parallel to his work, Faber 1974, Bloch 1983 pp. 70-71 and 161-63, Schnell 1984, Varty 1986, Brundage 1987 pp. 236-38, Thiry-Stassin and Thiry 1992, and Angenendt 1997 pp. 271-79.

[8] Contrast the silence of Erec's parents with the outspoken anger of Prophilias's parents when he returns to Rome with a wife acquired without their consent. But his new wife is of greater nobility than he, which finally decides the parents to accept her (*Athis* v. 1737-1810). Enide, the daughter of an impoverished vavassor, is not of the same status as Erec.

[9] Erec's change is typical of the kind of *causa* written in composition exercises that turn on a moral or social issue; see Edwards 1993.

speak for themselves on matters of consent. Each exemplifies solutions to a social and moral issue open to audience debate along the lines Matilda Bruckner sets forth in her major article on Chrétien's *Charrette*.

> A situation arises in which we cannot measure only the conduct of an individual; we must also measure the norm by which we usually judge his conduct. As an incident unfolds, for example, a given law may be shown to produce good and bad results: the weight itself is not giving true weight. One must then judge between norms, evaluating each in turn by a superior one.[10]

The law, the norm, and the judgment in contracting marriage in twelfth-century romance were hardly matters of general agreement. The Church and the aristocracy did not agree, for example, on whose consent was necessary for marriage to occur. Responses in these romances are not normative or uniform either.

Indeed, as Martine Thiry-Stassin and Claude Thiry ask: "Quel rôle peut jouer l'institution [du mariage] dans l'élaboration de l'*Histoire* ['et du roman,' one may add], et quelles libertés le poète se permet-il vis-à-vis de l'histoire?"[11] They find one answer by identifying the parameters which "peuvent nuancer l'expression littéraire ou esthétique de phénomènes à vocation sociale que nous étudions."[12] The parameters or limits in their text, *Guillaume le Maréchal*, are more tightly drawn than in most romances; as they point out, contemporary romances, despite their greater fictional freedom, can treat and develop "phénomènes à vocation sociale." In doing so they could expect diverse audience reactions to critical issues like marriage and consent.[13] Indeed, the two *gradus* of love and marriage were not necessarily conjoined; in the aristocratic tradition, marriage was a paternalistically patterned family affair, and love was often depicted as existing outside of marriage. We have seen echoes of this view in the *Troie*. But by the twelfth century the Church had introduced a troubling change in this relationship which brought the two *gradus* of love

---

[10] Bruckner 1986 p. 177; cf. Beltrami 1989. This is related to the "double-lens technique" by which the narrator and protagonists in a plot evaluate issues differently (Janssens 1988 pp. 34-39). On such "ambiguity" in the medieval Latin tradition, see Godman 1990a, esp. p. 613.

[11] Thiry-Stassin and Thiry 1992 p. 341; on the importance of marriage as a source of promotion but not as confirmation of lineage, see Peters 1993.

[12] Thiry-Stassin and Thiry 1992 p. 342.

[13] For an excellent survey of the topical potential of this theme in romance, see Hahn 1988.

and marriage together and revised their sequence. The novelty was conjugal consent. Although the consent of both the betrothed was now becoming a necessary stage in the marriage ceremony, according to the canonists, it was nonetheless not easily accepted by the families.

To understand how crucial consent might be for twelfth-century audiences, let us first look briefly at recent studies on medieval marriage and the issue of consent in the twelfth century. Traditionally, marriage was a contract struck between consenting families for the good of the families. Vassals required the approval of their lords in marriage. Repudiation by the husband as well as his absolute mastery over his wife were practices unquestioned by the Church; before the high Middle Ages, even manifestly unjust, violent, or criminal behavior on the husband's part rarely elicited ecclesiastical disapproval or censure.

The medieval Church gradually began to play a more significant role in marriages. The efforts of the clergy to control and regulate marriage led, for example, to the establishment of marriage as a sacrament during the course of the twelfth century. The issue of consent led to disputes between Church and Court. According to the Church, the consent of each of the affianced (the *épousailles*) and their consent to the consummation (the *noces*) became necessary stages in contracting marriage. Of course, the traditional issue of parental or family consent remains influential, but it may conflict with both ecclesiastical control and individual wishes both in historical record and in narrative fiction. These conflicts are central in the three romances to be studied here, although the particular circumstances in which consent is an issue are unusual, including those cases where it is — surprisingly — not an issue.

The Description of Consent in Gradus amoris

We may begin our discussion of the common place consent in *gradus amoris* with some differences noted in the last chapter between Joseph of Exeter's *Ylias* and Benoît de Sainte-Maure's *Roman de Troie*.

Perhaps one of the most moving moments for modern readers of the *Ylias* is the marriage of Hesione to Telamon. Described in terms of her pathos and his triumph, it is hardly a happy moment for her. To be sure, the marriage meets an objection raised by Benoît, who faults Telamon for not having married Priam's sister (*Troie* v. 2801-04). In his view, this would have made her position acceptable and, perhaps, tolerable as marriages go in the twelfth century. In Benoît's Troy, concubines are not inferior creatures; they actually enjoy a certain status along with their sons. But in Greece, their lot is another matter; forced concubinage for the Greeks is not a matter of love but of conquest.[14] For Benoît, marriage was a conventional means to unite enemies and terminate conflicts peacefully.[15] Could the marriage of Telamon and Hesione have stopped the Trojan War? Perhaps in the *Troie* but not in the *Ylias*. In fact, in the Latin poem the marriage of Hesione and Telamon is yet another cause — an *acheison* no longer *petite* — of the renewed hostilities, since it motivates Paris's abduction of Helen.

Joseph's amplification on Hesione's marriage suggests that, for him, marriage is not a solution to Greco-Trojan enmity. Antenor's mission shows that neither Priam nor most Trojans accept this marriage (*Ylias* Bk. II, v. 188-91, III, v. 1-4), and Priam's sister is forced into marriage without her consent. Telamon exercises absolute authority over his booty; he alone decides her fate and he alone is in charge. His behavior is not entirely different in this from Erec's after the dispute with his wife, although Enide's feelings are not the same as Hesione's. That is, Hesione is an object possessed as spoils of war; she is used more to shame the Trojan king than to satisfy Telamon's love: "Victori nubit Priameia *nostro* / Hesione" (*Ylias* Bk. II, v. 105-06; my emphasis) [Hesione, sister of Priam, is marrying *our triumphant* hero (Bate)]. Further, Telamon and the Greeks are unwilling to compromise on her fate in order to achieve peace. The issue is consent, but Hesione, although of noble family, is not free to accept or reject her husband: "iussa in thalamos timide ventura coactos" (*Ylias* Bk. II, v. 144) [going into a forced marriage afraid and under duress (Bate)]. In Benoît, consent is present for Medea, Briseida, and Polyxena. But the consequences for these women are less than cheerful, suggesting again, perhaps, Benoît's suspicions as to consent. Jason is unfaithful to Medea; Briseida is unfaithful to Troilus and she fears for her reputation; Polyxena regrets the failure of her marriage to Achilles,

---

[14] Hansen 1971 pp. 44-48. On this "war-spoils ethic" and its "brutality," see King 1985 (quote on p. 43).

[15] This justifies the projected marriage of Achilles and Polyxena in the *Troie*; see Chapter Four.

but, because she was a crucial pawn in Hecuba's vengeance on the Greek hero, she becomes the victim of Pyrrhus's revenge of his father's death.

Consent as motif has been largely overlooked in the interpretation of the three major romances treated here.[16] Still, it is a bright red thread that links them and identifies each as a rewriting of the consent model by using allusion to underscore rewriting of the consent motif.[17] The man's consent looms as large as the woman's although both point to the same contemporary problem: the place of consent in love and, especially, marriage. In the *Aeneid* Vergil ignores the issue as far as Lavinia is concerned; human fate is dependent on following the will of the gods and one's destiny, not on individual decision to marry one person or the other. But the issue of consent emerges in the rewriting of the *Aeneid* in the *Eneas*, which stands apart from its source principally because of the extensive amplification of Lavine's *gradus amoris*. And what other than Lavine's consent is at issue in this lengthy development?

Consent makes the expression of love in conjugal vows a sincere statement. Consent is also the realm in which different conceptions of marriage clash. To analyze the description of consent as a topos of romance, I shall examine three works that are related through allusions to one another and that all problematize consent. As stated earlier, they are the *Roman d'Eneas*, Chrétien de Troyes's *Erec et Enide*, and Renaut de Beaujeu's *Bel Inconnu*. The *Eneas* relates all of them to Vergil's epic and, thus at least indirectly, to Macrobius's analysis of the *Aeneid*. Since Macrobius nowhere raises the issue of consent, we can appreciate its relevance when it is inserted into the plot in the twelfth century. The link to the *Eneas* is explicit in *Erec* as well as in the *Bel Inconnu*, which alludes to both *Erec* and *Eneas*. These allusions justify our examining them together in the light of Macrobius's notion of description and in the context of consent as topos in a *gradus amoris* leading to marriage.

Since these romances model their plot on the *gradus amoris* topos, each *gradus amoris* can function like the banquet motif as Macrobius describes it in Homer and Vergil. There, certain commonplace elements such as the host, the guest, and the meal recur in each instance

---

[16] But see Varty 1986 and Kullmann 1993.

[17] Especially when all the works are brought together in the same manuscript; on the *recueil*, see Short 1988.

of the banquet motif, with replacements as the *materia* calls for them as well as with heterogeneous elements which the author adds to the motif in order to fit it into the new plot. Consent is crucial in all three romances. I shall treat them in chronological order, and including a look at Lavinia's marriage in Vergil's *Aeneid*. But before going into detail, I shall first summarize issues of consent as they emerge in all four narratives.

First, Vergil's *Aeneid*. Briefly put, Aeneas must forsake Dido and love for Rome, destiny, and dynasty. This is in conformity with the view of love and marriage we find in the *Troie*. In Italy, he finds that Lavinia is an important pawn in the struggle for dynasty. Although she makes it possible for Aeneas to fulfill his destiny, her views on the matter have no place in the epic, and the only evidence of her emotions suggests that she loves Turnus rather than Aeneas.

In the *Eneas*, on the other hand, Eneas forsakes Dido and love in Carthage for Lavine and another love in Rome. But marriage and dynasty are more troubled here than in the epic. Lavine's views on the choice of her husband loom large. Indeed, they take up much of the concluding narrative. The anonymous French author has added to the disagreement between her father and mother regarding a suitable spouse for their daughter the issue of their daughter's own consent. The marriage unites love and dynasty to provide a revised denouement to Vergil's plot.

Likewise, Chrétien de Troyes's *Erec et Enide* shows first the love, engagement, and marriage of the titular heroes; but a crisis ensues after the marriage which leads to Erec's departure. This "new Eneas" initially takes his Dido with him rather than repudiate her, and he marries her afterwards. In the first part Enide is a willing and loving daughter. Her marriage to Erec fits traditional family expectations — her father had been keeping his daughter in reserve for a prince like Erec — and, in the end, Erec presents his new parents-in-law with a virtual dowry of two castles. All this is conventional enough in both aristocratic and ecclesiastical views on marriage in the twelfth century. But Erec's role is different. Although he obviously consents to marry Enide — he asks for her hand — he does not ask his own father's permission to marry the comparatively low-born maiden, daughter of an impoverished vavassor, and place her on the throne next to him, prince and heir to a kingdom. Later, in the second part of the romance, when Enide hears Erec's men complain about his absence at tournaments, she virtually withdraws her consent or at least questions her conjugal duty, inspiring Erec to abandon his marriage bed. But not for tournaments.

Finally, in Renaut de Beaujeu's *Bel Inconnu*, the hero forsakes the Pucelle aux blanches mains, a "Dido" whom he meets on his way to a predetermined goal, the liberation of the Blonde Esmeree. But, unlike Eneas, the Inconnu returns to her because he loves her more than the Blonde Esmeree, the woman he consents to marry if Arthur approves and whom he actually does marry before the end of the romance. Yet Guinglain is a kind of Eliduc: he consents twice. The denouement depends on the consent of a third woman: the one Renaut is allegedly writing the romance for: "Quant vos plaira, dira avant, / U il se taira ore a tant" (*Bel Inc* v. 6253-54) [When you wish he will continue the story; otherwise he will leave it as it stands].

We have three romances that rewrite the motif of consent in *gradus amoris*. The *Eneas* incorporates it into his source. Although it maintains the titular hero's withdrawal of consent to Dido, it rewrites the conclusion to include the consent of Lavine. In *Erec*, only one woman is involved; the crisis turns on the issue of consent to intercourse in marriage. Finally, the *Bel Inconnu* returns to the *Eneas* scheme to relate a love encountered on a quest followed by another that emerges at the end of the quest. Although we are told that the Inconnu loves only the first woman, the second one gains his hand. His double consent is left hanging in the balance until the consent of a third, extradiegetic woman is obtained, but which is tacitly withheld.

Drawing parallels like these is hazardous. If we have recently come to recognize adaptations as original, which earlier scholars took to be corruptions, the identification of which works influenced a specific writer's adaptation is usually uncertain. Commonplace schemes may occur to otherwise independent writers by the very nature of topical adaptation. One did not need to read Matthew of Vendôme to construe a *gradus amoris*, especially when the writer was trained to think in terms of common places. Nonetheless, even if the analysis of such adaptations is, in specific instances, suspect or unconvincing, the principle of imitation as original description in Macrobius and the actual practice of the technique are fundamental to medieval writers trained in the school tradition. When one work specifically cites another, we have a basis for comparison.[18]

---

[18] Schmolke-Hasselmann 1980 chapter Six and Besamusca 1993 pp. 12-21. For an analysis of the *Eneas* as a model for Aimon de Varennes's *Florimont*, see Harf-Lancner 1994.

With the three romances examined here, we can observe a French vernacular tradition within which one author's work may echo in an audience's ears while hearing another work which alludes to, but rewrites some aspect of its predecessor. Thus, although the non-Latin public of the *Eneas* may very well be ignorant of Vergil's epic as Benoît's may have been of Dares and Dictys, this is not the case for Chrétien's audiences when they are reminded towards the end of *Erec et Enide* of major figures and situations in the *Roman d'Eneas* — for example:

> Comant Eneas vint de Troie,
> Comant a Cartage a grant joie
> Dido an son lit le reçut,
> Comant Eneas la deçut,
> Comant ele por lui s'ocist,
> Comant Eneas puis conquist
> Laurente et tote Lonbardie. (*Erec* v. 5339-45)

[How Eneas came from Troy to Carthage full of joy, and how Dido received him into her bed, how Eneas betrayed her and she committed suicide on his account, how Eneas then conquered Laurentium and all of Lombardy.]

The same is true in the *Bel Inconnu*'s echoes of *Erec*, beginning with the famous allusion to Chrétien's *bele conjointure* in terms of *roman* in the Prologue.[19]

> Cele qui m'a en sa baillie,
> Cui ja d'amors sans trecerie
> M'a doné sens de cançon faire,
> Por li veul un roumant estraire
> D'un molt biel conte d'aventure. (*Bel Inc* v.1-5)

[For her who has dominion over me and who inspired me to write a chanson I wish to draw a romance out of a very fine tale of adventure.]

Right away, an alert public may be on the look-out for issues raised in Chrétien that resurface in the *Bel inconnu*.

---

[19] Kelly 1992 p. 15.

Description of Consent in the Eneas

The *Roman d'Eneas* rewrites Vergil, using techniques that Macrobius identifies as description in Vergil's own adaptations of his predecessors; it thus has a place in the medieval tradition of imitation and transfer treated in Chapter Three.[20] In order to move beyond the mere formalities of descriptive imitation and transmission, I intend to show the originality of authors who rewrite antecedent motifs like the *gradus amoris* and its consent stage. I hope in this way to show the utility of medieval conceptions of imitation for interpretation, especially as description in Macrobius's sense of the term, and to show how specific masterpieces by those standards could have something new and important to say to contemporary audiences.

In the case of *Eneas* there can be no doubt that Vergil was the first author and the *Aeneid* the source.[21] But insofar as this romance has the same implied audience as the *Troie*, we cannot assume its knowledge of the Latin epic. The adaptations by the vernacular author can show his or her art of re-creation; the poet cannot build on its implied audience's appreciation of that art any more than Benoît could for the *Troie*. What those audiences would recognize, however, are the kinds of marriage problems current in their century. Let us then begin with the art, which we can compare in both works, and then pass on to what audiences of the *Eneas* could perceive in the rewritten vernacular poem.

To get our bearings on the *Eneas* authors's art, we can start by seeing how the anonymous French adapter rewrote passages in the *Aeneid* discussed by Macrobius. The *Eneas*, adapted from the *Aeneid* in about 1160, inserts new descriptive material into the broad lines of Vergil's plot. For example, as is well known, marvelous descriptive additions (*adiectio*) add to or replace (*immutatio*) many divine interventions found in Vergil.[22] There is a sharp reduction in some parts (*detractio*) — notably in the episodes involving the gods, certain sequences like Aeneas's voyage from Troy to Carthage and from

---

[20] Cormier 1973 pp. 88-93 and Foehr-Janssens 1997 analyze the *Eneas*'s rewriting of the *Aeneid* in the context of imitation and emulation.

[21] Of course, this does not identify what particular version or versions the French author used, or what role secondary sources and even commentaries, glosses, and scholia may have played; see Mora 1985 and Cormier 1988 and 1989.

[22] Faral 1913.

Carthage to Italy,[23] his descent into Hades, and the combats in
Latium (renamed Lombardy in the French romance) which tend to
be abbreviated and described in medieval rather than Roman
terms.[24] Other features are amplified (*adiectio*), such as Menelaus's
capture of Troy in the first lines and the Judgment of Paris episode
along with lavish descriptions of places, monuments, and objects, and
Ovidian loves at once violent and naive, orderly and overwhelming.[25]

> On peut voir en lisant l'*Eneas* combien la simple opération de transfert
> linguistique, avec le déplacement des contraintes stylistiques, a pu
> introduire de modifications sensibles d'une œuvre à l'autre, au point
> que si le modèle n'était pas expressément nommé, le lecteur pourrait
> hésiter à reconnaître l'épopée latine dans plusieurs passages de son
> adaptation romane.[26]

These words imply the very kind of camouflage in rewriting that
Macrobius discerns in Vergil: "hic opportune in opus suum quae
prior vates dixerat transferendo fecit ut sua esse credantur" (*Sat*
5.3.16) [he transferred into his work the earlier poet's words so appo-
sitely that they appeared to be his own]. As Horace states, infidelity
to sources is a major factor in original rewriting.

If we compare the two poems' treatment of the sea storm and
Dido's reception, episodes which Macrobius singled out and which
became paradigmatic in the reading of Vergil (see Chapters Two and
Three), we get a sense of the kind of adaptations the French author
made. Importantly, almost none of the passages Macrobius quotes
from the sea storm and banquet have left a trace in *Eneas*.

In eliminating these lines, the romance has practiced the commonplace operation of deletion in the rewriting of this description. Taking
our cue from *Sat* 5.2.13, where Macrobius invites his reader to make
his or her own comparisons: "versus utriusque qui volet conferat"
[whoever wishes can compare the lines in both authors], we can
extend the invitation to Vergil and his Old French rewriter. As we
have observed earlier, Vergil used a tripartite model for the sea

---

[23] Book III is compressed into five lines (v. 1192-96) whereas Book V takes up
scarcely more than one hundred (v. 2145-2252) in the French version. See Monfrin
1985 pp. 195-96.
[24] Schöning 1991 pp. 88-97, who notes that anachronism is not constant in the
romans d'antiquité. See also Logié 1996.
[25] Faral 1913 and Auerbach 1958 chap. 3.
[26] Mora-Lebrun 1994a p. 10; see also Zink 1984, Chênerie 1985, and Rousse
1985 p. 149.

storm: anger, winds, and intervention to calm the seas. In the *Eneas* the last two are partially deleted, partly modified (*detractio, immutatio,* and *transmutatio*). Vergil describes the wind's violent impact on the sea first (*Aen* Bk. I, v. 81-91), then its effect on Aeneas himself (v. 92-101), and finally on the ships (v. 102-23). The *Eneas* reduces the model from three agents to one: Juno herself causes the tempest (*Eneas* v. 183-89) and the storm subsides on its own after three days and nights (v. 264-69); Neptune is absent. The romance combines the storm's two-part effects on Aeneas and his ships into a whole, illustrating the punch by which the winds slap man, sea, and ships in the pitch-black storm (v. 190-209, 242-62). Only the "aquae mons" (*Aen* Bk. I, v. 105) survives as a wave that overwhelms Eneas's ship, an amplification that actually reduces the emphatic force of the original: "une vague li vint desore, / qui si la fiert a l'un des lez, / les borz a fraiz et decassez" (v. 246-48) [a wave washed over it, striking the ship on one side and breaking and shattering the broadside].

But Juno's anger is also amplified from the brief allusions to the wrongs committed against her that have their source in the *Aeneid* (Bk. I, v. 36), allusions that Roman audiences no doubt recognized immediately. These were detailed briefly in *Aeneid* v. 26-28 as the Judgment of Paris; her hatred of the descendants of Dardanus, the founding father of the Trojan line, because he was the son of one of Jupiter's lovers; and the favors Jupiter shows Ganymede, son of Tros and, therefore, also a member of the hated Trojan line.[27] In the *Eneas*, only Paris's judgment survives to explain Juno's anger. Perhaps because no French language version was available at the time the *Eneas* was written, the anonymous author recounts this episode at some length. Thus the Judgment passes from a brief allusion in the Latin to a major amplification and insertion in the French. The focus on Juno allows the *Eneas* author to transform his or her source, making Juno the prime mover of the storm. This sets up the striking opposition between Juno and Venus.

Venus won Paris's approval by promising him Helen.[28] The goddess continues to act according to conventional expectations in the

---

[27] Cf. *Aen* Bk. I, v. 28, and *Sat* 5.16.10-11. On Vergil's amplifications, see *Sat* 5.1.

[28] In Vergil Juno entices Aeolus in a similar way. For his services, she offers him her most beautiful nymph Deiopea as wife and mother of his children (*Aen* Bk. I, v. 72-75). Although this marriage is analogous to "feudal" marriages, the French romance leaves it out.

banquet scene, but details change. As with the sea storm, much is deleted, notably the ceremonial activities and the replacement of Ascanius by Cupid. Venus's central role in the *Eneas* thus mirrors her triumph in the Judgment of Paris. She gives Ascanius the power to instil love into Eneas and Dido, reserving Cupid for a more positive role at the end of the romance when Eneas and Lavine fall in love. "Mortal poison" (*Eneas* v. 811) replaces Cupid (*immutatio*); an amplification on this topic completes an earlier digression on the power of love (*Eneas* v. 764-76, 806-22). But Dido as Venus's instrument, audiences for the *Troie* will later note, does not enjoy Helen's fate as Venus's agent. As in Vergil, she commits suicide once she has served the goddess's purposes.

Critically, Venus's prominence marks a significant *mutatio*. Forefronting Venus in the Judgment of Paris and the banquet scene, the *Eneas* prepares for subsequent adaptations that emphasize her role. Indeed, the ubiquity of Eneas's mother after her victory in the Judgment of Paris enhances her concern for Eneas's destiny at Troy, at Carthage, and in "Lombardy." Abetted by Eneas's half-brother Cupid, Venus manipulates uncertain fortune to achieve established destiny and found the Roman dynasty. These developments entail considerable adaptation of Vergil's narrative. Acting as goddess of love and as a manifestation of good love — "Ele ot d'amor la poësté" (*Eneas* v. 769)[29] [she had dominion over love] — Venus motivates the major events in the narrative, assuring Eneas's safety in Carthage by "poisoning" Dido's heart with love (*Eneas* v. 811), and promoting his victory in Italy by love's beneficial influence on prowess. Rather than the labors of founding Rome as an illustration of rivalries among the gods and the realization of destiny through armed conflict, we see the removal of the Trojans to the West under the protection of Venus and through the power of love that here becomes necessary for the realization of dynasty.[30] In this way the French Venus links the 'mutated' parts of the *Aeneid*, and explains love as the prime mover in dynastic events. Her affair with Mars illustrates the union of love and arms and, therefore, the power of love to promote prowess.

Venus's interventions multiply through replacement (*immutatio*).

---

[29] The author no doubt sought to simplify his source, as Croizy-Naquet 1994 pp. 199-200 points out; but he had an informing intention too, as these illustrations show.

[30] Marchello-Nizia 1985 and Rousse 1985.

Rather than Hector, Venus warns Eneas in a dream to flee Troy; she, not her doves, guides him to the Golden Bough; and she, not the river Tiber, sends Eneas to seek Evander's help.[31] Vergil provides the model, however, when her promise to return to the marriage bed persuades her husband Vulcan to prepare the armor in which her son will defeat Turnus and the "Lombards." Finally, in a major transfer (*transmutatio*), after her son Cupid disappears from the Dido episode in the French, he emerges at the end of the romance.[32] No longer disguised as Ascanius in order to deceive Dido with kisses, Cupid assumes a more positive role to strike Lavine and Eneas with his arrows, advancing thereby the ends of destiny along the same lines his mother had followed.

> Amors l'a de son dart ferue;
> ainz qu'el se fust d'iluec meüe,
> i a changié cent foiz colors[33]:
> or est cheoite es laz d'amors,
> voille ou non, amer l'estuet. (*Eneas* v. 8057-61)[34]

[Love has struck her with his arrow. Before leaving the spot she blushed a hundredfold. Now she has fallen into love's snares: she must love whether she will or not.]

But she does will to love: "Eneas tien por mon ami, / ge l'ain" (v. 8300-01) [I take Eneas as my beloved; I love him]; Lavine consents. In this way, Vergil's epic is reshaped neatly and coherently, and love, Venus's domain, promotes the ends of dynasty. The conclusion to the *Eneas* emphasizes Venus's role in the founding of Rome, important from beginning to end:

---

[31] *Eneas* v. 1186-89, 2337-38, and 4573-82 respectively. Cf. Rockwell 1995 pp. 158-59.

[32] See Gaunt 1992 p. 13 and Deist 1994. But I cannot agree with Gaunt when he argues that Venus drops from the tale at the end; she is, as I hope to have shown, the agent of destiny, as are both her sons.

[33] In Vergil, Lavinia blushes because of Turnus, not of Aeneas (Bk. XII, v. 64-69).

[34] Lavine also speaks of love's poison (v. 8110). On Cupid's role here, see v. 8629-59. On Cupid's power over Eneas, see v. 8922-26 and 8940-55, who also refers to the "poison" in the letter attached to the arrow Lavine uses to attract his attention (v. 8954). Despite Lavine's and Eneas's resistance, both finally consent to the god of love's victory; the latter therefore completes Venus's plot and permits destiny to achieve its goals.

> Unques Paris n'ot graignor joie,
> quant Eloine tint dedanz Troie,
> qu'Eneas ot, quant tint s'amie
> en Laurente.... (*Eneas* v. 10109-12)[35]

[Paris had no greater joy when he held Helen in Troy than Eneas did when he held his beloved in Laurentium!]

Lavine does not suffer Dido's fate; she emerges from the conflict for her consent as unscathed as Helen does at the end of the *Troie*. But unlike Helen, she is her husband's *femme* and *amie*,[36] as the preceding quote shows.

These adaptations of Vergil's Venus and her role remind us of the Roman poet's own adaptations of Homeric material as Macrobius describes them. For example, Macrobius says that Vergil added the Dido encounter to his matter. Similarly, the *Eneas* drew the Lavine plot out to include almost one-third of his 10,000-line romance. But Lavine is not Dido.[37] Nor is Venus Vergil's headstrong goddess, majestic and beautiful, or Jean de Meun's rakish demiurge of sexual arousal. Rather, as the *Eneas* narrator exclaims, Lavine's love is beneficial: "Amors, molt dones vasalages! / Amors, molt faiz croistre corages" (*Eneas* v. 9063-64) [Love, you inspire courageous deeds, you fill hearts with courage].

Vergil's narrative, alternately abbreviated, amplified, and thus rewritten by inventive imitation, holds together in the romance through Venus's person. The wars Venus inspires are not just for a woman, as with Helen at Troy. The goddess is the guardian of dynasty. In the *Eneas*, love founds families and peoples. The dynasty Eneas founds is possible because his mother makes love beneficial in lineage and dynasty. To be sure, this is aristocratic love; that is, it is highly sensual in private because of the force of sincere attraction and essentially chivalric in public because it supports the commonweal and produces lineage (*Eneas* v. 2813-30, 2879-82, 2923-80, 10131-56). Thus, if the *Eneas* is less Augustan in conception than its model, it is more twelfth-century aristocrastic in context. Its author could write such a work by practicing Macrobian imitation as *mutatio* —

---

[35] See Baumgartner 1992. Schöning 1991 p. 291 points out that Turnus evokes the same image in terms of Eneas's labors near the romance's mid-point, v. 4177-79.

[36] Marchello-Nizia 1985 pp. 251-54.

[37] Huchet 1984 pp. 132-33.

mira imitatione descripta est. The *Eneas*, like the *Aeneid*, translates a work from one language into a new language, and it does so by rewriting its source so as to effect something new. The *Eneas* obviously retains the quest motif which Macrobius identified in the *Aeneid's iter* as the *navigatio* motif. But the French romance gives the motif a new, medieval significance: Venus has become the guide.

Where does she lead, and why? Here I wish to bring both formal and substantive arguments together in the context of description as topical invention. I hope in this way to show how the author of the *Eneas* invented the love of Lavine and Eneas by adapting his Vergilian material and models along with other sources available in his time. The analysis is based on the French author's use not only of a *gradus amoris*, but, more to the point in the *Eneas*, a *gradus amoris matromoniaeque* that requires the fiancée's consent. Consent is at issue in the marriage of Lavine.

Marriage is a commonplace motif in romance. Not that it appeared there for the first time. We find it in *chansons de geste* too.[38] If Olivier decides on his own, and without consulting his sister, whether Roland will marry her, he meets no opposition from "la belle Aude's" intended nor is her consent an issue. On the other hand, in Marie de France, a reader and an admirer of *romans d'antiquité*, consent, especially the woman's consent, is diversely problematized in almost every lay. No doubt, the most striking example is in *Le Chaitivel*,[39] but others are available. In Chrétien's romances, consent is also a major issue in *Erec*, *Cligés*, and *Yvain*; it is as well in Hue de Rotelande's *Ipomedon* (whatever one thinks of its solution to the problem), *Partonopeu de Blois*, Aimon de Varennes's *Florimont*, *Durmart le galois*, and Raoul de Houdenc's *Meraugis de Portlesguez* — to name just a few obvious examples among many.

However, Lavine's case is especially intriguing. It allows us to see how, in an early work, the *Eneas* author invents the narrative in which Vergil's "incomplete" version — incomplete because Lavinia's consent is missing[40] — is rewritten to include it. The *Eneas* author has, I suggest, simply added to the *gradus amoris* the stage or topos of consent, and then amplified on the implications of consent within the broader political and feudal framework of the founding of Rome and

---

[38] Kay 1995 treats marriage in French epic.
[39] See Bloch 1983 pp. 190-93; Gertz 1996 chap. 4 includes discussion of allusive description by the intertextual echoes and rewriting of Chrétien's *Charrette*.
[40] On *corronpre* in the sense of incomplete, see Kelly 1992 pp. 125-29.

the disposition of the Latin inheritance. In so doing, the author acts much as Matthew of Vendôme wanted his pupils to do when he said they should complete what ancient authors left incomplete — for example, in *gradus amoris*.

The *Eneas* contrasts two exemplary loves, that of Dido and Eneas and that of Eneas and Lavine. We can set aside Eneas's widowhood, which the French romance mentions only in passing, and not at the time of his first wife's disappearance during Eneas's flight from Troy, as in Vergil, but while he was still fighting the Greeks (*Eneas* v. 1180-84). Dido's widowhood is a different matter, as we shall see. The factors that define the relationship between Dido and Eneas and the marriage of Eneas and Lavine are his "twelfth-century marriage" to Lavine that makes possible his destiny as founding father.

In broad outline, the Dido-Eneas affair follows its Vergilian model rather closely. Venus causes Dido's passion, and Eneas is a willing partner. In fact, both he and Dido consent to their passion, the act, and the open affair. They are two exiles united by mutual consent. Even before Venus's intervention, Dido is willing to integrate Trojans and Carthaginians on equal status (*Eneas* v. 621-40, 653-62). The fatal kissing of Ascanius pushes her over the edge: "Ele ne set qui l'a sorprise: / mortel poison avoit beü" (v. 1258-59) [she didn't know what overcame her; she had drunk mortal poison[41]]. The consummation of their love in the cave witnesses Dido giving in to his and her desire: "tot li consent sa volenté; / pieça qu'el l'avoit desirré" (v. 1525-26) [she gave full consent to his desire; she herself had desired him for some time]. This is the consent to passion. Eneas and Dido illustrate here Matthew's final stage in a sensual *gradus amoris*, that is, consensual sex or "ad ultimum votiva duorum congressio" (*Ars vers* 4.13).

But there are, of course, obstacles to their love. Eneas's destiny stands in the way, and destiny is as powerful and impersonal a force in the *Eneas* as in *Troie*.[42] Furthermore, the widow Dido has herself

---

[41] For a subtle analysis of this image, see Angeli 1971 pp. 108-09. "Poison" seems a more accurate translation here than "potion," although audiences who knew some version of the Tristan legend might have noted "Tristanian" connotations in this word. Some versions of the Tristan legend were doubtless circulating at the time the *Eneas* was written; see Gallais 1967.

[42] Petit 1985b pp. 494-97. Patterson 1987 p. 192 recognizes the role of destiny, but prefers to use "history" as prime mover; see p. 181 on the "illogicality" of atemporal destiny. He may be right, but I am not sure the *Eneas* audiences would have thought so. See Dragonetti 1987 pp. 17-33.

contracted obligations willingly, and thus by consent, to her deceased husband. She swore eternal fidelity to him, and she feels the constraint of her oath. She says as much before the consummation: "se por ce non qu'a mon espos / pramis m'amor a mon vivant, / de lui [i.e., Eneas] feïsse mun amant" (v. 1304-06) [were it not that I promised to love my husband for the rest of my life, I would make Eneas my lover]. The same objection justified her earlier refusal to marry any of the Libyan barons (v. 1359-60). But Anna advises her to marry Eneas anyway, in part because Dido desires him, but also because, as a woman, she needs a man to defend her lands against those like the barons whom she had earlier deceived and spurned (v. 1347-64). Her advice would not have seemed unusual to twelfth-century barons. It is one of Laudine's reasons for consenting to marry Yvain (*Yvain* v. 1734-37, 2079-104). But Dido does not marry Eneas, she only makes him her lover (*amant*).

Now, the Libyan barons do constitute a rather formidable threat in the twelfth-century context. They may overrun Dido's lands and treat her as they see fit (v. 1721-31); we have seen this model in the *Troie*. The irony, perhaps, is that this is precisely what happens, not because the barons are laying waste her lands (v. 1415), but because of Eneas himself (v. 1416-32). Then, after his initial *recreantise* with Dido (v. 1573-78), the gods recall him to his duty and his destiny. For, although unmarried, Eneas "toz est livrez a male voe, / et terre et fame tient por soe" (v. 1613-14) [is off on the wrong tack — he's holding land and woman as if he owned them]. Dido, whom her subjects regard only as a concubine, dies without heir and abandons to an unspecified fate her land, or *enor*, and her vassals, or *barnage* (v. 2051-52). Her earlier prowess in outwitting and conquering the Libyan barons seems to be replaced by a *recreantise* that is ultimately suicidal.

As in Vergil, the Libyan barons gave her the land which, like Melusine later, she cleverly tricks them into granting. By a *jeu de verité*, or "angin" (v. 393), Dido requests as much land as a bull's hide can cover, then cuts the hide into fine strips which encompass an area large enough to hold the Carthage she plans to build. She then conquers those same barons by her *angin*, prowess, and wealth (v. 403-06). They become her vassals. As vassals they have a right to her hand in marriage; they also have a say in any marriage she makes and even in how she conducts her sex life. Those familiar with Laudine's circumstances in Chrétien's *Yvain* will recognize the same

forces at work in Dido's case. However, there are also major differences. Yvain marries Laudine with the consent of her vassals; her
new husband then leaves his wife for tournaments, precipitating later
the drama of their separation. In the *Eneas* there is no public marriage, the barons oppose the affair, and Eneas leaves permanently for
Lombardy.

In Lombardy Eneas falls in love with Lavine. Here too the vassal
barons have claims. Latin has already promised his lands and his
daughter's hand to Turnus. The *épousailles*, in twelfth-century terms,
have taken place.[43] Turnus reminds him of this in explicit terms after
her father, heeding destiny, changes his mind in favor of Eneas. He
insists on these facts because they are binding matrimonial procedure. Turnus's feudal rights and claims are unimpeachable, even if,
as he admits,

> ... et me quides metre a niant,
> si'n es vers moi par seirement:
> de ta terre m'as erité,
> o ta fille m'as tot doné;
> ge l'ai plevie et afiee;
> ne l'ai ancor pas esposee,
> et ne geümes an un lit,[44]
> encor remaint par ton respit;
> mais de la terre sui saisiz,
> et les chastiaus ai recoilliz,
> g'en ai les tors et les donjons
> et les homages des barons. (*Eneas* v. 3847-58)

[You think you can get rid of me, but you are bound by the oath
you swore to me. You have given me your lands in inheritance
— all of it along with your daughter. I have given my word and
sworn to the contract. I haven't yet consummated the marriage
in bed, but that is only because of your delaying tactics. But I

---

[43] Cf. "covenance", v. 3396 and 3424; "convent," "fiance," "seremant", v. 3493-
94; "covanz", v. 3883; "covenanz," v. 4153; "covenir", v. 4156, 4163; "homages", v.
3858, 4137; and "otroi", v. 4154. See Petit 1985a p. 115.

[44] That is, the *épousailles* have taken place, but not the *noces*. Note that in Erec's
case, his parents-in-law do not receive the castles he promised them until after the
épousailles but before the *noces*, and that Lac does not oppose the gift (*Erec* v. 1847-
1906). They are a virtual dowry for Enide; cf. as well *Erec* v. 2725-33, where Erec
requests that Enide receive half of Lac's land if she returns without her husband.

have taken possession of the land and castles, and I hold their walls and towers and the hommage of the barons.]

He has stronger, more fully established claims on Lavine and her inheritance than did Dido's barons.

But the situation is more complex than at Carthage for other reasons too. To some, the principle of consent allows for a change of mind if the consummation has not taken place.[45] To be sure, Latin did all the things Turnus said. But he had promised his daughter "estre mon gré / et ancontre ma volanté" (v. 3233-34) [against my will]. Here the father's consent is forced! Indeed, he did not truly consent. In fact, Latin was pushed into the marriage contract by his wife, who actively supported the feudal and conjugal contract with Turnus. Furthermore, Latin is not alone in having mental reservations. Lavine herself has trouble with the marriage even before she sees Eneas. She does not know what love is, which shows right away that she does not love Turnus. She will want Eneas as much as Dido did. But she lacks Dido's freedom to act.

Of course, none of this is in Vergil, where Lavinia, "causa mali tanti" (*Aeneid* XI, v. 480) [source of all that woe] — and therefore guilty too, somewhat like Helen and Polyxena (by the *Troie*'s standards) — is allowed scarcely a blush to express her feelings.[46] Rather, the *Eneas* informs the model with a *surplus de sen* not found on the surface at least in Vergil, but entirely comprehensible, problematic, and even controversial in the context of twelfth-century issues in marriage, feudalism, and love. There is no simple solution to the problem. The crux is consent. Turnus's claims are unimpeachable by traditional aristocratic procedure in contracting marriage.[47] He has the land and the sworn fidelity of Latin's vassals; he has the father's promise. But he does not have Lavine's consent. Does he need it?

Even though the French romance is set in a pagan, pre-Christian world, like the *Troie* it nonetheless raises issues of concern to twelfth-century nobility in the French-speaking world of France and England. Among these are the validity of marriage in relation to 1) the

---

[45] Duby 1981 pp. 183 and 196-97 and Brundage 1987 pp. 236-38 and 275. Destiny is also an overriding factor in evaluation of Turnus's feudal rights; see Ménétré 1994.

[46] *Aen* XII, v. 64-66; cf. Bk. XI, v. 479-80. Lavinia seems grieved at the prospect of Turnus's death; see *Aen* XII, v. 604-07.

[47] Cormier 1973 p. 194.

consent of vassals to the marriage, 2) parental consent, 3) consent of
the affianced to marry (*épousailles*), and 4) consent to sexual intercourse (*noces*). Let us review each of these issues in turn to see how the
Eneas evaluates its own positive and negative models in Eneas's relations with Dido and Lavine. Both affairs add significant social features to the topical *gradus amoris* by treating the feelings of Dido and
Lavine. These features explain why the *Eneas* author and his or her
public might deem Vergil's *Aeneid* incomplete in the same way that
Matthew of Vendôme found many of Ovid's love stories incomplete
(*Ars vers* 4.13): Vergil's Lavinia has virtually no *gradus amoris*. But
incompleteness may ensue not only from the absence of certain commonplace stages for falling in love. It may also occur because the
stages lack definition. By definition I mean the *surplus de sen* which, as
in a head-to-toe description of beauty, articulates an ideal (like
Helen's face), a defect (like Helen's liver), or — in the case of narrative schemes like the *gradus amoris* — approved or rejected custom or
ethics (like Helen's abduction). It is in the realm of custom and ethics
that we can detect issues and intentions that direct an artist's rewriting of an antecedent.

In the *Eneas*, two major issues distinguish Dido's fate from Lavine's
happy marriage. Eneas does not and cannot marry Dido, although
he does have a love affair with her — a love affair apparently as
sincere in its passion as, for example, Briseida's with Troilus in the
Troie, yet as impossible of happy resolution in the one case as in the
other. Nonetheless, the issue of marriage, regardless of its likelihood,
brings into play the four factors mentioned above: the consent of
vassals, parents, the affianced, and spouses. Let us conclude this
analysis of the *Eneas* by examining, in summary fashion, each of these
factors in the *gradus amoris* of Eneas, Dido, and Lavine.

1. The vassals' consent
In each of Eneas's love relationships the vassals play a role. In both
instances they oppose the love or marriage because Eneas is an out-
sider of lower nobility bent, they argue, on usurping a place and land
which, they think, should rightly go to one of them (*Eneas* v. 1582-88,
3361-69, 3881-96, 4185-98).[48] That place includes the marriage bed,
as Turnus says (v. 3852-54). The vassals condone neither Eneas's love

---

[48] Cormier 1973 p. 164.

affair nor his marriage, unlike, for example, Laudine's barons, who accept her marriage to Yvain.

2. Parental consent

Unlike Dido, Lavine must confront her parents' dissension about her marriage. Her mother has sided with Turnus, like the vassals. But Latin himself, who at first reluctantly agreed to the marriage and turned his lands and vassals over to Turnus, has a mental reservation which Eneas's arrival in Italy brings to the fore. The reservation is based on what Latin knows about Eneas's destiny to found Rome (v. 3337-50). But it also reflects paternal authority, traditional in the twelfth century, to choose his daughter's spouse (cf. v. 3252-54). Since Lavine's betrothal — the *épousailles* — has not been consummated by the *noces*, it can still be terminated. At least, Latin seems to think so. But there is a new element.

3. Lavine's consent

Latin does not take account of Lavine's feelings about either Turnus or Eneas. In this, he is the traditional father giving away his daughter for feudal reasons.[49] That is why the establishment of the great empire which is Eneas's destiny determines his preference. However, Lavine's mother knows that love is also a factor in marriage — and her words suggest that by love, she means what Dido herself felt. Because without love, there can be no consent. This is the crux of her debates with Lavine about the relative merits of Eneas and Turnus. Despite various devices she uses to move and even force Lavine's heart — Love's command, her mother's own peremptory "Aimme lou, fille!" (v. 7954) [love him, daughter!], Eneas's alleged homosexuality, conspiracy with Turnus himself — her stratagems fail. Lavine loves only Eneas and consents to marry him alone (v. 8300-34). Here is the real issue. This presentation would surely have agitated the *Eneas*'s audiences at a time when issues of consent were being debated within and between the aristocracy and the Church.

---

[49] Cf. Antigone in the *Thèbes*: "Parlez ent... a ma mere, / et par le conseill de mon frere, / qui voz parens connoist et vos, / soit acordez le plet de nous. / Se il l'agreent, je l'otroi" (v. 4183-87) [Speak to my mother about it; let the agreement between us be reached with my brother's advice, since he knows your family and you. If they come to terms, I consent]; however, she reserves implicitly her right to consent: "ja n'en seront desdit par moi" (v. 4188) [I won't oppose it]. Antigone is willing to marry; see Donovan 1975 pp. 145-47 and Rieger 1987 pp. 76-78.

4. Consent to consummation

In the *Eneas*, love serves dynasty by marriage and procreation.[50] Without offspring, marriage can be of no use in feudal policy. Consent to consummation in the *noces* becomes a major issue in a *gradus amoris* which, in the *Troie*, requires no more of consummation than that it produce descendants. In Dido's case it produces no heir, nor does it contribute to maintaining the realm. Dido neglects further building in Carthage, and her vassals revolt. She also violates the vow to her deceased husband, he who — we learn in Hades — has a greater claim on her love than does Eneas (v. 2656). By contrast, Lavine, in satisfying her erotic desire also contributes to the establishment of dynasty and empire (cf. v. 2923-96). Rome is literally built on her marriage to Eneas, and the marriage arises from her consent. The consummation confirms her consent to a full and complete — because voluntary and reciprocal[51] — *gradus amoris* whose last stage includes marriage.

The new, rewritten *Aeneid* is a *bele conjointure*[52] that expresses a topical truth about love and marriage in the twelfth century. In this, the *Eneas* imitates an extant model for marriage, a kind of imitation we have seen to be widely recognized in the twelfth century. Naturally, it is selective in using the source model. Some source material is set aside because it is not part of the new conception of the model's meaning. We have observed such abbreviation in the French romance's version of the sea storm and Dido's banquet, as well as its rewriting of *Aeneid* Books II and V. Lacunae in the sources are filled out, either to clarify the narrative or to complete the adaptation of the work and the expression of its model in a new context, as in the Lavine amplification which illustrates the role of love personified, principally by Venus in the *Eneas*, in a new configuration with love and consent as major topoi. This recalls Benoît's own additions to Dares, notably the story of Briseida's loves and the Greek return based on Dictys. The second half of the twelfth century may not have discovered love, but it surely uncovered its complexities when located and valorized in familiar social scenarios.

---

[50] Dido feels her love for Eneas is incomplete because there has been no male child (v. 1739-44, 2052). To her mind, the *gradus amoris* includes pregnancy and delivery of a son.

[51] Cormier 1973 pp. 258-68.

[52] On *Eneas* as *conjointure*, see Petit 1985b pp. 497-98.

Description of Consent in Chrétien de Troyes's Erec et Enide

Let me now move on to consent in *Erec et Enide*. Not only does Chrétien weave the work of fairies with the images of the four arts of the quadrivium in the coronation robe, he also draws explicit analogies with the *Aeneid*, or, more likely, given his audiences and his references, with the *Roman d'Eneas*, written shortly before his first Arthurian romance.[53] These analogies illustrate the art of emulation as the art of description that Macrobius taught Chrétien. I shall begin by comparing the treatment of material from the *Eneas* in *Erec et Enide*. Chrétien's audiences were probably like Benoît's: apparently, they did not know Latin, making the *Eneas* the lens through which they probably knew Vergil's epic.[54] I propose to explore this intertextual relationship in the context of Macrobius's art of description.

The stories about Erec and Enide told at court, from which Chrétien says he put together his *bele conjointure*, have not survived. As a result, we cannot study *Erec*'s sources as we did in analyzing the *Troie*'s and *Eneas*'s art of description; the kinds of adaptation Macrobius treats must necessarily escape us in the case of Chrétien's first romance. Even though some have argued for a significant influence of Vergil and other classical authors, it was not difficult for Jean Frappier to make short shrift of such attempts. Taking "source" in the usual sense of borrowing, he showed the unlikelihood of the proofs adduced for adaptation; most examples are too vague or commonplace,[55] so that, even if they are valid, only comparison with the lost *contes* would allow us to appreciate Chrétien's art of imitation and adaptation. And yet, if Chrétien "described" with the art we have found in Macrobius, then he may in fact have practiced the very *kinds* of adaptations which Frappier questions! But none is certain. We must therefore back up some and reconsider descriptions in *Erec* along the lines illustrated in Macrobius's *Saturnalia*.

Let us begin with Erec's quest. The quest is a prominent feature of the *Aeneid* according to Macrobius. As there is a quest for Rome in Vergil and the *Eneas*, so there is a quest in Chrétien.[56] Although

---

[53] Wetherbee 1972 pp. 237-40. If Chrétien had been in England or at an Anglo-Norman court at this time, as some have argued, the *Eneas* allusions would be more compelling. On *Eneas* allusions in the *Charrette*, see Beltrami 1989 pp. 246-51.

[54] This is "specific intertextuality" in Besamusca's sense of the term.

[55] Frappier 1959 on Ziltener 1957.

[56] There is none in *Thèbes*; the *Troie* contains the quest for the Golden Fleece, which includes a return, but not many adventures. It is noteworthy in assessing

Chrétien's *Erec et Enide* builds on the quest motif as Macrobius and even the Martianus Commentary depict it, its *figura* still reflects or mirrors the *Eneas* model — including a female companion who, in fact, problematizes the figure of the guide. Is Enide a guide? It follows that Vergil and the Old French romance could have served as models for motifs that were also present, implicit, or even absent from the tales Chrétien rewrote. What is new, or at least French, is the consent motif that *Erec* and *Eneas* share.

In her important study of the *Aeneid* traditions from antiquity to Chrétien de Troyes, Francine Mora-Lebrun has noted the importance of the *Eneas* for Chrétien's romances.[57] The *Eneas* obviously gives the quest for Rome a new, medieval signification. The marriage and inheritance are rewritten in a feudal context, and Eneas is in quest of marriage as much as he is of his inheritance. Especially from this perspective, Eneas's story is a sort of foil to Chrétien's as much as the Tristan legend is, and we shall have occasion in what follows to elaborate more thoroughly on these features.

Chrétien knew Eneas's story.[58] Since he alludes to it in two places towards the end of *Erec*, a little before the Macrobius reference, he projects the same knowledge into his implied audience.[59] There are plausible reasons for Chrétien's use of the *Eneas* as model in *Erec*. First, his French-speaking audiences could have understood his references to the French romance, with which they were more likely familiar than with the *Aeneid* itself. The *Eneas* offers a highly suggestive model of the nuptial quest.[60] Furthermore, audiences could have appreciated the contrasts between what Chrétien recalls and the adaptation of the motif in his narrative. This is a virtual *jeu-parti* the resolution of which is suggested by the way the Erec and Enide story both alters the *Eneas* illustration and continues on its own, different way to a denouement.

Chrétien's originality that the *Eneas* suppresses the adventures found in the *Aeneid* Book III, many features of which are characteristic of Chrétien's quests (see Kelly 1971 pp. 334-43).

[57] 1994b pp. 235-43, with references to the studies of its influence by other scholars.

[58] Lavine and Eneas are also named in *Perceval* v. 9059; however, the allusion there is comic, as one character likens Gauvain and his sister Clarissant to Lavine and Eneas in the hope that they will marry! See Ménard 1969 p. 336 n. 19.

[59] Frappier 1959 pp. 58-59 n. 44 accepts Chrétien's link with the *Eneas* and his originality in these passages. Cf. Cormier 1976.

[60] Baumgartner 1995 p. 54.

Chrétien's allusions to *Eneas* towards the end of *Erec* occur when his nearly completed romance is still fresh in his audience's mind. Chrétien first alludes to Eneas's arrival at "Laurente" in "Lonbardie" (*Erec* v. 5345) — hardly Vergilian place names, but they are constant in *Eneas*.[61] Moreover Chrétien extols the foundation of a kingdom and dynasty with which the *Eneas* also concludes. "Comant Eneas puis conquist / Laurente et tote Lonbardie / Don il fu rois tote sa vie" (*Erec* v. 5344-46) [how Eneas next conquered Laurentium and all of Lombardy, which he ruled over all his life.] But there are also striking differences, as there were for Macrobius in Vergil's imitation of Homer and early Latin authors. Above all, there is no Dido figure in *Erec*. To be sure, Erec and Enide's, shall we say, first love provokes murmurs among the vassals, just as Eneas and Dido's does, despite the otherwise universal recognition of Enide's beauty and its beneficial influence on Erec's prowess. But Erec does not leave Enide, although the vassals and Enide herself suggest at least temporary separations for tournaments. Still, the disastrous consequences associated with Eneas's love for Dido threaten Erec and Enide's marriage in the second part of Chrétien's romance. Importantly, no one threatens Erec's dynasty and destiny; only his prowess is in question.

Erec's first part is divided into two narrative sequences or *vers*: the White Stag and the Sparrow Hawk sections.[62] In the first sequence Enide's beauty inspires Erec's prowess, in the second it permits Arthur to maintain the custom of the White Stag by the kiss that all acknowledge should be bestowed on Enide as the most beautiful woman at court. Thus love serves private and public ends, as it does in the *Eneas* when Eneas wins Lavine. In both cases the narrative expresses, through adroit rewriting of source material (this is what Chrétien claims to do with his sources), a hitherto unsuspected, hidden beauty and meaning in a commonly told tale. Enide's beauty inspires Erec's prowess just as Lavine's does that of Eneas. The *figura*, *imago*, or informing model of both romances is strikingly similar. In the *Eneas*, that nuptial model informs the happy configuration of dynasty and love exemplified by the marriage of Eneas and Lavine.

---

[61] The Lombards were north of the Alps in Vergil's time; the people who gave their name to the Italian kingdom did not appear in Italy until the sixth century. Laurente is an even later name for a city near Vergil's Lavinium. "Laurenti... ab arce" [from the Laurentine citadel] appears Bk. VIII, v. 1; although the reference is not to a city, the *Eneas* author may have thought it was an urban reference.

[62] Kelly 1992 p. 17.

In Chrétien, the nuptial model adapts the incomplete, piecemeal tales of adventure to new chivalric and erotic ideals. For Enide does have some features in common with Dido as well as with the Lombard Lavine. Let us examine those features to see how Chrétien has rewritten them.

The *bele conjointure* of *Erec*'s first part is not complete with marriage. As in the Dido episode of *Eneas*, Erec must leave. But Erec does not abandon his wife for tournaments or even the quest, nor does Enide give in to the temptation to reject her husband, the one she loves, for little Turnuses like Galoain and Oringle de Limors whom she meets along the way to reconciliation with her husband. More strikingly, the two allusions to the *Eneas* plot offer hints on Chrétien's art of rewriting which is also an art of description. The first allusion is in the description of the saddle Enide receives after reconciliation with her husband, which relates a Roman story engraved by a Breton craftsman: "Uns brez taillierre, qui la fist, / Au taillier plus de set anz mist" (v. 5249-50) [A Breton carver who made it took more than seven years to complete his task]. Similarly, Erec's coronation robe mirrors the artistry of four fays — with the art of Macrobius.[63] The saddle engraving alludes to Eneas's love for and separation from Dido so as to pass on to Laurente, Lombardy, and kingship. This recalls Erec's trajectory too, except that he marries Enide rather than abandoning her, a fundamental rewriting of the Dido scenario. Later, Erec must leave, as Eneas must; in doing so he becomes cold to Enide, just as Eneas does to Dido. This comes about through Enide's acceptance of the men's condemnation of her husband's *recreantise*. Shouldn't Erec be accompanying them to tournaments rather then dallying in bed every day until after noon? (*Erec* v. 2434-42, 2446-49) Significantly, Erec does not abandon Enide for tournaments. Instead he takes her on a quest.

The second allusion likens the maiden in the garden of the Joie de la Cort to Lavine. But the differences are again striking and significant. An *amie* has succeeded in retaining her beloved in the Garden of Joy, but at great cost to his renown. Here the Dido model resurfaces. Erec and Enide correct it by convincing the *amie* that neither separation nor imprisonment is necessary to retain love. The two couples emerge from the Garden together. Erec and Enide go on to coronation, like Eneas and Lavine. The result is the happy *conjointure*

---

[63] On this juxtaposition of Celtic and Latin, see Kelly 1983.

of two previously mis-matched couples. And the making of old matter new with the original adaptation of a consent model of marriage.

We should not overlook, in this comparison between *Erec* and *Eneas*, the reflection in both works of that conflict between landed aristocracy and unestablished knights that Erich Köhler identified in early romance. Such conflict illustrates opposing points of view that the anonymous *Eneas* romancer and Chrétien might find in their audiences, and it confronts the two narratives. To the Latins and the Carthaginians, the Trojans, a dispossessed people bent on usurping land they do not have, should be driven away. "A tort s'i anbat Eneas," they exclaim, "mes ja par foi nel recevron, / n'estrange home sor nos n'avron." (*Eneas* v. 4186-88) [Eneas wrongly imposes himself on us. But we'll never accept him, nor have a foreign man dominate us.] But the Trojans came to Troy from Lombardy. By returning there, they attempt to join with the Latins in a manner acceptable to the gods and in harmony with their own self-interest (*Eneas* v. 3197-3215). Circumstances — the *petite acheison* common in the *Troie* — lead to battle, as does the killing of Silvia's tame stag during Ascanius's hunt.

> Por asez po de començaille
> sort l'acheisons de la bataille,
> et par molt petite avanture
> mut la guerre, qui tant fu dure,
> dont mil home furent ocis
> et altretant navré et pris. (*Eneas* v. 3519-24)

[From a very small beginning arises the cause of the battle, as a very small happening provoked the war which became so harsh and because of which thousands were killed and just as many wounded and captured.]

The violent amalgam of Trojans and Latins, of established aristocracy and foreign elements (that is, the unlanded young nobles with whom Eneas seeks to establish himself in Italy), becomes whole and complete through the love of Eneas and Lavine. "La josne gent" (v. 2177) become landed aristocracy and found a dynasty.

Something similar occurs in *Erec*'s second part. Erec stays in bed[64]

---

[64] On the bed as topos and its diverse amplifications, see the intriguing article by Angeli 1998, and, more generally, Lerchner 1993.

with his wife until noon, and the men, by which the text means Erec's father's vassals, murmur: he should be going to tournaments with them. The emotional estrangement of Erec and Enide arises because King Lac's men value tournaments more than, or at least on a par with, making love, and Enide believes them.[65] Surprisingly, husband and wife take leave not only of bed, but also of court and tournaments. Their quest relates their return to the unity and harmony of their first love. The conclusion, a narrative, thematic, and sexual *conjointure* — Enide again becomes *femme* and *amie*, as she and her husband reconsummate their union by mutual consent — relocates the couple at Arthur's court, where love is better understood than at Lac's. Lac's convenient, if fortuitous death allows for the coronation of Erec and Enide at Nantes in the robe Macrobius taught Chrétien how to describe. In fact, Enide functions in the *Erec* much as Venus does in the *Eneas*: she holds the romance together.[66]

In the *Eneas*, four topics are at issue in consent: the vassals, the parents, conjugal consent, and sexual consent. In *Erec*, these topics are all present too, but they are not described in the same way as in the *Eneas*. They constitute a *conjointure* of elements that play out various models for the romance's narrative.[67] The vassals want their lord to accompany them to tournaments, but he does not do so. Enide's father arranges her marriage in the conventional way, but she assents with no difficulty; surprisingly for the twelfth century, there is an "ellipse": Chrétien gives Erec's parents no voice in his marriage, and, just as surprisingly, they accept it without a murmur.[68] Enide's consent to both *épousailles* and *noces* is full and free before the marriage. But because she heeds Erec's vassals, she withdraws or at least calls into question her consent to lovemaking and even her marriage: "Lasse, con mar m'esmui / De mon païs! Que ving ça querre?" (*Erec* v. 2496-97) [Alas! how unfortunate that I left my country! What did I come here for?] She wants her husband to leave and take part in tournaments. The denouement provides the exemplary answer: Erec's and Enide's sex life begins again in earnest, he is crowned king at Arthur's court, he is never again at a tournament. The coronation

---

[65] But the tournament itself is morally ambiguous in the twelfth century; see Krüger 1985 and Stanesco 1988 p. 74-78.

[66] Kelly 1970 pp. 188-97.

[67] The best discussions of consent in *Erec* are Varty 1986 pp. 37-40 and Kullmann 1993 pp. 63-65.

[68] Cf. *Erec* v. 2329-433.

robe signals the triumph of consensual love in marriage. There is little mention of dynasty. There is no child — another "ellipse" — unlike in the *Eneas* or the fifteenth-century Burgundian adaptation of *Erec*.[69]

These two examples — *Eneas* and *Erec* — illustrate recomposition along the lines of description as Macrobius uses the term in the *Saturnalia*. Disparate narrative elements, derived from different sources — the different versions of the *conte d'avanture* about Erec and Enide — are woven together in a new combination made possible by an informing consent model. The combination models the narrative in a manner comprehensible to a specific kind of audience. Such a *conjointure* is analogous to what the Martianus commentator terms a *figura*. It gives shape to a sequence of events, making it credible, comprehensible, and coherent; the narrative has exemplary truth, as one author puts it in language familiar in other texts: "Pur essample issi ai fait / Pur l'estorie embelir, / Que as amanz deive plaisir." (*Tristan* Sneyd[2] v. 831-33) [I have made an exemplum, embellishing the story so that it might please lovers.] The marvelous embellishments of Breton story-tellers have become the topical embellishments of *conjointures*. They too use the art Chrétien learned by reading Macrobius's *Saturnalia*.

We know from Joseph of Exeter's use of ekphrasis that such description may be very significant for the meaning of a work. Erec's variegated coronation robe recalls Enide's last horse, the tri-colored palfrey which Guivret gives her after her reconciliation with Erec. The horse's saddle represents events in Eneas's voyage to Lombardy after the fall of Troy. Like the palfrey, colored white and black with a green stripe dividing the two colors, the *barbiolete* on Erec's scepter has a white head, black body, bright red back, green underbelly, and purple tail — it is a "contrefeites bestes" (*Erec* v. 6795)[70] [misshapen beast]. The robes of the man and woman are complex and diverse.[71] This contrasts remarkably with the marriage and coronation in *Eneas*, where we hear only of the founding of a lineage and a city.

---

[69] Wallen 1982 p. 194.

[70] The precise reading of this passage is uncertain. For consistency, I have followed my base edition. But, whatever the edition, all readings support my argument. On the text see Burgess and Curry 1989 and 1991. On green as the mean between black and white see Worstbrock 1985 p. 25.

[71] Liebertz-Grün 1994 pp. 308-11.

Description of Consent in Renaut de Beaujeu's Bel Inconnu[72]

Renaut de Beaujeu's *Bel Inconnu* is closer to the *Eneas* in its description of the titular hero's marriage to the Blonde Esmeree, although, according to the narrator, the marriage does not take place at the end of the projected romance. Moreover, the marriage is combined with a coronation, as in *Erec* and *Eneas*. However, the coronation uses the crown of the wife's parents in *Eneas*, whereas in *Erec* Arthur provides the crown and sceptor, much as Guenevere earlier provided Enide with her marriage dress. But the Inconnu's coronation and wedding are as succinctly described as in *Eneas*. As technique, the ceremonies suggest that an *adiectio* is present in *Erec* and a *detractio* in the *Bel Inconnu*. In *Eneas*, the emphasis is on founding a dynasty, in *Erec* on confirming a marriage, but in the *Bel Inconnu* on posing a problem which the narrator sets out in the Epilogue.

The *Bel Inconnu* contains a model of consent similar to that in the *Eneas* and *Erec*. Its second- or third-generation romance public could certainly recognize various citations, references, and adaptations from earlier works and begin to make the kind of mental comparisons common among the knowledgeable in antiquity. We have already noted the striking similarity between Eneas's *navigatio*, with the pause at Carthage, and the Inconnu's quest with the adventure at the castle of the Pucelle aux blanches mains. The following analogy may clarify the relations: Dido is to the Pucelle as Lavine is to the Blonde Esmeree. But the *Bel Inconnu* relies on an intermediary much like the Latin writers between Homer and Vergil. If Renaut is rewriting the *Eneas* model, he is also using *Erec* as intermediary. Thus, in Chrétien's romance, the encounter with Enide while seeking another goal, vengeance on Yder, leads to marriage. There is, consequently, an analogous relation between Enide, *fame* and *amie* and both the Pucelle as *amie* and the Blonde Esmeree as *fame*. Let us pursue these analogies to determine how, as *immutatio* or replacement, Renaut rewrote his antecedent models of consent in order to produce an original romance.

The *Bel Inconnu* follows a pattern not dissimilar to that of the *Eneas*. In a quest, the goal of which is the liberation of Blonde Esmeree from

---

[72] See Maddox 1996 on Renaut's imitation of Chrétien's romances; he uses the framework of topical invention to interpret the motif of custom. On the adaptation of other motifs in the *Bel Inconnu*, see Baumgartner 1996b and Dubost 1996.

a magic spell, the Inconnu encounters an adventure centered on the Pucelle aux blanches mains. After achieving that adventure, the reward for which is the maiden and her land, she provides some titillating and seductive gestures at the Inconnu's bedside. Had she remained, the consummation would have provided another illustration of Matthew of Vendôme's *votiva duorum congressio*. But she cuts short the scene to retire abruptly into her room in order to avoid lechery (*Bel inc* v. 2451). Unlike Dido, the Pucelle obviously wants some evidence of sincerity and commitment before giving herself to her knight errant. She wants a certain kind of consent. "Des que vos m'aiés esposee, / Lors vos serrai abandonnee." (*Bel Inc* v. 2453-54) [I will be yours as soon as you have married me.] The next morning justifies her prudence. The Inconnu slips away much as Eneas did from Carthage. But the Pucelle does not commit suicide, and the Inconnu does return to her.

Consent for the Pucelle is not just consent to sexual intercourse. The Pucelle's sentiments reflect those of Antigone in the *Thèbes*. She is not naive nor is she lacking in knowledge and foresight. Like the four fays in *Erec* she knows the seven arts, and like Venus in the *Eneas* she has magic powers (*Bel inc* v. 1933-36, 4937-41). In fact, like Eneas's mother the Pucelle has carefully orchestrated all the Inconnu's adventures. Indeed, she claims to know everything he does and will do, even when he is false to her! (*Bel Inc* v. 4979-82)

The Bel Inconnu himself must make a choice. The choice is whether or not to consent. The problem is that he consents twice, first to the Blonde Esmeree, and then to the Pucelle. To Esmeree he promises his hand if Arthur consents, illustrating the consent of *épousailles*; he then marries her and they celebrate their *noces*. To the Pucelle, however, he promises fidelity while the matter of marriage hangs in the air. His consent is articulated in two opposing arenas. In the one, consent is required of Esmeree's vassals (v. 3517-23) as well as of Arthur. Both vassals and Arthur give their approval, and the marriage takes place after a tournament, as in *Erec*. Moreover, like Erec, the Inconnu has also given his consent independently of any family member or lord. Without consulting his father, Gauvain, his mother, Blancemal, or Arthur, he promises fidelity to the Pucelle. She sets the terms of their contract, and he accepts them.

> ... tant que croire me vaurois,
> Ne vaurés rien que vos n'aiois;
> Et quant mon consel ne croirés
> Ce saciés bien, lors me perdrés. (*Bel Inc* v. 5013-16)

[As long as you trust me you will lack nothing you desire; but when you do not heed my advice you will lose me for sure.]

Which is precisely what happens. The Inconnu accepts these conditions, and his consent is unequivocal: "Ne feroie si grant folie / Que de vo comandement isse, / Ne ja mais anui vos fesisse" (*Bel Inc* v. 5020-22) [I would not be so foolish as to disobey you, nor would I ever displease you]. He does displease her, of course, and, of course, she knows that he will. He decides to go to the tournament against the Pucelle's wishes; he loses her by consenting to marry Blonde Esmeree. He seems to forget her very existence — a kind of ellipse.

The Inconnu seems to be as deficient in will power as Eliduc is in Marie de France's lay. But there is a complication in his case which is not explicit in Marie's lay, destiny.[73] The Inconnu's failures and inadequacies are known and determined by powers outside of him, powers which the Pucelle knows how to turn to her own ends. Thus his lack of will power in matters of consent actually gives her a certain control over him even when he leaves her. In other words, Renaut returns to destiny as a motif, which Chrétien set aside but which is very powerful in *romans d'antiquité* like the *Eneas*.[74]

The Inconnu's case also recalls the *Troie* paradigms where destiny is known and announced. Like Cassandra, the Pucelle possesses the arts whereby she can know and influence Guinglain's destiny.

---

[73] Marie uses destiny in the *gradus amoris* in four lays, *Guigemar*, *Equitan*, *Yonec*, and the *Deux Amants*; see Kelly 1999; for a broader discussion of the subject in the context of topical invention, see Krause and Martin 1998. On the personification of sexual desire as Love and, therefore, as a feature of destiny, see Schnell 1985 pp. 272-74 and 434-35.

[74] See Chapter Four and, for example, *Eneas* v. 1763, 3239-42, and 3340-48, which show that destiny depends on the will of the gods. *Destinee* comes up three times in the *Bel Inconnu* v. 2462, 4982, and 5423. I leave aside, because unprovable, the possibility that the Inconnu lacks will power precisely because the Pucelle controls his destiny; but see Baumgartner 1996b pp. 14 and 20.

> Ce so ge tot premierement
> L'aventure certainnement
> Que vos avés ici trovee,
> E tote vostre destinee;
> Je resavoie par mon sens
> Qu'a la cort venrïés par tens. (*Bel Inc* v. 4979-84)

[I was the very first to know for sure the adventure which you found here and your entire destiny. By my knowledge I knew that you would come to court at a certain time.]

She also knows how to manipulate destiny; she sets up both her encounter with the Inconnu and the quest for Blonde Esmeree. But she knows too that the success of her undertaking depends on the Inconnu's accommodation to his own destiny. She therefore does everything in her power to win him — which is to say, to obtain his consent to be her *ami* (*Bel Inc* v. 5005-08); she never insists on marriage after their reconciliation. This includes not only arranging encounters but also enhancing his desire by alternately teasing him sexually and playing hard-to-get. They finally come to terms after he consents to follow her counsels. She in turn consents to his every wish. If the Inconnu fails to keep this contract based on give-and-take, their relationship will terminate and he will lose the Pucelle. His assent leads to general recognition of his place as lord or "signor" of the Pucelle's lands (*Bel inc* v. 5052); her barons approve the arrangement (v. 5044-52).[75] The Inconnu and the Pucelle have a *Friedelehe* — that is, a union not sanctioned by the Church (despite the mass that follows their consummation, there is no marriage), but by the barons. *Muntehe* comes later, but with the Blonde Esmeree, not with the Pucelle aux blanches mains.

The Pucelle belongs to a significant intertextual nexus. As the narrator points out, she is more beautiful than Helen, Iseut, Biblis, Lavine, and Morgain la fée (*Bel Inc* v. 4344-50) — an unusual set of loving women. In a way, like Zeuxis's statue, the Pucelle's persona conjoins different features of these women.[76] She is learned and even

---

[75] As we have seen, similar approval is obtained from the Blonde Esmeree's barons, v. 3517-27.

[76] See, for example, *De inv* II.i.1-3. Cicero is here speaking of a selection of and from appropriate models that recalls Macrobius's own composition; see also *De inv* II.ii.4-5.

knows the magic arts, she is beautiful, she inspires combat for her person and realm, and she suffers for love. Biblis is, to be sure, a problematic figure because her passion for her brother is incestuous.[77] However, the incestuous desire aligns her with the Morgain tradition which seems to have been known by vernacular audiences at the time the *Bel inconnu* was written around 1200. Chrétien refers to her.[78] Morgain is also a *fée* like Blancemal, the Inconnu's mother; if the Pucelle herself is nowhere identified specifically as a fay, she has certainly acquired the powers of one! But like Lavine, she is the only child of her father, and thus his only heir; she is unmarried (*Bel Inc* v. 1939-40, 4935); and her lands are not in a marvelous Otherworld, they are a domain of which she is a lady as much as Laudine is. The man she marries will become lord of her castle (*Bel Inc* v. 2005-24, 2270-76).

By inserting consent into his model of the *gradus amoris*, Renaut has adapted the two narrative models found in the *Eneas* — extramarital consent leading to separation (the *Friedelehe*) and conjugal consent leading to marriage (the *Muntehe*)[79] — in, respectively, the Dido and Lavine sequences. But the Inconnu is not Eneas. After falling in love with Lavine, Eneas could reflect that this new love is greater than that for Dido.

> Se ge aüsse tel corage
> vers la raïne de Cartage,
> qui tant m'ama qu'el s'en ocist,
> ja mes cuers de li ne partist. (*Eneas* v. 9039-42)[80]

[Had I loved the queen of Carthage like this, she who loved me so much she killed herself for me, my heart would never have left her.]

But the Pucelle is not Dido either. Rather than be abandoned she takes the initiative. Similar to Enide, the Pucelle withdraws consent

---

[77] The name occurs in other romances; see Flutre 1962 p. 29 and West 1969 p. 18. On these names and the name topos in the *Bel Inconnu*, see Perret 1996.

[78] See *Erec* v. 1957, 4218, 4220; none of these references is to her beauty, although the first names "Guingomars" as her "amis". The name, including its variants, is common; see Flutre 1962 pp. 91 and 100 and West 1969 p. 84.

[79] See Gravdal 1996.

[80] Dido had already noted the difference between her affection and his (*Eneas* v. 1828-30); see Cormier 1973 pp. 128-36.

and sends her lover packing. But she does so knowlingly and with agency. The Inconnu leaves the Pucelle, triumphs in the tournament, and also consents to marry Esmeree, who does all that Arthur thinks suitable in a successful and well appointed *Muntehe*. She possesses a crown and the land which her husband conquered and saved as well as being a beautiful wife of high nobility who loves him and desires to receive him as her lord and husband (*Bel Inc* v. 6174-90). These are the public and private reasons for marriage which we have seen in the *Eneas*, although lineage is not an issue in the *Bel Inconnu*.

> Li rois et tuit l'ont tant proié
> Que Guinglains lor a otreié.[81]
> Il vit la dame et biele et saje,
> Se li plot molt en son corage.
> Li rois dist ses noces fera
> Et son neveu coronnera. (*Bel Inc* v. 6191-96)

[The king and everyone else pleaded so much with him to do this that Guinglain consented to their entreaties. He noted the lady's beauty and prudent demeanor, and she pleased him profoundly. The king announced that he would perform the marriage and crown his nephew.]

Apparently Arthur performs the ceremony; if this is so, Guinglain's marriage conforms to the feudal more than to the ecclesiastical model. But the Inconnu really loves the Pucelle whatever his feelings for Blonde Esmeree may be. He is like Tristan, who marries Iseut aux blanches mains while still in love with Iseut la Blonde, even though the Pucelle is not married and the epithets of the women — Blonde and Blanches Mains — are transferred (*immutatio*). This is an *estrange amor* like that which Thomas d'Angleterre condemns in his *Tristan*.[82]

Importantly, the dilemma in the *Bel Inconnu* is more complex as well. The narrator informs us that its plot has repercussions in his own life. Both the Inconnu's *gradus amoris* and Renaut's include the consent motif. If his lady shows him her approval, she will hear the rest of the romance's incomplete plot. He asks for her *biau sanblant* as a sign of her consent to continue.

---

[81] This constitutes the *épousailles* consent; the *noces* follow.

[82] See now Bertolucci Pizzorusso 1996.

Mais por un biau sanblant mostrer[83]
Vos feroit Guinglain retrover
S'amie, que il a perdue,
Qu'entre ses bras le tenroit nue.
Se de çou li faites delai,
Si ert Guinglains en tel esmai
Que ja mais n'avera s'amie. (*Bel Inc* v. 6255-61)

[But by showing your approval you will make Guinglain recover his beloved whom he has lost and hold her nude in his arms. But if you delay doing this, Guinglain will be in such distress that he will never again possess his beloved.]

There is something of the *jeu-parti* in this proposal, especially because we know that the Inconnu's marriage is and will be successful in terms of the marriage itself: he is crowned, married, and renowned as king: "Puis fu rois de molt grant mimore, / Si con raconte li istore" (*Bel Inc* v. 6245-46) [He subsequently become a king of great renown, as the story tells]. What his renown rests on we do not learn. Did it have anything to do with his promised return to the Pucelle?

At issue here are Renaut's autobiography and Renaut as example. The vexed question of Renaut's autobiographical allusions centers on an apparently unresponsive lady, perhaps a married lady (see *Bel Inc* v. 1248-71; I shall return to this matter below). If his story is true, his *gradus amoris* had no sequel because the *Bel Inconnu* has none. As the last lines of the *chanson* attributed to Renaut put it: "Et cil qui dit que m'amez, il se mant. / Ce poise moi, ire en ai et contraire: / Pleüst a Deu qu'il fussent voir disant" (*Bel Inc* p. 193, v. 33-35) [Whoever tells me that you love me is lying. This grieves, angers, and vexes me. Would to God they were telling the truth]. Now, the autobiographical validity of the *chanson*, like the narrator's interventions in the romance and the Occitan *vidas* and *razos* they recall,[84] cannot be unequivocally interpreted as documentation. What we can discuss and analyze in such statements is their exemplarity. As in Guillaume de Lorris's *Roman de la rose*, the truth of his love for a woman called

---

[83] Renaut is quite explicit, as the last two lines of the extant romance show: "Que ja mais jor n'en parlerai / Tant que le bel sanblant avrai" (*Bel Inc* v. 6265-66) [I shall tell no more of it until I have your approval]. *Bel sanblant* is here a sign of consent to continue the romance.

[84] On these texts, see Poe 1984, Meneghetti 1992, and Dronke 1994 pp. 66-70.

Rose is significant because it becomes the model for the art of love the romance purports to offer.

Renaut's epilogue puts his relation to the lady into the very context of consent problematized by the Inconnu's relations with the two women he is involved with. The Inconnu's will is certainly flighty and inconsequential; he betrays the Pucelle and breaks his word in doing so, since their relation was based on his consent to heed her counsel. But he is not portrayed as a self-conscious seducer. His actions may reflect the destiny the Pucelle knows and speaks of but of which we know only a part. His conduct certainly requires evaluation in the context of the *jeu-parti* Renaut proposes to his lady: is it preferable that he remain true to his *Muntehe* with the Blonde Esmeree or should he return to his *Friedelehe* with the Pucelle? The response Renaut's lady gives will reflect her own circumstances, as would be appropriate in audience responses to a *jeu-parti*. What are those circumstances?

Four different passages link Renaut's love life to the *Bel Inconnu*'s plot: the Prologue (v. 1-10), two interventions (v. 1237-71, 4828-61), and the Epilogue (v. 6247-66). The Prologue informs us that he loves a woman faithfully and that because of that love he has composed a *chanson*; now he wishes to write a romance for her to demonstrate his skill — "que faire sai" (v. 10). To those in his audience familiar with *Erec*, the Prologue would also allude to the beginning of Chrétien's first romance, of which the *Bel Inconnu* will provide additional motivational and thematic reminders. As mentioned earlier, Renaut rewrites Chrétien's *bele conjointure* reference just as he will rewrite some of his motifs. Whereas, according to *Erec*, the *conte d'avanture* is *depecié* and *corronpu*, but the romance *conjointure* is beautiful, in the *Bel Inconnu* the *conte d'avanture* is itself beautiful, but the new version is a *roman*. If these lines signal Chrétien's own *bele conjointure* in *Erec et Enide*, they also prepare the audience to heed the intertextual resonances and dissonances between the two romances as well as in Renaut's own paradoxical tale of love.

Renaut's first intervention after the Prologue is more circumstantial. He proclaims his fidelity while attacking false lovers. He illustrates his attack with a married lady ("dame," v. 1248) who, after having been seduced and betrayed, loses her "friends" or "tos ses amis" (v. 1255) — is this a reference to her own family?[85] — and her

---

[85] This would make her like Medea, whom Jason betrays in the *Troie* (v. 2036-40).

loving husband (v. 1256). Unlike such false lovers, however, Renaut promises total constancy even if it drives him mad. The second intervention returns to the lady to explain how lovers endure suffering for the sake of their ladies ("dames," v. 4835, 4838, 4849, 4654). Ladies dominate amorous relationships; their will must remain absolute and their honor intact. After a brief criticism of false lovers, Renaut concludes by exclaiming: "Ha! Dius, arai ja mon plaissir / De celi que je ainme tant?" (v. 4860-61) [Oh Lord! will I ever have pleasure from her whom I love so much?] From "her whom," or, more precisely in context, from that lady or *dame* who is among those ladies whose honor is in jeopardy and who have loving husbands. Is Renaut's lady married to a loving husband? She is in the exemplum. Obviously, such a lady's response to the Epilogue will be informed by these issues that are readily apparent; to audiences their implications extend beyond whatever autobiographical reality may lie behind the narrator's protestations to include individual choice and consent.

In the Epilogue, Renaut requests a "biau sanblant" (v. 6255 and 6266) if he is to continue his romance. That "sanblant" which is "biau" is consent not only to the continuation of the romance plot but also a stage in the *gradus amoris* that Renaut imagined earlier as leading to "plaissir" (v. 4860). Hitherto his lady has shown him no "sanblant" (v. 1269), and this is the source of his grief. Should she acquiesce? That is the question posed in the Epilogue. As with most *jeux-partis* the answer lies with the audience.[86] The stakes are clear despite her silence. They are high in part because she has a loving husband. The Inconnu himself represents, by his various actions, the unreliability of promises and even of sincere love, not only for him, since he has his "plaissir" from both women, but for the women themselves — the wife and the *amie*. Food for thought in a *jeu-parti* with real-life implications.

What if Renaut's lady does not grant a "biau sanblant"? Then the Inconnu remains in a good feudal marriage perhaps like her own; there is no indication that he is suffering any grief except the narrator's reference to his "esmai" or distress. But if the lady does grant a "biau sanblant," consenting to the continuation of the plot and the continuation of its *gradus amoris* beyond consummation — Andreas

---

[86] One possible scenario: Renaut is a kind of Bel Inconnu who did get his "sanblant" and, perhaps, even more; he then proved false by not completing the romance.

Capellanus's *continuatio amoris* — the Inconnu and Pucelle commit adultery despite a loving marriage. He is unfaithful whatever the plot may be. The lady can see herself in either role as the loser, whether as wife or as lover.

In the intratextual and intertextual contexts of the *Bel Inconnu* we are asked to reflect on potential answers to a narrative *jeu-parti* whose choices are illustrated by the Inconnu's own conduct and choices. They also elicit reflection on the romances evoked by allusions like those to the beautiful women the narrator compares the Pucelle to. For example, when he breaks his contract with the Pucelle by going to the tournament after which he marries the Blonde Esmeree, one recalls the tournaments Erec did not participate in because he stayed with his wife as "son mari qui l'[aime]" (*Bel Inc* v. 1256). In both cases there is a jolt: Enide falls from the status of *fame et amie* to that of wife alone; the Inconnu is dismissed. In effect, Enide withholds consent to the love life she knew with Erec by heeding the views of Erec's men, and her marriage slides into the male-dominated kind characteristic of twelfth-century mores, the more violent kinds of which are illustrated by Galoain and Limors. The return to conjugal bliss is a return to the happiness Eneas and Lavine know at the end of their romance. That bliss exists for the Belle Esmeree, but not for the Pucelle. How does Renaut's lady fit into this scenario?

Two factors stand out in these intertextual reflections and both are significant in the light of what we know now about the social context of twelfth-century romance audiences: the morality of tourneying and the purpose of marriage. Here recent studies can be enlightening.

First the tournament. The word tournament in twelfth-century French evolved from its original sense of *mêlée* in, for example, both the *Troie* and *Eneas*[87] to that of tournament in its current connotation, but with one major difference: the tournament, like the institution of marriage, was controversial. Although both *Erec* and the *Bel Inconnu* valorize the event, they do so against a social backdrop of ecclesiastical condemnation and actual conflict between *clergie* and *chevalerie*.[88] Furthermore, the tournament itself was outlawed in Plantagenêt England, a fact that would certainly be on the minds of audiences hearing tell of the tournament preceding Erec's marriage, the com-

---

[87] Mölk 1985.
[88] Parisse 1985; from the perspective of *Guillaume le maréchal*, see Peters 1993.

plaints of his men that their lord is not accompanying them to tournaments, and the fact that Erec never again takes part in a tournament after his marriage. There is none for his coronation. Individual
combat during a quest has superseded the general mêlée in this romance. When we turn to the *Bel Inconnu*, the problem is com-
pounded. To be sure, the Inconnu's marriage to Esmeree follows a
tournament, as in *Erec*; and the tournament was called to bring about
his marriage. But the marriage itself is as problematic as tournaments
were in Renaud's time precisely because of the Inconnu's double
consent and the unresolved denouement: he does not return to the
Pucelle.

This brings us to the second problem: the purpose of marriage in
these romances. Eneas, Erec, and Renaut's lady's husband are different kinds of distraught lovers. Eneas must leave a *Friedelehe* because of
his destiny and a marriage based on a greater love than he felt for the
queen of Carthage. Erec's marriage becomes problematic when martial obligations are perceived to be superior to or at least as important
as conjugal duty and pleasure. In the *Bel Inconnu*, the narrator evokes
an ideal marriage in which the wife goes wrong. It has become fash-
ionable to interpret the narrator's interventions and his Epilogue as a
modern game.[89] This may be true, although I would see it as a
double-edged *jeu-parti* without an obvious winner. But it may also be
true that the allusion is as autobiographically valid for the author's
love life as Michel Zink's is for his sense of translation when he
intervenes in his novel, *Le tiers d'amour*, to explain his dissatisfaction
with modern French translations of Occitan lyric.[90] The translations
no more catch the *beau samblant* of the troubadours' language than
Renaut, as lover or narrator, can win his lady's *beau samblant*. The *apo
koinu* solution is typical, it seems, not of a modern game, but of a
medieval *jeu-parti*. We can, I believe, escape the horns of this dilemma
if we turn to the exemplary character of the narrative and the relationship between Renaut and his lady as exemplary. What does it
exemplify? That is a big question and a bigger subject. I shall therefore make the motif of the last chapter the distraught husband. What
happens to the good husband whose wife commits adultery? What
becomes of him? What is his *gradus zelotypiae*?

---

[89] Stempel 1993 and Dubost 1996.
[90] *Tiers d'amour* p. 83.

CHAPTER SIX

NEW MODES OF DESCRIPTION IN
ROMANCE NARRATIVE

> Merlins lui dit: 'Tu, chetif geloux; ta galouzie
> t'occira. Car tous les geloux du monde ont le
> deable avecquez eulx, qui tousjours les semont
> de mal faire.'[1]

The romancers discussed in this chapter have three features in common that permit comparison in the context of description. First, they
practice what has come to be known as lyric insertions in narrative;
that is, they introduce pieces from vernacular lyric and other genres
into romance narrative. Second, they all locate their narratives in a
geography that we might loosely describe as a *matière de Lorraine*; that
is, the plots transpire in a region that extends from Maastricht and
Saint Trond in the north southwards between the Rhine valley and
the eastern border of the thirteenth-century kingdom of France to
Dijon, corresponding to a "literary space" analogous to that evoked
by Jehan Bodel's three matters of France, Rome, and Britain. This
space has been identified as a literary Lorraine or Lotharingia,
roughly embracing eastern France and the Rhine valley.[2] Third, they
forefront the lover or husband victim or apparent victim of his beloved's infidelities. Before examining these works in the context of their
so-called lyric insertions, it is necessary to understand what the term
insertion can refer to in medieval romance.

Insertions

The *Bel Inconnu* contains the virtual insertion of a lyric piece into its
Prologue (v. 3). Renaut says there that he has written a lyric for his

---

[1] Ms.103, ll. 131-33, in *Didot Perceval* p. 313: Merlin said to him: "You jealous
wretch, your jealousy will kill you. For all the jealous men in the world have the devil
with them urging them to do wrong."

[2] Walter 1990 and Baldwin 1997.

lady; his implied audience seems to include those who recall the song and mentally insert it into their reception of the romance he has begun for the same lady. If that lady existed she too is part of the audience, an implication the rest of the romance bears out. Such insertions may also be imbedded into the versification so that the fact of insertion may not be announced in Renaut's straightforward way, but will be perceived by connoisseurs whose memory is jogged by the similarities between the romance text and the original poem. This happens in *Joufroi de Poitiers* when its author inserts — indeed, imbeds — the rhetorical conceit of Guilhem d'Aquitaine's "Farai un vers de dreit nien" into the narrative sequence and versification.[3]

Obviously, insertions do not have to be lyric; they can be varied in a literary culture encouraging allusion and intertextuality in their diverse modes. For example, Martin Gosman has noted the amalgamation of the different versions of the Alexander legend as "tous ces efforts de réécriture qui ne sont que des tentatives d'insertion."[4] By this he means that different versions or episodes of the legend are brought together to form new wholes; these include adaptations of antecedent material that fit it into the new work. Such amalgams[5] become *conjointures* in Macrobius's sense of *conspiratio*, or the blending of matters that is aesthetically pleasing and meaningful — a *bele conjointure*. Macrobius too refers to Vergil's insertions of Greek and Latin imitations into his composition (*Sat* 5.13.33, 6.1.1, 6.4.1). These range from large blocks like Book IV, a rewriting of Medea from Apollonius of Rhodes's *Argonautica*, to briefer sections and finally words, especially words of Greek derivation (*Sat* 6.4.17). The practice of prosimetra might also inspire the insertion of lyric pieces into prose or narrative matter. But it also suggests a larger horizon. Not only might we consider the insertion of lyric passages into narrative, but also the investment of lyric with its narrative potential and, in general, the phenomenon of romance *conjointure* as *montage* or even *collage*.

---

[3] Stempel 1993 p. 280. Cf. Rieger 1987 on lyric motifs in the *Thèbes*, and Ziolkowski 1997 p. 56 on insertions and prosimetra.

[4] Gosman 1996 p. 8; see also Gosman 1992b, Brandsma 1995, Gaullier-Bougassas 1996, and Harf-Lancner 1996. A special case is the insertion of lyric pieces in one language into *chansonniers* written for an audience whose language is different; see Rosenberg 1998 (with additional bibliography).

[5] Kelly 1992 pp. 129-33. Butterfield 1987 (I thank Frank Willaert for calling this Cambridge disseration to my attention) and 1997 (with good bibliography pp. 94-98); and Harf-Lancner 1996. On exact quotation as a kind of *imitatio*, see Moos 1988a p. 740.

The insertion of new material is relatively homogeneous; for example, this is the case with the matter Gosman is interpreting, since it concerned the life of Alexander. The insertions are brought together in such a manner as, ideally, to hide the sutures, like the Medea episode adapted to and inserted into Vergil's narrative on Dido. As such these episodic insertions are different from most lyric insertions, which, although part of the plot of their romances, are usually distinct in lyric mode and versification from the narrative mode and versification that supports them. Let us start here with the broader sense of insertion like those in the Alexander romances. Two thirteenth-century romances, Huon de Mery's *Tournoiement Antechrist* and the anonymous *Cristal et Clarie*, are good illustrations.

Cristal et Clarie illustrates perhaps best Gosman's sense of insertions of excerpts from other narratives and lyric pieces, since it lifts almost verbatim from antecedents like Chrétien de Troyes.[6] Again, readers of the *Saturnalia* would perceive similarities between the anonymous romancer's insertions and that of Medea's story turned into Dido's in the *Aeneid,* just as those who knew Vergil would recognize in *Eneas* the love story of Eneas and Lavine remodeled on that of Dido and Eneas and inserted into the plot's conclusion. Some insertions are immediately recognizable even today. For example, there is a lengthy interpolation from Wace's *Brut* that describes the court held by Clarie's father towards the end of the romance.

> Plus erent cortois et vaillans
> N(e)is li povre home païsans
> Que chevalier en autres regnes
> Et altresi erent les femes.
> Ja ne veïssies chevalier,
> Qui de rien feïst a prisier,
> Qui armes et dras et ator
> Nen eüst tot d'une color.
> D'une color armé estoient
> Et d'une color se vestoient;
> Si erent les dames proisies
> D'une color aparreillies,

---

[6] Breuer ed. *Cristal* pp. xlix-lix and passim in notes and variants, Kelly 1984a pp. 42-44 and Busby 1989.

Ne ja chevalier n'i eüst,
De quel parage que il fust,
Que ja p(e)ust avoir druerie
Ne cortoise dame a amie,
Se il n'eüst trois fois esté
De cevalerie esprové.
Li chevalier mieus en valoient
Et en estor mieus le faisoient,
Et les dames plus en savoient
Et plus cortoisement vivoient. (*Cristal* v. 6871-92)[7]

[Even the poor peasants were more courteous and worthy than
knights in other kingdoms, and the same is true of the women.
No knight could be found who was at all estimable but that his
arms, dress, and outfit were of one color. They all wore arms and
apparel of the same color. Just so, the worthy ladies were dressed
in one color. Nor was there any knight, whatever his birth, who
could be loved by a courtly lady if he had not been tested three
times as a knight. For this reason, knights were more worthy and
more accomplished in combat and the ladies were knowledgeable in these matters and lived a life more worthy of court.]

These lines fit into the new plot; they justify the allegedly ten-year
quest during which Cristal establishes the prowess that makes him
known and worthy of loving and, finally, being loved by Clarie. The
three tests of knighthood may well be a model for Cristal's knightly
victories that win him the love of the three most beautiful women —
Narde, Olympe, and Clarie! But, of course, he is interested only in
the last one. Unlike the Bel Inconnu, Cristal has no conflict in giving
his consent to love Clarie.

Cristal's *gradus amoris* reminds the reader that the romance is written as an art of love (v. 1-14) with (like Guillaume de Lorris's *Roman
de la rose* or the *Bel Inconnu*) a real or projected love for the narrator (v.
83-90). The lengthy prologue sets up the *gradus amoris* model, then
rewrites it as narrative in major episodes modeled on earlier romances. The culmination of the *gradus amoris* interpolates the consummation in *Partonopeu de Blois*.[8] Shortly thereafter, Clarie shows

---

[7] Of course, Geoffrey of Monmouth is the *auctor* for this statement.
[8] Breuer ed. *Cristal* p. liv and lix.

herself to be as resourceful as Lunete and Lienor when confronting her father bent on catching Cristal in her bed; she keeps her father at bay by accusing him of incestuous designs on her, while Cristal blithely escapes using a magic ring that makes him invisible. The whole scene is obviously rewritten from *Yvain*.[9] In these and other examples the anonymous *Cristal* author has arranged extracts linked by his own inventions (*de suo*); he also smooths over the seams to weave a plot whole-cloth.

Let us pass now to Huon de Mery's *Tournoiement Antechrist*. This allegorical romance is most commonly mentioned to recall Huon's despair at emulating his two great predecessors, Raoul de Houdenc and, especially, Chrétien de Troyes. Huon asserts that he has tried to express himself in "le bel françois" (*Tournoiement* v. 3529), but that his formidable predecessors have so well harvested this field that, rich as it was, there is little left for him to choose from if he wants to be original. Huon is avoiding copy or close paraphrase; this is normal by the artistic standards of his and Macrobius's times. But he is speaking, on the level of Macrobius's Book VI, of fine language, not of the motifs and themes that Raoul and Chrétien used. In fact, in the domain of motifs and themes, Huon rewrites with considerable originality.

By 1236, the date of the composition of the *Tournoiement*, Huon's French-speaking audience seems fully adjusted to the allusive writing and reading typical of the Latin language tradition. He himself knows great predecessors and occasionally insists on his inability to emulate them — and not only in the well-known *bel françois* reference to Chrétien and Raoul de Houdenc, but also in references to the Bible, which may have seemed more familiar to his audiences. To describe the Virgin Mary means to emulate John's description in *Revelations*: "Cil la vit et descrit; et je / Serai dont tiex qui la descrive?" (v. 1418-19) [He saw and described her. Shall I too presume to describe her?] After summarizing *Revelations* (v. 1425), Huon goes on to describe those accompanying the Virgin, beginning with Virginity. Similarly, in another passage he comes to the image of the wounded heart.

> Mes qui le voir dire en vodroit,
> Crestïens de Troies dist miex

---

[9] Breuer ed. *Cristal* p. xlvi.

>Du cuer navré, du dart, des ex,
>Que je ne vos porroie dire. (v. 2600-03)

[But to tell the truth Chrétien de Troyes described the wounded heart, the arrow, and the eyes better than I could.]

But even here Huon has kept the model of the heart struck by an arrow after passing through the eyes.[10] So, although Huon cannot emulate Chrétien's achievement, he can use his text as model to treat the commonplace motif of the *coup de foudre*.

These passages also show that Huon is practicing the art of allusion. Not only does he refer to well-known authors which his implied audience knows, he also recalls their works (or works in the oral tradition) by naming well-known knights and ladies in the romance tradition. In this way his audience can catch an allusion to *Cligés* like that of the heart as well as authors' names, titles, and contents for Raoul's *Songe d'enfer* (v. 412-13, 822), *Voie de paradis* (v. 3514-25) and *Roman des ailes* (v. 1847-48), the Bible (reference to the "noces Archedeclin," v. 450), "Thobie" (v. 1389-94), Ezekiel (v. 3123), perhaps Gautier d'Arras's *Eracle* (v. 537), *Durmart le Galois* ("Bruns sans pitié," v. 704), and "ceus de la table roonde" (v. 1977-2015).[11]

Tout est dit!

>... qui bien trueve pleins est d'ire,
>Quant il n'a de matire point.
>Joliveté semont et point
>Mon cuer de dire aucun bel dit;
>Mais n'ai de quoi; car tot est dit,
>Fors ce qui de novel avient. (v. 4-9)

[Whoever writes well is filled with anger if there is nothing to write about. My high spirits urge and excite me to write something fine. But there's nothing to say. Everything has been said, except for current events.]

---

[10] Kelly 1995a p. 125.

[11] The names of Round Table knights, including Arthur son of Uterpendragon, Gauvain, Yvain, Cliges, Lancelot, "tuit li enfant le roi Lot" (v. 1992), Gorvain Cadrus, Meraugis, the king of Orkney, Perceval, and Keu (Lydoine is also named here), remind one of Chrétien's romances and Raoul's *Meraugis de Portlesguez*:

Huon therefore falls back on his own inventiveness to think up what no one has ever thought before (v. 16-21). He does so, it appears, by conjoining and amplifying the motif of the tournament and the image of Antichrist and thereby, by practicing Gosman's kind of insertion. Furthermore, Huon seems to be systematically evaluating Chrétien's habit of inserting new motifs into received matter. At least, this is the way Chrétien says he rewrote Erec's coronation robe woven by the fairies in his sources, but adorned with the quadrivium in his rewritten description.

Huon's *conjointure* is certainly new. But, as a *conjointure*, it still permits inserting old material into his "novel pensé" or the "matiere" he has contrived to express that thought (v. 18-19). He draws on what others have said and written (*mutuatio*), but the insertions are rewritten and arranged (*mutatio*) so as to treat the borrowed material originally. Various techniques allow for different kinds of insertion. Unlike the author of *Cristal et Clarie*, Huon does not practice verbatim insertion. Rather he practices the changes Macrobius speaks of. For example, he reminds us a propos of Despair that "Deseperance est la Monjoie / D'enfer, issi com Raoul dit" (v. 1232-33)[12] [Despair is Hell's Jerusalem, as Raoul tells us]. Huon cannot quibble with him. He merely effects a replacement (*immutatio*) in his insertion describing Hope.

> Mes s'il dit voir, sanz contredit
> Puis dire et par reson prover,
> Qu'autre surnon n'i puis trover
> A Esperance, ce m'est vis,
> Fors Monjoie de paradis:
> Tiex est li sornons sans doutance. (v. 1234-39)

[But if he is correct, I can indisputably say and rationally demonstrate that I can find no other surname for Hope, in my opinion, than Monjoie of Paradise. That is doubtless her surname.]

Elsewhere Huon borrows from and rewrites Chrétien's *Yvain* description of the Magic Fountain in Broceliande forest (v. 102-03).

It is indeed a fountain much as Chrétien described it. But Huon also emulates Chrétien's achievement, first by having the knight pour water on the Fountain's basin twice, thereby provoking not one, but

---

[12] See Mihm ed. *Songe d'enfer* v. 360 note (pp. 115-16).

two storms. The second is so violent that it opens Paradise, revealing
its inhabitants to the knight and the knight to the heavenly hosts! (v.
153-61) The storms are followed by fine weather and the singing
birds — "Souz le pin en ot plus assez, / Que n'en i vit Calogrinans"
(v. 194-95) [Under the pine were quite a few more than Calogrenant
saw], Huon exclaims, to remind us that his emulation is an *exaggeratio*,
or accumulation and enhancement.[13] Afterwards a Moor passes by,
combat ensues, and the knight surrenders to the Moor. Here a transformation begins in the context of Huon's "novel pensé": the Moor is
the son of Fornication and the Antichrist's chamberlain who keeps a
record of sins. He is en route to the Tournament which Antichrist
called against God.[14]

This passage is sufficient to show that the kinds of insertions Gosman identified in the Alexander amalgams recur in the *Tournoiement
Antechrist*. It also reflects procedures for adaptation characteristic of
medieval description and of the operations Macrobius identified in
Vergil's rewriting. Furthermore, it illustrates the technique of recom-
bination intended to produce a *bele conjointure*, a kind of structure for
which Chrétien and Raoul provided Huon with matter and models.
And finally, Huon shows that the traditional Latin procedures for
composition and recomposition that twelfth-century authors adapted
to vernacular writing have become an established part of audience
reception. But Huon is also pointing towards the future. His "novel
pensé" combined with old matter is the starting point for the even-
tual emergence of the late medieval Dit, an evolution that relies on
the subjectivity of first-person narrative characteristic of the allegorical mode in the *Roman de la rose* whereby the narrator's *persona* serves
to link diverse, often borrowed compositional blocks.[15]

Chrétien criticizes his oral antecedents for botching up Erec and
Enide's story. Yet whatever they told, Chrétien was able to put it
together as his *bele conjointure*, adding, subtracting, replacing, and ultimately transforming those tales into a new whole. Like the Alexander
insertions, these insertions fit into a meaningful design.[16] It is perhaps
not farfetched to recall how Macrobius says Vergil used the obscure

---

[13] On this device, see Kelly 1992 pp. 50, 160-62, and 166-67.
[14] An analogous replacement occurs in the tournament to describe the combat
between Abstinence and "Guersoi," or Drunkenness (v. 2235-49).
[15] Zink 1985 and Kay 1990.
[16] Gosman 1996 p. 23.

"Pisander." We don't know which Pisander he may have been referring to, but Vergil's borrowing of episodic material from him suggests Chrétien's own amalgamation of different *contes* in *Erec*: "unum ex diversis hiatibus temporum corpus effecerit, in quo opere inter historias ceteras interitus quoque Troiae in hunc modum relatus est, quae Maro fideliter interpretando fabricatus sibi est Iliacae urbis ruinam" (*Sat* 5.2.5) [he fashioned a single corpus out of diverse gaps in epoch, in which work among other events he also related the fall of Troy in the same way that Vergil constructed his own version of the destruction of Troy by faithfully rewriting his sources]. Book II on the Trojan War, Macrobius asserts, is constructed from Pisander in this way.

Similarly, Huon the Mery rewrote Chrétien in the *Tournoiement Antechrist*. We have seen how the thirteenth-century writer lifted motifs and themes from Chrétien's romances and reconstructed them in a new context, plot, and mode (allegorical). It was only on the minimal level of emulation — the small unit of discourse — that Huon despaired of emulating those he rewrote.

> Molt mis grant peine a eschiver
> Les diz Raol et Crestïen,
> C'onques bouche de crestïen
> Ne dist si bien com il disoient.
> Mes quant qu'il dirent il prenoient
> Le bel françois trestot a plein
> Si com il lor venoit a mein,
> Si qu'apres eus n'ont rien guerpi.
> (Tournoiement v. 3534-41)

[I took great care to avoid Raoul's and Chrétien's words, for never did Christian mouth speak so well as they did. But in all they said they drew abundantly on beautiful French as it came to them, with the result that they left nothing to glean.]

Still, Huon did find some ways by which he could emulate Chrétien even with very small units of discourse. In the biblical allusion in the *Tournoiement*'s last lines he admits that "Se j'ai trové aucun espi / Apres la mein as mestiviers, / Je l'ai glané molt volentiers" (v. 3542-44) [if I found any grain left by the harvesters, I gleaned it eagerly]. For example, since he found the motif of the wounded heart admirably treated by Chrétien, as *imitator* he merely named the motif without seeking to imitate or emulate his *auctor*.[17] But in another place he rewrites Chrétien's fountain in Broceliande forest by having Perceval (rather than Yvain) pour water on the stones and produce a storm that almost wipes out the knights of the Round Table on their way to the great tournament (*Tournoiement* v. 2016-30).

From Lyric Insertion to Narrative Investment

What Huon de Mery did with excerpts from Chrétien, Jean Renart did with excerpts from lyric pieces. Jean Renart "a composé son roman à partir des chansons. Voilà le fin mot du prologue et sa révélation."[18] This immediately forefronts the question of the *chansons' conjointure*, that is, their arrangement prior to their investment with the plot.[19] That *conjointure* was so successful that, as Jean Renart puts it,

> ... est avis a chascun et samble
> que cil qui a fet le romans
> qu'il trovast toz les moz des chans,
> si afierent a ceuls del conte. (*Dole* v. 26-29)

[It seems to each and everyone that he who made the romance invented the words of the songs so well that they fit those in the story.]

That is, the lyric pieces which appear to be part of the narrative are actually insertions. Indeed, as Zink shows, the narrative is itself modeled on the lyric pieces. The *trompe-l'œil* is possible by distinguishing how the romance is put together, or "composed," from the way it is related and read.[20] Such composition "embellishes" the *matière*, much as the jongleur Jouglet does for the emperor Conrad: "N'aprist pas hui si a descrire / qui l'embeli en tel meniere" (*Dole* v.

---

[17] Cf. Geoffrey of Vinsauf, *Doc* II.3.133: "in materia communi, si... describunt quid, ut ibi moram faciant in materia, non debemus ibidem immorari circa... descriptiones, sed breviter locum illum materiae transilire" [in common matter, if they describe anything by dwelling on that matter, we should not tarry long there in describing but briefly pass over that place]. Cf. Friis-Jensen 1990 pp. 353-54 (§ 131).

[18] Zink 1979 p. 29.

[19] Baumgartner 1981 p. 261 and Carmona 1988 pp. 23-24.

[20] Cf. Zink 1979 pp. 29-44.

711-12)[21] [He who embellished his material in this way was past master at description]. Like Jouglet, Jean Renart embellishes his lyrics with narrative. Jouglet's embellishment is description, and description is an art one can learn from Macrobius.

We stand here at the threshold of the modern notion of literature.[22] But we are also standing in the grand tradition from Macrobius to Chrétien de Troyes, a tradition in which authors imitate one another's works such that the rewriting appears to be original. The author identified by the name Jean Renart plotted his romance narrative line so well that it fits the words of the songs in the order in which he arranged them.

The narrative itself is adapted from some version of the wager tale, which recounts how a male "lover" (whether husband, *amant*, or relative) and another person wager privately on the ability of the latter to seduce the former's beloved. The would-be seducer fails; however, he does succeed in duping the lover after learning an intimate secret about the woman. Revealing that secret convinces the lover that his beloved has been untrue and that he has lost the wager. Later, the woman succeeds, by chance or by her own ingenuity, in reconfirming her innocence.[23]

As Zink also notes, Jean Renart makes major additions, deletions, replacements, and displacements in the wager tale itself. These adaptations are compatible with descriptive insertion characteristic of the Macrobian tradition. "En étendant ces considérations à l'ensemble du roman, on s'aperçoit qu'il est fait tout entier de substitutions et de déplacements, et que ces processus sont caractéristiques du conte de la gageure dans ses diverses versions."[24] Translated into Latin, "substitutions" and "déplacements" become *immutatio* and *transmutatio*. Clearly, we can detect evidence of the wager model in the plot of *Guillaume de Dole* even if we do not know what version or versions of it Jean Renart knew or used. We can also appreciate the originality of his rewriting: he deletes the wager as such, and "cette rupture dans l'enchaînement narratif a pour résultat que le roman tout entier dévie du schéma attendu."[25] It is indeed additional corroboration of Zink's

---

[21] See Zink 1979 p. 34.

[22] Zink 1979 p. 43; cf. Zink 1985.

[23] Paris 1903, Buffum ed. *Violette* p. liv. See Lecoy ed. *Dole* pp. x-xii.

[24] Zink 1979 p. 62; Zink refers there to the versions of the wager tale discussed in Paris 1903.

[25] Zink 1979 p. 47.

interpretation of this romance to discover that the operations Jean Renart used to rewrite his matter are consistent with commonplace notions of description in the Latin and French tradition contemporary with him, a tradition to which Chrétien de Troyes links his own romances by applying Macrobius's art of description to the plotting of vernacular narratives.[26] Jean Renart insists in his prologues that the *Dole*'s lyrics are insertions and that they are so well woven into the plot that they should appear to be whole cloth with it. But, as I hope to show, appearances — like Lienor herself — can deceive. So it is with Jean Renart's "insertions."

Before discussing his *Dole*, let us first look at the different kinds of insertions in two romances that come after Jean Renart's.

Lyric Insertions in the Narrative of Gerbert de Montreuil's Violette

Let us begin with a romance for which we can truly speak of lyric insertions in the usual sense of the term: Gerbert de Montreuil's *Roman de la violette*. The *Violette* may well be an imitation of *Guillaume de Dole*, but if it is, Gerbert was also either taken in by appearances or he was adapting his predecessor's art with originality. As Maureen Boulton has put it: "In contrast to Jean Renart's practice..., Gerbert's modifications of the insertion technique were in keeping with the more complex narrative situation of his work. The characters who sing their love are caught in situations more typical of the romance genre than is the courtly calm of *Guillaume de Dole*."[27] Gerbert's insertions fit given narrative moments; some appear even to have been modified to make them fit the narrative.[28] To be sure, it is difficult to be certain about most apparent modifications, given the divergence among variants, the absence of known antecedents for some songs, and the commonplace themes and motifs that appear in many of them, especially the refrains.[29] However, the close relation between content of song and narrative situation argues for either the choice of

---

[26] Cf. Zink 1979 pp. 121-22.

[27] Boulton 1993 p. 36; see also Carmona 1988 pp. 191-94 and 220-22, as well as Zink 1997. Butterfield 1987 p. 67 interprets the songs as giving voice to commonplace topics; the narrative serves "to wrest an individual meaning from [the song's] general character" (p. 58).

[28] Boulton 1993 p. 35 n. 12.

[29] Cf. Buffum ed. *Violette* pp. lxxxii-xci. On narrative allusions in the *Violette*, see Carmona 1988 esp. pp. 205-06.

the former to fit the latter, or for the actual adaptation of given lyric pieces to the narrative matter. The evidence argues in favor of the latter interpretation. For example, one song with a male voice is sung by a woman whose sentiments correspond to those he expresses.[30] Another even more striking specimen is the adaptation of a *chanson de mal mariée* so as to make it express Euriaut's constancy in a virtual *chanson de bien fiancée*.[31] The lyric pieces are obviously adapted to the narrative.

The songs usually serve to remind Gerard of his love amidst adventures that otherwise have little or nothing to do with it, but a lot to do with the prowess that makes him lovable.[32] Indeed, in one episode, Gerard is victim of a potion that makes him forget Euriaut and fall in love with Aiglente. Both Gerard and Euriaut are victims of deceptions. But this allows Gerbert to show the triumph of good love, in Euriaut's case over ignoble aristocrats like Lisiart or Meliatir who would rape or victimize her, and in Gerard's, over an unscrupulous woman like Aiglente who resorts to magic to win an otherwise constant lover. In fact, Gerbert uses the last example to introduce a kind of *jeu-parti* that proves the superiority of constancy as *fin'amour* over magic as source of *druerie*.

> Or verrons nous qui plus porra,
> Et tout apertement parra
> Se caraudes et sorcherie[33]
> Puet plus esprendre druerie,
> Et se ele est de millours mors
> Que n'est fine loiaus amors. (*Violette* v. 4289-94)

[Now we'll see which is stronger: it will be obvious whether charms and magic are more effective causes of love, and whether the ways of such love are better than true noble love.]

---

[30] Boulton 1993 pp. 36-37 — evidence that, as in the performance and reception of popular songs today, the gender of a lyric persona does not determine either the narrative or the extradiegetic gender. This *chanson* is found v. 324-31.

[31] Boulton 1993 pp. 37-38. The *chanson* is found v. 441-49.

[32] Abramowicz 1996 p. 101; cf. as well pp. 102-03 on the often autonomous, but relatively frequent insertion of traditional descriptions.

[33] Cf. Chrétien's reference to Enide's not using any magic power (v. 710), perhaps an allusion to one or the other *conte d'aventure* or to the *estoire* from which he says he drew the description of the coronation robe.

The choice is between glamor and love. This *fin'amour*, or "amours qui vient de volenté" (*Violette* v. 4301) [love that is willed], triumphs. This triumph is anticipated by Bernard de Ventadorn's lark song, which is inserted into the narrative like the lark that absconds with Euriaut's ring, but is caught by Gerard who recognizes the ring and is in this way reminded of Euriaut despite Aiglente's potion. Ironically, it is Aiglente who sings the lark song (*Violette* v. 4187-94) that precipitates the loss of her "enchanted" lover.

The *Violette* shares one song with the *Châtaleine de Vergi* — which is also the only song in this short narrative. Critically, the juncture with the narrative in each work is different, although the text in both works is essentially the same in all manuscripts. The differences are between the two songs and their independent adaptation to the plots in the two distinct narratives.[34] I shall set the two versions of the stanza side by side, highlighting the major differences in italics.

Par Diu! amours, grief m'est a consirer	Par Diu, Amours, grief m'est a consirer
Dou douch solas et de la compaignie,	Du douc soulas et de la compaignie
Et des *biaus mos* dont sot a moi *parler*	Et des *samblans* que m'i soloit *moustrer*
Cele qui m'ert dame, compaigne, amie,	Cele qui m'ert dame, compaigne, amie;
Et quant *recort* sa *simple* cortoisie	Et quant *regart* sa *douce* courtoisie
Et son douc *vis* et *son vïaire cler*,	Et ses dous *mos* qu'a *moi soloit parler*,
Comment me puet li cuers el cors durer?	Coment me puet li cuers u cors durer;
Que ne s'en part? certes, trop est malvais.	Que il ne part? Certes, trop est malvais!
(*Violette* v. 4624-31)	(*Vergi* v. 295-302)

[For God's sake, Love, it is grievous for me to be deprived of the sweet solace and lovely company and lovely conversations she used to have with me, she who was my lady, companion, and beloved. And when I recall her sincere courtesy, her sweet face and bright expression, how can my heart stay with me? Why doesn't it depart? It is surely most unworthy!]	[For God's sake, love, it is grievous for me to be deprived of the sweet solace and the company and of the glances that she used to give me, she who was my lady, companion, and beloved. And when I consider her sweet courtesy and the sweet words she used to utter to me, how can my heart stay with me? Why doesn't it depart? it is surely most unworthy!]

The differences illustrate how each lyric is made to fit a different narrative. There is an inversion of language and sight, as "Et des biaus mos dont sot a moi parler" moves to "et des samblans que m'i soloit moustrer"; more importantly, memory turns to sight: "Et quant recort sa simple cortoisie" becomes "Et quant regart sa douce

---

[34] The variants are not significant. The complete song appears in *Couci* v. 7347-98.

courtoisie." Each change has narrative significance. In the *Violette* Gerard is looking back to what he has lost; the poem therefore gives lyric expression to his grief. But in the *Vergi*, the loss has not yet occurred. Here, the knight envisages the potential or future loss of the person whose love he now enjoys and whom he can see; accordingly, "quant recort" quite understandably becomes "quant regart." The lyric text anticipates and, in effect, determines the narrative which will tell how he loses the Châtelaine. Unlike Euriaut, who saves Gerard's life by calling his attention to the dragon, the Châtelaine dies of a broken heart, her "douce cortoisie" having been betrayed by the knight who did not heed the warning of the lyric stanza. Euriaut is betrayed by a felon. But her "simple courtoisie" remains firm; there has been no deception on her part, although Gerard did not deal with her properly when he wagered on her fidelity.[35]

The *Châtelaine de Vergi* elaborates the narrative potential of the lyric. It is not inserted, as in the *Violette*; in fact, the narrative is molded and fitted to the lyric. The *Vergi* stanza finds exemplary illustration in the plot's violent conclusion: separation from the beloved followed by suicide and murder. The song is a model for narrative elaboration. It also calls for an explanation of the separation, which is provided by the moral lesson that makes the tale exemplify betrayal of one's word to the beloved, a betrayal that precipitates the sequence of deaths at the end of the *Châtelaine de Vergi*.

The Duchess of Burgundy unsuccessfully tries to seduce the anonymous knight who is the Châtelaine's lover. He rejects her proposition not only because she is his lord's wife (the reason he gives the Duchess) but also because he already has a liaison with a married woman (which he does not tell her).[36] The lovers have agreed to keep the liaison a secret to protect her, but the knight feels compelled to confess it to the Duke after the duchess accuses him of propositioning her. It is his only way to prove his innocence, since it is otherwise the duchess's word against his, and the duke is inclined to believe his

---

[35] This is clearly stated at the outset by the king (*Violette* v. 281-90); on the king, see Abramowicz 1996 pp. 115-16.

[36] She is married, as *Vergi* v. 706-08 shows, but her husband does not appear; indeed, his role is to be absent so that the lovers can meet. Knowledgeable members of the audience may note, for example, the divergence between this episode and the analogous one in Marie de France's "Lanval." Lanval tells the Queen that he has a lover, but his lover is not married.

wife. But, like Gerard in the *Violette*, the knight in the *Vergi* does not consult his lady on the agreement or even inform her of it. The duke betrays his word too by telling his wife about the liaison in order to justify not taking vengeance. The duchess then breaks her own word by letting the Châtelaine know that she has learned about the liaison. The duchess is entirely discrete: "vous estes bonne maistresse, / Qui aves apris le mestier / dou petit chienet afaitier" (*Vergi* v. 710-12) [you are a good trainer for having learned how to train your puppy]; only the Châtelaine can understand her veiled allusion to the puppy the lovers use as a signal for their assignations. The betrayal is enough to break the Châtelaine's heart, and she dies of sorrow. When the knight learns this, he commits suicide, as if to bring about an answer to the question posed in the inserted lyric: "coment me puet li cuers el cors durer?" If his heart is not literally eaten, it is certainly metaphorically removed. The duke kills the duchess in a fit of violent rage familiar from "Equitan" and the "Bisclavret" and analogous to Gerard's own murderous anger; the duke then departs to live and die in the Holy Land as penance for his sins — like the emperor's seneschal in *Guillaume de Dole*.

Of course, the *Vergi*'s plot does not turn on a wager as such. Furthermore it is inverted in the sense that the man's honor and word are suspect, not the woman's (if we set aside the Châtelaine de Vergi's adultery); however, the violent denouement comes about because of a woman's attempt to seduce a man followed by her claim that he tried in fact to seduce her. However, the Potiphar's wife tale is a variant of the wager tale used in *Guillaume de Dole* and the *Roman de la violette*, where a "gentleman's agreement" constitutes the betrayal and precipitates the denouement. Finally, the lyric question, "coment me puet li cuers el cors durer?" receives a quite literal answer when the same lyric is inserted into the *Roman du Châtelain de Couci*.

Lyric Insertions and Narrative in Jakames's Châtelain de Couci et Dame de Fayel

Jakamés's *Roman du Châtelain de Couci and de la Dame de Fayel* also takes place in the Lorraine region and includes inserted lyrics. In addition, it focuses in very interesting ways on the issue of adulterous love, including, like many works in the wager tale cycle, the tragic or dramatic features pursuant to discovery of an apparently ideal *fine amour*. Instead of the wager tale, the *Couci* uses a variety of the "cœur mangé" tale, which enters the plot only at the very end to provide a rather contrived denouement — a sort of final baseness in the husband's revenge on his wife's infidelity. The lyric pieces are distinctive as well. First, although there are fewer such pieces in this romance than in the others of comparable length treated here,[37] they are by and large quoted in full. Moreover, they are clearly treated as insertions understandable in the context of the plot rather than being necessary to make the plot comprehensible. For example, the first song, *Couci* v. 362-406, serves to inspire the Lady's love because she knows how well the Châtelain has been serving her. Similarly, the context of an inserted song (v. 2591-2614) serves to express the Châtelain's sentiments which the narrative has already described. Boulton rightly calls these pieces versions of the internal monologue.[38] To be sure, the *chansons* are the "very source" of the romance insofar as they preexisted, and "much of the plot... is constructed to account for the composition of the songs."[39] However, as insertions, "the songs are supposed to grow out of the development of the plot,"[40] which justifies the new feature of quoting them in full. Using, at least implicitly, the principle of the Occitan *vida*, then, the songs are chosen from the actual corpus of the trouvère, the historical Châtelain de Couci — at least, that is the evidence based on what is known today[41] — but they are chosen selectively[42] and arranged so as to be sung at critical topical junctures in the romance plot's *gradus amoris* and *conservatio amoris*. They therefore fit a plot whose denouement is the "cœur mangé" episode appended like Dictys to Dares in the *Roman de Troie*. Still, *conjointure* is an obvious feature of the combination of *matières* in this *matière de Lorraine*.

Quoting the insertion in its entirety lengthens in fact the amount of quoted material to quantities familiar from other romances in this group. It also obliges the author to account for more features of the quoted song, as in the Occitan *razo*. In order to understand these operations better in the *Couci*, I should like to propose a comparative

---

[37] Perhaps even fewer than the first author intended, since two places in the two extant manuscripts have rather obvious lacunae; see Matzke-Delbouille ed. *Couci* p. lxiv.

[38] Boulton 1993 Chapter Two, esp. pp. 61-66 on *Couci*.

[39] Boulton 1993 p. 61.

[40] Boulton 1993 p. 62.

[41] *Couci* ed. Matzke-Delbouille p. lxv and Boulton 1993 p. 61.

[42] See Lerond ed. *ChansonCouci*, esp. pp. 36-44.

hypothesis for interpretation. The *Couci* postdates two works with which it shares major motifs, Jean Renart's *Lai de l'ombre* and the anonymous *Châtelaine de Vergi*; it also shares with the latter the third stanza of the song by the trouvère who gave his name to Jakemes's romance, the Châtelain de Couci himself, which is discussed above. Did Jakemes know these two works and, by using procedures for rewriting and allusion common in his time, bring them together in a new *conjointure* and a new romance?

Although the *Lai de l'ombre* contains no lyric insertions, it does begin much as the *Couci* does: a knight falls in love with a lady by *ouï-dire*, visits her while her husband is away, and declares his love (it is also inserted as a resumé in Jean Renart's *Guillaume de Dole* v. 658-74). But unlike the *Couci*, the lady's *gradus amoris* in the lay is brief. She is literally *surprise d'amour* by the knight's gesture of throwing the ring she refuses to her reflection in the water, since that reflection represents the lady he loves most after her. The *Couci* Lady falls in love more gradually, making her analogous to Briseida and Guenevere rather than to the typical *coup de foudre* that so often begins medieval narratives — for example, like that experienced by the lady in the *Lai de l'ombre*.[43] I shall return to her below.

But first we must look again at the *Vergi*. In this tale, we discover what might be the conclusion to the affair begun in the *Lai de l'ombre*. To be sure, the lady in the lay hardly seems to be concerned with *qu'en dira-t-on* as she passionately embraces the knight beside the fountain in her courtyard. Yet surely her marriage must make secrecy imperative if the affair is to continue. The *Vergi* and *Couci* share the secret door motif as the lover's entrance,[44] including a signal — an upright stone replaces the puppy — that the husband is absent and the road clear for a night together. The love death is also a motif they share, as is the rival woman's vengeance and the male lover's violent death. If Jakemes rewrote this material, he did so by inserting the "cœur mangé" much as, for example, Vergil introduced the Medea material in order to write Dido's story. On the other hand, if these tales are actually independent of one another, we can observe nonetheless how the different authors rewrote conventional motifs with

---

[43] See my 1995b pp. 236-37 and n. 32.

[44] See Matzke-Delbouille ed. *Couci* p. lx: "mais sans aucune ressemblance précise dans le détail," that is, without any actual borrowing by the later author from the earlier one — but is he altering the source in order to hide it?

originality in the context of an adulterous triangle and then inserted them into a new *conjointure*.

It is important to note one other feature of Jakemes's rewriting before concluding with an examination of his narrative gradation: plagiarism. We have observed how *Cristal et Clarie* lifts material from one work and inserts it almost verbatim into a new plot and arrangement, thus effecting an original *conjointure* of antecedent matter. This variety of the *cento* occurs with the inserted lyrics themselves. So do the borrowings from Jacques Bretel's *Tournoi de Chauvency* that have been identified in the *Couci*.[45] Now, verbatim liftings (actually disallowed by Macrobius but not unknown in the medieval tradition, as we have seen) tend to be commonplaces — they are descriptions and, as such, they are suitable in any commonplace context. This includes motifs. They are not narrative material as such, but descriptive in the sense of "un schéma d'ensemble... dont le dessein est de manifester, plus ou moins concrètement et artificiellement, le développement de séquences où un savoir est transmis."[46] Their originality emerges from their placement in a new *conjointure*. We need, consequently, to consider originality in the *Châtelain de Couci*.

We need not dwell long on the Châtelain himself. As has been suggested in comparing this romance with the *Lai de l'ombre* and the *Châtelaine de Vergi*, the Châtelain's *gradus amoris* is conventional, as is the *conservatio amoris* that follows. Or rather they would have been conventional topical sequences had the Dame de Fayel and her husband not been such original descriptions. Jakames has linked the lyric pieces and the plot largely with the husband as an instance of *jointure*. The songs realize in the narrative the topical potential they possess in isolation.[47] That is to say that lyric pieces in the tradition of the *grand chant courtois* not infrequently locate themselves at some point in a *gradus amoris*, although less often in the *conservatio amoris*, by which the *Couci* also reveals its originality. The romancer merely invents the narrative potential inherent in the chosen lyrics.

The first insertion, at v. 362-406, expresses the Châtelain's happiness that he has declared his love to the Dame de Fayel. Although she refuses to acquiesce out of fidelity to her husband, the Châtelain does not despair. Rather he devotes himself to enhancing his stature

---

[45] Matzke-Delbouille ed. *Couci* pp. lix-lx, lxi n. 1, and the "Notes" to the edition.
[46] Croizy-Naquet 1994 pp. 70-71; see as well Carmona 1988 pp. 116-18.
[47] On the topical potential of the *grand chant courtois* see Kelly 2000.

in her eyes and ears by winning renown in tournaments. He is filled with joy, and the inserted song expresses that joy and his hope for the progress of his "good" love. It has been suggested that this song has little to do with the plot.[48] Yet, apart from its function as an expression of the Châtelain's love, it has two additional links to the plot: it moves the Lady to love and it anticipates the Dame de Vermandois, the Lady's jealous rival. Let us begin with its immediate effect on the Lady.

When the Dame de Fayel first hears the song and learns that the Châtelain composed it, she moves in her own *gradus amoris* from refusal to a feeling of love, which, by its nature, is the beginning of consent. Her refusal is phrased as follows:

> Castellains, pour noient parlés,
> Car je n'ai voloir ne maniere
> Que je face vostre priyere;
> Mais de tant vous conforterai,
> Que je nul baceler ne sai
> Pour qui mie je vous cangaisse
> Se jou amer nullui cuidaisse.
> Mais vous ne autrui n'amerai,
> Fors le singnour qu'espousé ai. (*Couci* v. 274-82)

[Châtelain, you are wasting your time. For I have neither the will nor the inclination to do as you ask. But I will offer you this much consolation: I know of no young man whom I would prefer to you were I disposed to love anyone. But I will love neither you nor anyone else except the husband I married.]

Yet her inclination to comfort him is only an inclination. Still, word of the Châtelain's triumphs in tournaments finds her heart inclined to listen with pleasure.

> La dame moult souvent ooit
> Maint recort qu'al coer li toucoit;
> Mais encor n'estoit pas ferue
> Dou dar de quoi Amours argüe
> Les siens, mes forment li plaisoit
> Cou que dou castellain ooit. (*Couci* v. 347-52)

---

[48] Matzke-Delbouille ed. *Couci* p. lxiv; but see Boulton 1993 p. 62-63.

[The lady often heard news which touched her heart. But she had not yet been struck by the arrow with which Love torments her subjects; still, what she heard about the Châtelain pleased her immensely.]

It is the song that finally wins her heart.

> ... la dame l'oÿ.
> Et quant sot que cius l'avoit fait
> Qui maint travail a pour li trait,
> Amours le coer li atenrie
> Pour la valeur qu'elle a oÿe
> Dou castellain, et moult li plest
> De ce que en son siervice est. (*Couci* v. 414-20)

[... the lady heard it. When she found out that he had composed it who endured much hardship for her sake, Love softens her heart because of the qualities that she heard tell about the Châtelain, and she is very much pleased by what she hears.]

The second link between the song and the plot anticipates its future development, after their love has been consummated and preserved intact for some time. In the song, the Châtelain distinguishes between the worthy lady, or "dame de valour," and the deceitful, profligate lover, or "Fausse drue habandonnee." The designation "drue" recalls the *Violette*'s own distinction between *fine amour* as a product of will and *druerie* as occurring by magic or overpowering passion. The "drue" in the Châtelain's song encourages both good and bad lovers whereas the "dame de valour" accepts only the true lover. Thus, the song anticipates the later contrast between the Dame de Fayel and the Dame de Vermandois. The latter is perfectly willing to be false to her husband; indeed, like the duchess of Burgundy in the *Vergi*, she propositions the potential lover herself. But she and the duchess are alike as well in that they are prepared to betray lovers out of jealousy when their own desires are not met. The Dame de Vermandois reveals his wife's infidelity to the Sire de Fayel. Her shame and the vengeance the Châtelain exacts from her are clearly circumscribed in the song's second stanza. The Châtelain assumes the guise of false lover in order to seduce the Dame de Vermandois.

Dame tieng a esgaree
Qui croit faus dru vanteour,
Car honte a longe duree
Qui avient par tel folour,
Et joie a povre savour
Qui en teil lieu est gastee,
S'elle a tant en li valour
Que hace sa deshonnour. (*Couci* v. 370-77)

[I hold that lady mad if she believes the words of a false, boasting lover. For shame is long lived when it follows on such folly, and joy has little savor when it is wasted in this way if she is worthy enough to hate being dishonored.]

The Châtelain and the Dame de Vermandois are on the verge of consummating their apparent passion, when he stands up, loudly reprimands her infidelity and betrayal of the Lady of Fayel, and makes it appear as if others have observed the seduction, making her fear for her reputation and dread her husband's reaction when he hears gossip about it — just as in the song.

We hear no more in the romance about the Dame de Vermandois's fate. But there is a third figure of great importance in the *Couci* plot, one who is present *in absentia* as well in both the *Lai de l'ombre* and the *Châtelaine de Vergi*: it is the sire de Fayel, husband of the Châtelain's lady. His story is perhaps the most original, and problematic, rewriting in this romance. Commonly, when the adulterous woman appears, her husband is either not in evidence, as in the *Ombre* and the *Vergi*, or she is a *mal-mariée*, which puts the blame for her conduct on the husband whose age, jealousy, or abuse constitutes a betrayal of his wife and, thus, grounds for her own infidelity. But the sire de Fayel is like none of these husbands. He is rather like the husband in Marie de France's "Equitan": a correct spouse. But also like the husband in Marie's lay, he is prone to violence when he learns of his wife's infidelity.[49] Yet when the Dame de Vermandois reveals the adultery to him, he does not immediately react. Let us therefore examine the sire de Fayel's *gradus zelotypiae*.[50]

---

[49] Of course, Equitan and the seneschal's wife plot to murder her husband.
[50] His reaction is not without analogies to those of the husband in the first book of Helisenne de Crenne's *Angoysses douloureuses*; see Debaisieux 1998.

I believe we perceive in him even better than in his wife what Matzke-Delbouille call "la fine simplicité des analyses psychologiques."[51] "Analyses psychologiques," here as elsewhere, implies the topical psychology of medieval literature. A *gradus* model for narrative elaboration uses a sequence of topoi that, in the husband's case, marks the progress of his jealousy from discovery to vengeance. There are several stages in the Sire de Fayel's passage from faultless husband to a man gone mad with jealousy. He appears first as his wife describes him: a good husband. He evinces none of the characteristics typical of the husbands of *mal-mariées* in the romance and lyric tradition. Before learning of his wife's infidelity he is not old, impotent, jealous, or abusive. They seem to love one another honestly and sincerely; as far as she is concerned, "J'ai marit preu, vaillant et sage, / Que pour homme ne fausseroie, / Ne autrui que lui n'ameroie." (*Couci* v. 220-22) [I have a worthy husband who is valiant and prudent; I wouldn't be untrue to him for anyone's sake, nor would I love anyone except him.] There is no reason to suppose that these sentiments are insincere. For his part, her husband allows the Châtelain to stay in his castle with his wife even when he is away; he himself participates in tournaments and is respected for his prowess and courtesy. There are no constraints during his absence like, for example, the seclusion which Guillaume imposes on Lienor while he is away.[52] The Dame de Fayel has complete freedom of movement and can receive anyone she wishes and go to any event that interests her. Hence, the Lady is distraught at the course her own sentiments are taking — "Elle ne se seit conseillier" (*Couci* v. 808) [she doesn't know what to do]— and she turns to her cousin for advice. The cousin's response is set in the context of her good marriage. Yes, she will assist the Dame de Fayel if she wants to have an affair, but

> ... moult m'esmierveille par m'ame
> De vous qui iestes haute dame,
> S'avés mari preu et vaillant,
> Et sour cou faites autre amant. (*Couci* v. 2346-49)

---

[51] Matzke-Delbouille ed. *Couci* p. lxi.

[52] Contrast the Dame de Fayel's freedom of movement with the constraints imposed on wives in, for example, *Flamenca* and Marie de France's *Guigemar* and *Yonec*.

[I truly marvel, in faith, that you, a noble lady endowed with a worthy, valiant husband, wish to take a lover in addition to what you have.]

To encourage a young man ("baceler," v. 2350-61) in what seems to be a platonic relationship is one thing and, indeed, seems entirely reasonable; but one must preserve one's honor above all things. Yet by an about-face as surprising as it is sudden, the cousin then agrees to help the Lady if she has really set her mind on having a lover. "Et nompourquant, se vous l'amés, / S'en faites vostres volentés" (*Couci* v. 2360-61) [However, if you do love him, follow your inclination]. The Dame de Fayel is already in love, and her cousin aids her to the bitter end, without as much as a glance back at the morality of the love she so sternly rebuked. The lovers take advantage of the husband's trust; they are, in fact, so discrete that the husband remains blissfully ignorant until the Dame de Vermandois tells him what is going on (*Couci* v. 4165-69).

With that news, the Sire de Fayel begins his gradual change of character from faultless husband to vengeful, jealous husband. He passes from doubts to certainty while spying on the lovers, who largely succeed in covering their tracks with some skillful spur-of-the-moment deceptions that maintain his doubts for a time and thus protect the Lady. But even when he can no longer doubt, the husband observes a certain reticence in taking vengeance on his wife in the usual, abusive ways of the *chanson de mal-mariée*. The grounds for reticence on his part are feudal. Although the Sire de Fayel verbally abuses his wife, she does not have to endure physical abuse thanks to her family.

> Mais n'ose pas son mautalant
> Moustrer ne batre par haussage,
> Car elle estoit de grant linage;
> Si portoit en lui son maiscief,
> U li fust lait, u li fust grief.
> Longement ce mautalent tint....[53] (*Couci* v. 6185-90)

---

[53] See as well v. 5806-15, in which the Dame de Vermandois is outraged by the Châtelain's preference for the Dame de Fayel because the latter is inferior to her in *lignage*.

[But he didn't dare reveal his anger or physically abuse her in his arrogance, for she came from a very noble family. He kept his misfortune to himself, whether it displeased or grieved him. He restrains his anger for a long time....]

The narrator's ominous tone explains the gradual disintegration of his character that culminates in the cannibalism of the final scene when he has his wife eat her lover's heart unbeknownst to her. Although his angry jealousy curtails his movement away from the castle (*Couci* v. 5304-08, 5601-05), his wife keeps up the pretense of light-heartedness, service, and innocence; even their sexual relations do not come to a full stop (*Couci* v. 6430-35). Yet his jealousy continues to eat away internally, resulting in a kind of madness in his gleeful revenge on her (*Couci* v. 7998, 8004). Like the Duke of Burgundy, the Sire de Fayel leaves his domain after her death to do penance in the Holy Land.

The conclusion of the story is heavy with the irony of this perplexing romance: "tel doivent iestre," we are told, "et si fait / Tout cil qui sont amant parfait"! (*Couci* v. 8195-96) [that is how all should be who are perfect lovers], whereupon the narrator evokes in the epilogue his own faithful love.

What are we to make of this? Let's return to the elements Jakemes brought together in order to spin out his narrative: the lyric pieces and some version or versions of the "cœur mangé" tale. The latter appears only for the denouement, as we have seen; furthermore, it is a truly triangular narrative making the lover, the wife, and the husband equally important. To make his plot fuller, Jakemes also does as Matthew of Vendôme advised his pupils: he fills out the stages that are missing in the original. We do not know what "cœur mangé" tales he may have known. But we can see that his version includes the husband's *gradus zelotypiae*. We have already observed the steps in his developing jealousy, including special features like the higher birth and family of his wife and the resultant interiorizing and deepening of his anger because he does not dare vent it physically on her.

Without the husband, of course, the plot could have had a happy ending, or it could have a different dramatic denouement, as in the *Châtelaine de Vergi*, where the husband plays no role in the plot, but which includes a rejected woman. Jakemes chose to link his triumph to the lyric pieces, and, notably, he makes the husband the juncture between these pieces and the "cœur mangé" motif.

With the exception of three rondeaux, Jakemes attributes all the lyric pieces to the Châtelain.[54] He invents and sings them first; as messages to his lady, they communicate his feelings and concerns. They are related to his own and the lady's *gradus amoris* by identifying certain stages that the plot (as if following Matthew's injunctions) fills out and makes complete. We have seen that the first song (v. 362-406) makes the Dame de Fayel begin to love in earnest. The third (v. 2591-614) evokes the period of trial the Lady puts the Châtelain through by making him wait outside her secret door in the cold: "elle me fait a teil doulour languir" (v. 2608) [she makes me languish so grievously]. He tries to put the best face on her motives by telling himself that "felons" and "maisdisans" (v. 2609-10) keep her from being open with him. But he is not convinced in his heart of hearts. "Mierveilles ai dont vient ceste ocoisanz / Qu'elle me fait a teil doulour languir" (v. 2607-08) [I wonder what causes her to make me languish so grievously]. Matters are eventually sorted out, and the *gradus amoris* is consummated and completed soon enough. The joy of this topical denouement produces a song that appears to have disappeared from the manuscripts — was it perhaps too bold for some scribe? — but which sprang from love "de volenté jolie" (v. 3700) [of joyful will]. The same is true for the second missing lyric (v. 4947[a]). The goal of the Châtelain's love is indeed to "enjoy" the Dame de Fayel, and the goal is quite explicit.

1. "Espoirs li dist que par siervir / Pora de sa dame joïr" (v. 745-46) [Hope tells him that by his service he can enjoy his lady].

2. After the separation caused by the Dame de Vermandois, "Amours... / Li dist... / Qu'encore de sa douce amie / Goÿra, cou le tient en joie" (v. 4941-44) [Love tells him that he will enjoy his beloved once more, which keeps him in high spirits].

3. The single stanza in v. 7005-11 is almost as explicit: "Que celle k'aim entre mes bras nuette / Tiengne une fois ains que voise outre mer!" (v. 7010-11)[55] [May I embrace her whom I love one more time in the nude before going abroad], a wish which is granted for two days. "Mais poi y eut solas ne giu" (v. 7327) [but they had little solace or play], so depressed were they at his imminent departure for the Holy Land.

---

[54] On these attributions, see Matzke and Delbouille ed. *Couci* pp. lxiii-lxvi. The rondeaux are sung, but not composed, by a lady (v. 987-88), the Dame de Vermandois (v. 3830-31), and the Dame de Fayel (v. 3851-56).

[55] Cf. v. 6602-04.

The Dame de Fayel's evolution and goals are more circumspect. As we saw above, the stages by which she slips into love are discretely delineated and the description itself more circumstantial. She does not fall in love by the conventional *coup de foudre*; her love occurs rather as a gradual emotional deepening after her initial astonishment at the Châtelain's declaration, as she admires his physical features, his character, and his martial achievements in tourneys. Inner consent completes this sequence provoked by his first song about good and bad lovers. After that, consent to love advances to consent to consummate that love after a series of trials which the Dame de Fayel partially imposes and partially endures: she keeps him out for one night, but then is tortured by the thought that his terrible illness may have been caused by that very cruelty; however, she repeats the test the next time he is allowed to come to her door in order to test his sentiments by overhearing his words when he thinks she has betrayed him again:

> Nous voliens savoir entresait
> Vo pensee et que vous diriés
> De cou qu'entrer ens ne poyiés;
> Et bien saciés, s'euissiés dit
> Cose qui tournast a despit,
> Vous n'i fuissiés entrés huimais. (*Couci* v. 3482-87)

[We wanted to find out for sure what you were thinking and what you would say about not being let in. And rest assured that if you had said anything derogatory you would never have gotten in.]

But henceforth her desire for her knight is as intense as his for her, and just as dependent on embraces and sexual gratification.[56]

The Châtelain's songs begin again during the Crusade. The first asks: "Coment me poet li coers el corps durer"? (v. 7369) [how can my heart stay in my body?] which we have already heard in the *Châtelaine de Vergi*. Here, of course, his heart will indeed pass from his body into his lady's by way of the "cœur mangé" denouement. His last song, composed while he is returning home and cognizant that

---

[56] *Couci* v. 3577-78, 3745-48, 6257-59, and 6361-67; only the depressing prospect of their separation because of the Crusade tempers their ardor, as we have seen.

death is imminent (v. 7564-608), is a final praise of the lady he must leave, evoking the analogy between his death by poison and love. After this comes the link with the husband in Jakemes's own version of the "cœur mangé" tale.

The songs themselves, like the tales in the *Lai de l'ombre* and the *Châtelaine de Vergi*, contain only an absent husband. He is implicit in the lyric addresses to a "dame,"[57] which implies a married woman, and, perhaps, in *losengiers* and others who betray a good love, including not only the husband, but also the Dame de Vermandois and the Fayel castle servants who inform their Lord of what occurs during his absences (v. 6177-78). Nonetheless, his role in the denouement requires some preparation. This is where the husband of the *Ombre* and the *Vergi*, who seemed harmless enough, is rewritten into the vicious husband of the Dame de Fayel.

The husband's metamorphosis begins with the discovery of his wife's infidelity. The discovery is two-fold, but at first uncertain. His doubts lead to overwrought worry as he hovers between hope and suspicion, keeping everything to himself while spying on his wife. Catching her in *flagranti delicto* would permit him to exact immediate revenge. However, the Dame de Fayel's indisposition keeps her away when the Châtelain next enters the castle through the secret door (v. 4519-22); he uses the subterfuge, which had been prepared in case of need, that he is actually having an affair with Ysabel, the Dame de Fayel's cousin and servent. Nonetheless, the Sire de Fayel's suspicions do not evaporate. He sinks into chronic jealousy (v. 4824, 5304-08), with the side effect of *recreantise*, so that he can keep constant watch on his wife (v. 5307-08, 5601-05). He would like to take vengeance on her, but he fears her family and therefore refrains from physical, but not verbal abuse. He resorts to dissimulation while seeking a way to separate the lovers permanently. He finally succeeds, getting the Châtelain away on the Crusade. He also becomes more gracious to his wife, again by dissimulation; they apparently renew their sexual pleasures (v. 6429-35). His violence, however, is finally displaced into the "cœur mangé" denouement.

The description of the jealous husband is also an insertion in the two senses of the term we have identified here. First, it develops the background to the "cœur mangé" denouement, and as such provides

---

[57] *Couci* v. 402, 2598, 5968, 5974, 5984, 7387, 7397, and 7565 (therefore, three times in this refrain).

another link between that tale and the romance plot, thereby conforming to Gosman's sense of the insertion. But it also has Tristan-like implications, not only in the motifs of the clandestine visit and the role of the cousin Ysabel as a 'replacement love' analogous to Brengien, as well as in the *cœur mangé* episode itself to which Iseut alludes when she sings the "lai de Gudrun" in Thomas's version,[58] but also explicitly in the Tristan allusion in one of the lyric pieces: "onques Tristans qui but le buverage / Si loiaument n'ama sans departir" (v. 834-35) [Tristan who drank the potion never loved so constantly].

It is noteworthy that "insertions," whether as lyric pieces or as excerpts from or allusions to other narratives, are descriptions in that they fill out a common place with meaning specific to the context and significance of the new romance. They identify the topical places and narrative potential of lyric moments and descriptive stasis. Furthermore, by actually quoting an antecedent text, lyric or descriptive, the medieval romance allows greater freedom than Macrobius seems to have for "flores" and "ornamenta" for such quotation (see above, chap. 2). The verbatim aspect is there. But also the originality of *cento* rearrangement permits a fuller, even original reading of the quoted material.

Finally, we note as well the essentially open significance of the narrative of the kind that Bruckner identified in the *Charrette*. The mixture of lessons is not always consistent, and such inconsistency must provoke a degree of receptive "distanciation" in audiences. We may fall back again on the maiden's observation in Froissart's *Meliador*, another romance with inserted lyrics. For on one of these lyrics, whose composition she admires, she nonetheless has reservations: "Ceste parole n'est pas mienne, / Car onques n'amai par tel art"[59] [I don't agree with that poem, for it doesn't represent my art of love]. She is not prepared to evolve into love like the Dame de Fayel or to change her mind like Ysabel, who, after reprimanding her Lady for thinking of loving outside a good marriage, nonetheless agrees to help her if she firmly intends to have an affair. As we have seen, Ysabel is even prepared to lose her reputation, and does so, to cover up the Dame de Fayel's tracks.

---

[58] See Matzke-Delbouille *Couci* p. lx, Boulton 1993 p. 64, Bertolucci Pizzorusso 1998 pp. 106-08, Riquer and Simó 1998 pp. 1109-10 and 1119. Cf. Vincensini 1996 pp. 335-72.

[59] *Meliador* v. 20353-54; see Kelly 1978 pp. 248-52.

Other episodes in the *Couci* raise similar moral and social problems. Perhaps we can set the issue best by quoting the Châtelain's own words to the Dame de Vermandois when he exacts "honniestre vengement" (v. 4985) [honorable revenge]. Could not his reprimand be addressed to the Dame de Fayel herself?

> Dame, or esgardés!
> Il ne demeure pas en vous
> Que vostres maris ne soit couls.
> Vous li iestes de pute foi... (v. 5757-60)

[See here, my lady! you are hardly standing in the way of your husband's becoming a cuckold! You have the fidelity of a slut...]

On the other hand, can the sympathy one might feel for the Sire de Fayel hold out against his own deterioration into chronic jealousy and deceit? Deceit is indeed the one characteristic common to all these figures. They oblige the public to think for itself, an expectation that seems to remain constant in all the romances we have examined here. The thirteenth-century Lorraine romances reconfirm the place of individual judgment in diverse audiences and individuals.

Narrative Description of Lyric Pieces in Jean Renart's Rose *or* Guillaume de Dole

Maureen Boulton has analyzed the "dialogic" relationship between the lyric insertion and the romance narrative that contains such insertions.[60] Let us begin with the insertion. "The insertion of a lyric poem... into a narrative context"[61] seems to imply that the narrative existed before the poems were inserted into it. However, this is not the case in Jean Renart's *Roman de la rose* or *Guillaume de Dole*, the romance on which the burden of Professor Boulton's argument rests. Not only do we know that the various insertions were extant prior to Jean Renart's romance, he tells his audience that they were[62] and, therefore, there can be no misunderstanding on that score: "est avis a chascun et samble / que cil qui a fet le romans / qu'il trovast toz

---

[60] Boulton 1987 p. 81.
[61] Boulton 1987 p. 75.
[62] Zink 1979 p. 29.

les moz des chans" (*Dole* v. 26-28) [it seems to everyone that the author of the romance wrote the songs] — which is to say that he did not.[63] Thus, it is appropriate to speak not only of lyric insertions, but also of narrative investment or increment. I sense that Professor Boulton was aware of this because, in her definition quoted above, she refers to "the insertion... into a narrative *context*" (my emphasis).[64] That "context" embraces and is prior to both the lyric before insertion and the narrative that is written for the lyric pieces. It is in this "context" that the dialogism occurs through the addition of narrative wrapping to songs selected (*mutuatio*) and prearranged (*transmutatio*). The wager tale itself is rewritten, like the *chanson de mal mariée* in the *Violette* that becomes a *chanson de bien fiancée*, in order to fit the lyric context of the songs.

Dialogism is a term Professor Boulton borrows from current critical terminology. As she uses the term, it refers to the way authors like Jean Renart "compose their works with images of different types of language, and engage in a sort of 'dialogue' with these languages."[65] She goes on to note astutely that dialogism was a feature of medieval theoretical discourse, one which has already been discussed above: the *genera dicendi*, and more specifically, their medieval variety known as Material Style,[66] or a kind of decorum such that language is adapted to social circumstances that a given work presents. "Il conte d'armes et d'amors / et chante d'ambedeus ensamble." (*Dole* v. 24-25) [He tells of arms and love and sings of both together.] These lines evoke the narrative context, *armes et amors*, and the 'dialogism' of the lyric matter and the narrative.[67] Although the *Dole* appears to be a romance with lyric insertions, it is, in fact, a mosaic of lyric pieces

---

[63] Frequent allusions to the lyric authors remind the reader that the songs antedate the romance (see *Dole* v. 844-45, 1451-52, 3620, 3878-79, 4123-24, 5229); others would no doubt have been recognized by nostalgic amateurs of the *chanson d'histoire* like those sung "ça en arriers" (v. 1148) [in the past] by ladies and queens. Here the allusion is made obvious by the quotation of the lyric material alluded to; on this "doubling function," see Jewers 1996 p. 912.

[64] Boulton 1997 p. 86; see also Jewers 1996 p. 923 on "accommodating narrative."

[65] Boulton 1987 p. 81. For example, the epic language of *Gerbert de Metz* adumbrates the role of Liénor in the *Dole*; see Boulton 1997 p. 93 and Psaki 1997 pp. 134-36.

[66] Kelly 1991 pp. 71-78 and 1992 pp. 52-56.

[67] Cf. *Violette*, v. 39-41: "... si est si bien acordans / Li cans au dit, les entendans / En trai a garant que di voir." [The song is in harmony with the words, and I call the audience to witness to the truth of this statement.]

held together by interlacing narrative insertions modeled on the lyric context.

There are therefore two matters at issue in Jean Renart's use of "insertions." First is the way in which his implied audience was expected to receive his romance. They should, he suggests, perceive the lyric and other pieces as so finely woven into the narrative fabric that they produce a work of one piece. The audience is forewarned, and the audience will judge. The new *conjointure*, which makes the familiar new, will, if successful by its own standards, seem so because the words of the insertions "afierent a ceus del conte." This, as Professor Boulton, observes, raises two questions: "Why were *songs* inserted into *stories* in the thirteenth and fourteenth centuries?" and "Why were *these* songs inserted into *this* story?"[68] These are questions that pertain to our mode of reading this romance.

But what did Jean Renart actually do when he wrote the romance that produces the *illusion* of lyric insertions? He says he made it *appear* as if he wrote them. But he didn't write them. In fact, the lyric pieces either preceded the narrative which was added to them or else the two, lyrics and narrative, come together from their separate existence into the new work. Indeed, it would be more accurate to say that Jean wrote *Guillaume de Dole* by combining lyrics and narratives, since the romance contains narrative and lyrico-narrative material from a *chanson de geste* and from several *chansons de toile* as well as from a wager tale.[69] Furthermore, these different modes of writing are truncated, that is, incomplete by themselves (*detractio*). The lyrics in the manuscript do not include all known stanzas of each piece, except for some refrains; the excerpt from the *chanson de geste* is only a laisse; and the wager motif itself is incomplete because it lacks a wager.[70] To be sure, as Boulton points out, the lyric pieces are monologues in lyric mode. Nonetheless, if it is true that "a medieval author could introduce significant innovations while remaining within the literary tradition,"[71] it is also true that the most significant innovations and, therefore, in the broad sense of the word we have been using in this study, the most significant descriptions, modify the wager narrative in order to make it conform to its lyric matter. "A context must be created

---

[68] Boulton 1993 p. xiv; her emphasis.
[69] See Lecoy ed. *Dole* pp. xxii-xxix for a catalogue of all these pieces.
[70] Zink 1979 pp. 46-49.
[71] Boulton 1987 p. 82.

for" the insertion, "and this necessity has narrative consequences."[72] The narrative is therefore formed — "created" in the pre-Christian sense of the word — to fit a specific, predetermined array of lyric and narrative excerpts that themselves make a context, but are unchanged except through abbreviations by emphasis or deletion by cutting.[73]

The way by which Conrad falls in love illustrates the narrative's dependence on descriptive insertions. The name Liénor (v. 791) is the first stage in Conrad's *gradus amoris*. Jouglet's description of her, itself a digression inserted into the wager plot, derives apparently from the *Lai de l'ombre*, another tale of love beginning by *ouï-dire* (v. 657-74); for the *Ombre*'s lady, Jouglet invents a description just as he will do for Liénor (v. 687-722): "N'aprist pas hui si a descrire / qui l'embeli en tel meniere" (*Dole* v. 711-12) [he was no apprentice in the art of description, he who beautified her in this way], comments the narrator. Conrad himself alludes to the same words upon hearing the analogous description of Liénor.

> — Si te consaut Dieus,
> or me rembeliz la pucele.»
> Cil s'aperçoit mout bien que cele
> li plesoit ja par oïr dire,
> et au samblant que il remire
> li est avis qu'il l'aime ja.[74] (*Dole* v. 803-08)

["So help you God, embellish the maid for me." He, Jouglet, perceived well enough that she pleased the emperor already just by hearing her name; upon considering the king's appearance he concludes that he is already in love with her.]

One is reminded of the commentary in Gide's *Faux-monnayeurs*: "L'analyse psychologique a perdu pour moi tout intérêt du jour où je

---

[72] Boulton 1993 p. 287. Space precludes considering the effect on reception among audiences who knew the parts of each lyric piece that were deleted. On poetics of allusion in this kind of narrative, see Boulton 1993 pp. 289-93.

[73] See Allen 1982 p. 100 on "normative array": "exempla arrayed under a given topic... in fact relate to and define that topic." In Jean Renart's *Rose*, the poems and extracts chosen are arrayed in relation to the topic love. As Allen points out elsewhere, "a medieval person who wishes to be ethically good could achieve that condition by acting as if he were in a story" (p. 292). Similarly, Conrad acts "as if he were in a story" in order to become in love with Liénor; see Zink 1979 p. 32.

[74] Cf. Zink 1979 pp. 32-35.

me suis avisé que l'homme éprouve ce qu'il s'imagine éprouver. De là
à penser qu'il s'imagine éprouver ce qu'il éprouve." — Conrad might
well have added: "Je le vois bien avec mon amour" (*Faux-monnayeurs*
p. 76). That his love is more an object of his imagination than of his
emotions is quite evident when Liénor appears before him to defend
herself. The emperor fails to recognize the beautiful woman he imagines he loves and, accordingly in Jean Renart's fictional world, does
indeed love.

These factors bring us back to Boulton's questions which I referred
to above. Her questions are elicited by the completed work, not by its
composition, or the putting together of the completed work. From
the latter point of view, we may ask of the composition of *Guillaume de
Dole*: "Why was this story adapted to these songs?" and "Why were
these songs chosen, why were they arranged in the order we find
them in, and what effect did they have on the story written around
them?"

Two lyric pieces in particular are crucial to answering these questions about the romance's composition. The first in effect restates the
wager in such a way as to make the emperor responsible for, but
innocent of, his seneschal's plot. Conrad's seneschal has become jealous of the emperor's special attention to Guillaume. When he over-
hears his lord sing an anonymous song, he realizes that Guillaume
enjoys favor because of his sister. "De ce sui je toz fiz," the seneschal
concludes, "que n'est pas por chevalerie / qu'il li porte tel druerie: /
ce n'est que por sa seror non." (v. 3200-03) [Of this I am quite sure:
the affection he shows him has nothing to do with his knighthood; his
sister is the sole reason for it.] Speaking these two stanzas is a *pechié*,
not in the sense of a sin, but of what Lecoy translates as a "force
obscure et néfaste qui pousse à l'erreur ou à la faute."[75] Not only do
the two stanzas reveal to the seneschal the relationship binding together Conrad, Guillaume, and Lienor, they also set up the model
for the seneschal's plot. In a sense, the seneschal is a male Dame de
Vermandois. In the song the emperor sings, love is all the singer
desires; yet he cannot escape grief because of the *losengiers* who prevent him from serving love as he would. Up to this point, there have
been no *losengiers*. But the type fits the seneschal, whose plot to accuse

---

[75] *Dole* p. 221 s.v. *pechiez*. If we apply the standards by which Helen is responsible
for the fall of Troy, must we not also make the emperor responsible for Lienor's
alleged "fall"?

Lienor of not being a virgin and hence making the love impossible, springs from that song. Loss of virginity is an insurmountable obstacle in this romance: "je la cuidai a feme avoir, / mes or voi que pas ne puet estre" (v. 3684-85), for "la hautece de cest roiaume / ne s'i acordast a nul fuer" (v. 3690-91) [I thought that she would be my wife but I now see that it is impossible... The high nobility of this kingdom would in no way accept it]. We are in the social context of Laudine's and Lavine's marriages: the consent of the barons is necessary.

The seneschal's accusation is a slander ("mesdire," v. 3193) that springs from "grant envie" (v. 3162). But a slanderer can only slander, he cannot actually accomplish anything. This holds in the seneschal's case too. Learning the secret about Lienor's birthmark makes his claim to have seduced her credible. But he is impotent; the seneschal never even sees Lienor, which allows her to reveal his slander when she appears at the emperor's court to prove her innocence. And she succeeds, for indeed the seneschal

> ot nïé et dit
> qu'il onques mes jor ne me vit
> ne ne me fist descovenue
> par qoi honte me soit creüe.
> Si m'aït Dex, ce ne fist mon! (v. 5079-83)

[denied that he had ever seen me or done me any wrong that would have caused me shame. So help me God, he definitely did not!]

This is because, as the refrains in the emperor's song repeat, *bone amor* counters slander, or, "ne riens fors li ne m'en puet fere aïe" (v. 3187) and "ne riens fors li ne me puet geter d'ire" (v. 3195) [it alone can help me in this matter... it alone can release me from anxiety].

The second lyric piece crucial to the narrative is sung after the seneschal has hatched his plot, and it is succeeding for a while. The emperor seeks solace by singing two stanzas of another song. His reading of the song's words conforms to the seneschal's scenario since, to the emperor's mind, his and Lienor's experience corresponds to that expressed at the end of the first stanza. "Por c'en chasti tote gent / q'el m'a mort et li traïe" (v. 3889-90) [for this reason I caution everyone because it, love, has slain me and betrayed her]. The betrayal follows the seneschal's alleged seduction, which in turn is responsible for Conrad's grief. Even if, as the second stanza puts it, his words have gone too far — "j'ai dit par ma folie, / ... grant outrage" (v. 3891-92) [my foolishness has made me speak outrageously] — his delay in speaking earlier of his love has made the betrayal possible. But the emperor's outburst after singing the song gets it right. "Ha!... bele Lïenors, / Com m'a traï li seneschaus" (v. 3900-01) [Ah!... lovely Lienor, how the seneschal has betrayed me]. The double-entendre for the reader implies the correction of the song and love's responsibility in the emperor's misfortune. Indeed, love is still alive, and the emperor is not dead. Yet, he continues to condemn the absent Lienor, "Touz li pechiez et toz li maus / est de vos et de vostre frere" (v. 3902-03) [all the sin/wrong and the evil/harm comes from/to you and your brother[76]], applying to them both the un-motivated fault we saw in Helen's case.

These lines are no doubt deliberately ambiguous. Does the emperor really believe both brother and sister to be responsible for the calamity? Or does he merely mean that it is their concern, not his? Since both readings are possible, his words suggest some confusion in his mind regarding his own sense of the situation. This is borne out by his will to wed Lienor despite its impossibility.

> Or sachiez que li emperere
> la desirast mout a avoir,
> mes or ne l'ose mes voloir,
> qu'il set bien que ne porroit estre. (v. 3904-07)

[Rest assured that the emperor would have liked very much to have her as wife, but he doesn't dare to wish for that now because he knows that it would be impossible.]

We recall that the emperor has still not seen Lienor except in his imagination, that is, in images spurred through the sound of her name. Yet his wish will be granted.

Jean Renart is rewriting the wager tale. He has eliminated the wager as such, but not the deception. He takes up the wager model to project a permanent separation despite love; all the while, the reader knows the seneschal's deception. The song Conrad has sung

---

[76] This translation reflects the two major meanings of *pechié* in Old French.

plots a successful betrayal but it also allows for action by Lienor, given the fact that both men who are victims of the betrayal are incapable of action.

Both Guillaume and the emperor do little more than mope about, leaving action to others. Guillaume buries his head in his cape (v. 3734-36) and gives himself over to his grief. The emperor can only sing: "chanter m'estuet, car plus ne m'en puis taire, / por conforter ma cruel aventure / qui m'est tornee a grant mesaventure" (v. 4131-33) [I must sing since I can no longer keep silent about it, in order to assuage my cruel adventure which has turned into my great misfortune]. But even if they cannot act, Lienor can:

> Mar acointai sa tres douce feture
> por tel dolor ne por tel mal atrere,
> qui ce me fet que nus ne puet deffere,
> fors ses fins cuers.... (v. 4136-39)

[Woe is me for coming to know her sweet self since it has brought such grief and misfortune on me; it affects me this way so that none can undo it except her gentle heart....]

That gentle heart will indeed manifest the required finesse: "Onqes n'en fu nule si sage" (v. 4072) [no woman was ever more level-headed].

Lienor's success is modeled on the *chanson de toile* concerning the exploits of a Bele Aiglentine. Michel Zink has shown how Jean Renart rewrote this poem, the most extensively quoted lyric piece in the romance, for the conclusion of *Guillaume de Dole*.[77] The song is sung as the knights gather for the tournament at Saint Trond. The emperor has not yet declared his love or asked for Lienor's hand. Thus, the chanson's plot can be a model only for what follows. But the model is close enough to fit the kind of scheme Macrobius identified in Vergil's rewrite of Medea's story in the *Aeneid* Book IV. The mother discovers Aiglentine's pregnancy after her daughter makes a wound — a mark — on herself while sewing. Aiglentine confesses her love for a courteous mercenary, "le preu Henri" (v. 2261). Her mother asks her daughter to meet Henri and rectify the situation. Here are the broad lines of the plot Jean Renart rewrites in his

---

[77] Zink 1978 and 1979.

romance: the tell-tale mother, the wronged maiden, the mother's intervention, the voyage to court to rectify the situation, and the rectification.[78] Jean adds from his other sources a new figure, the *male mere* (cf. "male maistre," v. 1183), who, however, is bad only by inadvertancy, as she, rather than her daughter, is seduced by the seneschal's apparent courtesy and betrays her daughter's secret.[79] Wicked *losengiers* reappear in the person of the seneschal. The innocent woman, falsely accused because of a mark, which would be true evidence if, as in the case of Bele Aiglentine, it actually signalled her loss of virginity.

Other *chansons de toile*[80] echo Lienor's story too: "L'amor Doon vos covient oublier" (v. 1165), her mother tells the Bele Aude, even though "Tant bon'amor fist bele Aude en Doon" (v. 1166) [you must forget love for Doon... Lovely Aude had found a fine love in Doon]. Immediately afterwards Bele Aude is violently abused because she loves a foreign mercenary. Still another song echoes Bele Doe's loneliness because Doon delays coming to see her.

All these elements come together in the narrative, a narrative fashioned both to fit the broad lines of lyric models while redefining the topoi that identify it in the new story: the mercenary becomes an emperor, the *male mere* does not intentionally mistreat her daughter, and the latter's fault is non-existent. What we note, however, is that the wager story is rewritten to fit the lyric model of the "bad mother" rather than having the lyric conform to the predetermined narrative scheme. This means that the lyric model of the "bad mother" was set up — "com-posed" — before the narrative matter that was subsequently adapted to it, all of which fully confirms Zink's observation that the romance is an elaborate *razo* or, indeed, *vida* since it is put together using material found in some forty-six lyric pieces, a *laisse* from a *chanson de geste*, and a number of suggestive allusions to fictional characters like Perceval, Graelant Muer, and Alexander: "voilà que l'on peut soupçonner une supercherie," — a *conspiratio* — "ou plutôt que la présentation semble entièrement tirée des chansons elles-mêmes, à la manière de *razos* des troubadours, qui tirent le plus

---

[78] Cf. Stanesco 1988 p. 110. Except for the social status, the *chanson*'s plot conforms to that in the Eighth Nouvelle of the *Cent nouvelles nouvelles*, insofar as in both a wronged maiden goes to her former fiancé and rectifies the wrong she is blamed for.

[79] Zink 1979 p. 58.

[80] On embroidery as an image in the *Dole*, see Dragonetti 1987 pp. 159-67, Walter 1990 pp. 199-200, Jewers 1996, and Jones 1997.

souvent du poème lui-même les éléments biographiques qui veulent en rendre compte."[81] We may therefore identify several steps in the composition or putting together of *Guillaume de Dole*, steps that are characteristic of the Macrobian tradition of descriptive rewriting.

On the one hand stands the lyric tradition on which Jean Renart draws in order to appear to insert certain poems into his narrative. On the other hand stands the narrative itself, the so-called *conte de la gageure* or wager tale in folklore traditions that emerge in the romance tradition in Jean Renart's romance.[82] But, as we have seen, this *conte*[83] is rewritten to fit the lyrics, not the other way around.[84] Does this not imply that, as is the case with the *vidas* and *razos* which Zink refers to, the lyrics come before the amplification of their narrative potential? According to Jean Renart's prologue the lyric pieces mesh so well with the narrative that the whole appears to be of one cloth, with words and song blending into a tale of arms and love. This is indeed a *conspiratio* in Macrobius's sense: "in unum conspirata" or song blending different voices (*Sat* praef. 10).

But the *conspiratio* is also a conspiracy, a deception or "supercherie" in Zink's words. For, in fact, it appears that Jean Renart actually invented the words of the story so as to fit the model found in the songs. From this we may conclude that Jean Renart chose his songs to fit a preconceived model, a poetic archetype or blueprint that patterns the disposition of the songs in such a way that the narrative could be made to fit that disposition by the very operations of addition, deletion, replacement, and transposition which we have already observed in the relation of narrative to some key lyric pieces, especially "Bele Aiglentine" and other *chansons de toile* and *de femme*. The example of Bele Aiglentine provides that model.

Let us now examine the disposition of songs in the plot. There is a circular arrangement of the kinds of songs that are sung in *Guillaume de Dole* — or, more accurately, there is a spiral sequence. The ro-

---

[81] Zink 1978 p. 3 and Baumgartner 1981 p. 261; cf. Boulton 1997 pp. 98-99.

[82] Paris 1903 pp. 487-90.

[83] We cannot, of course, know what actual tale or tales Jean may have known or used any more than we can know the *conte d'avanture* Chrétien rewrote in *Erec*. In both cases, however, we can delineate with some accuracy these authors' rewriting by examining how they describe the tale or tales, like *depecier* and *corronpre* in Chrétien or Jean Renart's claim to weave songs and words so nicely that they seem to be written by the same author.

[84] There is, of course, some rewriting in the lyrics in the sense that lines have been lost or suppressed.

mance begins with the festivities in the woods accompanied by dancing, singing, feasting, and promenades. The jealous husbands who
are deceived in the songs are projected into those who are off in the
woods hunting while their wives and *amies* sport with attractive young
men. Similarly, at the end of the romance, dancing and singing evoke
the marriage of Lienor and the emperor after the would-be deceiver,
the seneschal, has been unmasked and punished. In between, we find
the *laisse* from a *chanson de geste* which is displaced into the tournament
Guillaume de Dole wins. *Chansons* in the *grand chant courtois* tradition
also evoke the emperor's state of mind as he falls in love with Lienor
and proposes to marry her. These virtual interior monologues follow
the emperor as he falls in love, doubts and fears, hopes and despairs
before the happy denouement. The "chançons d'istoire," as they are
called (v. 1151), provide plot outlines that are rewritten in the narrative in some of the different ways discussed above.

   In addition, the cycle of songs resembles a spiral as far as the plot
is concerned. For the jealous husbands mocked by the young lovers
in the initial forest scene acquire a more positive patina. The emperor has evolved, especially in term of the ages of life scheme, so
that he too falls into the class of those once boorish husbands who
tramped around in the woods while he joined the more courteous,
light-hearted youth for fun and games. First comes the change.

> Se j'ai eü le cuer volage,
> ç'a esté enfance et jonece.
> Ou a folie ou a parece
> le tendroit on des ore mes.
> Une foiz est bien que ge les
> mon voloir por fere le lor (v. 3496-3501)

[If I have been light hearted, it was because of my youth or
young manhood. People would consider such conduct foolish or
idle now. It's high time I leave doing what I want in order to do
what they wish...]

— that is: take a wife. Thus, Gace Brulé's song on jealousy which
causes one to "encerchier... / ce qu'en ne voudroit trover" (v. 3630-
31) [seek out what one wouldn't want to find] prefigures the deception that threatens the jealous husbands and the fiancé as well. Like
them, the emperor now spends his time hunting rather than with

"déjeuners sur l'herbe," which is no doubt another sign that he has left youth and early manhood and entered the prime of life.

> Il sejourna a ses chastiaus
> a deduit de chiens et d'oisiaus
> et a plenté de chevaliers;
> et si ooit mout volentiers
> a son couchier menestereuls. (v. 3393-97)

[He passed his time in his castle with hunting and throngs of knights. He gladly listened to minstrels singing when he retired to bed.]

Thus the denouement reverses the evaluation of the *entrée en matière*. The young emperor has become the mature husband; his wife is not a *mal mariée* seeking escape with Doon or Gui, nor is the seneschal a foreign mercenary or young *bachelier*[85] in the woods. Each type has been rewritten to fit the songs the story is written around.

The use of lyric pieces brings about a change in descriptions too, especially under the influence of the *chanson d'histoire*.[86] The common archetypal pattern in the lyric and narrative modes is the amorous triangle. There had always been such triangles. What the *chanson d'histoire* brings to the triangle is new types. The triangle may be pre- or post-conjugal. In the lyric modes this differentiates between the *chanson de femme* and the *chanson de mal-mariée*.[87] The former often includes a mother or father figure who impedes or furthers the desires of the daughter, the latter an undesirable husband. The active figure

---

[85] Of course, the seneschal does have his own potential romance with the Châtelaine de Dijon (cf. *Dole* v. 4297-4304, and 4397-4420); this gets him in trouble when Lienor uses that romance to advance her own self-defense.

[86] In what follows, I am using the descriptions by Pierre Bec 1977 for these kinds of lyric; the descriptions are quoted in the notes. A *chanson d'histoire* "possède une trame narrative, généralement simple et tragique, avec des personnages qui y sont imbriqués" (Bec 1977 p. 109).

[87] *Chansons de femme* include "un corpus assez varié de genres poétiques globalement caractérisés par un monologue lyrique, à connotation douloureuse, placé dans la bouche d'une femme" (Bec 1977 p. 57); the principal subject is love in its emotional and situational diversity (p. 58). They include the *chansons de mal-mariée*, which represent "une femme malheureuse en ménage et qui se plaint, soit de sa condition en soi, soit de son mari qu'elle méprise pour diverses raisons (en particulier parce qu'elle a été mariée contre son gré)" and who seeks "des compensations" from a real or imaginary lover (Bec 1977 p. 70).

is the woman herself who, rather than submit to the wishes of her parents or husband and thus realize the conventional aristocratic marriage model, either brings one or both parents around to her point of view, or revolts against them by attempting or carrying out an abduction, elopement, or flight to the beloved.[88] The desired man remains more static. As object of desire, he either happens on the scene and whisks away the woman or else is the goal of her flight. The post-conjugal phase of the *mal-mariée* leads to adultery. Both of these types occur in the romances which I have examined here.

The New Mode of Writing Romance

The figure who has received the most attention since the reevaluation of these works began with Michel Zink's studies of *Guillaume de Dole* is the woman. Lienor finds herself in the unwanted pseudo-triangle containing herself, the emperor, and the emperor's seneschal. To restore her honor and public recognition of her virginity, she carries off the spectacular visit to the emperor's court that proves her innocence and catches the seneschal in the web of his own deceit. The denouement is happy and she and her husband presumably live happily ever after. The two other romances discussed here, *Violette* and *Couci*, are more conventional romance variants on this scheme. Euriaut successfully resists attempts to seduce, marry, or rape her; however, unlike Lienor, she undertakes nothing to restore her honor. Rather, she resists, enduring until Gerard finally returns and they are reunited. The Châtelaine de Vergi and the Dame de Fayel are involved in extramarital affairs. The revelation of the truth destroys lovers as well as others. Here we meet the distraught male lover, who is also quite prominent in these narratives.

Of course, jealous lovers or husbands are not unknown in twelfth-century narratives. Marie de France has a number of them. They all react violently when they discover their wife's infidelity, as seen in "Guigemar" and "Equitan" as well as in "Bisclavret," "Le Laüstic," and "Yonec." Only when the husband does not learn of a real or intended infidelity do the adulterous lovers escape his revenge, as in

---

[88] Perhaps this is what Joseph of Exeter had in mind when referring to Helen's "fuga." However, he was hardly sympathetic to Helen's escapade, which her flight becomes.

"Lanval" and "Milun." Chrétien de Troyes offers only one such husband: Alis in *Cligés*, who dies of frustrated anger when he learns the truth about his unconsummated marriage and his wife's affair.[89] Arthur never learns about Guenevere and Lancelot in the *Charrette* and is therefore analogous to himself in "Lanval." His reaction is of course different in the prose romances, although he does more real harm to Guenevere through his own infidelities and misprisions than by any real action taken against her. He even seems reluctant to discover the truth during much of the *Mort Artu*.

The *chansons de mal-mariée* have their violent husbands too. These become the violent fiancés in the *Violette*, in which Gerard plans to kill Euriaut, but decides only to abandon her in the woods when she saves his life from a dragon.[90] The knight's responses in the *Vergi* are hardly "virtuous": he does not keep his word, nor does he confide in the Châtelaine; he commits suicide when he discovers the Châtelaine dead of a broken and betrayed heart. His potential violence is displaced when the Duke of Burgundy kills the Duchess. The Duchess has in fact assumed the role of the lying seneschal in *Guillaume de Dole*. But like the seneschal, the Duke goes to the Holy Land to atone for his sins. In some ways, the *Vergi* is the denouement to the affair between a knight and married woman that began in Jean Renart's *Lai de l'ombre*. The major "ellipse" in both these narratives is the husband, who exists but never appears, as in "Milun."

There is, however, a major difference between *Guillaume de Dole* and other versions of the wager tale: the virtual impotence of the men confronted by the real or imagined infidelity of the woman they love. The emperor mopes about, struggling with a love he cannot get over but about which he can do little more than sing; his major worry appears to be Guillaume and the barons whom he has assembled to announce his wish to marry Lienor (*Dole* v. 3690-91, 4598-99, 4664-73, 4704-05). Guillaume buries his head in his cape and cries, leaving a nephew to do the dirty work, that is, take vengeance on his sister in an excess of verbal and physical abuse. Indeed, had the latter

---

[89] However, the violence can be seen as displaced. The doctors from Salerno know Fenice's infidelity and torture her to make her confess. Yet they fail and are themselves defenestrated by a band of women.

[90] The *Fille du Comte de Pontieu* contains the variant of the wife who violently attacks her husband because he failed to protect her from rape; she is punished by being abandoned at sea. Later, the plot rebounds as she leaves the Sultan's harem to rejoin her husband. This short tale contains no lyric pieces in any of its extant versions.

not slipped and fallen Lienor would have suffered Virginia's fate. It is Lienor who acts sensibly.

The inactivity of men is characteristic of the *chanson d'histoire*. The difference is borne out by Lienor's own coronation robe. This robe was made by a fay (*Dole* v. 5324). Rather than depicting the quadrivium, however, it portrays the story of Helen of Troy. When Paris abducted Helen the Greeks acted. Troy is overcome. The conclusion is missing because the surviving manuscript is corrupt.[91] However, enough survives as inserted allusion to show that both Conrad and Guillaume are as powerless as Helen in rectifying or even coming to terms with their apparent misfortunes. Jean Renart has in fact introduced into the romance tradition an interesting new phenomenon: the distraught, impotent male lover — impotant because he cannot rectify a situation in which he is victim. The one exception, the sire de Fayel, is more active than either the emperor or Guillaume in Jean Renart's very original romance.

Twelfth-century romance by and large reduces such men to jealous husbands or angry but spurned lovers like Troilus and Turnus. Marc is, of course, an exception, but one which proves the rule. It is difficult to analyze the description of his character because of the fragmentary state of the romances that depict him, especially Thomas d'Angleterre's version. Beroul depicts him as a largely violent, but erratic figure: "Senpres est ci e senpres la." (*Tris*B v. 3433) The situation is, to be sure, analogous to that in *Guillaume de Dole* insofar as there is a nephew, a fiancé, and a maiden loved by both, who themselves are either *ci* or *la*. The relationship is rewritten, and the Prose *Tristan* gives Marc a major place, of course, but that is after Jean Renart's time.[92]

---

[91] See *Dole* v. 5350 and var. (p. 177).
[92] See now Trachsler 1996 chap. 4.

CONCLUSION

Se non è vero, è ben trovato.

This is a rather long book to draw out from a single, passing reference to Macrobius in Chrétien's *Erec*. But as Geoffrey of Vinsauf has remarked, "Sic surgit permulta seges de semine pauco" (*Poetria nova* v. 687) [In this way, plentiful harvest springs from a little seed (Nims)]. Geoffrey is expressing a commonplace truism Chrétien himself adapts in the *Conte del graal*:

> ... qui auques requeillir velt,
> En tel liu sa semence espande
> Que fruit a .c. doubles li rande;
> Car an terre qui riens ne valt
> Bone semence seche et faut.[1] (*Perceval* v. 2-6)

[And whoever wishes to reap something should sow in a field that will yield a double hundred crop. For good seed withers and dies in worthless land.]

In critical scholarship, the significance of a small discovery lies in its showing the way towards the solution of larger issues. The Macrobius allusion has indeed led to the larger discussion of that late Roman author's treatment of description and its relevance to the art of composition taught in schools when Chrétien could have studied the *Saturnalia* and its detailed treatment of description. But, as Chrétien also remarks in the the *Conte du graal* prologue, "Ki petit semme petit quelt" (*Perceval* v. 1) [who sows little harvests little]. The fruit of the enterprise is contained in the seed, and abundance alone is often indicative of fruitful beginnings. We needed therefore to see whether in fact Chrétien and his contemporaries actually applied the principles of imitation and invention — including the art of description they learned in the schools and from Macrobius — to the treatment of the matter of their own works. It must be admitted that, if

---

[1] On the sowing metaphor in romance, see Kelly 1992 pp. 19-20 and Jewers 1996 pp. 909-11.

Chrétien did not read Macrobius as we have read him, he certainly opened many of the doors to rewriting that the fifth-century author also opened in reading Vergil.

Medieval practice stressed original rewriting of canonical works over writing of new material. There were, to be sure, different poetic traditions, some of which — during the seventy-five to a hundred years I have been examining in my last three chapters — do not become seriously intertwined with scholastic rewriting. The last chapter, for example, has noted a blending of lyric and narrative modes. *Chansons de geste* still maintained a largely independent line of evolution, although, as Sarah Kay has noted, interference between them and romances began to make itself felt by the beginning of the thirteenth century.[2] In this book, I have concentrated on romance rewriting, whether it was rewriting the same matter as in the case of twelfth-century adaptations of Dares's version of the Trojan War, or of the same motif, as with the place of consent in love and marriage in works containing different plots that, however, allude to one another. Finally, it was possible to predicate French assimilation of the procedures of rewriting and allusion and their application to rewriting narrative to fit lyric pieces as models.

I think, moreover, that there are larger issues raised by rewriting, and I should like to turn to those issues briefly in this conclusion. To do so, I shall begin with a question raised by Roger Pensom about medieval literary invention and its relation to divine creation — that is, "the rational mastery of poetry" illustrated by preceptive treatises that "coexists uneasily with the Neo-Platonic doctrine of the 'archetypus' and the 'vitalis spiritus' put forward by Matthew of Vendôme and Geoffrey of Vinsauf."[3] Uneasy coexistence suggests two equally valid areas of competence. But creation and art, and the intervening realm represented by nature, do not co-exist in this way in the medieval philosophical and arts traditions. They are part of a hierarchy based on analogy rather than simple co-existence. This means that the artistic analogy that imitates the archetype can be only a blueprint that distantly mirrors but never reproduces that archetype. This is the eternal inadequacy of art vis à vis divine creation and natural

---

[2] See Kay 1995 as well as Zink 1981 pp. 6-8, Suard 1992 and 1993, and Jones 1993. An example among the romances treated here is the function of the *Gerbert de Metz* laisse in *Dole* v. 1332-67.

[3] Pensom 1993 p. 532.

procreation that, among others, Nature develops so eloquently in Jean de Meun's *Roman de la rose*. Indeed, Macrobius likens *mutatio* as rewriting to procreation, which also recalls his neoplatonic analogy among creation, procreation, and artistic re-creation.[4]

Thus, although topical invention may seek to perfect a given matter or subject,[5] that perfection will be limited to the possibilities the writer perceives in the subject-matter and thereby to the limitations of human art and invention. Rewriting is always possible, but it does not necessarily replace the antecedent matter; similarly, the given work not only proposes a meaning, it also provokes the audience, including writers and non-writers, to contemplate different, more personal evaluations of the work. Such understanding can include correction by a new author or by a new audience. This, it seems to me, is the import of Matilda Bruckner's answer to the question: "Why are there so many interpretations of the *Charrette*?" In easy coexistence with this question would be another: "Why is there so much rewriting of medieval romance?"

The medieval writers were aware of the ultimate inadequacy of their own inventions. Indeed, they may have included a kind of imperfection in their inventions, a deliberate flaw in the Chinese vase. Bernardus Silvestris could leave the denouement to his *Mathematicus* open because human freedom vis à vis human destiny is an open question to which a reader may or may not provide a provisional answer, just as authors like Benoît de Sainte-Maure and Joseph of Exeter could leave ellipses in their Trojan matter and point to human inability to resolve contested issues peacefully. The sense of provisional rewriting survives the passage of the art from Latin to French writing. Marie de France said that the Ancients left their words partially obscure for the sake of those who might come after and would fill out their meaning. Does not Marie de France herself do the same, she who, as time passes — and it would pass quickly enough — would also join the ranks of the Ancients?[6] At issue is whether a gap in a text is a potential, a topos that can be the seedbed of new growth, or a lacuna indicative of poor artistry, as in the *conte d'aventure* whose oral versions Chrétien criticizes in the *Erec* prologue. In any case, these are antecedent "places," "lieux" — and, as

---

[4] *Sat* 5.1.18-20 and 5.11.16; see Curtius 1954 p. 442.
[5] On this kind of perfection in romance, see Kelly 1992 pp. 134-35.
[6] On the meanings for "Ancients" in the Middle Ages, see Gössmann 1974.

such, "le concept de lieu est peut-être le plus important de toute la rhétorique."[7] It is the locus of original invention.

The reader of medieval literature sees him- or herself confronted with the very bifurcation that Matilda Bruckner found in the *Charrette* and its readers. The reader as scholar can recover the exemplary context of the text and set it out for others. But the reader as private person will, like the maiden in Froissart's *Meliador*, ask more personal questions that involve one's own life and views. It is the latter, I think, that the vernacular authors were trying to reach with the art that they had at their disposal.

---

[7] Molinié 1992 p. 191. Cf. McKeon 1987 p. 36: "commonplaces of invention may open up the perception of new meanings and applications even in a familiar text, which in turn uncovers previously unperceived lines of arguments to unnoticed conclusions which were not there until they were made facts by discovery"; and Moos 1988b p. 196: "Der Topos dient einer Methode des Problemdenkens und der kommunikativen Verständigung (*logica probabilis*)." See as well Abramowska 1985 and Dragonetti 1996 p. 28.

BIBLIOGRAPHY

Primary Works

Where more than one edition is indicated in this Bibliography, references are always to the first one named after the abbreviation; for example, *Sat* refers to Marinone's edition. Whenever another edition is referred to, the editor's name is given together with the abbreviation, as in ed. Willis *Sat*. If the introduction or other material written by the editor is referred to, the editor's name is given before the abbreviation, as in Marinone ed. *Sat* or Willis ed. *Sat*. Translations are listed in this Bibliography under the appropriate abbreviation; when they are cited, the translator's name appears after the translation; for example, "veri sacra fides" (*Ylias* Bk. 1 v. 7) [sacred truth (Bate)]. Otherwise translations are taken from editions containing a translation, except where I alter them; such alterations are shown in italics. All other translations are my own.

Accessus. Accessus ad auctores — *Bernard d'Utrecht* — *Conrad d'Hirsau: Dialogus super auctores*. Ed. R. B. C. Huygens. Leiden: Brill, 1970.

Ad Her. [*Cicero*] *ad C. Herennium de ratione dicendi (Rhetorica ad Herennium)*. Ed. and trans. Harry Caplan. Loeb Classical Library. Cambridge, MA: Harvard University Press, London: Heinemann, 1954.

Aen. Virgil. Ed. and trans. H. Rushton Fairclough. Loeb Classical Library. 2 vols. Rev. ed. Cambridge, MA: Harvard University Press, London: Heinemann, 1960.

Alex. Gautier de Châtillon. *Alexandreis.* Ed. Marvin L. Colker. Thesaurus mundi 17. Padua: Antenore, 1978.

Anth. A Thirteenth-Century Anthology of Rhetorical Poems: Glasgow MS Hunterian V.8.14. Ed. Bruce Harbert. Toronto Medieval Latin Texts, 4. Toronto: Pontifical Institute of Mediaeval Studies, 1975.

Anticlaudianus. Alain de Lille. *Anticlaudianus.* Ed. R. Bossuat. Textes philosophiques du moyen âge, 1. Paris: Vrin, 1955.

ArsGM. Gervase of Melkley. *Ars poetica [= versificaria].* Ed. Han-Jürgen Gräbener. Forschungen zur romanischen Philologie, 17. Münster: Aschendorff, 1965.

ArsPoet. Horace. *Satires, Epistles and Ars Poetica.* Ed. and trans. H. Rushton Fairclough. Loeb Classical Library. Cambridge, MA: Harvard University Press, London: Heinemann, 1961. Pp. 450-89.

Ars vers. Matthew of Vendôme. *Ars versificatoria.* In Vol. III: *Mathei Vindocinensis opera.* Ed. Franco Munari. Storia e Letteratura, 171. Rome: Edizioni di Storia e Letteratura, 1988.

——. Matthew of Vendôme. *The Art of Versification.* Trans. Aubrey E. Galyon. Ames: Iowa State University Press, 1980.

ArtOmer. Saint Omer Art of Poetry: A Twelfth-Century Anonymous Ars Poetica from a Manuscript of Saint-Omer. Ed. and trans. Henrik Specht and Michael Chesnutt. Odense University Series in English, 10. Odense: Odense University Press, 1987.

Athis. Li romanz d'Athis et Prophilias (L'estoire d'Athenes). Ed. Alfons Hilka. Gesellschaft für romanische Literatur 29 and 40. 2 vols. Dresden: Gesellschaft für romanische Literatur, 1912-16.

Beiträge. Beiträge zur Kunde der lateinischen Literatur des Mittelalters aus Handschriften gesammelt. Ed. Jakob Werner. Aarau: Sauerländer, 1905.

Bel Inc. Renaut de Beaujeu. *Le Bel Inconnu.* Ed. G. Perrie Williams. CFMA 38. Paris: Champion, 1929.

Biblionomia. Richard de Fournival. *La Biblionomia du manuscrit 636 de la Bibliothèque de la Sorbonne. Texte et facsimilé avec la transcription de Léopold Delisle.* Ed. H. J. Vleeschauwer. Mousaion, 62. Pretoria: Mousaion, 1965.

Brugge. Is Brugge groot? Ed. and trans. Corrie de Haan and Johan Oosterman. Griffioen. Amsterdam: Querido, 1996.

ChansonCouci. Chansons attribuées au Chastelain de Couci (fin du XIIe—début du XIIIe siècle). Ed. Alain Lerond. Publications de la Faculté des Lettres et Sciences humaines de Rennes, 7. Paris: Presses Universitaires de France, 1964.

Chemin. Christine de Pizan. *Le livre du chemin de long estude.* Ed. Robert Püschel. Berlin 1887; repr. Geneva: Slatkine, 1974.

Chronique. Guillaume de Tyr. *Chronique.* Ed. R. B. C. Huygens. Corpus Christianorum: continuatio mediaeualis, 63-63A. 2 vols. Turnhout: Brepols, 1986.

Cité. Christine de Pizan. "The Livre de la Cité des dames of Christine de Pisan: A Critical Edition". Ed. Maureen Cheney Curnow. Diss. Vanderbilt 1975.

ComBS. Commentum quod dicitur Bernardi Silvestris super sex libros Eneidos Virgilii / The Commentary on the First Six Books of the "Aeneid" of Vergil Commonly Attributed to Bernardus Silvestris. Ed. Julian Ward Jones and Elizabeth Frances Jones. Lincoln, NE, London: University of Nebraska Press, 1977.

ComCP. Saeculi noni auctoris in Boetii Consolationem Philosophiae commentarius. Ed. Edmund Taite Silk. Papers and Monographs of the American Academy in Rome, 9. Rome: American Academy in Rome, 1935.

Comédie. La "comédie" latine en France au XIIe siècle. General ed. Gustave Cohen. Collection Budé. 2 vols. Paris: Belles Lettres, 1931.

ComMC. The Commentary on Martianus Capella's "De nuptiis Philologiae et Mercurii" Attributed to Bernardus Silvestris. Ed. Haijo Jan Westra. Studies and Texts, 80. Toronto: Pontifical Institute of Medieval Studies, 1986.

Comput. Philippe de Thaon. *Comput (MS BL Cotton Nero A.V).* Ed. Ian Short. Anglo-Norman Text Society: Plain Texts Series, 2. London: Anglo-Norman Text Society, from Birkbeck College, 1984.

ComSS. Macrobius. *Commentarii in Somnium Scipionis.* Ed. Jacob Willis. Leipzig: Teubner, 1963.

Cos. Bernardus Silvestris. *Cosmographia.* Ed. Peter Dronke. Textus minores, 53. Leiden: Brill, 1978.

———. Bernardus Silvestris. *The "Cosmographia".* Trans. Winthrop Wetherbee. New York, London: Columbia University Press, 1973.

Couci. Jakames. *Le roman du Castelain de Couci et de la Dame de Fayel.* Ed. John E. Matzke and Maurice Delbouille. SATF. Paris: SATF, 1936.

Cristal. Cristal und Clarie. Ed. Friedrich Apfelstedt, Hugo von Feilitzen, and Hermann Breuer. Gesellschaft für romanische Literatur, 36. Dresden: Gesellschaft für romanische Literatur, Halle: Niemeyer, 1915.

De cons. Boethius. *Philosophiae consolatio.* Ed. Ludovicus Bieler. Corpus Christianorum: series latina, 94. Turnhout: Brepols, 1984.

De exc. Dares Phrygius. *De excidio Troiae historia.* Ed. Ferdinand Meister. Leipzig: Teubner, 1873.

De inv. Cicero. *De inventione. De optimo genere oratorum. Topica.* Ed. and trans. H. M. Hubbell. Loeb Classical Library. Cambridge, MA: Harvard University Press, London: Heinemann, 1949. Pp. 1-345.

Didot Perc. The Didot "Perceval" According to the Manuscripts of Modena and Paris. Ed. William Roach. Philadelphia: University of Pennsylvania Press, 1941.

Doc. Geoffrey of Vinsauf. *Documentum de modo et arte dictandi et versificandi* [short version]. Ed. Edmond Faral. In Faral 1924. Pp. 263-320.

Dogma. Guillaume de Conches. *Das Moralium dogma philosophorum: lateinisch, altfranzösisch und mittelniederfränkisch.* Ed. John Holmberg. Arbeten uitgivna med understöd av Vilhelm Ekmans Universitetsfond, Uppsala, 37. Uppsala: Almqvist & Wiksells, 1929.

Dole. Jean Renart. *Le roman de la rose ou de Guillaume de Dole.* Ed. Félix Lecoy. CFMA, 91. Paris: Champion, 1979.

Eneas. Eneas. Ed. J.-J. Salverda de Grave. CFMA, 44 and 62. 2 vols. Paris: Champion, 1925-29.

——. *Le roman d'Eneas.* Ed. and trans. Aimé Petit. Lettres Gothiques: Livre de poche, 20. Paris: Librairie Générale Française, 1997.

Ephem. Dictys Cretensis. *Ephemeridos belli troiani.* Ed. Werner Eisenhut. Leipzig: Teubner, 1973.

Erec. Chrétien de Troyes. *Erec et Enide.* Ed Wendelin Foerster. Halle: Niemeyer, 1890.

——. Chrétien de Troyes. *Erec et Enide.* Ed. Mario Roques. CFMA, 80. Paris: Champion, 1966.

——. Chrétien de Troyes. *Erec and Enide.* Ed. and trans. Carleton W. Carroll. Garland Library of Medieval Literature, 25A. New York, London: Garland, 1987.

——. Chrétien de Troyes. *Erec et Enide: édition critique d'après le manuscrit B. N. fr. 1376.* Ed. and trans. Jean-Marie Fritz. Lettres Gothiques: Livre de Poche, 17. Paris: Librairie Générale Française, 1992.

——. Chrétien de Troyes. *Erec et Enide.* Ed. and trans. Peter F. Dembowski. In Chrétien de Troyes. *Œuvres complètes.* Under the direction of Daniel Poirion. Bibliothèque de la Pléiade. Paris: Gallimard, 1994. Pp. 1-169 and 1053-1114.

Eulalie. In *Altfranzösisches Übungsbuch (die ältesten Sprachdenkmäler mit einem Anhang) zum Gebrauch bei Vorlesungen und Seminarübungen.* Ed. W. Foerster and E. Koschwitz. 5th ed. by Wendelin Foerster. Leipzig: Reisland, 1915. Cols. 47-52.

Faux-monnayeurs. André Gide. *Les faux-monnayeurs.* Collection Folio, 879. Paris: Gallimard, 1925, 1997.

Glosae. Bernard of Chartres. *The "Glosae super Platonem".* Ed. Paul Edward Dutton. Studies and Texts, 107. Toronto: Pontifical Institute of Medieval Studies, 1991.

GramLat. Grammatici latini. Ed. Heinrich Keil. 7 vols.: Leipzig: Teubner, 1857-80.

Historia. Guido de Columnis. *Historia destructionis Troiae.* Ed. Nathaniel Edward Griffin. The Mediaeval Academy of America Publication, 26. Cambridge, MA: The Mediaeval Academy of America, 1936.

Hist Troy. Anonymi Historia *troyana Daretis Frigii.* Ed. Jürgen Stohlmann. Beihefte zum "Mittellateinischen Jahrbuch," 1. Wuppertal, Ratingen, Düsseldorf: Henn, 1968.

Iliad. Homer. *The Iliad.* Ed. and trans. A. T. Murray. Loeb Classical Library. 2 vols. Cambridge, MA: Harvard University Press, London: Heinemann, 1960-63.

In Anti: Radulphus de Longo Campo. *In Anticlaudianum Alani commentum.* Ed. Jan Sułowski. Źródła do dziejów nauki i techniki, 13. Wrocław, Warsaw, Cracow, Gdańsk: Zakład Narodowy Imienia Ossolińskich: Wydawnictwo Polskiej Akademi Nauk, 1972.

Laborintus. Eberhard the German. *Laborintus*. In Faral 1924. Pp. 337-77.

Lais. Marie de France. *Les lais*. Ed. Jean Rychner. CFMA 93. Paris: Champion, 1968.

Manekine. Philippe de Remi. *La Manekine*. Ed. and trans. Irene Gnarra. Garland Publications in Comparative Literature. New York, London: Garland, 1988.

Meliador. Jean Froissart. *Meliador*. Ed. Auguste Longnon. Société des Anciens Textes français. 3 vols. Paris: Firmin Didot, 1895-99.

Metalogicon. John of Salisbury. *Metalogicon*. Ed. J. B. Hall and K. S. B. Keats-Rohan. Corpus Christianorum: continuatio mediaeualis, 98. Turnhout: Brepols, 1991.

MGH. Poetae latini aevi carolini. In *Monumenta Germaniae historica unde ab anno Christi quingentesimo usque ad annum millesimum et quingentesimum*. Ed. Ernst Dümmler, Ludwig Traube, and Paul von Winterfeld. Monumenta Germaniae historica. 4 vols. Berlin: Weidmann, 1880-99.

Odyssey. Homer. *The Odyssey*. Ed. and trans. A. T. Murray. Loeb Classical Library. 2 vols. Cambridge, MA: Harvard University Press, London: Heinemann, 1960.

Opera Bedae. Bede. *Opera disdascalica*. In his *Opera*. Ed. Ch. W. Jones. Corpus Christianorum: series latina, 123. 3 vols. Turnhout: Brepols, 1975-80.

Partonopeu. *Partonopeu de Blois*. Ed. Joseph Gildea and Leon Smith. 2 vols. Villanova: Villanova University Press, 1967-70.

Perceval. Chrétien de Troyes. *Le roman de Perceval ou Le conte du graal*. Ed. Keith Busby. Tübingen: Niemeyer, 1993.

Philomena. Chrétien de Troyes. *Philomena*. Ed. and trans. Anne Berthelot. In Chrétien de Troyes. *Œuvres complètes*. Ed. under the direction of Daniel Poirion. Bibliothèque de la Pléiade. Paris: Gallimard, 1994. Pp. 915-52 and 1391-1410.

Philosophie. Alard de Cambrai. *Le livre de philosophie et de moralité*. Ed. Jean Charles Payen. Bibliothèque française et romane, B9. Paris: Klincksieck, 1970.

PNCom. An Early Commentary on the "Poetria Nova" of Geoffrey of Vinsauf. Ed. Marjorie Curry Woods. Garland Medieval Texts, 12. New York, London: Garland, 1985.

Poetria nova. Geoffrey of Vinsauf. *Poetria nova*. In Faral 1924. Pp. 197-262.

——. Trans. Margaret F. Nims. Toronto: Pontifical Institute of Mediaeval Studies, 1967.

Rose. Guillaume de Lorris and Jean de Meun. *Le roman de la rose*. Ed. Félix Lecoy. Classiques français du moyen âge, 92, 95, 98. 3 vols. Paris: Champion, 1965-70.

Sat. Macrobius. *I Saturnali*. Ed. Nino Marinone. Classici Latini. Turin: Unione Tipografico-Editrice Torinese, 1967.

——. Macrobius. *Saturnalia*. Ed Jacob Willis. Leipzig: Teubner, 1963.

——. Macrobius. *Opera quae supersunt*. Ed. Ludwig Jan. 2 vols. Quedlinburg, Leipzig: Bassius, 1848-52.

——. Macrobius. *The Saturnalia*. Trans. Percival Vaughan Davies. Records of Civilization: Sources and Studies, 79. New York, London: Columbia University Press, 1969.

Scholia. Scholia in Horatium. Ed. H. J. Botschuyver. Amsterdam: Van Bottenburg, 1935-42. Vols. I and III-IV.

Songe d'enfer. Raoul de Houdenc. *The "Songe d'enfer"*. Ed. Madelyn Timmel. Beihefte zur Zeitschrift für romanische Philologie, 190. Tübingen: Niemeyer, 1984.

Thèbes. Le roman de Thèbes. Ed. Guy Raynaud de Lage. CFMA, 94, 96. 2 vols. Paris: Champion, 1968-71.

Tiers d'amour. Michel Zink. *Le tiers d'amour: un roman des troubadours*. Paris: Fallois, 1998.

Timaeus. Timaeus a Calcidio translatus commentarioque instructus. Ed. J. H. Waszink. In *Plato latinus*. Vol. 4. Ed. Raymundus Klibansky. London: Warburg Institute, Leiden: Brill, 1962.

Top. Boethius. *"De topicis differentiis": Translated, with Notes and Essays on the Text.* Ed. and trans. Eleanore Stump. Ithaca, NY, London: Cornell University Press, 1978.

Tournoiement. Huon de Mery. *Li tornoiemenz Antecrit.* Ed. Georg Wimmer. Ausgaben und Abhandlungen aus dem Gebiete der romanischen Philologie, 76. Marburg: Elwert, 1888.

*Tris*B. Beroul. *The Romance of Tristran.* Ed. A. Ewert. 2 vols. Oxford: Blackwell, 1939-70.

Tristan. Thomas. *Les fragments du roman de Tristan.* Ed. Bartina H. Wind. TLF, 92. Geneva: Droz, Paris: Minard, 1960.

Troie. Benoît de Sainte-Maure. *Le roman de Troie.* Ed. Léopold Constans. SATF. 6 vols. Paris: Firmin-Didot, 1904-12.

Vergi. La chastelaine de Vergi: édition critique du ms. B. N. f. fr. 375 avec Introduction, Notes, Glossaire et Index, suivie de l'édition diplomatique de tous les manuscrits connus du XIIIᵉ et du XIVᵉ siècle. Ed. René Ernst Victor Stuip. Diss. Amsterdam. The Hague, Paris: Mouton, 1970.

Vetula. Pseudo-Ovidius De vetula: Untersuchungen und Text. Ed. Paul Klopsch. Mittellateinische Studien und Texte, 2. Leiden, Cologne: Brill, 1967.

Vindobonensia. Scholia Vindobonensia ad Horatii Artem poeticam. Ed. Josephus Zechmeister. Vienna: [n.p.], 1877.

Violette. Gerbert de Montreuil. *Le roman de la Violette ou de Gerart de Nevers.* Ed. Douglas Labaree Buffum. SATF. Paris: Champion,1928.

Vita Boetii. Anicii Manlii Severini Boetii Philosophiae consolationis libri quinque accedunt eiusdem atque incertorum opuscula sacra. Ed. Rudolfus Peiper. Lepizig: Teubner, 1871.

Ylias. Joseph Iscanus. *Werke und Briefe.* Ed. Ludwig Gompf. Mittellateinische Studien und Texte, 4. Leiden, Cologne: Brill, 1970.

——. "The Text of Joseph of Exeter's *Bellum Troianum.*" Ed. Geoffrey Blundell Riddehough. Diss. Harvard University, 1951.

——. "Joseph of Exeter's *Bellum Troianum*: A Literary Study and English Translation." Trans. Carol Clemeau Esler. Diss. Bryn Mawr, 1965.

——. Joseph of Exeter. *Trojan War I-III.* Ed. and trans. A. K. Bate. Warminster, Wiltshire: Aris & Phillips, 1986.

Yvain. Chrétien de Troyes. *Yvain (Le Chevalier au lion).* Ed. Wendelin Foerster and T. B. W. Reid. French Classics. Manchester: Manchester University Press, 1942.

Secondary Works

Abramowicz, Maciej 1996: *Réécrire au moyen âge: mises en prose des romans en Bourgogne au xv-e siècle.*

Abramowska, Janina 1985: "Le topos et quelques lieux communs des études littéraires." *Literary Studies in Poland—Etudes littéraires en Pologne* 13: 23-50.

Abrams, M. H. 1993: *A Glossary of Literary Terms.* 6th ed. Fort Worth, TX: Harcourt Brace.

Allen, Judson Boyce 1982: *The Ethical Poetic of the Later Middle Ages: A Decorum of Convenient Distinction.* Toronto, Buffalo, London: University of Toronto Press.

Anderson, David 1988: *Before the Knight's Tale: Imitation of Classical Epic in Boccaccio's "Teseida".* Middle Ages Series. Philadelphia: University of Pennsylvania Press.

Andrieux-Reix, Nelly 1987: *Ancien français: fiches de vocabulaire.* Etudes littéraires, 17. Paris: Presses Universitaires de France.

Angeli, Giovanna 1971: *L'"Eneas" e i primi romanzi volgari.* Documenti di filologia, 15. Milan, Naples: Ricciardi.

Angeli, Giovanna 1998: "Le dialogue nocturne conjugal: entre 'cadre' et *topos*." In *Miscellanea mediaevalia: mélanges offerts à Philippe Ménard*. Ed. J. Claude Faucon, Alain Labbé, and Danielle Quéruel. Nouvelle Bibliothèque du moyen âge, 46. 2 vols. Paris: Champion. Vol. I, pp. 51-63.

Angelucci, Paolo 1984: "La tipologia macrobiana dei rapporti tra poeta e modelli nella poesia esametrica latina." *Rivista di cultura classica e medioevale* 26: 93-115.

Angelucci, Paolo 1990. *Teoria e prassi del rapporto con i modelli nella poesia esametrica latina.* Rome: Herder.

Angenendt, Arnold 1997: *Geschichte der Religiosität im Mittelalter*. Darmstadt: Wissenschaftliche Buchgesellschaft.

Astell, Ann W. 1999: "Cassiodorus's *Commentary on the Psalms* as an *Ars rhetorica*." *Rhetorica* 17: 37-75.

Atkinson, J. Keith 1994: "Manuscript Context as a Guide to Generic Shift: Some Middle French Consolations." In *Medieval Codicology, Iconography, Literature, and Translation: Studies for Keith Val Sinclair*. Ed. Peter Rolfe Monks and D. D. R. Owen. Litterae textuales. Leiden, New York, Cologne: Brill. Pp. 321-32.

Attridge, Derek 1999: "Innovation, Literature, Ethics: Relating to the Other." *PMLA* 114: 20-31.

Auerbach, Erich 1958. *Literatursprache und Publikum in der lateinischen Spätantike und im Mittelalter*. Bern: Francke.

Badel, Pierre-Yves 1980. *Le Roman de la rose au XIVe siècle: étude de la réception de l'œuvre*. Publications romanes et françaises, 153. Geneva: Droz.

Baldwin, John W. 1997: "'Once There Was an Emperor...': A Political Reading of the Romances of Jean Renart." In *Jean Renart and the Art of Romance: Essays on "Guillaume de Dole"*. Ed. Nancy Vine Durling. Gainesville: University Press of Florida. Pp. 45-82.

Bamberg 1895: *Katalog der Handschriften der königlichen Bibliothek zu Bamberg*. Bamberg: Buchner.

Barbero, Alessandro 1987: *L'aristocrazia nella società francese del medioevo: analisi delle fonti letterarie (segoli X-XIII)*. Studi e Testi della Storia medioevale, 12-13. Bologna: Cappelli.

Barker-Benfield, B. C., and P. K. Marshall 1983: "Macrobius." In L. D. Reynolds, ed. *Texts and Transmission: A Survey of the Latin Classics*. Oxford: The Clarendon Press. Pp. 222-35.

Baswell, Christopher 1985: "The Medieval Allegorization of the 'Aeneid': MS Cambridge, Peterhouse 158." *Traditio* 41: 181-237.

Baswell, Christopher 1995: *Virgil in Medieval England: Figuring the "Aeneid" from the Twelfth Century to Chaucer*. Cambridge Studies in Medieval Literature, 24. Cambridge: Cambridge University Press.

Batany, Jean 1992: "Benoît, auteur anticlérical? De Troïlus à Guillaume Longue-Épée." In *Le roman antique au moyen âge*. Actes du Colloque du Centre d'Etudes Médiévales de l'Université de Picardie, Amiens 14-15 janvier 1989. Ed. Danielle Buschinger. Göppinger Arbeiten zur Germanistik, 549. Göppingen: Kümmerle. Pp. 7-22.

Bate, A. Keith 1971: "Joseph of Exeter — Religious Poet." *Medium Aevum* 40: 222-29.

Bate, Keith 1991. "La littérature latine d'imagination à la cour d'Henri II d'Angleterre." *Cahiers de civilisation médiévale* 34: 3-21.

Baumgartner, Emmanuèle 1981: "Les citations lyriques dans le *Roman de la Rose* de Jean Renart." *Romance Philology* 35: 260-66.

Baumgartner, Emmanuèle 1987: "Vocabulaire de la technique littéraire dans le *Roman de Troie* de Benoît de Sainte-Maure." *Cahiers de lexicologie* 51.2: 39-48.

Baumgartner, Emmanuèle 1988: "Peinture et écriture: la description de la tente dans les romans antiques au XIIe siècle." In *Sammlung—Deutung—Wertung: Ergebnisse, Probleme, Tendenzen und Perspektiven philologischer Arbeit. Mélanges de littérature médiévale et de linguistique allemande offerts à Wolfgang Spiewok à l'occasion de son soixantième anniversaire par ses collègues et amis.* Ed. Danielle Buschinger. [Amiens:] Université de Picardie, Centre d'Etudes médiévales, Stuttgart: Sprint. Pp. 3-11.

Baumgartner, Emmanuèle 1992: "Sur quelques versions du *Jugement de Pâris.*" In *Le roman antique au moyen âge.* Actes du Colloque du Centre d'Etudes Médiévales de l'Université de Picardie, Amiens 14-15 janvier 1989. Ed. Danielle Buschinger. Göppinger Arbeiten zur Germanistik, 549. Göppingen: Kümmerle. Pp. 23-31.

Baumgartner, Emmanuèle 1994: "Le roman de *Tristan* en prose et le cercle des bretthes estoires." In *Cyclification: The Development of Narrative Cycles in the Chansons de geste and the Arthurian Romances.* Proceedings of the Colloquium, Amsterdam, 17-18 December, 1992. Ed. Bart Besamusca, Willem P. Gerritsen, Corry Hogetoorn, and Orlanda S. H. Lie. Koninklijke Nederlandse Akademie van Wetenschappen: Verhandelingen, Afd. Letterkunde, n. s. 159. Amsterdam, Oxford, New York, Tokyo: North-Holland. Pp. 7-20.

Baumgartner, Emmanuèle 1995. *Le récit médiéval XIIe-XIIIe siècles.* Contours littéraires. Paris: Hachette.

Baumgartner, Emmanuèle 1996a: "Benoît de Sainte-Maure et *l'uevre de Troie.*" In *The Medieval "Opus": Imitation, Rewriting, and Transmission in the French Tradition.* Proceedings of the Symposium Held at the Institute for Research in Humanities October 5-7 1995, The University of Wisconsin-Madison. Ed. Douglas Kelly. Faux Titre, 116. Amsterdam, Atlanta: Rodopi. Pp. 15-28.

Baumgartner, Emmanuèle 1996b: "Féerie—fiction: le *Bel Inconnu* de Renaud de Beaujeu." In *Le Chevalier et la merveille dans "Le Bel Inconnu" ou le beau jeu de Renaut.* Ed. Jean Dufournet. Unichamp, 52. Paris: Champion. Pp. 7-21.

Baumgartner, Emmanuèle 1998: "La musique pervertit les mœurs." In *Miscellanea mediaevalia: mélanges offerts à Philippe Ménard.* Ed. J. Claude Faucon, Alain Labbé, and Danielle Quéruel. Nouvelle Bibliothèque du moyen âge, 46. 2 vols. Paris: Champion. Vol. I, pp. 75-89.

Beaujouan, Guy 1982: "The Transformation of the Quadrivium." In *Renaissance and Renewal in the Twelfth Century.* Ed. Robert L. Benson, Giles Constable, and Carol D. Lanham. Cambridge, MA: Harvard University Press. Pp. 463-87.

Beaune, Colette 1985: *Naissance de la nation France.* Bibliothèque des histoires. Paris: Gallimard.

Bec, Pierre 1977: *La lyrique française au moyen âge (XIIe-XIIIe siècles): contribution à une typologie des genres poétiques médiévaux. Etudes et textes. Vol. I: Etudes.* Publications du Centre d'Etudes Supérieures de Civilisation Médiévale de l'Université de Poitiers, 6. Paris: Picard.

Becker, Gustavus 1885. *Catalogi bibliothecarum antiqui.* Bonn: Cohen.

Beltrami, Pietro G. 1989: "Lancelot entre Lanzelet et Eneas: remarques sur le sens du 'Chevalier de la charrete'." *Zeitschrift für französische Sprache und Literatur* 99: 234-60.

Berlioz, Jacques 1985: "Virgile dans la littérature des *exempla* (XIIIe-XVe siècles)." In *Lectures médiévales de Virgile.* Actes du Colloque organisé par l'Ecole française de Rome (Rome, 25-28 octobre 1982). Collection de l'Ecole française de Rome, 80. Rome: Ecole française de Rome. Pp. 65-120.

Bernabei, Richard 1970: "The Treatment of Sources in Macrobius' *Saturnalia,* and the Influence of the *Saturnalia* during the Middle Ages." Diss. Cornell University.

Berschin, Walter 1988: *Greek Letters and the Latin Middle Ages: From Jerome to Nicholas of Cusa*. Trans., rev. and expanded by Jerold C. Frakes. Washington, DC: Catholic University of America Press.

Bertolucci Pizzorusso, Valeria 1996: "La 'clergie' di Thomas: l'intertesto agiografico-religioso." In *Ensi firent li ancessor: mélanges de philologie médiévale offerts à Marc-René Jung*. Ed. Luciano Rossi, Christine Jacob-Hugon, and Ursula Bähler. 2 vols. Alessandria: dell'Orso. Vol. 1, pp. 335-48.

Bertolucci Pizzorusso, Valeria 1998: "L'arpa d'Isotta: variazioni testuali e figurative." In *Miscellanea mediaevalia: mélanges offerts à Philippe Ménard*. Ed. J. Claude Faucon, Alain Labbé, and Danielle Quéruel. Nouvelle Bibliothèque du moyen âge, 46. 2 vols. Paris: Champion. Vol. I, pp. 101-19.

Besamusca, Bart 1993: *Walewein, Moriaen en de Ridder metter mouwen: Intertekstualiteit in drie Middelnederlandse Arturromans*. Middeleeuwse studies en bronnen, 39. Hilversum: Verloren.

Bestul, Thomas H. 1975: "The *Saturnalia* of Macrobius and the *Praecepta artis rhetoricae* of Julius Severianus." *Classical Journal* 70.3: 10-16.

Binkley, Peter. *See* Rigg. A. G.

Bischoff, Bernhard 1966-81: *Mittelalterliche Studien: ausgewählte Aufsätze zur Schriftkunde und Literaturgeschichte*. 4 vols. Stuttgart: Heisemann.

Blänsdorf, Jürgen 1995: "Ancient Genres in the Poem of a Medieval Humanist: Intertextual Aspects of the 'De sufficientia votorum suorum' (C.126H) of Baudri de Bourgueil (1046-1130)." *International Journal of the Classical Tradition* 1: 209-18.

Bloch, R. Howard 1983: *Etymologies and Genealogies: A Literary Anthropology of the French Middle Ages*. Chicago, London: University of Chicago Press.

Blons-Pierre, Catherine 1993: "L'esthéthique de la description des personnages chez Chrétien de Troyes." *Bien dire et bien aprandre* 11: 55-68.

Bodenham, C. H. L. 1985: "The Nature of the Dream in Late Mediaeval French Literature." *Medium Aevum* 54: 74-86.

Bornscheuer, Lothar 1976: *Topik: zur Struktur der gesellschaftlichen Einbildungskraft*. Frankfurt: Suhrkamp.

Boulton, Maureen 1987: "E. R. Curtius, the Medieval Theory of Styles, and the Rhetorical Innovations of *Guillaume de Dole*." *Annals of Scholarship* 4.3: 75-85.

Boulton, Maureen Barry McCann 1993: *The Song in the Story: Lyric Insertions in French Narrative Fiction, 1200-1400*. Middle Ages Series. Philadelphia: University of Pennsylvania Press.

Boulton, Maureen Barry McCann 1997: "Lyric Insertions and the Reversal of Romance Conventions in Jean Renart's *Roman de la rose* or *Guillaume de Dole*." In *Jean Renart and the Art of Romance: Essays on "Guillaume de Dole"*. Ed. Nancy Vine Durling. Gainesville: University Press of Florida. Pp. 85-104.

Bourgain, Pascale 1985: "Virgile et la poésie latine du bas moyen âge." In *Lectures médiévales de Virgile*. Actes du Colloque organisé par l'Ecole française de Rome (Rome, 25-28 octobre 1982). Collection de l'Ecole française de Rome, 80. Rome: Ecole française de Rome. Pp. 167-87.

Boutemy, André 1937: "Notice sur le recueil poétique du manuscrit Cotton Vitellius A xii, du British Museum." *Latomus* 1: 278-313.

Boutemy, André 1939: "Notice sur le manuscrit 749 de la Bibliothèque Municipale de Douai." *Latomus* 3: 183-206 and 264-98.

Brandsma, Frank 1995: "Opening Up the Narrative: The Insertion of New Episodes in Arthurian Cycles." *Queeste* 1: 31-39.

Brinkmann, Hennig 1980: *Mittelalterliche Hermeneutik*. Darmstadt: Wissenschaftliche Buchgesellschaft.

Brooke, Christopher 1989: *The Medieval Idea of Marriage*. Oxford, New York: Oxford University Press.

Bruckner, Matilda Tomaryn 1980: *Narrative Invention in Twelfth-Century French Romance: The Convention of Hospitality (1160-1200)*. French Forum Monographs, 17. Lexington, KY: French Forum.

Bruckner, Matilda Tomaryn 1986: "An Interpreter's Dilemma: Why Are There So Many Interpretations of Chrétien's *Chevalier de la charrette*." *Romance Philology* 40: 159-80.

Bruckner, Matilda Tomaryn 1987: "Intertextuality." In *The Legacy of Chrétien de Troyes*. Vol. I. Ed. Norris J. Lacy, Douglas Kelly, and Keith Busby. Faux Titre, 31. Amsterdam: Rodopi. Pp. 223-65.

Bruckner, Matilda Tomaryn 1993. *Shaping Romance: Interpretation, Truth, and Closure in Twelfth-Century French Fictions*. Middle Ages Series. Philadelphia: University of Pennsylvania Press.

Brundage, James A. 1987: *Law, Sex, and Christian Society in Medieval Europe*. Chicago, London: University of Chicago Press.

Brunner, Horst 1989: "Von der stat Troya vrsprung, päwing, streyten vnd irer zerstörung: literarische Formen der Vermittlung historischen Wissens an nicht-lateinkundiges Publikum im Hoch- und Spätmittelalter und in der frühen Neuzeit." *Der Deutschunterricht* n.s. 1: 55-73.

Büchner, Karl 1961: "Überlieferungsgeschichte der lateinischen Literatur des Altertums." In *Geschichte der Textüberlieferung der antiken und mittelalterlichen Literatur*. Vol. I. Zürich: Atlantis. Pp. 309-422.

Burgess, Glyn S., and John L. Curry 1989: "'Si ont berbïoletes non' (*Erec et Enide*, l. 6739)." *French Studies* 43: 129-39.

Burgess, Glyn S., and John L. Curry 1991: "*Berbiolete* and *Dindialos*: Animal Magic in Some Twelfth-Century Garments." *Medium Aevum* 60: 84-92.

Burgess, Glyn S. 1994: "The Term 'Chevalerie' in Twelfth-Century French." In *Medieval Codicology, Iconography, Literature, and Translation: Studies for Keith Val Sinclair*. Ed. Peter Rolfe Monks and D. D. R. Owen. Litterae textuales. Leiden, New York, Cologne: Brill. Pp. 343-58.

Burton, Rosemary 1983: *Classical Poets in the "Florilegium Gallicum"*. European University Studies. Ser. I: German Language and Literature, 633. Frankfurt-am-Main, Bern: Lang.

Busby, Keith 1989: "*Cristal et Clarie*: A Novel Romance?" In *Convention and Innovation in Literature*. Ed. T. D'haen, R. Grübel, and H. Lethen. Utrecht Publications in General and Comparative Literature, 24. Amsterdam, Philadelphia: Benjamins. Pp. 77-103.

Butterfield, Ardis 1987: "Interpolated Lyric in Medieval Narrative Poetry." Diss. University of Cambridge.

Butterfield, Ardis 1997: "*Aucassin et Nicolette* and Mixed Forms in Medieval French." In *Prosimetrum: Crosscultural Perspectives on Narrative in Prose and Verse*. Ed. Joseph Harris and Karl Reichl. Cambridge: Brewer. Pp. 67-98.

Camargo, Martin 1992: "A Twelfth-Century Treatise on 'Dictamen' and Metaphor." *Traditio* 47: 161-213.

Camargo, Martin 1994: "Beyond the *Libri Catoniani*: Models of Latin Prose Style at Oxford University ca. 1400." *Mediaeval Studies* 56: 165-87.

Cambridge 1980: *A Catalogue of Manuscripts Preserved in the Library of the University of Cambridge*. Cambridge; repr. Munich: Kraus-Thomson, Hildesheim: Olms.

Cameron, Alan 1966: "The Date and Identity of Macrobius." *Journal of Roman Studies* 56: 25-38.

Cameron, Alan 1977: "Paganism and Literature in Late Fourth Century Rome." In *Christianisme et formes littéraires de l'Antiquité tardive en Occident.* Vandœuvres-Genève, 23-28 août 1976. Ed. Manfred Fuhrmann. Entretiens sur l'Antiquité Classique, 23. Geneva: Fondation Hardt. Pp. 1-30.

Carmona, Fernando 1988: *El Roman lírico medieval.* Estudios Románicos. Barcelona: PPU.

Carton, Mary Josepha 1965: "Vat. Lat. 3417 and Its Relationship to the Text of Macrobius' *Saturnalia 7.*" *Transactions and Proceedings of the American Philological Association* 96: 25-30.

Castellani, Marie-Madeleine 1993: "La description du héros masculin dans *Erec et Enide* de Chrétien de Troyes." *Bien dire et bien aprandre* 11:105-17.

Castellani, Marie-Madeleine 1996: "Version longue — version brève: l'exemple d'*Athis et Prophilias.*" *Bien dire et bien aprandre* 14: 101-11.

Champion, Pierre 1907: *Le manuscrit autographe des poésies de Charles d'Orléans.* Paris: Champion.

Chênerie, Marie-Luce 1985: "Le motif des présents dans le Roman d'Énéas." In *Relire le "Roman d'Énéas".* Ed. Jean Dufournet. Unichamp, 8. Paris: Champion. Pp. 43-61.

Chenu, M.-D. 1927: "Auctor, actor, autor." *ALMA* 3: 81-86.

Cizek, Alexandru 1989: "Der 'Charakterismos' in der *Vita Adalhardi* des Radbert von Corbie." *Rhetorica* 7:185-204.

Cizek, Alexandru N. 1994: *Imitatio et tractatio: die literarisch-rhetorischen Grundlagen der Nachahmung in Antike und Mittelalter.* Rhetorik-Forschungen, 7. Tübingen: Niemeyer.

Cohen, Adolf Emile 1941. *De Visie op Troje van de westerse middeleeuwse Geschiedschrijvers tot 1160.* Diss. Leiden. Assen: Van Gorcum.

Colby, Alice M. 1965: *The Portrait in Twelfth-Century French Literature: An Example of the Stylistic Originality of Chrétien de Troyes.* Histoire des idées et critique littéraire, 61. Geneva: Droz.

Combarieu, Micheline de 1996: "Un exemple de réécriture: le franchissement du pont de l'épée dans le *Chevalier de la charrete* de Chrétien de Troyes et dans le *Lancelot en prose.*" *Bien dire et bien aprandre* 13:113-31.

Contamine, Philippe 1980: *La guerre au moyen âge.* Nouvelle Clio. Paris: Presses Universitaires de France.

Copeland, Rita 1991: *Rhetoric, Hermeneutics, and Translation in the Middle Ages: Academic Traditions and Vernacular Texts.* Cambridge Studies in Medieval Literature, 11. Cambridge: Cambridge University Press.

Cormier, Raymond J. 1973: *One Heart One Mind: The Rebirth of Virgil's Hero in Medieval French Romance.* Romance Monographs, 3. University, MS: Romance Monographs.

Cormier, Raymond J. 1976: "Remarques sur le *Roman d'Enéas* et l'*Erec et Enide* de Chrétien de Troyes." *Revue des langues romanes* 82: 85-97.

Cormier, Raymond J. 1988: "Qui détient le rameau d'or devant Charon (*Enéide*, VI.405-407)." *Rheinisches Museum für Philologie* n.s. 131: 151-56.

Cormier, Raymond J. 1989: "An Example of Twelfth Century *adaptatio*: The *Roman d'Eneas* Author's Use of Glossed *Aeneid* Manuscripts." *Revue d'histoire des textes* 19: 277-89 + plates VI-IX.

Courcelle, Pierre 1948: *Les lettres grecques en Occident de Macrobe à Cassiodore.* Bibliothèque des Ecoles Françaises d'Athènes et de Rome, 159. Paris: De Boccard.

Courcelle, Pierre 1984: *Lecteurs païens et lecteurs chrétiens de l'Énéide.* Vol. I: *Les témoignages littéraires.* Institut de France: Mémoires de l'Académie des Inscriptions et Belles-Lettres, n.s. 4. Paris: Imprimerie Gauthier-Villars.

Croizy-Naquet, Catherine 1994: *Thèbes, Troie et Carthage: poétique de la ville dans le roman antique au XIIe siècle*. Nouvelle Bibliothèque du moyen âge, 30. Paris: Champion.

Croizy-Naquet, Catherine 1997: "Pyrrhus, Andromaque et ses fils dans le *Roman de Troie*." In *Entre fiction et histoire: Troie et Rome au moyen âge*. Ed. Emmanuèle Baumgartner and Laurence Harf-Lancner. Paris: Presses de la Sorbonne Nouvelle, 1997. Pp. 73-96.

Curcio, Gaetano 1907: "Commenti medio-evali ad Orazio." *Rivista di filologia e d'istruzione classica* 35.4: 43-64.

Curtius, E. R. 1938: "Dichtung und Rhetorik im Mittelalter." *Deutsche Vierteljahrsschrift für Literaturwissenschaft und Geistesgeschichte* 16: 435-75.

Curtius, Ernst Robert 1954: *Europäische Literatur und lateinisches Mittelalter*. 2nd ed. Bern: Francke.

Dahan, Gilbert 1980: "Notes et textes sur la poétique au moyen âge." *Archives d'histoire doctrinale et littéraire du moyen âge*. 55: 171-239.

Debaisieux, Martine 1998: "Cruels effets du désir adultère: scénario de la violence dans *Les Angoysses douloureuses*." In *Violence et fiction jusqu'à la Révolution*. Travaux du IXe Colloque International de la Société d'Analyse de la Topique Romanesque (SATOR) (Milwaukee—Madison, septembre 1995). Ed. Martine Debaisieux and Gabrielle Verdier. Tübingen: Narr. Pp. 143-53.

Deist, Rosemarie 1994: "The Kiss of Ascanius in Vergil's *Aeneid*, the *Roman d'Enéas*, and Heinrich von Veldeke's *Eneide*." *The German Quarterly* 67: 463-69.

Delhaye, Philippe 1958: "'Grammatica' et 'Ethica' au XIIe siècle." *Recherches de théologie ancienne et médiévale* 25: 59-110.

Demats, Paule 1973. *Fabula: trois études de mythographie antique et médiévale*. Publications romanes et françaises, 122. Geneva: Droz.

Dembowski, Peter F. 1994: "Textual and Other Problems of the Epilogue of *Erec et Enide*." In *Conjunctures: Medieval Studies in Honor of Douglas Kelly*. Ed. Keith Busby and Norris J. Lacy. Faux Titre, 83. Amsterdam, Atlanta: Rodopi. Pp. 113-27.

De Paolis, Paolo 1986-88: "Macrobio 1934-1984." *Lustrum* 28-29: 107-254. "Addendum." *Lustrum* 30: 7-9.

Deproost, Paul-Augustin 1992: "La tempête dans l'*Historia Apostolica* d'Arator: sources et exégèse d'un cliché littéraire." In *De Tertullien aux Mozarabes: mélanges offerts à Jacques Fontaine*. Ed. Louis Holtz, Jean-Claude Fredouille, and Marie-Hélène Jullien. Collection des Etudes Augustiniennes. 3 vols. Paris: Institut d'Etudes Augustiniennes. Vol. 1, pp. 479-509.

De Rentiis, Dina 1996: *Die Zeit der Nachfolge: zur Interdependenz von ‹imitatio Christi› und ‹imitatio auctorum› im 12.-16. Jahrhundert*. Beihefte zur Zeitschrift für romanische Philologie, 273. Tübingen: Niemeyer.

Dion, Marie-Pierre ed. 1990: *La Cantilène de sainte Eulalie*. Actes du Colloque de Valenciennes 21 mars 1989. Lille: ACCES and Bibliothèque Municipale de Valenciennes.

Donati, Maria Teresa 1990: "Metafisica, fisica e astrologia nel XII secolo: Bernardo Silvestre e l'introduzione 'Qui celum' dell''Experimentarius'." *Studi medievali* ser. 3, 31: 649-703.

Donovan, L. G. 1975: *Recherches sur "Le roman de Thèbes"*. Paris: Société d'Edition d'Enseignement Supérieur.

Dragonetti, Roger 1987: *Le mirage des sources: l'art du faux dans le roman médiéval*. Paris: Seuil.

Dragonetti, Roger 1996: "Les chemins de l'inconnaissance: entretien avec Roger Dragonetti." *Cahiers de la Faculté des Lettres, Université de Genève*. Pp. 26-30.

Dronke, Peter 1974: *Fabula: Explorations into the Uses of Myth in Medieval Platonism*. Mittellateinische Studien und Texte, 9. Leiden, Cologne: Brill.

Dronke, Peter 1985: *"Integumenta Virgilii."* In *Lectures médiévales de Virgile.* Actes du Colloque organisé par l'Ecole française de Rome (25-28 octobre 1982). Collection de l'Ecole française de Rome, 80. Rome: Ecole française de Rome. Pp. 313-29.

Dronke, Peter 1986: "Dido's Lament: From Medieval Lyric to Chaucer." In *Kontinuität und Wandel: lateinische Poesie von Naevius bis Baudelaire. Franco Munari zum 65. Geburtstag.* Ed. Ulrich Justus Stache, Wolfgang Maaz, and Fritz Wagner. Hildesheim: Weidmann. Pp. 364-90.

Dronke, Peter 1994: *Verse with Prose from Petronius to Dante: The Art and Scope of the Mixed Form.* Cambridge, MA, London: Harvard University Press.

Dubost, Francis 1996: *"Tel cuide bien faire qui faut*: le 'beau jeu' de Renaut avec le merveilleux." In *Le Chevalier et la merveille dans "Le Bel Inconnu" ou le beau jeu de Renaut.* Ed. Jean Dufournet. Unichamp, 52. Paris: Champion. Pp. 23-56.

Duby, Georges 1981: *Le chevalier, la femme et le prêtre: le mariage dans la France médiévale.* Pluriel. Paris: Hachette.

Dunkle, J. Roger 1987: "Satirical Themes in Joseph of Exeter's *De bello troiano.*" *Classica et Mediaevalia* 38: 203-13.

Dziatzko, C. 1895: "Αρχέτυπου." In *Paulys Real-Encyclopädie der classischen Altertunmswissenschaft.* Stuttgart: Metzler. Vol. 2.1 col. 460-61.

Eastwood, Bruce 1994: "Manuscripts of Macrobius, *Commentarii in Somnium Scipionis,* before 1500." *Manuscripta* 38: 138-55.

Edwards, Robert R. 1993: "Poetic Invention and the Medieval *Causae.*" *Mediaeval Studies* 55: 183-217.

Eisenhut, Werner 1983: "Spätantike Troja-Erzählungen — mit einem Ausblick auf die mittelalterliche Trojaliteratur." *Mittellateinisches Jahrbuch* 18:1-28.

Eley, Penny 1994: "How Long Is a Trojan War? Aspects of Time in the *Roman de Troie* and Its Sources." In *Shifts and Transpositions in Medieval Narrative: A Festschrift for Dr. Elspeth Kennedy.* Ed. Karen Pratt. Cambridge: Brewer. Pp. 139-50.

Englisch, Brigitte 1994: *Die artes liberales im frühen Mittelalter (5.-9. Jh.): das Quadrivium und der Komputus als Indikatoren für Kontinuität und Erneuerung der exakten Wissenschaften zwischen Antike und Mittelalter.* Sudhoffs Archiv: Zeitschrift für Wissenschaftsgeschichte, Beiheft 33. Stuttgart: Steiner.

Escorial 1910-23: *Catálogo de los códices latinos de la Real Biblioteca del Escorial.* 5 vols. Madrid: Helénica.

Esposito, Mario 1913: "Miscellaneous Notes on Mediaeval Latin Literature." *Hermathena* 17: 104-14.

Faber, Birgitta Maria 1974: *Eheschließung in mittelalterlicher Dichtung vom Ende des 12. bis zum Ende des 15. Jahrhunderts.* Diss. Bonn. Bonn: Rheinische Friedrich-Wilhelms-Universität.

Faral, Edmond 1913: *Recherches sur les sources latines des contes et romans courtois du moyen âge.* Paris: Champion.

Faral, Edmond 1924: *Les arts poétiques du XIIᵉ et du XIIIᵉ siècle: recherches et documents sur la technique littéraire du moyen âge.* Bibliothèque de l'Ecole des Hautes Etudes: Sciences historiques et philologiques, 238. Paris: Champion.

Faral, Edmond 1936: "Les manuscrit 511 du 'Hunterian Museum' de Glasgow: notes sur le mouvement poétique et l'histoire littéraire en France et en Angleterre entre les années 1150 et 1225." *Studi medievali* n.s. 9: 18-121.

Fichte, Joerg 1995: "Von der Historie zur Tragödie: Macht und Ohnmacht des Schicksals über Troilus und Cressida." In *Fortuna.* Ed. Walter Haug and Burghart Wachinger. Fortuna Vitrea, 15. Tübingen: Niemeyer. Pp. 192-215.

Fiocchi, Laura 1981: "Progetto di analisi della tradizione indiretta in Macrobio." In *La Cultura in Italia fra tardo antico e alto medioevo.* Atti del Convegno tenuto a

Roma, Consiglio Nazionale delle Ricerche, dal 12 al 16 novembre 1979. 2 vols. Rome: Herder. Vol. 1, pp. 423-32.

Flamant, Jacques 1977: *Macrobe et le néo-platonisme latin, à la fin du IV* siècle*. Etudes préliminaires aux religions orientales dans l'Empire Romain 58. Leiden: Brill.

Fleming, John V. 1993: "The *Fidus Interpres*, or from Horace to Pandarus." In *Interpretation: Medieval and Modern*. The J. A. W. Bennett Memorial Lectures, Perugia 1992. Ed. Piero Boitani and Anna Torti. Cambridge: D. S. Brewer. Pp. 189-200.

Flutre, Louis-Ferdinand 1962: *Table des noms propres avec toutes leurs variantes figurant dans les romans du moyen âge écrits en français ou en provençal et actuellement publiés et analysés*. Publications du C. E. S. C. M., 11. Poitiers: Centre d'Etudes Supérieures de Civilisation Médiévale.

Foehr-Janssens, Yasmina 1997: "La reine Didon: entre fable et histoire, entre Rome et Troie." In *Entre fiction et histoire: Troie et Rome au moyen âge*. Ed. Emmanuèle Baumgartner and Laurence Harf-Lancner. Paris: Presses de la Sorbonne Nouvelle, 1997. Pp. 127-46.

Fourrier, Anthime 1960. *Le courant réaliste dans le roman courtois en France au moyen-âge. Tome I: Les débuts (XII* siècle)*. Paris: Nizet.

Fraker, Charles F. 1993: "*Oppositio* in Geoffrey of Vinsauf and Its Background." *Rhetorica* 11: 63-85.

Frappier, Jean 1959: "Virgile source de Chrétien de Troyes?" *Romance Philology* 13: 50-59.

Frappier, Jean 1968: *Chrétien de Troyes*. Connaissance des lettres, 50. Paris: Hatier.

Fredborg, Karin Margareta 1987: "The Scholastic Teaching of Rhetoric in the Middle Ages." *Cahiers de l'Institut du Moyen-Age grec et latin, Université de Copenhague* 55: 85-105.

Friedman, Lionel J. 1965: "Gradus amoris." *Romance Philology* 19: 167-77.

Friis-Jensen, Karstens 1987: *Saxo grammaticus as Latin Poet: Studies in the Verse Passages of the Gesta Danorum*. Analecta Romana Instituti Danici: supplementum, 14. Rome: L'Erma di Bretschneider.

Friis-Jensen, Karsten 1988: "Horatius liricus et ethicus: Two Twelfth-Century School Texts on Horace's Poems." *Cahiers de l'Institut du moyen-âge grec et latin, Université de Copenhague* 57: 81-147.

Friis-Jensen, Karsten 1990: "The *Ars Poetica* in Twelfth-Century France: The Horace of Matthew of Vendôme, Geoffrey of Vinsauf, and John of Garland." *Cahiers de l'Institut du moyen-âge grec et latin, Université de Copenhague* 60: 319-88 and 61:184.

Friis-Jensen, Karsten 1995a: "Commentaries on Horace's *Art of Poetry* in the Incunable Period." *Renaissance Studies* 9: 228-39.

Friis-Jensen, Karsten 1995b: "Horace and the Early Writers of Arts of Poetry." *Sprachtheorien in Spätantike und Mittelalter*. Ed. Sten Ebbesen. Geschichte der Sprachtheorie, 3. Tübingen: Narr. Pp. 360-401.

Friis-Jensen, Karsten 1997: "Medieval Commentaries on Horace." In *Medieval and Renaissance Scholarship*. Proceedings of the Second European Science Foundation Workshop on the Classical Tradition in the Middle Ages and the Renaissance (London, The Warburg Institute, 27-28 November 1992). Ed. Nicholas Mann and Birger Munk Olsen. Mittellateinische Studien und Texte, 21. Leiden, New York, Cologne: Brill. Pp. 51-73.

Fuhrmann, Manfred. 1967: "Die lateinische Literatur der Spätantike: ein literarhistorischer Beitrag zum Kontinuitätsproblem." *Antike und Abendland* 13: 56-79.

Galand-Hallyn, Perrine 1994: *Le reflet des fleurs: description et métalangage poétique d'Homère à la Renaissance*. Travaux d'Humanisme et Renaissance, 283. Geneva: Droz.

Gallais, Pierre 1967: "Bleheri, la cour de Poitiers et la diffusion des récits arthuriens sur le Continent." In *Moyen âge et littérature comparée*. Société Française de Littérature Comparée: Actes du Septième Congrès National, Poitiers 27-29 mai 1965. Paris: Didier. Pp. 47-79.

Gally, Michèle 1996: "Variations sur le *locus amoenus*: accords des sens et esthétique poétique." *Poétique* 106: 161-77.

Gaullier-Bougassas, Catherine 1996: "La réécriture inventive d'une même séquence: quelques versions du voyage d'Alexandre sous la mer." *Bien dire et bien aprandre* 14: 7-19.

Gaunt, Simon 1992: "From Epic to Romance: Gender and Sexuality in the *Roman d'Enéas*." *Romanic Review* 83: 1-27.

Genicot, Léopold 1975: "Princes territoriaux et sang carolingien: la *Genealogia comitum Buloniensium*." In his *Etudes sur les principautés lotharingiennes*. Université de Louvain: Recueil de travaux d'histoire et de philologie, ser. 6, 7. Louvain: Publications Universitaires de Louvain. Pp. 217-306.

Gerritsen, W. P. 1973: "Rhetorica en litteratuur in de middeleeuwen." Three Lectures at the Rijksuniversiteit Groningen. 22 en 29 November, 13 December.

Gerritsen, W.P. 1995: "Een avond in Ardres: over middeleeuwse verhaalkunst." In *Grote Lijnen: syntheses over Middelnederlandse letterkunde*. Nederlandse Literatuur en cultuur in de middeleeuwen, 11. Amsterdam: Prometheus. Pp. 157-72 and 220-23.

Gertz, SunHee Kim 1996: *Poetic Prologues: Medieval Conversations with the Literary Past*. Analecta Romanica, 56. Frankfurt: Klostermann.

Ghellinck, J. de 1946: *L'essor de la littérature latine au XIIᵉ siècle*. 2 vols. Museum Lessianum: section historique, 4-5. Brussels: Edition Universelle, Paris: Desclée de Brouwer.

Gibson, Margaret 1975: "The Continuity of Learning circa 850-circa 1050." *Viator* 6: 1-13.

Gier, Albert 1977: *Der Sünder als Beispiel: zu Gestalt und Funktion hagiographischer Gebrauchstexte anhand der Theophiluslegende*. Bonner romanistische Arbeiten, 1. Frankfurt, Bern, Las Vegas: P. Lang.

Glauche, Günter 1970: *Schullektüre im Mittelalter: Entstehung und Wandlungen des Lektürekanons bis 1200 nach den Quellen dargestellt*. Münchener Beiträge zur Mediävistik und Renaissance-Forschung, 5. Munich: Arbeo.

Godman, Peter 1987: *Poets and Emperors: Frankish Politics and Carolingian Poetry*. Oxford: Clarendon Press.

Godman, Peter 1990a: "Ambiguity in the 'Mathematicus' of Bernardus Silvestris." *Studi medievali* ser. 3, 31: 583-648.

Godman, Peter 1990b: "Literary Classicism and Latin Erotic Poetry of the Twelfth Century and the Renaissance." In *Latin Poetry and the Classical Tradition: Essays in Medieval and Renaissance Literature*. Ed. Peter Godman and Oswyn Murray. Oxford-Warburg Studies. Oxford: Clarendon Press. Pp. 149-82.

Goetz, Georg 1890: *Commentatiuncula Macrobiana*. Index scholarum aestivarum publice et privatim in Universitate Litterarum Ienensi 21 April-31 August 1890. Jena: Neuenhahn.

Gosman, Martin 1992a: "L'Historia malmenée: l'idéalisation du pouvoir dans les 'romans antiques'." *Bien dire et bien aprandre* 10: 51-63.

Gosman, Martin 1992b: "Le *Roman d'Alexandre*: les interpolations du XIIIᵉ siècle." In *Le roman antique au moyen âge*. Actes du Colloque du Centre d'Etudes Médiévales de l'Université de Picardie, Amiens 14-15 janvier 1989. Ed. Danielle Buschinger. Göppinger Arbeiten zur Germanistik, 549. Göppingen: Kümmerle. Pp. 61-72.

Gosman, Martin 1996: "Le 'Roman d'Alixandre' et ses versions du XIIe siècle: une réécriture permanente." *Bien dire et bien aprandre* 13: 7-23.

Gössmann, Elisabeth 1974: *Antiqui und Moderni im Mittelalter: eine geschichtliche Standortbestimmung.* Veröffentlichungen des Grabmann-Institutes, n.s. 23. Munich, Paderborn, Vienna: Schöningh.

Gouttebroze, Jean-Guy 1995: "Entre les historiographes d'expression latine et les jongleurs, le clerc lisant." In *Le clerc au moyen âge.* Senefiance, 37. Aix-en-Provence: CUER MA. Pp. 215-30.

Gravdal, Kathryn 1996: "Pouvoir féodal et objets matériels dans *Le Bel Inconnu.*" In *Le Chevalier et la merveille dans "Le Bel Inconnu" ou le beau jeu de Renaut.* Ed. Jean Dufournet. Unichamp, 52. Paris: Champion. Pp. 57-67.

Greif, Wilhelm 1886: *Die mittelalterlichen Bearbeitungen der Trojanersage: ein neuer Beitrag zur Dares- und Dictysfrage.* Ausgaben und Abhandlungen aus dem Gebiete der romanischen Philologie, 61. Marburg: Elwert.

Gruber, Joachim 1981: "Einflüße verschiedener Literaturgattungen auf die prosimetrischen Werke der Spätantike." *Würzburger Jahrbücher für die Altertumswissenschaft* n.s. 7: 209-21.

Grundmann, Herbert 1958: "Litteratus—illitteratus: der Wandel einer Bildungsnorm vom Altertum zum Mittelalter." *Archiv für Kulturgeschichte* 40: 1-65.

Hahn, Stacey Layne 1988: "Patterns of Diversity: Hierarchy and Love in the Prose *Lancelot.*" Diss. Wisconsin.

Haidu, Peter 1983: "The Episode as Semiotic Module in Twelfth-Century Romance." *Poetics Today* 4: 655-81.

Hajdú, István 1993: "Ein Zürcher Kommentar aus dem 12. Jahrhundert zur Ars poetica des Horaz." *Cahiers de l'Institut du moyen-âge grec et latin, Université de Copenhague* 63: 231-93.

Halász, Katalin 1992: *Images d'auteur dans le roman médiéval (XIIe-XIIIe siècles).* Studia romanica de Debrecen: series litteraria, 17. Debrecen: Kossuth Lajos Tudományegyetem.

Halm, Carolus, and Gulielmus Meyer ed. 1969: *Catalogue codicum latinorum Bibliothecae Monacensis.* Munich; repr. Wiesbaden: Harrasowitz.

Hamasse, Jacqueline 1990: "Le vocabulaire des florilèges médiévaux." *Méthodes et instruments du travail intellectuel au moyen âge: études sur le vocabulaire.* Ed. Olga Weijers. CIVICIMA: Etudes sur le vocabulaire intellectuel du moyen âge, 3. Turnhout: Brepols. Pp. 209-30.

Hansen, Inez 1971: *Zwischen Epos und höfischem Roman: die Frauengestalten im Trojaroman des Benoît de Sainte-Maure.* Beiträge zur romanischen Philologie des Mittelalters, 8. Munich: Fink.

Harf-Lancner, Laurence 1994: "D'Enéas à Florimont: sens et fonction de la féerie dans le *Florimont* d'Aimon de Varennes." *Bien dire et bien aprandre* 12: 123-34.

Harf-Lancner, Laurence 1996: "De la biographie au roman d'Alexandre: Alexandre de Paris et l'art de la conjointure." In *The Medieval "Opus": Imitation, Rewriting, and Transmission in the French Tradition.* Proceedings of the Symposium Held at the Institute for Research in Humanities October 5-7 1995, The University of Wisconsin-Madison. Ed. Douglas Kelly. Faux Titre, 116. Amsterdam, Atlanta: Rodopi. Pp. 59-74.

Hart, Thomas Elwood 1981: "Chrestien, Macrobius, and Chartrean Science: The Allegorical Robe as Symbol of Textual Design in the Old French *Erec.*" *Mediaeval Studies* 43: 250-96.

Hartmann, Wilfried 1970: "Manegold von Lautenbach und die Anfänge der Frühscholastik." *Deutsches Archiv für Erforschung des Mittelalters* 26: 47-149.

Hathaway, Neil 1989: "Compilatio: From Plagiarism to Compiling." *Viator* 20: 19-44.

Haug, Walter 1989: "Literatur und Leben im Mittelalter: eine neue Theorie zur Entstehung und Entwicklung des höfischen Romans." *Der Deutschunterricht* 41.1: 12-26.

Haug, Walther 1992: *Literaturtheorie im deutschen Mittelalter: von den Anfängen bis zum Ende des 13. Jahrhunderts*. 2nd rev. ed. Darmstadt: Wissenschaftliche Buchgesellschaft.

Haye, Thomas 1997: *Das lateinische Lehrgedicht im Mittelalter: Analyse einer Gattung*. Mittellateinische Studien und Texte, 22. Leiden, New York, Cologne: Brill.

Henkel, Nikolaus 1993: "Kurzfassungen höfischer Erzähldichtung im 13./14. Jahrhundert: Überlegungen zum Verhältnis von Textgeschichte und literarischer Interessenbildung." In *Literarische Interessenbildung im Mittelalter*. DFG-Symposion 1991. Ed. Joachim Heinzle. Germanistische Symposien: Berichtsbände, 14. Stuttgart, Weimar: Metzler. Pp. 39-59.

Herescu, N. I. 1932: "Sur une répétition virgilienne (*Aen.*, I, 103-16)." *Revue des études latines* 10: 322-23.

Herman, József 1996: "The End of the History of Latin." *Romance Philology* 49: 364-82.

Herter, H. 1935: "Nemesis." *Paulys Real-Encyclopädie der classischen Altertumswissenschaft*. Stuttgart: Metzler. Vol. 16 col. 2338-80.

Herzog, Reinhart 1975: *Die Bibelepik der lateinischen Spätantike: Formgeschichte einer erbaulichen Gattung*. Vol. 1. Theorie und Geschichte der Literatur und der schönen Künste: Texte und Abhandlungen, 37. Munich: Fink.

Hexter, Ralph 1988: "The Metamorphosis of Sodom: The Ps-Cyprian 'De Sodoma' as an Ovidian Episode." *Traditio* 44: 1-35.

Hofer, Stefan 1928: "Kristian und Macrobius." *Zeitschrift für romanische Philologie* 48: 130-31.

Holtz, Louis 1981: *Donat et la tradition de l'enseignement grammatical: étude sur l'"Ars Donati" et sa diffusion (IVᵉ-IXᵉ siècle) et édition critique*. Documents, études et répertoires. Paris: Centre National de la Recherche Scientifique.

Holtz, Louis 1985: "La redécouverte de Virgile aux VIIIᵉ et IXᵉ siècles d'après les manuscrits conservés." In *Lectures médiévales de Virgile*. Actes du Colloque organisé par l'Ecole française de Rome (Rome, 25-28 octobre 1982). Collection de l'Ecole française de Rome, 80. Rome: Ecole française de Rome. Pp. 9-30.

Holtz, Louis 1991: "La transmission des classiques latins: de l'antiquité tardive à l'époque carolingienne." In *Itinerari dei testi antichi*. Ed. Oronzo Pecere. Saggi di storia antica, 3. Rome: "L'Erma" di Bretschneider. Pp. 85-104.

Homeyer, Helene 1970: "Der Dichter zwischen zwei Welten: Beobachtungen zur Theorie und Praxis des Dichtens im frühen Mittelalter." *Antike und Abendland* 16: 141-52.

Homeyer, H. 1982: "Beobachtungen zum Weiterleben der trojanischen Abstammungs- und Gründungssagen im Mittelalter." *Res Publica Litterarum* 5.2: 93-123.

Hooley, D. M. 1997: *The Knotted Thong: Structures of Mimesis in Persius*. Ann Arbor: University of Michigan Press.

Hübner, Wolfgang 1995: "Die vier Elemente in den Vergleichen von Dantes 'Paradiso'." *International Journal of the Classical Tradition* 1: 5-14.

Huchet, Jean-Charles 1984: *Le roman médiéval*. Littératures modernes, 36. Paris: Presses Universitaires de France.

Hunt, R. W. 1971: "The Deposit of Latin Classics in the Twelfth-Century Renaissance." In *Classical Influences on European Culture A. D. 500-1500*. Proceedings of an International Conference Held at King's College, Cambridge, April 1969. Ed. R. R. Bolgar. Cambridge: Cambridge University Press. Pp. 51-55.

Hunt, Tony 1978a: "Chrestien and the *comediae*." *Mediaeval Studies* 40: 120-56.

Hunt, Tony 1978b: "Redating Chrestien de Troyes." *Bulletin bibliographique de la Société Internationale Arthurienne — Bibliographical Bulletin of the International Arthurian Society* 30: 209-37.

Hunt, Tony 1981-82: "Chrestien and Macrobius." *Classica et Mediaevalia* 33: 211-27.

Hunt, Tony 1991: *Teaching and Learning Latin in Thirteenth-Century England.* 3 vols. Cambridge: Brewer.

Huot, Sylvia 1987: *From Song to Book: The Poetics of Writing in Old French Lyric and Lyrical Narrative Poetry.* Ithaca, London: Cornell University Press.

Hurst, Peter F. 1995: "On the Interplay of Learned and Popular Elements in the 'De Phyllide et Flora' (Carm. Bur. 92): A Preliminary Study." *Mittellateinisches Jahrbuch* 30.2: 47-59.

Hüttig, Albrecht 1990: *Macrobius im Mittelalter: ein Beitrag zur Rezeptionsgeschichte der Commentarii in Somnium Scipionis.* Freiburger Beiträge zur mittelalterlichen Geschichte: Studien und Texte, 2. Frankfurt, Bern, New York, Paris: P. Lang.

Irvine, Martin 1994. *The Making of Textual Culture: 'Grammatica' and Literary Theory, 350-1100.* Cambridge Studies in Medieval Literature, 19. Cambridge: Cambridge University Press.

Jaeger, C. Stephen 1994: *The Envy of Angels: Cathedral Schools and Social Ideals in Medieval Europe, 950-1200.* Philadelphia: University of Pennsylvania Press.

Jaffe, Samuel 1985: "Antiquity and Innovation in Notker's *Nova rhetorica*: The Doctrine of Invention." *Rhetorica* 3: 165-81.

James, Montague Rhodes ed. 1912: *A Descriptive Catalogue of the Manuscripts in the Library of Corpus Christi College Cambridge.* Vol. 1. Cambridge: University Press.

Janssens, Jozef D. 1988: *Dichter en publiek in creatief samenspel: over interpretatie van middelnederlandse ridderromans.* Leuvense Studiën en Tekstuitgaven, n.s. 7. Leuven, Amersfoort: Acco.

Jappé, Françoise 1996: "Adaptation et création dans le conte de *Narcisse*." *Bien dire et bien aprandre* 14: 155-67.

Jeauneau, Edouard 1960: "Macrobe, source du platonisme chartrain." *Studi medievali* ser. 3, 1: 3-24.

Jeauneau, Edouard 1971: "La lecture des auteurs classiques à l'école de Chartres durant la première moitié du XIIᵉ siècle. Un témoin privilégié: les 'Glosae super Macrobium' de Guillaume de Conches." In *Classical Influences on European Culture A. D. 500-1500.* Proceedings of an International Conference Held at King's College, Cambridge, April 1969. Ed. R. R. Bolgar. Cambridge: Cambridge University Press. Pp. 95-102.

Jeauneau, Edouard 1975: "L'héritage de la philosophie antique durant le haut moyen âge." In *La cultura antiqua nell'Occidente latino dal VII al'XI secolo, 18-24 aprile 1974.* Settimane di Studio del Centro Italiano di Studi sull'Alto Medioevo, 22. 2 vols. Spoleto: La Sede del Centro. Vol. I, pp. 15-54.

Jeudy, Colette, and Yves-François Riou 1989: *Les manuscrits classiques latins des bibliothèques publiques de France.* Vol. 1: *Agen-Evreux.* Documents, Etudes et Répertoires publiés par l'Institut de Recherche et d'Histoire des textes. Paris: Editions du Centre National de la Recherche Scientifique.

Jewers, Caroline 1996: "Fabric and Fabrication: Lyric and Narrative in Jean Renart's *Roman de la rose.*" *Speculum* 71: 907-24.

Jones, Catherine M. 1993: *The Noble Merchant: Problems of Genre and Lineage in "Hervis de Mes".* North Carolina Studies in the Romance Languages and Literatures, 241. Chapel Hill: University of North Carolina Department of Romance Languages.

Jones, Nancy A. 1997: "The Uses of Embroidery in the Romances of Jean Renart: Gender, History, Textuality." In *Jean Renart and the Art of Romance: Essays on "Guillaume de Dole"*. Ed. Nancy Vine Durling. Gainesville: University Press of Florida. Pp. 13-44.

Jongen, Ludo 1994: "Achilles as Anti-Hero: A Thirteenth-Century Middle Dutch View of the Fall of Troy." *Amsterdamer Beiträge zur älteren Germanistik* 40: 111-29.

Jongkees, A. G. 1967: "Translatio Studii: les avatars d'un thème médiéval." In *Miscellanea Mediaevalia in memoriam Jan Frederik Niermeyer*. Groningen: Wolters. Pp. 41-51.

Jung, Marc-René 1996: *La légende de Troie en France au moyen âge: analyse des versions françaises et bibliographie raisonnée des manuscrits*. Romanica Helvetica, 114. Basel, Tübingen: Francke.

Jung, Marc-René 1997: "L'histoire grecque: Darès et les suites." In *Entre fiction et histoire: Troie et Rome au moyen âge*. Ed. Emmanuèle Baumgartner and Laurence Harf-Lancner. Paris: Presses de la Sorbonne Nouvelle, 1997. Pp. 185-206.

Kay, Sarah 1990: *Subjectivity in Troubadour Poetry*. Cambridge Studies in French. Cambridge: Cambridge University Press.

Kay, Sarah 1995: *The "Chansons de geste" in the Age of Romance: Political Fictions*. Oxford: Clarendon Press.

Kelly, Douglas 1966: "The Scope of the Treatment of Composition in the Twelfth- and Thirteenth-Century Arts of Poetry." *Speculum* 41: 261-78.

Kelly, Douglas 1969a: "*En uni dire (Tristan* Douce 839) and the Composition of Thomas's *Tristan*." *Modern Philology* 66: 9-17.

Kelly, Douglas 1969b: "Theory of Composition in Medieval Narrative Poetry and Geoffrey of Vinsauf's *Poetria Nova*." *Mediaeval Studies* 31: 117-48.

Kelly, Douglas 1970: "The Source and Meaning of *Conjointure* in Chrétien's *Erec* 14." *Viator* 1: 179-200.

Kelly, Douglas 1971. "La forme et le sens de la quête dans l'*Erec et Enide* de Chrétien de Troyes." *Romania* 92: 326-58.

Kelly, Douglas 1978: *Medieval Imagination: Rhetoric and the Poetry of Courtly Love*. Madison, London: University of Wisconsin Press.

Kelly, Douglas 1983: "The Logic of the Imagination in Chrétien de Troyes." In *The Sower and His Seed: Essays on Chrétien de Troyes*. Ed. Rupert T. Pickens. French Forum Monographs, 44. Lexington, KY: French Forum. Pp. 9-30.

Kelly, Douglas 1984a: "Obscurity and Memory: Sources for Invention in Medieval French Literature." In *Vernacular Poetics in the Middle Ages*. Ed. Lois Ebin. Studies in Medieval Culture, 16. Kalamazoo: Medieval Institute Publications, Western Michigan University. Pp. 33-56.

Kelly, Douglas 1984b: "The Rhetoric of Adventure in Medieval Romance." In *Chrétien de Troyes and the Troubadours: Essays in Memory of the Late Leslie Topsfield*. Ed. Peter S. Noble and Linda M. Paterson. Cambridge: St. Catharine's College. Pp. 172-85.

Kelly, Douglas 1987: "The Art of Description." In *The Legacy of Chrétien de Troyes*. Vol. I. Ed. Norris J. Lacy, Douglas Kelly, and Keith Busby. Faux Titre 31. Amsterdam: Rodopi. Pp. 191-221.

Kelly, Douglas 1988: "Le patron et l'auteur dans l'invention romanesque." In *Théories et pratiques de l'écriture au moyen âge*. Actes du Colloque Palais du Luxembourg-Sénat, 5 et 6 mars 1987. Ed. Emmanuèle Baumgartner and Christiane Marchello-Nizia. Littérales, 4. Paris: Centre de Recherches du Département de Français de Paris X-Nanterre, Fontenay-Saint Cloud: Centre Espace-Temps-Histoire de l'E.N.S. Pp. 25-39.

Kelly, Douglas 1991: *The Arts of Poetry and Prose*. Typologie des sources du moyen âge occidental, 59. Turnhout: Brepols.

Kelly, Douglas 1992: *The Art of Medieval French Romance*. Madison, London: University of Wisconsin Press.

Kelly, Douglas 1995a: *Internal Difference and Meanings in the "Roman de la rose"*. Madison, London: University of Wisconsin Press.

Kelly, Douglas 1995b: "The Invention of Briseida's Story in Benoît de Sainte-Maure's *Troie*." *Romance Philology* 48: 221-41.

Kelly, Douglas 1997a: "The *Fidus interpres*: Aid or Impediment to Medieval Translation and *Translatio?*" In *Translation Theory and Practice in the Middle Ages*. Ed. Jeanette Beer. Studies in Medieval Culture, 38. Kalamazoo: Medieval Institute Publications, Western Michigan University. Pp. 47-58.

Kelly, Douglas 1997b: "Guerre et parenté dans le *Roman de Troie*." In *Entre fiction et histoire: Troie et Rome au moyen âge*. Ed. Emmanuèle Baumgartner and Laurence Harf-Lancner. Paris: Presses de la Sorbonne Nouvelle, 1997. Pp. 53-71.

Kelly, Douglas 1998a: "Horace et le *Roman de Troie* de Benoît de Sainte-Maure." In *Miscellanea mediaevalia: mélanges offerts à Philippe Ménard*. Ed. J. Claude Faucon, Alain Labbé, and Danielle Quéruel. Nouvelle Bibliothèque du moyen âge, 46. 2 vols. Paris: Champion. Vol. I, pp. 723-31.

Kelly, Douglas 1998b: "The Scope of Medieval Instruction in the Art of Poetry and Prose: Problems of Documentation and Interpretation." *Studies in Medieval and Renaissance Teaching*. 6.2: 49-68.

Kelly, Douglas 1999: "Forlorn Hope: The Mutability Topoi in Some Medieval Narratives." In *The World and Its Rival: Essays on Literary Imagination in Honor of Per Nykrog*. Pp. 59-77. Amsterdam, Atlanta: Rodopi.

Kelly, Douglas 2000: "The Poem as Art of Poetry: The Rhetoric of Imitation." In *Medieval Lyric Genres in Historical Context*. Ed. William D. Paden. Champagne-Urbana: University of Illinois Press. Forthcoming.

Kennedy, Elspeth 1986: *Lancelot and the Grail: A Study of the Prose "Lancelot"*. Oxford: Clarendon Press.

King, Katherine Callen 1985: "Achilles amator." *Viator* 16: 21-64.

Klebs, Elimar 1899: *Die Erzählung von Apollonius aus Tyrus: eine geschichtliche Untersuchung über ihre lateinische Urform und ihre späteren Bearbeitungen*. Berlin: Reimer.

Klopsch, Paul 1980: *Einführung in die Dichtungslehren des lateinischen Mittelalters*. Das lateinische Mittelalter. Darmstadt: Wissenschaftliche Buchgesellschaft.

Klopsch, Paul 1985: "Mittellateinische Bukolik." In *Lectures médiévales de Virgile*. Actes du Colloque organisé par l'Ecole française de Rome (Rome, 25-28 octobre 1982). Collection de l'Ecole française de Rome, 80. Rome: Ecole française de Rome. Pp. 145-65.

Knapp, Fritz Peter 1975. *Similitudo: Stil- und Erzählfunktion von Vergleich und Exempel in der lateinischen, französischen und deutschen Großepik des Hochmittelalters*. Philologia Germanica 2. Vienna, Stuttgart: Braumüller.

Köhn, Rolf 1986: "Schulbildung und Trivium im lateinischen Hochmittelalter und ihr möglicher praktischer Nutzen." In *Schulen und Studium im sozialen Wandel des hohen und späten Mittelalter*. Ed. Johannes Fried. Vorträge und Forschungen: Konstanzer Arbeitskreis für mittelalterliche Geschichte, 30. Sigmaringen: Thorbecke. Pp. 203-84.

Krause, Virginia, and Christian Martin 1998: "Topoï et utopie de l'amour dans les *Lais* de Marie de France." *Dalhousie French Studies* 42: 3-15.

Krüger, Sabine 1985: "Das kirchliche Turnierverbot im Mittelalter." In *Das ritterliche Turnier im Mittelalter: Beiträge zu einer vergleichenden Formen- und Verhaltensgeschichte des*

Rittertums. Ed. Josef Fleckenstein. Veröffentlichungen des Max-Planck-Instituts für Geschichte, 80. Göttingen: Vandenhoeck & Ruprecht. Pp. 401-22.

Kruger, Steven F. 1992: *Dreaming in the Middle Ages*. Cambridge Studies in Medieval Literature, 14. Cambridge: Cambridge University Press.

Kullmann, Dorothea 1993: "Chrétien de Troyes et la doctrine ecclésiastique du mariage." In *Epica, romanzo, altra letteratura, storia della civiltà*. Qfr, 10. Bologna: Pàtron. Pp. 33-74.

Lacy, Norris J. 1996: "Motif Transfer in Arthurian Romance." In *The Medieval "Opus": Imitation, Rewriting, and Transmission in the French Tradition*. Proceedings of the Symposium Held at the Institute for Research in Humanities October 5-7 1995, The University of Wisconsin-Madison. Ed. Douglas Kelly. Faux Titre, 116. Amsterdam, Atlanta: Rodopi. Pp. 157-68.

La Penna, Antonio 1953: "Studi sulla tradizione dei *Saturnali* di Macrobio." *Annali della Scuola Normale Superiore di Pisa: lettere, storia e filosofia* ser. 2, 22: 225-52.

Latzke, Therese 1979: "Der Fürstinnenpreis." *Mittellateinisches Jahrbuch* 14: 22-65.

Lauer, Ph. 1940: *Bibliothèque Nationale: Catalogue général des manuscrits latins*. Vol. 2. Paris: Bibliothèque Nationale.

Lausberg, Heinrich 1960. *Handbuch der literarischen Rhetorik: eine Grundlegung der Literaturwissenschaft*. 2 vols. Munich: Hueber.

Le Goff, Jacques 1982: "Quelques remarques sur les codes vestimentaire et alimentaire dans *Érec et Énide*." In *La chanson de geste et le mythe carolingien: mélanges René Louis*. 2 vols. Saint-Père-sous-Vézelay: Musée Archéologique Régional. Vol. II, pp. 1243-58.

Lehmann, Paul 1935: "Eine Sammlung mittellateinischer Gedichte aus dem Ende des 12. Jahrhunderts." *Historische Vierteljahrschrift* 30: 20-58.

LeMoine, Fannie 1972. *Martianus Capella: A Literary Re-evaluation*. Münchener Beiträge zur Mediävistik und Renaissance-Forschung, 10. Munich: Arbeo.

Lennartz, Klaus 1993: "Marginalien zur 'Summa metrica' des Matheus von Vendôme." *Mittellateinisches Jahrbuch* 28.2: 47-49.

Leonardi, Claudio 1959-60: "I codici di Marziano Capella." *Aevum* 33: 443-89, 34: 1-99, 411-524.

Leonardi, Claudio 1961: "Nuove voci poetiche tra secolo IX e XI." *Studi medievali* ser. 3, 2: 139-68.

Leotta, Rosario 1988: "Il 'De ornamentis verborum' di Marbodo di Rennes." *Studi medievali* ser. 3, 29: 103-27.

Lerchner, Karin 1993: *Lectulus floridus: zur Bedeutung des Bettes in Literatur und Handschriftenillustration des Mittelalters*. Pictura et poesis, 6. Cologne, Weimar, Vienna: Böhlau.

Lerer, Seth 1982: "John of Salisbury's Virgil." *Vivarium* 20: 24-39.

Lesne, Emile 1938-40: *Histoire de la propriété ecclésiastique en France*. Vol. IV: *Les livres: 'scriptoria' et bibliothèques du commencement du VIIIᵉ à la fin du XIᵉ siècle*. Vol. V: *Les écoles de la fin du VIIIᵉ siècle à la fin du XIIᵉ*. Mémoires et Travaux publiés par les Professeurs des Facultés Catholiques de Lille, 46 and 50. Lille: Facultés Catholiques.

Leupin, Alexandre 1988: "'Arte callidissima et occulta': la *Séquence de sainte Eulalie* en ancien français." *Romania* 109: 447-71.

Lieberg, Godo 1969: "Seefahrt und Werk: Untersuchungen zu einer Metapher der antiken, besonders der lateinischen Literatur von Pindar bis Horaz." *Giornale italiano di filologia* 21: 209-40.

Liebertz-Grün, Ursula 1994: "Kampf, Herrschaft, Liebe: Chrétiens und Hartmanns Erec- und Iweinromane als Modelle gelungener Sozialisation im 12. Jahrhundert." In *The Graph of Sex and the German Text: Gendered Culture in Early Modern*

Germany 1500-1700. Ed. Lynne Tatlock. Chloe: Beihefte zum Daphnis, 19. Amsterdam: Rodopi. Pp. 297-328.

Lindsey, W. M. 1900: "A Bodleian MS. of Macrobius." *Classical Review* 14: 260-61.

Linke, Hugo 1880: *Quaestiones de Macrobii Saturnaliorum fontibus*. Diss. Breslau. Breslau: Koebner.

Lögdberg, Gunnar 1936: *In Macrobii Saturnalia adnotationes*. Diss. Uppsala. Uppsala: Almqvist & Wiksell.

Logié, Philippe 1996: "Le traitement du livre VI de l'*Énéide* dans l'*Énéas*: propositions méthodologiques." *Bien dire et bien aprandre* 14: 41-51.

Loomis, Roger Sherman ed. 1959: *Arthurian Literature in the Middle Ages: A Collaborative History*. Oxford: Clarendon Press.

Lord, Mary Louise 1996: "The Use of Macrobius and Boethius in Some Fourteenth-Century Commentaries on Virgil." *International Journal of the Classical Tradition* 3: 3-22.

Lottin, Odan D. 1942-49: *Psychologie et morale aux XIIe et XIIIe siècles*. 3 vols. Louvain: Abbaye du Mont César, Gembloux: Duculot.

Lowe, E. A. 1963: *Codices latini antiquiores: A Paleographical Guide to Latin Manuscripts Prior to the Ninth Century*. Oxford: Clarendon Press. Vol. 10.

Luscombe, David Edward 1989: "Trivium, Quadrivium and the Organisation of Schools." In *L'Europa dei secoli XI e XII fra novità e tradizione: sviluppi di una cultura*. Atti della decima Settimana internazionale di studio, Mendola, 25-29 agosto 1986. Pubblicazioni dell'Università Cattolica del Sacro Cuore: Miscellanea del Centro di Studi Medioevali, 12. Milan: Vita e Pensiero. Pp. 81-100.

Luttrell, Claude 1974: *The Creation of the First Arthurian Romance: A Quest*. Evanston: Northwestern University Press.

Maddox, Donald 1996: "Inventing the Unknown: Rewriting in *Le Bel Inconnu*." In *The Medieval "Opus": Imitation, Rewriting, and Transmission in the French Tradition*. Proceedings of the Symposium Held at the Institute for Research in Humanities October 5-7 1995, The University of Wisconsin-Madison. Ed. Douglas Kelly. Faux Titre, 116. Amsterdam, Atlanta: Rodopi. Pp. 101-23.

Manitius, M. 1893: *Analekten zur Geschichte des Horaz im Mittelalter (bis 1300)*. Göttingen: Dieterich.

Manitius, Max 1911-31: *Geschichte der lateinischen Literatur des Mittelalters*. Handbuch der Altertumswisenschaft, 9.2.1-3. 3 vols. Munich: Beck.

Manitius, Max 1935: *Handschriften antiker Autoren in mittelalterlichen Bibliothekskatalogen*. Ed. Karl Manitius. Zentralblatt für Bibliothekswesen, 67. Leipzig: Harrassowitz.

Marchello-Nizia, Christiane 1985: "De l'*Énéide* à l'*Eneas*: les attributs du fondateur." In *Lectures médiévales de Virgile*. Actes du Colloque organisé par l'Ecole française de Rome (Rome, 25-28 octobre 1982). Collection de l'Ecole française de Rome, 80. Rome: Ecole française de Rome. Pp. 251-66.

Marinone, Nino 1975: "Frammenti di storiografi latini in Macrobio." *Studi Urbinati* 49/n. s. B 1: 493-527.

Marinone, Nino 1987: "Macrobio." In the *Enciclopedia virgiliana*. Rome: Istituto della Enciclopedia Italiana. Vol. 3, pp. 299-304.

Marshall, P. K. *See* Barker-Benfield, B. C.

Martin, Henri ed. 1886: *Catalogue des manuscrits de la Bibliothèque de l'Arsenal*. Paris: Plon, Nourrit.

Martin, Hervé 1996: *Mentalités médiévales: xie-xve siècle*. Nouvelle Clio. Paris: Presses Universitaires de France.

Martin, Janet 1979: "The Uses of Tradition: Gellius, Petronius, and John of Salisbnury." *Viator* 10: 57-76.

Massaro, Matteo 1978: "Un commento medievale inedito ad Orazio." *Atene e Roma* n.s. 23: 190-93.

Mayer, Marcos 1976: "De nuevo sobre la tradición biográfica virgiliana (A propósito di MACR. *sat*, 5,2,1)." *Anuario de filología* (Universidad de Barcelona, Facultad de filología) 2: 99-111.

Mazal, Otto, and Franz Unterkircher ed. 1965: *Katalog der abendländischen Handschriften der österreichischen Nationalbibliothek: "series nova" (Neuerwerbungen). Teil I.* Museion. Vienna: Prachner.

McGregor, James H. 1978: "Ovid at School: From the Ninth to the Fifteenth Century." *Classical Folia* 32: 29-51.

McKeon, Richard 1987: *Rhetoric: Essays in Invention and Discovery.* Woodbridge, CT: Ox Bow.

McKitterick, Rosamond 1989: *The Carolingians and the Written Word.* Cambridge: Cambridge University Press.

Mégier, Elisabeth 1997: "*Fortuna* als Kategorie der Geschichtsdeutung im 12. Jahrhundert am Beispiel Ordericus' Vitalis und Ottos von Freising." *Mittellateinisches Jahrbuch* 32: 49-70.

Méla, Charles 1989: "'Poetria nova' et 'homo novus'." *Littérature* 74: 4-26.

Ménard, Philippe 1969: *Le rire et le sourire dans le roman courtois en France au moyen âge (1150-1250).* Publications françaises et romanes, 105. Geneva: Droz.

Meneghetti,, Maria Luisa 1992: *Il pubblico dei trovatori: la ricezione della poesia cortese fino al XIV secolo.* Saggi, 759. Turin: Einaudi.

Ménétré, Annie 1994: "Conduite politique et destin d'un chef de guerre: Turnus, le déshérité." In *Le monde des héros dans la culture médiévale.* Ed. Danielle Buschinger and Wolfgang Spiewok. WODAN: Greifswalder Beiträge zum Mittelalter/ Etudes médiévales de Greifswald, 35. Ser. 3: Tagungsbände und Sammelschriften/Actes de colloques et ouvrages collectifs, 18. Greifswald: Reineke. Pp. 215-26.

Milin, Gaël 1995: *Le roi Marc aux oreilles de cheval.* Publications romanes et françaises, 197. Geneva: Droz.

Minnis, A. J. 1984: *Medieval Theory of Authorship: Scholastic Literary Attitudes in the Later Middle Ages.* London: Scolar Press.

MitW: Mittellateinisches Wörterbuch bis zum ausgehenden 13. Jahrhundert. Munich: Beck, 1967-.

Molinié, Georges 1992: *Dictionnaire de rhétorique.* Livre de Poche, 16. Paris: Librairie Générale Française.

Mölk, Ulrich 1985: "Philologische Aspekte des Turniers." In *Das ritterliche Turnier im Mittelalter: Beiträge zu einer vergleichenden Formen- und Verhaltensgeschichte des Rittertums.* Ed. Josef Fleckenstein. Veröffentlichungen des Max-Planck-Instituts für Geschichte, 80. Göttingen: Vandenhoeck & Ruprecht. Pp. 163-74.

Monfrin, Jacques 1985: "Les *Translations* vernaculaires de Virgile au moyen âge." In *Lectures médiévales de Virgile.* Actes du Colloque organisé par l'Ecole française de Rome (Rome, 25-28 octobre 1982). Collection de l'Ecole française de Rome, 80. Rome: Ecole française de Rome. Pp. 189-249.

Moores, Elizabeth 1990: "The Long and the Short of the *Contemptus sublimitatis*: A Medieval Text in the Making." *Manuscripta* 34: 216-32.

Moos, Peter von 1976: "*Poeta* und *historicus* im Mittelalter: zum Mimesis-Problem am Beispiel einiger Urteile über Lucan." *Beiträge zur Geschichte der deutschen Sprache und Literatur* (Tübingen) 98: 93-130.

Moos, Peter von 1988a: "*Fictio auctoris*: eine theoriegeschichtliche Miniatur am Rande der Institutio Traiani." In *Fälschungen im Mittelalter. Teil I: Kongreßakten und Festvorträge—Literatur und Falschung.* Internationaler Kongreß der Monumenta

Germaniae Historica München, 16.-19. September 1986. Monumenta Germaniae Historica: Schriften, 33.1. Hannover: Hahn. Pp. 739-80.

Moos, Peter von 1988b: *Geschichte als Topik: das rhetorische Exemplum von der Antike zur Neuzeit und die "historiae" im "Policraticus" Johanns von Salisbury.* Ordo, 2. Hildesheim, Zürich, New York: Olms.

Moos, Peter von 1991: "Zwischen Schriftlichkeit und Mündlichkeit: dialogische Interaktion im lateinischen Hochmittelalter (Vorstellung des neuen Teilprojektes H im SFB 231)." *Frühmittelalterliche Studien* 25: 300-14.

Moos, Peter von 1993: "Was galt im lateinischen Mittelalter als das Literarische an der Literatur? eine theologisch-rhetorische Antwort des 12. Jahrhunderts." In *Literarische Interessenbildung im Mittelalter.* DFG-Symposion 1991. Germanistische Symposien: Berichtsbände 14. Ed. Joachim Heinzle. Germanistische Symposien: Berichtsbände, 14. Stuttgart, Weimar: Metzler. Pp. 431-51.

Mora, Francine 1985: "Sources de l'Énéas: la tradition exégétique et le modèle épique latin." In *Relire le "Roman d'Eneas".* Ed. Jean Dufournet. Unichamp, 8. Paris: Champion. Pp. 83-104.

Mora-Lebrun, Francine 1994a: *L'"Enéide" médiévale et la chanson de geste.* Nouvelle Bibliothèque du moyen âge, 23. Paris: Champion.

Mora-Lebrun, Francine 1994b: *L'"Enéide" médiévale et la naissance du roman.* Perspectives littéraires. Paris: Presses Universitaires de France.

Mora, Francine 1996: "De l'*Énéide* à l'*Énéas*: le traducteur médiéval à la recherche d'une nouvelle stylistique." *Bien dire et bien aprandre* 14: 21-40.

Mora-Lebrun, Francine 1997: "Mythe troyen et histoire thébaine: le manuscrit S du *Roman de Thèbes.*" In *Entre fiction et histoire: Troie et Rome au moyen âge.* Ed. Emmanuèle Baumgartner and Laurence Harf-Lancner. Paris: Presses de la Sorbonne Nouvelle, 1997. Pp. 23-51.

Morris, Rosemary 1988: "Aspects of Time and Place in the French Arthurian Verse Romances." *French Studies* 42: 257-77.

Mueller, L. 1895: "Handschriftliches zu Macrobius." *Berliner philologische Wochenschrift* 15: col. 27-29, 60-61.

Munk Olsen, Birger 1973: "Note sur quelques préfaces de florilèges latins du XIIᵉ siècle." *Revue romane* 8: 190-96.

Munk Olsen, Birger 1979-80: "Les classiques latins dans les florilèges médiévaux antérieurs au XIIIᵉ siècle." *Revue d'histoire des textes* 9: 47-121, and 10: 115-64.

Munk Olsen, Birger 1982. "Les florilèges d'auteurs classiques." In *Les genres littéraires dans les sources théologiques et philosophiques médiévales: définition, critique et exploitation.* Actes du Colloque International de Louvain-la-Neuve 25-27 mai 1981. Université Catholique de Louvain: Publications de l'Institut d'Etudes Médiévales, 2ᵉ série: Textes, Etudes, Congrès 5. Louvain-la-Neuve: Université Catholique de Louvain. Pp. 151-64.

Munk Olsen, Birger 1982-89: *L'étude des auteurs classiques latins aux XIᵉ et XIIᵉ siècles.* Documents, études et répertoires publiés par l'Institut de Recherche et d'Histoire des textes. 3 vols. Paris: Editions du Centre National de Recherche Scientifique.

Munk Olsen, Birger 1985: "Virgile et la Renaissance du XIIᵉ siècle." In *Lectures médiévales de Virgile.* Actes du Colloque organisé par l'Ecole française de Rome (Rome, 25-28 octobre 1982). Collection de l'Ecole française de Rome, 80. Rome: Ecole française de Rome. Pp. 31-48.

Munk Olsen, Birger 1991a: *I classici nel canone scolastico altomedievale.* Fondazione Ezio Franceschini: Quaderni di cultura mediolatina, 1. Spoleto: Centro Italiano di Studi sull'Alto Medioevo.

Munk Olsen, Birger 1991b: "L'étude des textes littéraires classiques dans les écoles pendant le haut moyen âge." In *Itinerari dei testi antichi*. Ed. Oronzo Pecere. Saggi di storia antica, 3. Rome: "L'Erma" di Bretschneider. Pp. 105-14.

Munk Olsen, Birger 1992: "Les poètes classiques dans les écoles au IXᵉ siècle." In *De Tertullien aux Mozarabes: mélanges offerts à Jacques Fontaine*. Ed. Louis Holtz, Jean-Claude Fredouille, and Marie-Hélène Jullien. Collection d'Etudes Augustiniennes. 3 vols. Paris: Institut d'Etudes Augustiniennes. Vol. 2, pp. 197-210.

Murphy, James J. 1961: "The Arts of Discourse, 1050-1400." *Mediaeval Studies* 23: 194-205.

Newton, Francis L. 1962: "Tibullus in Two Grammatical *Florilegia* of the Middle Ages." *Transactions and Proceedings of the American Philological Association* 93: 253-86.

NGlos. Novum Glossarium mediae latinitatis ab anno DCCC usque ad annum MCC. Copenhagen: Munksgaard, 1957-.

Niermeyer, J. F. 1984: *Mediae latinitatis lexicon minus*. Leiden: Brill.

Nolan, Barbara 1992: *Chaucer and the Tradition of the "Roman Antique"*. Cambridge Studies in Medieval Literature, 15. Cambridge: Cambridge University Press.

Ogilvy, J. D. A. 1936: *Books Known to Anglo-Latin Writers from Aldhelm to Alcuin (670-804)*. Studies and Documents, 2. Cambridge, MA: Mediaeval Academy of America.

Ogilvy, J. D. A. 1967: *Books Known to the English, 597-1066*. Cambridge, MA: Mediaeval Academy of America.

Olmont, H. 1907: "Nouvelles acquisitions du Département des Manuscrits de la Bibliothèque Nationale pendant les années 1905-1906." *Bibliothèque de l'Ecole des Chartes* 68: 5-74.

Otis, Brooks 1936: "The *Argumenta* of the So-Called Lactantius." *Harvard Studies in Classical Philology* 47: 131-63.

Pabst, Bernhard 1994: *Prosimetrum: Tradition und Wandel einer Literaturform zwischen Spätantike und Spätmittelalter*. Ordo, 4. 2 vols. Cologne, Weimar, Vienna: Böhlaus.

Pack, Roger A. 1981: "A Medieval Critic of Macrobius' Cosmometrics." *Vivarium* 19: 146-51.

Paris, Gaston 1903: "Le cycle de la gageure." *Romania* 32: 481-551.

Parisse, Michel 1985: "Le tournoi en France, des origines à la fin du XIIIᵉ siècle." In *Das ritterliche Turnier im Mittelalter: Beiträge zu einer vergleichenden Formen- und Verhaltensgeschichte des Rittertums*. Ed. Josef Fleckenstein. Veröffentlichungen des Max-Planck-Instituts für Geschichte, 80. Göttingen: Vandenhoeck & Ruprecht. Pp. 175-211.

Parkes, Malcolm 1994: "Le pratiche di lettura." Trans. Fabio De Propris. In *Lo spazio letterario del medioevo. 1: Il medioevo latino*. Ed. Guglielmo Cavallo, Claudio Leonardi, and Enrico Menestò. Vol. II: *La circolazione del testo*. Ed. Francesco Stella. Rome: Salerno Editrice. Pp. 465-86.

Pasquali, Giorgio 1951: *Stravaganze quarte e supreme*. Venice: Pozza.

Patterson, Lee 1987: *Negotiating the Past: The Historical Understanding of Medieval Literature*. Madison, London: University of Wisconsin Press.

Pecere, Oronzo 1991. "Antichità tarda e trasmissione dei testi: qualche riflessione." In *Itinerari dei testi antichi*. Ed. Oronzo Pecere. Saggi di storia antica, 3. Rome: "L'Erma" di Bretschneider. Pp. 55-83.

Peden, Alison M. 1985: "Macrobius and Mediaeval Dream Literature." *Medium Aevum* 54: 59-73.

Pellegrin, Elisabeth 1973: "Possesseurs français et italiens de manuscrits latins du fonds de la Reine à la Bibliothèque Vaticane." *Revue d'histoire des textes* 3: 271-97.

Pellegrin, Elisabeth [et alii] 1975-82: *Les manuscrits classiques latins de la Bibliothèque Vaticane*. Documents, Etudes et Répertoires. 3 vols. Paris: Centre National de la Recherche Scientifique.

Pensom, Roger 1993: Review of Kelly 1992. *Notes and Queries* n. s. 40: 532-34.

Perret, Michèle 1996: "Statut du nom propre dans *Le Bel Inconnu*." In *Le Chevalier et la merveille dans "Le Bel Inconnu" ou le beau jeu de Renaut*. Ed. Jean Dufournet. Unichamp, 52. Paris: Champion. Pp. 91-109.

Peters, Ursula 1993: "Ritterbiographie und Familiengeschichte: das Beispiel der 'Histoire de Guillaume le Maréchal'." In *Literarische Interessenbildung im Mittelalter*. DFG-Symposion 1991. Ed. Joachim Heinzle. Germanistische Symposien: Berichtsbände, 14. Stuttgart: Metzler. Pp. 180-99.

Petit, Aimé 1985a: "L'anachronisme dans les romans antiques, et plus particulièrement dans le Roman d'Énéas." In *Relire le "Roman d'Énéas"*. Ed. Jean Dufournet. Unichamp, 8. Paris: Champion. Pp. 105-48.

Petit, Aimé 1985b: *Naissances du roman: les techniques littéraires dans les romans antiques du XIIe siècle*. 2 vols. Lille: Atelier National Reproduction des thèses Université de Lille III, Paris, Geneva: Slatkine.

Petit, Aimé 1996: "Les avatars du *Roman d'Énéas* dans un manuscrit du XIVe siècle." *Bien dire et bien aprandre* 14: 53-61.

Pickens, Rupert T. 1985: *"Le Conte du graal (Perceval)."* In *The Romances of Chrétien de Troyes: A Symposium*. Ed. Douglas Kelly. The Edward C. Armstrong Monographs on Medieval Literature, 3. Lexington, KY: French Forum. Pp. 232-86.

Pieri, Alieto 1977: *Lucrezio in Macrobio: adattamenti al testo virgiliano*. Biblioteca di cultura contemporanea, 126. Messina, Florence: D'Anna.

Pigman, G. W., III 1980: "Versions of Imitation in the Renaissance." *Renaissance Quarterly* 33: 1-32.

Poe, Elizabeth Wilson 1984: *From Poetry to Prose in Old Provençal: The Emergence of the "Vidas," the "Razos," and the "Razos de trobar"*. Birmingham, AL: Summa.

Poirion, Daniel 1978: "De l'*Énéide*' à l'*Eneas*': mythologie et moralisation." *Cahiers de civilisation médiévale* 19: 213-29.

Poirion, Daniel 1986. *Résurgences: mythe et littérature à l'âge du symbole (XIIe siècle)*. Ecriture. Paris: Presses Universitaires de France.

Pope, M. K. 1952. *From Latin to Modern French with Especial Consideration of Anglo-Norman: Phonology and Morphology*. Rev. ed. Publications of the University of Manchester, 229: French Series, 6. Manchester: Manchester University Press.

Possamaï-Perez, Marylène 1997: "Troie dans l'*Ovide moralisé*." In *Entre fiction et histoire: Troie et Rome au moyen âge*. Ed. Emmanuèle Baumgartner and Laurence Harf-Lancner. Paris: Presses de la Sorbonne Nouvelle, 1997. Pp. 97-109.

Pratt, Karen 1991: "Medieval Attitudes to Translation and Adaptation: The Rhetorical Theory and the Poetic Practice." In *The Medieval Translator II*. Ed. Roger Ellis. Westfield Publications in Medieval Studies, 5. London: Centre for Medieval Studies, Queen Mary and Westfield College, University of London. Pp. 1-27.

Prill, Paul E. 1987: "Rhetoric and Poetics in the Early Middle Ages." *Rhetorica* 5: 129-47.

Psaki, Regina 1997: "Jean Renart's Expanded Text: Lïenor and the Lyrics of *Guillaume de Dole*." In *Jean Renart and the Art of Romance: Essays on "Guillaume de Dole"*. Ed. Nancy Vine Durling. Gainesville: University Press of Florida. Pp. 122-41.

Purcell, William M. 1987: "*Transsumptio*: A Rhetorical Doctrine of the Thirteenth Century." *Rhetorica* 5: 369-410.

Purcell, William M. 1991. "*Identitas, Similitudo*, and *Contrarietas* in Gervasius of Melkley's *Ars poetica*: A *Stasis* of Style." *Rhetorica* 9: 67-91.

Purcell, William M. 1993: "Eberhard the German and the Labyrinth of Learning: Grammar, Poesy, Rhetoric, and Pedagogy in *Laborintus*." *Rhetorica* 11: 95-118.

Quadlbauer, Franz 1962: *Die antike Theorie der genera dicendi im lateinischen Mittelalter.* Österreichische Akademie der Wissenschaften: philosophisch-historische Klasse, 241.2. Graz, Vienna, Cologne: Böhlaus.

Quadlbauer, Franz 1974: "Zur 'invocatio' des Iuvencus (praef. 25-27)." *Grazer Beiträge* 2: 189-212.

Quadlbauer, Franz 1977: "Lukan im Schema des ordo naturalis / artificialis: ein Beitrag zur Geschichte der Lukanbewertung im lateinischen Mittelalter." *Grazer Beiträge* 6: 67-105.

Quadlbauer, Franz 1980a: "Primo ne medium, medio ne discrepet imum: zu Hor. ars 152 und seiner Nachwirkung in der spät- und mittellateinischen Literartheorie und in der 'Ecbasis'." In *Symmicta philologica Salisburgensia Georgio Pfligersdorffer sexagenario oblata.* Ed. Joachim Dalfen [et alii]. Filologia e critica, 33. Rome: Ateneo. Pp. 125-46.

Quadlbauer, Franz 1980b: "'Purpureus pannus': zum Fortwirken eines horazischen Bildes in Spätantike und lateinischem Mittelalter." *Mittellateinisches Jahrbuch* 15: 1-32.

Quadlbauer, Franz 1984: "Optimus Orator / Perfecte Eloquens: zu Ciceros formalem Rednerideal und seiner Nachwirkung." *Rhetorica* 2: 103-19.

Quadlbauer, Franz 1986: "Ovidkritik bei Matthaeus von Vendôme und ihre poetologisch-rhetorischen Hintergründe." In *Kontinuität und Wandel: lateinische Poesie von Naevius bis Baudelaire. Franco Munari zum 65. Geburtstag.* Ed. Ulrich Justus Stache, Wolfgang Maaz, and Fritz Wagner. Hildesheim: Weidmann. Pp. 424-45.

Quadlbauer, Franz 1989: "Zur Literaturtheorie des 10. Jahnhunderts." In *Tradition und Wertung: Festschrift für Franz Brunhölzl zum 65. Geburtstag.* Ed. Günter Bernt, Fidel Rädle, and Gabriel Silagi. Sigmaringen: Thorbecke. Pp. 119-40.

Quint, Maria-Barbara 1988: *Untersuchungen zur mittelalterlichen Horaz-Rezeption.* Studien zur klassischen Philologie, 39. Frankfurt-am-Main, Bern, New York, Paris: P. Lang.

Rabuse, Georg 1958: *Der kosmische Aufbau der Jenseitsreiche Dantes.* Graz, Cologne: Böhlaus.

Rabuse, Georg 1976: "Die Identifikation der Spuren des Macrobius in Dantes Göttliche Komödie." In his *Gesammelte Aufsätze zu Dante: als Festgabe zum 65. Geburtstag des Verfassers.* Ed. Erika Kanduth, Fritz Peter Kirsch, and Siegfried Loewe. Wiener romanistische Arbeiten: Sonderband. Vienna, Stuttgart: Braumüller. Pp. 288-95.

Raby, F. J. E. 1966: "Some Notes on Dante and Macrobius." *Medium Aevum* 35: 117-21.

Ratkowitsch, Christine 1991. *Descriptio picturae: die literarische Funktion der Beschreibung von Kunstwerken in der lateinischen Großdichtung des 12. Jahrhunderts.* Wiener Studien: Arbeiten zur mittel- und neulateinischen Philologie, Beiheft 15. Vienna: Verlag der Österreichischen Akademie der Wissenschaften.

Renaud, Geneviève 1976: "Les miracles de Saint Aignan d'Orléans XIᵉ siècle." *Analecta Bollandiana* 94: 245-74.

Riddehough, Geoffrey B. 1947: "A Forgotten Poet: Joseph of Exeter." *Journal of English and Germanic Philology* 46: 254-59.

Riddehough, Geoffrey B. 1949: "Joseph of Exeter: The Cambridge Manuscript." *Speculum* 24: 389-96.

Rieger, Dietmar 1987: "'Aufgehobene' Genera: Gattungszitate und Gattungsinstrate im altfranzösischen *Thebenroman*." *Vox romanica* 46: 67-86.

Rigg, A. G. 1977-90: "Medieval Latin Poetic Anthologies." *Mediaeval Studies* 39: 281-330, 40: 387-407, 41: 468-505, 43: 472-97, 49: 352-90 (with David Townsend), and, by Peter Binkley, 52: 221-54.

Riquer, Isabelle de, and Meritxell Simó 1998: "Cor de dona, dolça vianda." In *Miscellanea mediaevalia: mélanges offerts à Philippe Ménard*. Ed. J. Claude Faucon, Alain Labbé, and Danielle Quéruel. Nouvelle Bibliothèque du moyen âge, 46. Paris: Champion. Vol. II, pp. 1109-22.

Roberts, Michael 1985: *Biblical Epic and Rhetorical Paraphrase in Late Antiquity*. ARCA Classical and Medieval Texts, Papers and Monographs, 16. Liverpool: Cairns.

Roberts, Michael 1989: *The Jeweled Style: Poetry and Poetics in Late Antiquity*. Ithaca, NY, London: Cornell University Press.

Rockwell, Paul Vincent 1995: *Rewriting Resemblance in Medieval French Romance: "Ceci n'est pas un graal"*. Garland Studies in Medieval Literature, 13 / Garland Reference Library of the Humanities, 1908. New York, London: Garland.

Rockwell, Paul 1997: "Remembering *Troie*: The Implications of *Ymages* in the *Roman de Troie* and the Prose *Lancelot*." *Arthuriana* 7.3: 20-35.

Rollo, David 1995: "Benoît de Sainte-Maure's *Roman de Troie*: Historiography, Forgery, and Fiction." *Comparative Literature Studies* 32: 191-225.

Rosenberg, Samuel N. 1998: "French Songs in Occitan Chansonniers: An Introductory Report." *Tenso* 13: 18-32.

Rouse, R. H. 1973: "Manuscripts belonging to Richard de Fournival." *Revue d'histoire des textes* 3: 253-69.

Rouse, R. H. and M. A. 1976: "The *Florilegium Angelicum*: Its Origin, Content and Influence." In *Medieval Learning and Literature: Essays Presented to Richard William Hunt*. Ed. J. J. G. Alexander and M. T. Gibson. Oxford: Clarendon Press. Pp. 66-114.

Rousse, Michel 1985: "Le pouvoir, la prouesse et l'amour dans l'Énéas." In *Relire le "Roman d'Énéas"*. Ed. Jean Dufournet. Unichamp, 8. Paris: Champion. Pp. 149-67.

Sanford, Eva Matthews 1924: "The Use of Classical Latin Authors in the Libri Manuales." *Transactions and Proceedings of the American Philological Association* 55: 190-248.

Sarradin, A. 1878. *De Josepho Iscano, Belli Trojani XII° post Christum sæculo poeta*. Diss. Paris. Versailles: Cerf.

Schmidt, Paul Gerhard 1977. "Weltliche Dichtung des lateinischen Mittelalters und ihr Publikum." *Gymnasium* 84: 167-83.

Schmolke-Hasselmann, Beate 1980: *Der arthurische Versroman von Chrestien bis Froissart: zur Geschichte einer Gattung*. Beihefte zur Zeitschrift für romanische Philologie, 177. Tübingen: Niemeyer.

Schmolke-Hasselmann, Beate 1983: "Der französische Artusroman in Versen nach Chrétien de Troyes." *Deutsche Vierteljahrsschrift für Literaturwissenschaft und Geistesgeschichte* 57: 415-30.

Schnell, Rüdiger 1984: "Literatur als Korrektiv sozialer Realität: zur Eheschliessung in mittelalterlichen Dichtungen." *Non Nova, sed Nove: mélanges de civilisation médiévale dédiés à Willem Noomen*. Ed. Martin Gosman and Jaap van Os. Mediaevalia Groningana, 5. Groningen: Bouma. Pp. 225-38.

Schnell, Rüdiger 1985: *Causa amoris: Liebeskonzeption und Liebesdarstellung in der mittelalterlichen Literatur*. Bibliotheca Germanica, 27. Bern, Munich: Francke.

Schöning, Udo 1991: *Thebenroman-Eneasroman-Trojaroman: Studien zur Rezeption der Antike in der französischen Literatur des 12. Jahrhunderts*. Beihefte zur Zeitschrift für romanische Philologie, 235. Tübingen: Niemeyer.

Schwartz, W. 1944: "The Meaning of *Fidus interpres* in Medieval Translation." *The Journal of Theological Studies* 45.2: 73-78.

Sedgwick, Walter Bradbury 1928: "The Style and Vocabulary of the Latin Arts of Poetry of the Twelfth and Thirteenth Centuries." *Speculum* 3: 349-81.

Sedgwick, Walter Bradbury 1930. "The *Bellum Troianum* of Joseph of Exeter." *Speculum* 5: 49-76.
Short, Ian 1988: "L'avènement du texte vernaculaire: la mise en recueil." In *Théories et pratiques de l'écriture au moyen âge*. Actes du Colloque Palais du Luxembourg-Sénat, 5 et 6 mars 1987. Ed. Emmanuèle Baumgartner and Christiane Marchello-Nizia. Littérales, 4. Paris: Centre de Recherches du Département de Français de Paris X-Nanterre, Fontenay-Saint Cloud: Centre Espace-Temps-Histoire de l'E.N.S. Pp. 11-24.
Silvestre, Hubert 1963: "Note sur la survie de Macrobe au moyen âge." *Classica et Mediaevalia* 24: 170-80.
Simpson, James 1992: "The Information of Alan of Lille's 'Anticlaudianus': A Preposterous Interpretation." *Traditio* 47: 113-60.
Sinclair, Brent W. 1982: "Vergil's *sacrum poema* in Macrobius' *Saturnalia*." *Maia* 34: 261-63.
Stackelberg, Jürgen von 1956: "Das Bienengleichnis: ein Beitrag zur Geschichte der literarischen *Imitatio*." *Romanische Forschungen* 68: 271-93.
Stahl, William H. 1965: "To A Better Understanding of Martianus Capella." *Speculum* 40: 102-15.
Stahl, William Harris 1971-77: *Martianus Capella and the Seven Liberal Arts*. Vol. I: *The Quadrivium of Martianus Capella: Latin Tradition in the Mathematical Sciences 50 B. C.-A. D. 1250, with a Study of the Allegory and the Verbal Disciplines*, by Richard Johnson with E. L. Burge. Vol. II: *The Marriage of Philology and Mercury*. Trans. William Harris Stahl and Richard Johnson with E. L. Burge. Records of Civilization: Sources and Studies, 84. 2 vols. New York: Columbia University Press.
Stanesco, Michel 1988: *Jeux d'errance du chevalier médiéval: aspects ludiques de la fonction guerrière dans la littérature du moyen âge flamboyant*. Brill's Studies in Intellectual History, 9. Leiden, New York, Copenhagen, Cologne: Brill.
Stempel, Wolf-Dieter 1993: "La 'modernité' des débuts: la rhétorique de l'oralité chez Chrétien de Troyes." In *Le passage à l'écrit des langues romanes*. Ed. Maria Selig, Barbara Frank, and Jörg Hartmann. ScriptOralia, 46. Tübingen: Narr. Pp. 275-98.
Stiennon, Jacques 1995: *L'écriture*. Typologie des sources du moyen âge occidental, 72. Turnhout: Brepols.
Stock, Brian 1972: *Myth and Science in the Twelfth Century: A Study of Bernard Silvester*. Princeton: Princeton University Press.
Stock, Brian 1983: *The Implications of Literacy: Written Language and Models of Interpretation in the Eleventh and Twelfth Centuries*. Princeton: Princeton University Press.
Strasbourg 1923: *Catalogue général des manuscrits des bibliothèques publiques de France*. Vol. 47. Paris: Plon-Nourris.
Suard, François 1992: "De l'épopée au roman." *Bien dire et bien aprandre* 10: 171-84.
Suard, François 1993: "La description dans la chanson de geste." *Bien dire et bien aprandre* 11: 401-17.
Sullivan, Penny 1985: "Translation and Adaptation in the *Roman de Troie*." In *The Spirit of the Court*. Selected Proceedings of the Fourth Congress of the International Courtly Literature Society (Toronto 1983). Ed. Glyn S. Burgess and Robert A. Taylor. Cambridge: Brewer. Pp. 350-59.
Szövérffy, Joseph 1983: "Lateinische Hymnik zwischen Spätantike und Humanismus: kulturgeschichtliche und geschichtliche Bemerkungen." *Wiener Studien* n.s. 17: 210-47.
Taylor, Jane H. M. 1996: "Melusine's Progeny: Patterns and Perplexities." In *Melusine of Lusignan: Founding Fiction in Late Medieval France*. Ed. Donald Maddox and Sara Sturm-Maddox. Athens, GA, London: University of Georgia Press. Pp. 165-84.

Thiry-Stassin, Martine, and Claude Thiry 1992: "Mariage et lignage dans l'*Histoire de Guillaume le Maréchal*." In *Femmes: mariages—lignages XIIᵉ-XIIIᵉ siècles. Mélanges offerts à Georges Duby*. Bibliothèque du Moyen Age, 1. Brussels: De Boeck Université. Pp. 341-59.

ThLL. Thesaurus linguae latinae. Leipzig: Teubner, 1900-.

Thomson, Rodney M. 1975: "The Reading of William of Malmesbury." *Revue bénédictine* 85: 362-94.

Thraede, K. 1962: "Epos." In the *Reallexikon für Antike und Christentum: Sachwörterbuch zur Auseinandersetzung des Christentums mit der antiken Welt*. Stuttgart: Hiersemann. Vol. 5 col. 983-1042.

Thurot, Ch. 1964: *Extraits de divers manuscrits latins pour servir à l'histoire des doctrines grammaticales au moyen âge*. Paris 1869; repr. Frankfurt: Minerva.

Tilliette, Jean-Yves 1985: "*Insula me genuit*: l'influence de l'*Énéide* sur l'épopée latine du XIIᵉ siècle." In *Lectures médiévales de Virgile*. Actes du Colloque organisé par l'Ecole française de Rome (Rome, 25-28 octobre 1982). Collection de l'Ecole française de Rome, 80. Rome: Ecole française de Rome. Pp. 121-42.

Tilliette, Jean-Yves 1993: "La *Descriptio Helenae* dans la poésie latine du XIIᵉ siècle." *Bien dire et bien aprandre* 11: 419-32.

Tilliette, Jean-Yves 1995: "Le sens et la composition du florilège de Zurich (Zentralbibliothek, ms. C 58): hypothèses et propositions." In *Non recedet memoria eius: Beiträge zur lateinischen Philologie des Mittelalters im Gedenken an Jakob Werner (1861-1944)*. Akten der wissenschaftlichen Tagung vom 9./10. September 1994 am Mittellateinischen Seminar der Universität Zürich. Ed. Michele C. Ferrari and Peter Stotz. Lateinische Sprache und Literatur des Mittelalters, 28. Bern, Berlin, Frankfurt-am-Main, New York, Paris, Vienna: P. Lang. Pp. 147-67.

Tobler-Lommatzsch. *Tobler-Lommatzsch Altfranzösisches Wörterbuch*. Berlin: Wiedmann, Wiesbaden: Steinen, 1925-.

Tohill, Kathleen 1978: "Extracts from Macrobius in Codex Vaticanus Palatinus Latinus 886." *Manuscripta* 22: 104-08.

Trachsler, Richard 1996: *Clôtures du cycle arthurien: études et textes*. Publications romanes et françaises, 215. Geneva: Droz.

Triaud, Annie 1985: "Survie de l'Énéas dans une version tardive." In *Relire le "Roman d'Énéas"*. Ed. Jean Dufournet. Unichamp, 8. Paris: Champion. Pp. 169-87.

Trimpi, Wesley 1983: *Muses of One Mind: The Literary Analysis of Experience and Its Continuity*. Princeton: Princeton University Press.

Tuve, Rosemond 1966: *Allegorical Imagery: Some Mediaeval Books and Their Posterity*. Princeton: Princeton University Press.

Uitti, Karl D. 1981: "A propos de philologie." *Littérature* n° 41: 30-46.

Urbanek, Ferdinand 1995: "Die drei antik-mittelalterlichen Genera dicendi in weiterer Aufgliederung." *Mittellateinisches Jahrbuch* 30.2: 1-27.

Vance, Eugene 1987: *From Topic to Tale: Logic and Narrativity in the Middle Ages*. Theory and History of Literature, 47. Minneapolis: University of Minnesota Press.

Varty, Kenneth 1986: "The Giving and Withholding of Consent in Late Twelfth-Century French Literature." *Reading Medieval Studies* 12: 27-49.

Vernet, André 1975: "La transmission des textes en France." In *La cultura antica nell'Occidente latino dal VII all'XI secolo: 18-24 aprile 1974*. 2 vols. Settimane di studio del Centro Italiano di Studi sull'Alto Medioevo, 22. Spoleto: La Sede del Centro. I: 89-123.

Viarre, Simone 1975: "Cosmologie antique et commentaire de la création du monde. Le chaos et les quatre éléments chez quelques auteurs du haut moyen âge." In *La cultura antica nell'Occidente latino dal VII al'XI secolo*, 18-24 aprile 1974.

Settimane di Studio del Centro Italiano di Studi sull'Alto Medioevo, 22. 2 vols. Spoleto: La Sede del Centro. Vol. II, pp. 541-73.

Vielliard, Françoise 1994: "La traduction du De excidio Troiæ de Darès le Phrygien par Jean de Flixecourt." In *Medieval Codicology, Iconography, Literature, and Translation: Studies for Keith Val Sinclair*. Ed. Peter Rolfe Monks and D. D. R. Owen. Litterae textuales. Leiden, New York, Cologne: Brill. Pp. 284-95.

Vietti, Maria 1979: "Pathos virgiliano e retorica in Macrobio." *Atti della Accademia delle Scienze di Torino. II: Classe di scienze morali, storiche e filologiche* 113: 219-43.

Villa, Claudia 1992a: "Il lessico della stilistica fra XI e XIII sec." In *Vocabulaire des écoles et des méthodes d'enseignement au moyen âge*, Actes du colloque Rome 21-22 octobre 1989. Ed. Olga Weijers. CIVICIMA: Etudes sur le vocabulaire intellectuel du moyen âge, 5. Turnhout: Brepols. Pp. 42-59.

Villa, Claudia 1992b: "Per una tipologia del commento mediolatino: l'Ars poetica' di Orazio." In *Il commento ai testi*. Atti del Seminario di Ascona 2-9 ottobre 1989. Ed. Ottavio Besomi and Carlo Caruso. Fonte verità: Proceedings of the Centro Stefano Franscini, Ascona. Basel, Boston, Berlin: Birkhäuser. Pp. 19-42.

Villa, Claudia 1993: "La tradizione medioevale di Orazio." In: *Atti del Convegno di Venosa 8-15 novembre 1992*. Venosa: Osanna. Pp. 193-202.

Villa, Claudia 1994: "I manoscritti di Orazio. III." *Aevum* 68: 117-46.

Villa, Claudia 1997: "I commenti ai classici fra XII e XV secolo." In *Medieval and Renaissance Scholarship*. Proceedings of the Second European Science Foundation Workship on the Classical Tradition in the Middle Ages and the Renaissance (London, The Warburg Institute, 27-28 November 1992). Ed. Nicholas Mann and Birger Munk Olsen. Mittellateinische Studien und Texte 21. Leiden, New York, Cologne: Brill. Pp. 19-32.

Vinaver, Eugène 1964: "From Epic to Romance." *Bulletin of the John Rylands Library*. 46: 476-503.

Vincensini, Jean-Jacques 1996: *Pensée mythique et narrations médiévales*. Nouvelle Bibliothèque du moyen âge, 34. Paris: Champion.

Vogt-Spira, Gregor 1994: "Ars oder Ingenium? Homer und Vergil als literarische Paradigmata." *Literaturwissenschaftliches Jahrbuch im Auftrage der Görres-Gesellschaft*. N. s. 35: 9-31.

Wagner, David L., ed. 1986: *The Seven Liberal Arts in the Middle Ages*. Bloomington: Indiana University Press.

Wallen, Martha 1982: "Significant Variations in the Burgundian Prose Version of *Erec et Enide*." *Medium Aevum* 51: 187-96.

Walter, Philippe 1990: "Tout commence par des chansons... (Intertextualités lotharingiennes)." In *Styles et valeurs: pour une histoire de l'art littéraire au moyen âge*. Ed. Daniel Poirion. Moyen âge. Paris: CDU et SEDES. Pp. 187-209.

Walther, Hans 1926: "Kleine mittellateinische Dichtungen aus zwei Erfurter Handschriften (Amplon. Q.12 und Q.345)." In *Mittelalterliche Handschriften: paläographische, kunsthistorische, literarische und bibliotheksgeschichtliche Untersuchungen. Festgabe zum 60. Geburtstage von Hermann Degering*. Leipzig: Hiersemann. Pp. 296-315.

Ward, John Oastler 1972: "*Artificiosa eloquentia* in the Middle Ages: A Study of Cicero's *De inventione*, the *Ad Herennium* and Quintilian's *De institutione oratoria* from the Early Middle Ages to the Thirteenth Century, with Special Reference to the Schools of Northern France." Diss. Toronto.

Ward, John O. 1990: "Rhetoric and the Art of Dictamen." In *Méthodes et instruments du travail intellectuel au moyen âge: études sur le vocabulaire*. CIVICIMA: Etudes sur le vocabulaire intellectuel du moyen âge, 5. Turnhout: Brepols. Pp. 20-61.

Ward, John O. 1995: *Ciceronian Rhetoric in Treatise, Scholion and Commentary*. Typologie des sources du moyen âge occidental, 58. Turnhout: Brepols.

Wattenbach, W. 1893: "Beschreibung einer Handschrift der Stadtbibliothek zu Reims." *Neues Archiv der Gesellschaft für ältere deutsche Geschichtskunde* 18: 491-526.
Wattenbach, W. 1896: *Das Schriftwesen im Mittelalter.* 3rd ed. Leipzig: Hirzel.
Webb, Clement C. J. 1897: "On Some Fragments of Macrobius' *Saturnalia.*" *Classical Review* 11: 441.
Wendehorst, Alfred 1986: "Wer konnte im Mittelalter lesen und schreiben?" In *Schulen und Studium im sozialen Wandel des hohen und späten Mittelalters.* Ed. Johannes Fried. Vorträge und Forschungen: Konstanzer Arbeitskreis für mittelalterliche Geschichte, 30. Sigmaringen: Thorbecke. Pp. 9-33.
West, G. D. 1969: *An Index of Proper Names in French Arthurian Verse Romances 1150-1300.* University of Toronto Romance Series, 15. Toronto: University of Toronto Press.
Wetherbee, Winthrop 1972: *Platonism and Poetry in the Twelfth Century: The Literary Influence of the School of Chartres.* Princeton: Princeton University Press.
Willaert, Frank 1992: "Het zingende hof: Ontstaan, vertolking en onthaal van hoofse minnelyriek omstreeks 1400." In *Een zoet akkoord: Middeleeuwse lyriek in de Lage Landen.* Ed. Frank Willaert. Amsterdam: Prometheus. Pp. 109-22, 348-55.
Williams, Clem C., Jr. 1984: "A Case of Mistaken Identity: Still Another Trojan Narrative in Old French Prose." *Medium Aevum* 53: 59-72.
Willis, J. A. 1954: "De Macrobii codice Montepessulano." *Rheinisches Museum für Philologie* n.s. 97: 287.
Willis, J. A. 1957: "De codicibus aliquot manuscriptis Macrobii Saturnalia continentibus." *Rheinisches Museum für Philologie* n.s. 100: 152-64.
Wills, Jeffrey 1996: *Repetition in Latin Poetry: Figures of Allusion.* Oxford: Clarendon Press.
Wlosok, Antonie 1990: *Res humanae—res divinae: kleine Schriften.* Ed. Eberhard Heck and Ernst A. Schmidt. Bibliothek der klassischen Altertumswissenschaften, n.s. 2, 84. Heidelberg: Winter.
Woods, Marjorie Curry 1991: "A Medieval Rhetoric Goes to School — and to the University: The Commentaries on the *Poetria nova.*" *Rhetorica* 9: 55-65.
Worstbrock, Franz Joseph 1963: "Zur Tradition des Troiastoffes und seiner Gestaltung bei Herbort von Fritzlar." *Zeitschrift für deutsches Altertum und deutsche Literatur* 92: 248-74.
Worstbrock, Franz Josef 1965: "Translatio artium: über die Herkunft und Entwicklung einer kulturhistorischen Theorie." *Archiv für Kulturgeschichte* 47:1-22.
Worstbrock, Franz Josef 1985: "Dilatatio materiae: zur Poetik des 'Erec' Hartmanns von Aue." *Frühmittelalterliche Studien* 19: 1-30.
Wright, Neil 1995: *History and Literature in Late Antiquity and the Early Medieval West: Studies in Intertextuality.* Collected Studies Series. Aldershot, Hampshire, Brookfield, VT: Variorum.
Wright, Roger 1982: *Late Latin and Early Romance in Spain and Carolingian France.* ARCA: Classical and Medieval Texts, Papers and Monographs, 8. Liverpool: Cairns.
Wright, Roger 1997: "Translation between Latin and Romance in the Early Middle Ages." In *Translation Theory and Practice in the Middle Ages.* Ed. Jeanette Beer. Studies in Medieval Culture, 38. Kalamazoo: Medieval Institute Publications, Western Michigan University. Pp. 7-32.
Ziltener, Werner 1957: *Chrétien und die Aeneis: eine Untersuchung des Einflusses von Vergil auf Chrétien von Troyes.* Graz, Cologne: Böhlaus.
Zink, Michel 1978: *Belle: essai sur les chansons de toile suivi d'une édition et d'une traduction.* Musical Transcription by Gérard Le Vot. Paris: Champion.
Zink, Michel 1979: *Roman rose et rose rouge: Le Roman de la rose ou de Guillaume de Dole de Jean Renart.* Paris: Nizet.

Zink, Michel 1981: "Une mutation de la conscience littéraire: le langage romanesque à travers des exemples français du XIIe siècle." *Cahiers de civilisation
médiévale* 24: 3-27.

Zink, Michel 1984: "Héritage rhétorique et nouveauté littéraire dans le 'roman
antique' en France au moyen âge: remarques sur l'expression de l'amour dans
le roman d'*Eneas*." *Romania* 105: 248-69.

Zink, Michel 1985: *La subjectivité littéraire: autour du siècle de saint Louis.* Ecriture. Paris:
Presses Universitaires de France.

Zink, Michel 1996: "Traduire Saint Bernard: quand la parabole devient roman." In
The Medieval "Opus": Imitation, Rewriting, and Transmission in the French Tradition.
Proceedings of the Symposium Held at the Institute for Research in Humani-
ties October 5-7 1995, The University of Wisconsin-Madison. Ed. Douglas
Kelly. Faux Titre, 116. Amsterdam, Atlanta: Rodopi. Pp. 29-42.

Zink, Michel 1997: "Suspension and Fall: The Fragmentation and Linkage of Lyric
Insertions in *Le roman de la rose (Guillaume de Dole)* and *Le roman de la violette*." In
Jean Renart and the Art of Romance: Essays on "Guillaume de Dole". Ed. Nancy Vine
Durling. Gainesville: University Press of Florida. Pp. 105-21.

Zintzen, Clemens 1988: "Bemerkungen zur Nachwirkung des Macrobius in Mittelalter und Renaissance." In *Roma renascens: Beiträge zur Spätantike und Rezeptionsgeschichte. Ilona Opelt von ihren Freunden und Schülern zum 9.7.1988 in Verehrung
gewidmet.* Ed Michael Wissemann. Frankfurt, Bern, New York, Paris: Lang. Pp.
415-39.

Ziolkowski, Jan 1985: *Alan of Lille's Grammar of Sex: The Meaning of Grammar to a Twelfth-
Century Intellectual.* Speculum Anniversary Monographs, 10. Cambridge, MA:
The Medieval Academy of America.

Ziolkowski, Jan 1997: "The Prosimetrum in the Classical Tradition." In *Prosimetrum:
Crosscultural Perspectives on Narrative in Prose and Verse.* Ed. Joseph Harris and Karl
Reichl. Cambridge: Brewer. Pp. 45-65.

Zumthor, Paul 1978: "Le texte-fragment." *Langue française* 40: 75-82.

Zundel, Eckart 1989: *Clavis Quintilianea: Quintilians "Institutio oratoria (Ausbildung des
Redners)" aufgeschlüsselt nach rhetorischen Begriffen.* Darmstadt: Wissenschaftliche
Buchgesellschaft.

INDEX OF TITLES

INDEX OF NAMES

INDEX OF PLACES

INDEX OF SUBJECTS

Studies in the History
of Christian Thought

EDITED BY HEIKO A. OBERMAN

46. GARSTEIN, O. *Rome and the Counter-Reformation in Scandinavia.* 1553-1622. 1992
47. GARSTEIN, O. *Rome and the Counter-Reformation in Scandinavia.* 1622-1656. 1992
48. PERRONE COMPAGNI, V. (ed.). *Cornelius Agrippa, De occulta philosophia Libri tres.* 1992
49. MARTIN, D. D. *Fifteenth-Century Carthusian Reform.* The World of Nicholas Kempf. 1992
50. HOENEN, M. J. F. M. *Marsilius of Inghen.* Divine Knowledge in Late Medieval Thought. 1993
51. O'MALLEY, J. W., IZBICKI, T. M. and CHRISTIANSON, G. (eds.). *Humanity and Divinity in Renaissance and Reformation.* Essays in Honor of Charles Trinkaus. 1993
52. REEVE, A. (ed.) and SCREECH, M. A. (introd.). *Erasmus' Annotations on the New Testament.* Galatians to the Apocalypse. 1993
53. STUMP, Ph. H. *The Reforms of the Council of Constance (1414-1418).* 1994
54. GIAKALIS, A. *Images of the Divine.* The Theology of Icons at the Seventh Ecumenical Council. With a Foreword by Henry Chadwick. 1994
55. NELLEN, H. J. M. and RABBIE, E. (eds.). *Hugo Grotius – Theologian.* Essays in Honour of G. H. M. Posthumus Meyjes. 1994
56. TRIGG, J. D. *Baptism in the Theology of Martin Luther.* 1994
57. JANSE, W. *Albert Hardenberg als Theologe.* Profil eines Bucer-Schülers. 1994
59. SCHOOR, R.J.M. VAN DE. *The Irenical Theology of Théophile Brachet de La Milletière (1588-1665).* 1995
60. STREHLE, S. *The Catholic Roots of the Protestant Gospel.* Encounter between the Middle Ages and the Reformation. 1995
61. BROWN, M.L. *Donne and the Politics of Conscience in Early Modern England.* 1995
62. SCREECH, M.A. (ed.). *Richard Mocket, Warden of All Souls College, Oxford, Doctrina et Politia Ecclesiae Anglicanae.* An Anglican Summa. Facsimile with Variants of the Text of 1617. Edited with an Introduction. 1995
63. SNOEK, G.J.C. *Medieval Piety from Relics to the Eucharist.* A Process of Mutual Inter-action. 1995
64. PIXTON, P.B. *The German Episcopacy and the Implementation of the Decrees of the Fourth Lateran Council, 1216-1245.* Watchmen on the Tower. 1995
65. DOLNIKOWSKI, E.W. *Thomas Bradwardine: A View of Time and a Vision of Eternity in Fourteenth-Century Thought.* 1995
66. RABBIE, E. (ed.). *Hugo Grotius, Ordinum Hollandiae ac Westfrisiae Pietas (1613).* Critical Edition with Translation and Commentary. 1995
67. HIRSH, J.C. *The Boundaries of Faith.* The Development and Transmission of Medieval Spirituality. 1996
68. BURNETT, S.G. *From Christian Hebraism to Jewish Studies.* Johannes Buxtorf (1564-1629) and Hebrew Learning in the Seventeenth Century. 1996
69. BOLAND O.P., V. *Ideas in God according to Saint Thomas Aquinas.* Sources and Synthesis. 1996
70. LANGE, M.E. *Telling Tears in the English Renaissance.* 1996
71. CHRISTIANSON, G. and T.M. IZBICKI (eds.). *Nicholas of Cusa on Christ and the Church.* Essays in Memory of Chandler McCuskey Brooks for the American Cusanus Society. 1996
72. MALI, A. *Mystic in the New World.* Marie de l'Incarnation (1599-1672). 1996
73. VISSER, D. *Apocalypse as Utopian Expectation (800-1500).* The Apocalypse Commentary of Berengaudus of Ferrières and the Relationship between Exegesis, Liturgy and Iconography. 1996
74. O'ROURKE BOYLE, M. *Divine Domesticity.* Augustine of Thagaste to Teresa of Avila. 1997
75. PFIZENMAIER, T.C. *The Trinitarian Theology of Dr. Samuel Clarke (1675-1729).* Context, Sources, and Controversy. 1997
76. BERKVENS-STEVELINCK, C., J. ISRAEL and G.H.M. POSTHUMUS MEYJES (eds.). *The Emergence of Tolerance in the Dutch Republic.* 1997
77. HAYKIN, M.A.G. (ed.). *The Life and Thought of John Gill (1697-1771).* A Tercentennial Appreciation. 1997
78. KAISER, C.B. *Creational Theology and the History of Physical Science.* The Creationist Tradition from Basil to Bohr. 1997
79. LEES, J.T. *Anselm of Havelberg.* Deeds into Words in the Twelfth Century. 1997
80. WINTER, J.M. VAN. *Sources Concerning the Hospitallers of St John in the Netherlands, 14th-18th Centuries.* 1998

81. TIERNEY, B. *Foundations of the Conciliar Theory*. The Contribution of the Medieval Canonists from Gratian to the Great Schism. Enlarged New Edition. 1998

82. MIERNOWSKI, J. *Le Dieu Néant*. Théologies négatives à l'aube des temps modernes. 1998

83. HALVERSON, J.L. *Peter Aureol on Predestination*. A Challenge to Late Medieval Thought. 1998.

84. HOULISTON, V. (ed.). *Robert Persons, S.J.: The Christian Directory (1582)*. The First Booke of the Christian Exercise, appertayning to Resolution. 1998

85. GRELL, O.P. (ed.). *Paracelsus*. The Man and His Reputation, His Ideas and Their Reputation. 1998

86. MAZZOLA, E. *The Pathology of the English Renaissance*. Sacred Remains and Holy Ghosts. 1998.

87. 88. MARSILIUS VON INGHEN. *Quaestiones super quattuor libros sententiarum*. Super Primum. Bearbeitet von M. Santos Noya. 2 Bände. I. Quaestiones 1-7. II. Quaestiones 8-21. 2000

89. FAUPEL DREVS, K. *Vom rechten Gebrauch der Bilder im liturgischen Raum*. Mittelalterliche Funktionsbestimmungen bildender Kunst im *Rationale divinorum officiorum* des Durandus von Mende (1230/1-1296). 1999

90. KREY, P.D.W. and SMITH, L. (eds.). *Nicholas of Lyra*. the Senses of Scripture. 2000

92. OAKLEY, F. *Politics and Eternity*. Studies in the History of Medieval and Early-Modern Political Thought. 1999

93. PRYDS, D. *The Politics of Preaching*. Robert of Naples (1309-1343) and his Sermons. 2000

94. POSTHUMUS MEYJES, G.H.M. *Jean Gerson – Apostle of Unity*. His Church Politics and Ecclesiology. Translated by J.C. Grayson. 1999

95. BERG, J. VAN DEN. *Religious Currents and Cross-Currents*. Essays on Early Modern Protestantism and the Protestant Enlightenment. Edited by J. de Bruijn, P. Holtrop, and E. van der Wall. 1999

96. IZBICKI, T.M. and BELLITTO, C.M. (eds.). *Reform and Renewal in the Middle Ages and the Renaissance*. Studies in Honor of Louis Pascoe SJ. 1999

97. KELLY, D. *The Conspiracy of Allusion*. Description, Rewriting, and Authorship from Macrobius to Medieval Romance. 1999